Indians, Fire, and the Land
in the Pacific Northwest

Praise for Indians, Fire, and the Land in the Pacific Northwest

". . . by far the most comprehensive survey of North American Indian fire practices available. . . a rich broth of data and disciplines . . . The book can well serve as a model for other regions or for any part of the world where aboriginal economies, broadly interpreted, thrive."
—Stephen J. Pyne, *H-Net Reviews*

"The chapters range from northern California to British Columbia, and summarize nearly everything that is known about Pacific Northwest Indian use of fire in the environment. . . . *Indians, Fire, and the Land* is the most valuable resource to date on Indian burning in the region, and should provide valuable evidence for every reader for his or her next campfire debate. It should be equally usable by archeologists, anthropologists, ecologists, and historians. This is more than a 'recommend'—buy this one—you need it for your library."
—James K. Agee, *Northwest Science*

"*Indians, Fire, and the Land* should be read by every restorationist in the Pacific Northwest and Intermountain region of the Northern Rockies—it's that important and that good. Moreover, it puts in black-and-white, what people such as Dennis Martinez and Kat Anderson have been telling the restoration community for years—namely, that Native American peoples have much to teach the rest of us about how to manage the land properly."
—David Egan, *Ecological Restoration*

"*Indians, Fire, and the Land* adds significant depth to our knowledge of how original peoples utilized fire to create unique landscapes all across the Pacific Northwest . . . Boyd's collection brings to us for the first time a coherent treatment of the role that anthropogenic fire played in the shaping and forming of a unique ecosystem and points to the great contribution that archaeology, paleobotany, and palynology can make to our historical understanding of early human landscape manipulation."
—Bruce Shelvey, *Western Historical Quarterly*

"Although the book's focus is on Native American use of fire at the time of white contact, interesting observations reach back into early Indian fire use and the changes that came with Euro-American settlement and fire suppression policies. The result not only provides valuable insights into Pacific Northwest Indian history, but the book also casts light on significant questions and themes surrounding current debates over public land management policies, particularly the use of prescriptive fire."
—Robert Bunting, *Oregon Historical Quarterly*

Indians, Fire, and the Land
in the Pacific Northwest

Robert Boyd, Editor

Oregon State University Press
Corvallis, Oregon

Cover photo: Painting by Father Nicolas Point, c. 1840. Full credit on page 54.

The paper in this book meets the guidelines for permanence and durability of the Committee on Production Guidelines for Book Longevity of the Council on Library Resources and the minimum requirements of the American National Standard for Permanence of Paper for Printed Library Materials Z39.48-1984.

Library of Congress Cataloging-in-Publication Data
Indians, fire, and the land in the Pacific Northwest / Robert Boyd, editor
   p.   cm.
Includes bibliographical references (p.) and index.
ISBN 0-87071-459-7 (alk. paper)
1. Indians of North America—Agriculture—Northwest, Pacific.
2. Indians of North America—Northwest, Pacific—Social life and customs. 3. Human ecology—Northwest, Pacific. 4. Fire ecology—Northwest, Pacific. 5. Prescribed burning—Northwest, Pacific.
6. Northwest, Pacific—Social life and customs. I. Boyd, Robert, Ph.D.
E78.N77I53 1999
577'.2—dc21
                        98-54743
                            CIP

Oregon State University Press
101 Waldo Hall
Corvallis OR 97331-6407
541-737-3166 •fax 541-737-3170
http://.osu.orst.edu/dept/press

Table of Contents

Introduction

Basic Issues

I n May and June of 1792, George Vancouver's British-sponsored exploring expedition entered the uncharted waters of Puget Sound. Expecting a forested wilderness inhabited by unsophisticated natives, they were surprised at what they found. At Penn Cove, on Whidbey Island:

> The surrounding country, for several miles in most points of view, presented a delightful prospect consisting chiefly of spacious meadows elegantly adorned with clumps of trees; among which the oak bore a very considerable proportion, in size from four to six feet in circumference. In these beautiful pastures . . . the deer were seen playing about in great numbers. Nature had here provided the well-stocked park, and wanted only the assistance of art to constitute that desirable assemblage of surface, which is so much sought in other countries, and only to be acquired by an immoderate experience in manual labour. [1]

Among the "pine forests" of Admiralty Inlet, Joseph Whidbey noted "clear spots or lawns . . . clothed with a rich carpet of Verdure." The "verdure" of these "lawns" included "grass of an excellent quality," tall ferns "in the sandy soils" and several other plants: "Gooseberrys, Currands, Raspberrys, & Strawberrys were to be found in many places. Onions were to be got almost everywhere." Whidbey was nostalgic: the lawns had "a beauty of prospect equal to the most admired Parks of England."[2]

Nearly two centuries later, in 1979, well after the "lawns" observed by Vancouver's party had been converted to agriculture, the "pine forests" partially cut and managed for timber production, many indigenous species supplanted by Eurasian varieties, and the villages and seasonal camps of the Native Americans replaced by the cities and farms of Euro-American newcomers, anthropologist Jay Miller

> went into the Methow Valley [north-central Washington] with a van load of [Methow Indian] elders, some of whom had not been there for fifty years. When we had gone through about half the valley, a woman started to cry. I thought it was because she was homesick, but, after a time, she sobbed, 'When my people lived here, we took good care of all this land. We burned it over every fall to make it like a park. Now it is a jungle.' Every Methow I talked to after that confirmed the regular program of burning.[3]

Separated by 187 years of systemic, region-wide ecological change in the Pacific Northwest, these two sets of observations address several themes central to this volume.

The Pacific Northwest at first contact with Euro-Americans was not exclusively a forested wilderness. West of the Cascades, as documented in the Vancouver journals, there were large and small prairies scattered throughout a region that was climatically more suited to forest growth. And east of the mountains, as the Methow passage suggests, the forests of the past were quite different, with a minimum of underbrush and clutter. Other differences in local environments were present both east and west.

Vancouver believed that "Nature" alone was responsible for the "luxuriant lawns" and "well-stocked parks"; there is nothing in any of the expedition's journals suggesting that the Native inhabitants of the "inland sea" had any hand in their existence. Until relatively recently, most anthropologists believed this as well. The traditional stereotype of non-agricultural foraging peoples was that they simply took from the land and did not have the tools or knowledge to modify it to suit their needs. We now know better. Indigenous Northwesterners did indeed have a tool—fire—and they knew how to use it in ways that not only answered immediate purposes but also modified their environment. We now know that the "lawns" that Vancouver observed on Whidbey Island, the prairies that early trappers and explorers described in the Willamette Valley, and the open spaces that led the Hudson's Bay Company to select the site of Victoria for their headquarters in 1845 had been actively manipulated and managed, if not actually "created," by their Native inhabitants. Anthropogenic (human-caused) fire was by far the most important tool of environmental manipulation throughout the Native Pacific Northwest.

This does not mean, of course, that fire was ubiquitous in the pre-contact Northwest, that all peoples used it, nor that all environments were shaped by it. The "interior valleys" province[4] and the ponderosa pine forests of the east were most heavily affected; in contrast, fire use in the coastal wet forests appears to have been relatively limited. The amount of environmental modification practiced by Northwest Native Americans did not begin to approach the magnitude of change instituted by their Euro-American successors, or for that matter, the great majority of agricultural peoples. But the change they did create was much greater than has been assumed.

In almost all cases, the immediate reason for environmental fire use in the Northwest related to the food quest. Northwest Native Americans used fire in fire drives of deer and elk and in gathering species such as grasshoppers and tarweed. But more than this, they used it to create environments suitable for some of their most-favored food plants, such as camas and other root crops and many species of wild berries. Firing in the camas beds, huckleberry fields, oak groves, and tule flats, as well as other environments, took place *after* harvest, as a kind of post-use cleanup process, with ecological consequences in following seasons. Although reliable evidence is sparse, snippets of information such as that from the elderly Methow woman suggest that local

Native Americans may have shared with their Euro-American successors an aesthetic that favored open, manicured spaces, and deplored weedy clutter.

We have underestimated not only the Native Americans' ability to modify their environment, but their knowledge of it as well. Anthropologists have been very late in appreciating this information, and in most of the Pacific Northwest, much too late to collect it. The elders who retained the ecological knowledge have, for the most part, passed on. The fieldwork of several of the contributors to this volume[5] not only has captured a great deal of this remaining "traditional ecological knowledge," but (by implication) has given us a hint of the vast well of information that already has been lost.

Although we can't know exactly what was in the heads of these original environmental managers, we can look at the fruits of their labor—the environments first reported by early explorers—and gain some idea of what their knowledge included. There are only so many ways to produce open prairies in environments suitable for coniferous forests or bunchgrass plains where sagebrush and juniper are more likely to grow. Native Americans understood the concept of plant succession. They knew that the creative use of fire reverted the successional sequence to its early stages, and they favored fleshy annual plants with easily accessible nutrients instead of longer-growing, later-stage species that locked up nutrients in hard-to-utilize packages. Native Americans probably knew as much if not more about specific plant sequences in local communities as contemporary forest and rangeland specialists.

Although Northwest Indians were not agricultural, it is clear that they also understood that fertilizer—whether ash in tobacco plots or seaweed in clover beds—improved the growth of subsequent crops. Studies of camas plot exploitation from several separate areas suggest an understanding of the benefits of transplanting, weeding, and aerating the soil. And in recent times, Indian women in different areas have trimmed and cut back different berry species to enhance growth. Although we must recognize and control for the possibility that some of these practices have been influenced by post-contact exposure to White techniques, chances are most of them are aboriginal.[6]

Other ecological effects of burning and other traditional management practices that are apparent today may not have been so obvious or primary in the world of the Native Americans. The beneficial effects of understory and spot burning in several forest types as a preventive to wildfires, disease outbreaks, and extensive forest burns, now so apparent to Northwest forest managers, have become timely because of the ill-advised, unnatural (and culturally specific) practice of fire suppression. Likewise, Native Americans may not have understood contemporary ecologists' concept of "edge environments." But the effects of creating more ecological "borders" through selective burning were the same: to increase the number and variety of species in any given area. Native Americans also were not concerned with species depletion and loss and overall biodiversity: these are problems and issues of our own practices and times.

Patterns of Indian Burning in the Pacific Northwest

The papers in this volume summarize virtually everything that is known about Pacific Northwest Indian use of fire in the environment. Since the greater part of what the Indians knew has been lost, we are left with only a few early descriptions of fire-influenced environments and the few details elders were able to recall about former cultural systems of fire. But what remains shows a notable consistency—in species interactions, landscape consequences, and cultural patterning of fire use. Wherever mountain huckleberries were gathered, fire appears to have been applied in similar ways; wherever ponderosa pine forests occurred, the effects of anthropogenic fire appear to have been the same; wherever the fire drive was used to hunt deer, it was conducted in a similar fashion. Topographical, climatic, and ecological characteristics limited how fire could be safely and efficiently used in different ecosystems. Cross-cultural similarities in fire use may represent optimal ways of using fire to produce particular desired results, invented once or several times and spread to other cultures. Viewed together, these limitations and similarities constitute what the acknowledged expert on anthropological fire, Henry Lewis, would call "patterns" of Indian burning.

The Pacific Northwest, however, is not a unified environment, nor were its indigenous cultures all alike. There were numerous regional environments, and local cultures varied in the mix of elements that made up their total cultural systems. In the early 1980s, when I was collecting data for my paper on Willamette Valley Indian fire use, I noted that cultural patterns of fire in the Pacific Northwest tended to fall into identifiable regional clusters. In 1993, forest ecologist James Agee described the varying fire ecologies of major ecosystems in the Pacific Northwest.[7] As might be expected, many regional cultural patterns of fire use correspond closely to the ecosystems discussed by Agee. What follows is an attempt to expand and refine this discussion of regional patterns of fire use, incorporating the new, broader database on Indian fire represented by the papers in this volume, plus the greatly improved (since 1985) understanding of Pacific Northwest fire ecology.

The discussion will be organized by "ecoregions," defined as "regions of relative homogeneity in ecological systems or in relationships between organisms and their environments." There currently is no region-wide consensus on the exact delineation of ecoregions (Maps 2 and 3).[8] Those used here are broadly defined and vary from strictly biological systems by including humans among other organisms and indigenous cultures as forms

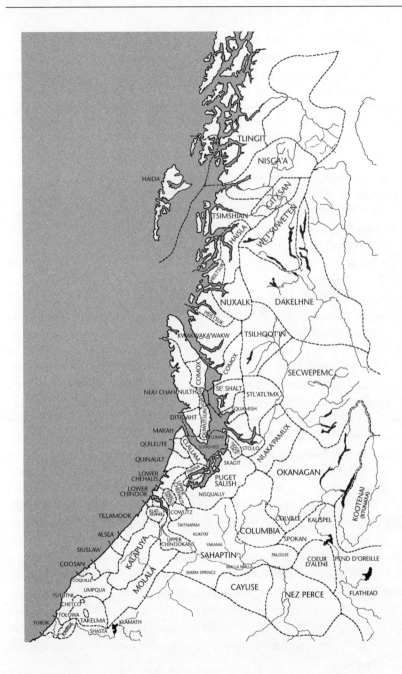

Map 1. Peoples of the Northwest Coast and Plateau culture areas. Map by David Myhrum, based on map by Wayne Suttles, Native Languages of the North Pacific Coast of North America. Copyright Cameron Suttles, 1978. British Columbia First Nations names from "First Nations of British Columbia" map, UBC Museum of Anthropology, 1996.

of adaptation to differing environments. Anthropologists divide the Pacific Northwest into two large "culture areas": "Northwest Coast" west of the Coastal-Cascade crest, and "Plateau" east of it, in the upper drainages of the Fraser and Columbia rivers (Map 1). Within these two major groupings, researchers have defined different subareas, mostly on the basis of clusterings of important culture traits.[9] The following discussion, of course, takes into account variations in only one cultural subsystem—the use of fire. Within the framework of eight "ecoregions," there is a summary of major vegetation types, an inventory of recorded indigenous fire uses, and a definition (where the evidence will allow) of the regional cultural "pattern" of fire use.

Coast Ecoregion

The Coast ecoregion is discussed (for British Columbia) in Nancy Turner's "'Time to Burn': Traditional Use of Fire to Enhance Resource Production." Called the "Coast Range ecoregion" in the U.S., in B.C. it corresponds to the "Coastal Western Hemlock vegetation zone," including most ecoregions of the "Coast and Mountains ecoprovince." Extending along the entire coast from 42° to 58°, there is considerable latitudinal variation in species composition. Major tree species are Sitka spruce (*Picea sitchensis*), Western hemlock (*Tsuga heterophylla*), red cedar (*Thuja plicata*), and Douglas-fir (*Pseudotsuga menziesii*) in the south. Understories include swordfern (*Polystichum munitum*) and salal (*Gaultheria shallon*), and mosses and Alaska blueberry (*Vaccinium alaskaense*) in the north. Indigenous cultures include all the peoples with Pacific coastal frontage: Tlingit, the coastal Tsimshian peoples, Haida, Heiltsuk, Nuxalk, Kwakwaka'wakw, Nuu-chah-nulth, Makah, Quileute, Quinault, Chinook, Tillamook, Siuslawan, Coosan, and Tututni. The high precipitation (200–300 cm/yr) and importance of marine resources probably explain the relative lack of historic or anthropological documentation of anthropogenic burning in this region. Yet it did occur. Early explorers attributed autumn smoke at both Cape Flattery and the mouth of the Rogue to Indian-caused fires.[10] Three coastal peoples (Coos, Tillamook [probable], and Quileute) burned back brush to facilitate deer hunting.[11] Burning of limited areas to encourage berry growth seems to have been the most common use, however: Turner reports it for all coastal B.C. peoples from Haida to Nuu-chah-nulth; and anthropologist Elizabeth Jacobs verified it among the Tillamook:

> every few years the berry pickers would burn over the salal or shot huckleberry (*Vaccinium ovatum*) patch. That meant no berries there next season, but a greatly improved crop the second year. This was done to improve blackberry patches as well; these vines bore more lavishly the immediately following season.[12]

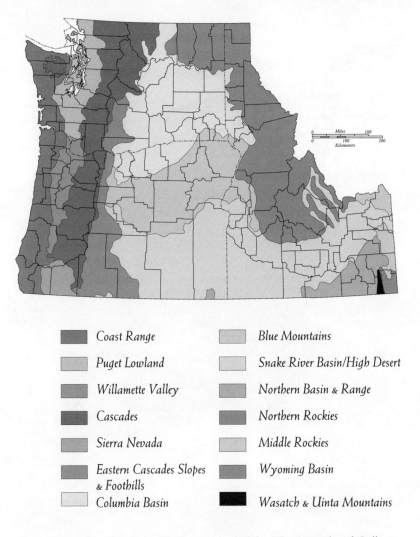

<table>
<tr><td>Coast Range</td><td>Blue Mountains</td></tr>
<tr><td>Puget Lowland</td><td>Snake River Basin/High Desert</td></tr>
<tr><td>Willamette Valley</td><td>Northern Basin & Range</td></tr>
<tr><td>Cascades</td><td>Northern Rockies</td></tr>
<tr><td>Sierra Nevada</td><td>Middle Rockies</td></tr>
<tr><td>Eastern Cascades Slopes & Foothills</td><td>Wyoming Basin</td></tr>
<tr><td>Columbia Basin</td><td>Wasatch & Uinta Mountains</td></tr>
</table>

Map 2. Ecoregions of Oregon, Washington, and Idaho. The Omernik and Gallant classification (1986), from Atlas of the Pacific Northwest, edited by Philip L. Jackson and A. Jon Kimerling, published by Oregon State University Press, 1993.

Agee states that fire is, indeed, rare in this zone, and that when it does occur, shrubs including salal, red huckleberry (*Vaccinium parvifolium*), salmonberry (*Rubus spectablis*), and vine maple (*Acer circinatum*) are early colonizers.[13] The limited ethnographic citations mention burning for the first two species more than once.

Along the Olympic Peninsula coast, burning may have maintained prairies at Quillayute and Forks, where important food sources such as bracken were concentrated.[14] The Tillamook area presents an interesting case. It has been

Map 3. Ecoprovinces of British Columbia. Map by Ric Vrana after original by Dennis Dimarchi, courtesy of Province of British Columbia, Ministry of Environment, Lands and Parks.

suggested that Tillamooks also may have burned to open up areas for camas (*Camassia quamash*), which on archaeological evidence appears to have been formerly much more widespread.[15] On the coast itself, anthropogenic fire use may have been locally intense, as the following notation indicates:

> October 1856. At this time there was not a bush or tree to be seen on these hills (Bay City) as the Indians kept them burned off every spring, but when the whites came they stopt the fires.[16]

But at the same time, there is no ethnographic or historic evidence of patterned Indian use of fire in the forested interior of Tillamook County, an area dominated by seral stands of Douglas-fir. Throughout the Coastal ecoregion, Indian subsistence was oriented to the sea, and the few reasons for fire use recorded by anthropologists do not indicate interior exploitation.[17]

Puget Sound Ecoregion

The Puget Sound ecoregion combines three overlapping ecosystems in Agee: Western hemlock, Douglas-fir, and Oregon oak; and corresponds to the "Georgia Depression" ecoprovince of British Columbia. Ecologists characterize this as an area of mixed communities: "Prairie, oak woodland, and pine forest are encountered."[18] Microclimatic differences and glacial soils are important influences. Cultures are all Coast Salish, including Quwutsun', Sto:lo, Lummi, Lushootseed (Puget Salish), Upper Chehalis, and Cowlitz speakers. Anthropogenic burning was concentrated in the prairies of the middle section of this region, which dotted the landscape from the Cowlitz River in the south to the Tsolum River on Vancouver Island. The prairies, their maintenance by fire, and their important plant species are discussed in Richard White's "Indian Land Use and Environmental Change: Island County, Washington, a Test Case," Estella Leopold and Robert Boyd's "An Ecological History of Old Prairie Areas in Southwestern Washington," and Nancy Turner's 'Time to Burn'.[19]

Although the origin of the prairies dates to a warm, dry period between 9500 and 4500 B.P., their maintenance was due to patterned seasonal burning by the Salishan peoples. Firing of the prairies every year before the first autumn rains is documented in Hudson's Bay Company journals at Forts Nisqually and Victoria, by early settlers on Whidbey Island, and in ethnographic accounts from all areas. On the Nisqually Plains there was definite patterning to the late summer/early fall fires. Journal references from several years consistently fall during the dry time from August 13 to September 12, with intermittent blazes in the preceding and following months, apparently dependent on annual climatic variations.[20]

Economically important plants were concentrated on prairies; fire was used in the management of important species such as camas, blackberries (*Rubus ursinus*), and bunchgrass (*Festuca idahoensis*); and virtually all the other prairie species used by Indians are fire followers (e.g. bracken, *Pteridium aquilinum*) or benefit from frequent low-level fire (e.g., acorn production). One of the area's earliest ethnographers provides a clear picture of the productivity of the western Washington prairies and how their major crops were gathered:

> the kamas . . . are found in great quantities . . . in the prairies
> . . . and they were formerly a great article of trade with the interior.
> Besides these, the roots of the sunflower [*Balsamorhiza deltoidea*] and
> fern are largely used, and a small white root of rather insipid taste
> [probably chocolate lily, *Fritillaria lanceolata*]. From the fern, they make
> a species of flour which is baked into bread. The kamas season is in
> the latter part of May and June, and then as well as in the fall when
> the sunflower is dug, the prairies are dotted over with squaws, each
> armed with a sharp stick and a basket, busily engaged in digging

them. At these times, camps are generally found near the skirts of timber which border the open lands for the convenience of gathering and preserving. The kamas are baked in the ground.[21]

Burning the prairies in early autumn before the rains allowed a second growth of the native bunchgrass, providing year-round pasture for deer and (in later years) horses.

Everywhere, in this part of the country [Nisqually in 1841], the prairies open wide, covered with a low grass of a most nutritious kind, which remains good throughout the year. In September there are slight rains, at which time the grass commences a luxuriant growth, and in October and November, there is an abundance of green grass, which remains until the ensuing summer, about June, it is ripe, and drying without being wet, is like our hay in New England; in this state, it remains until the Autumn rains begin to revive it.[22]

The western Washington prairies were a major feature of the "managed landscape" of the pre-White Pacific Northwest.

Willamette Valley Ecoregion

The Willamette Valley ecoregion is discussed in Robert Boyd's "Strategies of Indian Burning in the Willamette Valley." It includes valley wet prairies and oak savannas, riverine deciduous (ash, [*Fraxinus latifolia*] and alder [*Alnus rubra*]) corridors, and encircling foothill conifer (Douglas-fir and Western hemlock) forests. Dominant tree species are Oregon oak (*Quercus garryana*), Douglas-fir, and bigleaf maple (*Acer macrophyllum*). The indigenous valley grasses were displaced early and are not well known; they probably included native bunchgrasses *Deschampsia cespitosa* in the wet prairies and *Festuca rubra* in the savannas. Forbs (flowering plants) accompanied the prairie grasses; various shrub species grew in the borders and forest understories. Cultures include Kalapuya and Klikitat (intrusive) in the valley and Molala in Cascade conifer forests.

As in western Washington, prairies were central to Indian settlement and subsistence. But the Willamette Valley, prairies were more continuous and of much greater extent than in western Washington. According to analyses of 1850s land survey maps,[23] prairies covered the greater part of the valley and its lower elevation foothills. Lightning fires are rare in western Washington and northwestern Oregon, but plentiful historical records substantiate extensive indigenous burning in late August–early September, and apparently spottily and earlier in special microenvironments. Burning was a constituent part of many food-getting activities, including the deer drive and tarweed (*Madia* spp.) and grasshopper gathering; otherwise it was apparently used after harvest with secondary benefits for acorn, root, and berry (various species, notably camas and blackberry) production. Fire also was important in the production of basketry materials (e.g. hazel, *Corylus cornuta*) and in tobacco cultivation. The particulars of the cultural management of all these species are largely unknown and must be surmised given the termination of aboriginal burning in the 1850s. But the ubiquity of fire in the subsistence quest and environment has led one researcher to term the indigenous valley life-style a "pyroculture."[24] The Willamette Valley was the most intensively fire-managed environment in the aboriginal Northwest.

Upper Rogue Ecoregion

The Upper Rogue ecoregion is described in Jeff LaLande and Reg Pullen's "Burning for a 'Fine and Beautiful Open Country': Native Uses of Fire in Southwestern Oregon." The Upper Rogue ("Sierra Nevada" on Map 2) is characterized by mixed Douglas-fir and hardwood forests with considerable altitudinal variation: oak and ponderosa pine predominate in the savannas; Douglas-fir with several other species mid-range; and white fir (*Abies concolor*) is important in higher elevations. Shrub composition is highly mixed and variable with hazel, poison oak (*Rhus diversiloba*), blackberry, and wild rose (*Rosa gymnocarpa*) common. Fire-resistant species and open understories were typical in most associations. The Upper Rogue is transitional, both environmentally and culturally, between the Willamette Valley and California.[25] It is drier with more lightning fires; there is a greater variety of ecosystems and a more diverse assemblage of economically important fire-affected species. Cultures included Takelman-speaking Takelma and Cow Creek Umpqua, and several Athapascan-speaking peoples on Rogue tributaries and the middle Umpqua river.

Firing was not limited to the valley savannas but occurred in higher-elevation mixed woodlands and (apparently) along trails and ridges as well. Early historical accounts describe "chains of prairies" along trails and grass-covered ridgetops, reminiscent of fire-maintained "yards" and "corridors" known from the southern Washington Cascades, northwest California, and several other regions.[26] All the "reasons" for burning in the Willamette Valley were duplicated here, with some variation: less concentration on roots and more on seeds, burning for both hazelnuts and basketry material, and in the utilization of mid-elevation species such as the sugar pine (*Pinus lambertiana*). And there is more surviving ethnographic data on the social direction of firing activities.

Cascade Ecoregion

The Cascade ecoregion (Pacific and Cascade Ranges ecoregion of the "Coast and Mountains" ecoprovince in B.C.) is discussed in two papers: David French's "Aboriginal Control of Huckleberry Yield in the Northwest"; and Helen Norton, Robert Boyd, and Eugene Hunn's "The Klikitat Trail of South-Central Washington: A Reconstruction of Seasonally Used Resource Sites." The ecoregion includes lower-elevation conifer forests and high-elevation subalpine communities. The forests are dominated by Douglas-fir with Western hemlock and Western red cedar in old-growth areas. Understories include salal, rhododendron, Oregon grape (*Berberis nervosa*), vine maple, and oceanspray (*Holodiscus discolor*). Subalpine trees include silver and subalpine fir (*Abies amablis and A. lasiocarpa*) and Engelmann spruce (*Picea engelmannii*). Plant communities are locally dominated by Cascade blueberry (*Vaccinium deliciosum*), black alpine sedge (*Carex nigricans*) and *Saxifraga tolmiei*. Cultures: includes the higher elevations of all the Pacific Coast B.C. peoples and most Coast Salish, Northwest Sahaptin Taitnapam and Klikitat, Upper Chinookans, and Molala in the States.

Burning of black mountain huckleberry patches (*Vaccinium membranaceum*) was the prominent activity in the subalpine zone, with the particulars and effects well known, since the practice survived until recent times, well within the memories of living informants. Autumn burns took place after the berry harvest; the ecological effects on huckleberries and other vegetation were well understood and manipulated by the Indians. Productivity was enhanced by managed fire; fire prevented invasion by shrubs and trees. Burned over areas were limited in extent and, particularly in the southern half of the Northwest, apparently dotted along trails that traversed both subalpine and lower forested zones. Other useful species (e.g. various *Vaccinium*, beargrass [*Xerophyllum tenax*], and kinnikinnick [*Arctostaphylos uva-ursi*]) were available altitudinally in these "yards." In post-contact times, the openings along trails picked up an added function as pasture for horses. Most peoples who exploited this region visited it seasonally when desired species were ripe; a few southern Pacific Northwest peoples, in particular the Molala of the western Oregon Cascade foothills and the Taitnapam and Klikitat of the southern Washington Cascades, spent much of their annual round in the prairies and openings of the subalpine zone and neighboring forests. Like other Northwest peoples who occupied more extensive grasslands, these latter three also could be called "prairie peoples."[27]

Columbia Basin Ecoregion

The Columbia Basin is discussed in William Robbins's "Landscape and Environment: Ecological Change in the Intermontane Northwest." Most researchers divide the basin into three zones, but considering the cultural adaptation, it is better viewed as a single region, with significant environmental differences varying by altitude. Geographically, the ecoregion centers on the steppeland of eastern Oregon and Washington and coincides with the southern, western, and central portions of the Columbia Basin. Ecologists characterize the central, driest portion as sagebrush (*Artemisia*) steppe. Sagebrush, however, is very vulnerable to fire, while the three dominant annual bunchgrasses (*Festuca idahoensis, Agropyron spicatum* and *Poa sandbergii*), found throughout the ecoregion, are not. The steppe also included a medley of assorted forbs: besides the dominant yarrow (*Achillea millefolium*), there were economically important species such as the *Lomatiums* and certain lilies valued for their roots. In higher elevations were ponderosa pine forests, usually a narrow strip between the treeless steppes and montane coniferous forests but fairly large in the Yakima and Grande Ronde Valleys. Camas and balsamroot (*Balsamorhiza sagittata*) were common components of the ponderosa pine zone.

Indigenous cultures included some Upper Chinookans, Sahaptin,[28] Nez Perce, and Columbia Salish. These peoples were seasonally mobile and their subsistence quest took them to different locations as wild foods became available. As far as plant foods were concerned, the sequence was roughly altitudinal: dry land roots (e.g. *Lomatium cous, Lewisia rediviva*) in April and May, camas in June through September, and black mountain huckleberry in August–September.[29] Most extant evidence on fire use from this region is historical and suggests that burning also followed an altitudinal gradient: low-lying areas (near villages?) "lately burnt," with new grass or clover (*Trifolium*) in May and early June; open prairie land (from Walla Walla, the Palouse region, Wascopam, and Umatilla) during August; higher areas (in the Grande Ronde or the Blue Mountains) in late August.[30] The best source on reasons for fire use in this area comes from anthropological "culture element" inventories: five peoples burned to gather "sunflower seeds"; four "burned brush to drive game out."[31] The most frequently mentioned "reason" for burning in the historical literature is for a new growth of grass, followed by the deer drive, animal forage, and seed gathering. One source mentions grasshoppers; it is likely that the early White observers, who saw the fires but didn't ask "why," missed many more reasons. The dating of the historical citations *suggests* post-harvest "clean-up." Alan Marshall's Nez Perce informants "asserted that the firing of prairies . . . was intentional and common because it improved the quality and quantity" of the three most important Nez Perce plant foods: *Lomatium cous, L. canbyi,* and camas. Marshall notes that the intentional burning of these root patches, along with harvest-associated disturbance of the soil and replanting of unsatisfactory roots, resembled "swidden techniques" used elsewhere by horticultural peoples.[32]

Northern Rockies Ecoregion

The Northern Rockies ecoregion ("Southern Interior Mountains" ecoprovince in B.C.) is discussed in Stephen Barrett's and Stephen Arno's "Indian Fires in the Northern Rockies: Ethnohistory and Ecology" and John Ross's "Protohistorical and Historical Spokan Prescribed Burning and Stewardship of Resource Areas." Geographically, the region includes northeast Washington, southeast B.C., the Idaho panhandle, and Montana west of the continental divide. Ponderosa pine was found in the valleys; Douglas-fir and lodgepole pine (*Pinus contorta*) at mid elevations; grand and supalpine firs (*Abies grandis* and *A. lasiocarpa*) higher up. Important understory species include the three Plateau grasses, camas, and sunflower in the ponderosa zone; Oregon boxwood (*Pachistima myrsinites*), pinegrass (*Calamagrostis rubescens*), and several economically valuable plants: black mountain huckleberry, grouseberry (*V. scoparium*), beargrass, and wild rose in the mountains. Cultures: the larger part of the ranges of the Salish (Flathead, Pend d'Oreille, Kalispel), Spokan, Coeur d'Alene, and Colville Interior Salish and Kootenai.

In western Montana, burning clearly was concentrated in the valleys where settlements occurred, with less frequent firing intervals at higher elevations. Fire was frequent enough that it kept forest understories in the ponderosa zone clear and prevented succession to closed Douglas-fir stands. These findings seem to be borne out by the several uses documented ethnographically for the Spokan: "clean-up" around villages and springs and in tule stands; to create deer browse and horse pasture; for camas, cous, sunflower seeds, and pinenuts in the "piney woods." Deer drives probably extended into the lower elevation forests. In higher elevations, campsites and trails as well as mountain huckleberry patches were burned. Individuals with special "powers" and knowledge directed the deer drive[33] and huckleberry patch burning.

Middle Fraser Ecoregion

The middle Fraser ("Southern Interior" ecoprovince) is discussed in Nancy Turner's "'Time to Burn': Traditional Use of Fire to Enhance Resource Production by Aboriginal Peoples in British Columbia." From Hope upstream, the Fraser River drainage is a highly dissected plateau with canyons and mountain ridges. Vegetational zones shift rapidly with elevation: there are bunchgrass associations on the middle Fraser, the Thompson, and along the Okanagan (which, although in the Columbia drainage, probably should be considered an outlier of this ecoregion). A thin ponderosa pine belt surrounds all these areas, with interior Douglas-fir forests on the plateau and Engelmann spruce/subalpine fir associations in the mountains. Cultures include Stl'atl'imx (Lillooet), Nlaka'pamux (Thompson), Secwepemc (Shuswap), and Okanagan.

The subsistence round here was, as might be expected, highly altitudinal, though people apparently did not follow a strictly uphill sequence, instead moving back and forth between zones as need dictated. Roots and berries were important foods, though with a different selection than in the Columbia Basin: camas and cous were absent, and serviceberry (*Amelanchier alnifolia*) was the most important berry species. Indians burned every few years to manipulate crops of montane roots (avalanche lily, tiger lily, spring beauty; *Erythronium grandiflorum, Lilium columbianum,* and *Claytonia lanceolata*) and, less frequently, the black mountain huckleberry. In the lower elevations, burning is not as well documented, though it certainly occurred. "Blueberries" (various *Vaccinium* species), onions (*Allium*), raspberries (*Rubus idaeus*), and blackcaps (*Rubus leucodermis*), all managed by fire, are found here, and Turner notes that serviceberry is a fire follower, producing best in twenty to forty-year-old burns. Hazel bushes were burned in the lowest elevations.[34] More information on lower-elevation burning may be preserved in early historical records, such as the Hudson's Bay Company's Fort Kamloops Journal.

Gitxsan Interior Cedar-Hemlock Zone

This zone (corresponding to the Nass Basin and Nass Ranges ecoregions of the Coast and Mountains ecoprovince) is described by Leslie Johnson in "Aboriginal Burning for Vegetation Management in Northwest British Columbia." The northern-most region covered in this book, it is (as Johnson notes) "transitional between the northwest coast and boreal interior" and is named after the co-dominant red cedar and hemlock. Unlike virtually all other forested regions in the Northwest, this area lacks Douglas-fir. Mosses are important, as are subalpine fir, bunchberry (*Cornus canadensis*), and the black mountain huckleberry. The Gitxsan people are located wholly within this zone; neighboring Wet'suwet'en territory is a part of the sub-boreal Central Interior ecoprovince, dominated by Engelmann spruce, with mosses and bunchberry.

Burning to manipulate berry crops (black mountain huckleberry, low bush blueberry [*V. caespitosum*], and soapberry [*Shepherdia canadensis*]) was most important here, and unlike in the south, most berry patches were not far from villages. Berry burning occurred in autumn; patches were burned every four years. Gitxsan also burned floodplains in spring (originally probably to manage riceroot, *Fritillaria camschatcensis*), and around villages. Johnson suggests that the seral plant communities of the area may have been influenced by Indian burning.

Background Research on Anthropogenic Fire

In-depth studies of fire use by indigenous peoples such as those of the Pacific Northwest are recent, resulting from the convergence of several lines of research: in geography, anthropology, environmental studies, and history. Early on paleoanthropologists recognized that fire use was an important technological advance in human cultural evolution. By providing artificial warmth, fire allowed early humans to expand into cold environments, and through cooking, to break down tough plant and animal tissues, thus increasing food supplies. The "domestication" of fire traditionally has been set at around 500,000 years ago, concurrent with the first evidence of occupation of the colder latitudes of Eurasia by *Homo erectus*. There is archaeological evidence that the fire drive in hunting grazing animals was used at this time too. But traditionally, anthropologists considered this solely a technological advance.[35]

Geography

Studies of the role of anthropogenic fire in the environment were instead initiated by geographers, most notably Carl Sauer at the University of California (Berkeley), in the 1930s and 1940s. Sauer and his students noted that many "savannas, steppes, and prairies," particularly in the Americas, were shaped by what he called aboriginal "fire economies," in which fire was a major and recurring tool of the food quest. Sauer considered the savannas of Middle America, the tall grass prairies of the Midwest, and the open deciduous forests of the early contact East Coast all to have been shaped by anthropogenic fire. His theories have been confirmed by later geological studies.[36] In the Northwest, a watershed geographical study was Carl Johannessen *et al.*'s 1971 "The Vegetation of the Willamette Valley," which documented the role of anthropogenic fire in the maintenance of valley prairies. In recent years, several geographers have returned to the theme of anthropogenic effects on the landscape in pre-Columbian America, with particular attention to the role of fire.[37]

Anthropology: Stewart and Lewis

Anthropological studies of fire use also began at the University of California, but were approached from a different perspective. Beginning in the late 1930s, the anthropology department began an ambitious "culture element survey" of virtually all the Indian cultures of the West Coast. Informants were questioned about the presence or absence of various traits: technological, social organization, subsistence, etc., and comparative lists were constructed from their answers. One ethnographer, Omer Stewart, who was responsible for most Great Basin peoples, noted what previous ethnographers had missed: aboriginal fire use was ubiquitous throughout the interior west, often with significant environmental effects. In 1953, he completed an 800-page comparative study (as yet unpublished), and several articles on Indian fire use followed. As an anthropologist, Stewart was concerned with the role of fire in culture: he wanted to know *why* Indians burned—what were their reasons? But ecological effects were important too: like Sauer, Stewart believed that the Great Plains were maintained largely by anthropogenic fire.[38]

The seminal paper in the anthropological literature on fire, Henry Lewis's 1973 *Patterns of Indian Burning in California*, combined the ecological awareness of Sauer with the anthropological sensibility of Stewart (as well as practical knowledge derived from experience as a fire-fighter in northern California's national forests). Lewis brought together ethnographic, ethnohistoric, and ecological evidence that made it clear that Indian fire use strongly influenced the pre-White environments of northern California, from grassland through chaparral to redwood forests, setting back natural successions, clearing underbrush, and producing open areas in the forest. Since 1973, Lewis has written on many aspects of aboriginal fire use, including the role of anthropogenic fire in plant and animal resource management and domestication, the technology of burning and cross-culturally valid types of burned areas, and "traditional ecological knowledge." Beyond northern California, he has conducted fieldwork on fire use among northern Alberta Indians and Australian aborigines. His fieldwork with living informants who until recently practiced aboriginal burning has allowed him to flesh out the bare bones of practices that were otherwise known only through historical accounts of surviving pyrogenic environments, and to fill in a gap that earlier anthropologists had overlooked.[39]

Anthropology: Resource Management

The anthropological perspective on fire use also includes a consideration of its role in the native food quest, or subsistence pattern. Sauer's list of "reasons" for burning included examples where fire was not only a tool that produced immediate results in hunting and gathering, but also a way of modifying the environment to attract wild animals or to produce greater future yields of plants. The latter kind of fire use is very important in West Coast ethnography, where *none* of the Native peoples (with the exception of a few in southern California) practiced "true" agriculture, where the ground is broken and plants are grown from seeds or cuttings, and where there is demonstrable genetic change in species tended by humans. West Coast peoples *understood* the concept of planting (many grew tobacco from seed), but none used it with food plants. In the 1930s it was pointed out that one southern Basin group, the Owens Valley Paiute, *irrigated* crops (wild hyacinth and yellow nutgrass), although they did not plant them. Later studies among Nevada Paiutes uncovered other forms of what was initially termed "environmental manipulation," including broadcasting seeds and burning to improve future growth. The earliest "ethnobotanical" studies in the Great Basin, California, and the Northwest inventoried the vast range of wild plants available to and used by Native peoples. More recent studies are much more sophisticated, and despite the rapidly diminishing pool of native knowledge, or "ethnoscience," try to uncover the myriad ways these wild resources were managed in lieu of true agriculture.[40]

In California, for instance, ecologist Kat Anderson has found, through interviews with Native American elders, that plant species used in basketry (such as deer grass and redbud) were either burned over or pruned to cause regrowth of straight, long stems or branches; sedge plots were weeded, spaced, and left fallow to produce rhizomes suitable for baskets; and plots of lilaceous bulbs were dug selectively, aerating the soil and severing and leaving smaller bulbs to grow back. The California researchers now use the word "environmental management" to refer to this bundle of sophisticated techniques, and recognize that Indians not only were causing significant alterations in their environment, as Lewis has shown, but also were probably directing change in the gene pool of selected species, as Anderson has suggested. In 1993, several significant California papers were published in *Before the Wilderness: Environmental Management by Native Californians*, an inspiration for this volume.[41]

For the Pacific Northwest, the problem of indigenous plant management was addressed at a symposium, "Was the Northwest Coast Agricultural?", at the 1997 meeting of the American Association for the Advancement of Science. The proceedings of that symposium, edited by Douglas Deur and Nancy Turner, are to be published as a volume tentatively titled *"Keeping it Living": Traditional plant tending and cultivation on the Northwest Coast*. Papers address several topics relevant to the contributions in this volume: the foraging-cultivation continuum and the definition of "agriculture"; management of two important wild root crops: camas among the Coast Salish and wapato (*Sagittaria latifolia*) among Chinookans; and plant management among two North Coast peoples, Tlingit and Tsimshian. Nancy Turner and Sandra Peacock, in "Anthropogenic Plant Communities of the Northwest Coast," discuss (for British Columbia) several of the management techniques Kat Anderson has studied in California, including tilling, weeding and clearing, pruning, replanting and transplanting, and "gardening" of owned plots of important species, using a combination of techniques. They also survey eight "anthropogenic plant communities" in British Columbia, where the precontact vegetation cover was altered by human activities.

New Directions in Archaeology

A few of the papers in *"Keeping it Living"* address specifically archaeological subjects. Douglas Deur discusses the archaeological evidence for Kwakwa̱ka̱'wakw management of springbank clover (*Trifolium wormskjoldii*) in rock-lined plots along the coast, where they were "fertilized" by seaweed deposited at high tide; and for camas in Tillamook County (Oregon), where archaeological remains suggest a much wider distribution in pre-contact times, perhaps facilitated by burning to create suitable environments.[42] And Dana Lepofsky and colleagues from Simon Fraser University, in an innovative paper, describe their project to determine the antiquity of anthropogenic burning among the Sto:lo people of the lower Fraser River. Lepofsky *et al.* combine several research methodologies used by the contributors to *Indians, Fire, and the Land . . .* , including ethnographic interviews with elders, fire ecology (place and time of burns), carbon lenses in soil profiles, and palynological studies of changing vegetation.[43]

"Documenting Precontact Plant Management on the Northwest Coast: An Example of Prescribed Burning in the Central and Upper Fraser Valley, British Columbia" is significant not only for its methodology, but for what it hopes to find. Lepofsky *et al.* hypothesize that burning represented a form of "resource intensification" similar to that known archaeologically for salmon and camas, when improved knowledge and technology created increases in food supply, contributing indirectly to population growth and overall cultural complexity. They anticipate that the record will show evidence for increased burning and "burning specialists" (e.g., Ross, this volume) coincident with the appearance of more complex hierarchical social systems 2,500 year ago. Not mentioned, but possibly as important, may be the pronounced climatic cooling and retreat of productive dryland environments that occurred in the Northwest about the same time (Leopold and Boyd, this volume). As many important species became less common, knowledge of ways to maximize their growth may have been at a premium (LaLande and Pullen, this volume). In the southern Plateau, this "cooling down" period has been associated with several changes in adaptation, demography, and cultural complexity.[44] Holistic studies such as Lepofsky *et al.* hold great promise for future research.[45]

Fire Ecology

Fire ecology itself is a new field. Development of the field was stymied for many years by what has been called the "Smokey the Bear syndrome": a pervasive belief, peculiar to Western cultures, that fire was a destructive force, particularly in forests, that had to be contained or eliminated. During the 1960s, the (non-governmental) annual Tall Timbers fire ecology conference was the only place where one might encounter researchers who were interested in the positive effects of fire on the environment. With the growth of the field of ecology itself in the 1970s, it became apparent that fire was an integral part of an interrelated system of plants, animals, and the land. Its ecological benefits of cleansing, fertilizing, altering succession patterns, and creating mosaics high in species diversity emerged as a counterbalance to the more readily perceived problems of economic loss of timber and wildfire destructiveness. We now know that many forest and rangeland species, particularly in western North America, are adapted to regular low-level, recurrent fires, and that the raging wildfires characteristic of the post-settlement West are abnormal—a product, ironically, of the very policies that were instituted to prevent them. Forest and range managers just now are beginning to play catch-up with what the original inhabitants of the American West knew all along. Prescribed fire, mimicking pre-contact conditions, is a large part of the U.S. government's Northwest Forest Plan, in both coastal and interior lands. In the past fifteen years there have been several high-visibility conferences on fire ecology, and Stephen Pyne's books (*Fire in America,* 1981, and *World Fire: the culture of fire on earth,* 1995) have introduced the field to a broad audience. In the Pacific Northwest, two important volumes on fire ecology have appeared recently: John Walstad *et al.*'s 1990 *Natural and Prescribed Fire in Pacific Northwest Forests* and James Agee's 1993 *Fire Ecology of Pacific Northwest Forests.* In all of these more recent volumes there is a growing appreciation of the role of Native Americans in pre-settlement fire ecology; Agee in particular devotes several pages to it.[46]

Environmental History

American historians also came to the topic of Indian fire use late, concurrent with the rise of the new subfield, environmental history, in the 1970s. Most environmental histories limit themselves to the relationship between the European colonists of North America and the land, but a few have adopted a more holistic approach, and have backtracked to consider the relationships of Native Americans and the land as well. Two of the most influential books in the sub-field, Richard White's *Land Use, Environment, and Social Change: the shaping of Island County, Washington* and William Cronon's *Changes in the Land: Indians, Colonists and the Ecology of New England* do just that, and lay considerable importance on the Indian use of fire in shaping the environment (White has said, "No single Indian practice contributed to more dramatic changes in North American environments."). These environmental historians have adopted (consciously or intuitively) the anthropological concept of "ecological transition," an abrupt shift in systemic relations, which like the more familiar concepts of demographic transition, epidemiological transition (or even scientific revolution) signifies a revolutionary change in the way things are ordered. Regional environmental histories with this long historical perspective continue to be written: from the Northwest, three important works are Peter Boag's *Environment and Experience: settlement culture in nineteenth century Oregon*, Robert Bunting's *The Pacific Raincoast: environment and culture in an American Eden, 1778–1900*, and William Robbins's *Landscapes of Promise: the Oregon story, 1800–1940*.[47]

Introduction to the Papers

As a result of the post-contact "ecological transition" in the Pacific Northwest, most of the environments first encountered by the Whites are gone or radically changed, and the knowledge that lay behind their active management has disappeared with them. We, the current inhabitants of the Northwest, need to know what these earlier environments were like—what their possibilities are—so we can best manage them for today. Most of the original ethnohistorical data on pre-White Northwest fire environments, scattered in early historical records, is not readily available. Much of that data is reprinted here. Since the early 1970s, regional anthropologists, their blinders to the effect of hunter/gatherer/fisherfolk on their environments removed, have documented the indigenous use of fire, both by recording early historical observations and by interviewing the few surviving native peoples who understood the patterns and remember some of the techniques. Again, we need to do our best to record and recreate this knowledge so it can serve us today. The papers reproduced here include the larger part of what is known about Indian environmental fire use in the Northwest.

The papers represent several different disciplines and approach the problem of aboriginal fire from several perspectives, each with its own methodology. Of the twelve, six are by anthropologists, three are by historians, two by botanists, and one by professional foresters. Several of the contributors are ethnobotanists; three are environmental historians; one of the anthropologists is an ethnohistorian; one of the botanists a palynologist. The papers come from all parts of the Native Northwest: northern B.C., British Columbia in general, the Montana Rockies, northeast Washington, the Columbia Plateau, Whidbey Island, southwestern Washington, the Willamette Valley, and southwestern Oregon. In addition, there is a comparative paper which considers indigenous burning in northern Alberta, northern California, Australia, and western Washington.

Nine of the papers originally were published elsewhere; the majority of these have been revised and updated. Three of the papers have not been published previously: two were prepared especially for this volume. The papers are presented in chronological order of first appearance. Ordering them in this fashion shows how and when ideas first appeared, were picked up by different disciplines and applied to different areas, and how the pool of knowledge grew and the case for indigenous fire management in the Northwest became stronger.

All the papers reproduced here date from the second half of the twentieth century. But the oldest analytical work on regional fire use predates them by a century. This is James G. Cooper's "Report on the Botany of the Route," in volume 12 of the *Report of the Pacific Railroad surveys of 1853–55*.[48] Like many of the earliest explorers of the Northwest, Cooper *noted* the effects of Indian fires, but then went a step beyond to incorporate this observation in his *theory* of the origin of the "dry prairies" of western Washington. They were, he held, maintained by regular Indian burning.[49] Cooper also collected some 150 species of plants native to these managed prairies, and noted that their floral composition tied them to prairies in California and the Midwest. But as Richard White observes (in this volume), Cooper's insights were ignored for a century.

The first paper on anthropogenic fire printed here, David French's 1957 "Aboriginal Control of Huckleberry Yield in the Northwest" had different roots. French was aware of Omer Stewart's papers on the role of Indian fire in cultural evolution and shaping the environment, but his immediate concern was with what today would be called the "foraging-agricultural continuum," and the origins of agriculture itself. French's Indian informants, though not technically "agricultural," understood the principle of planting, and "managed" (although he did not use this word) a wild crop, the black mountain huckleberry, through burning. French's paper, though influential among local anthropologists, has never been published. The second paper, Richard White's "Indian Land Use and Environmental Change: Island County Washington, a Test Case" built on different precedents. White, a historian, had read Carl Sauer's works on environmental modification through fire, as well as Cooper's "Botany of the Route." Combined with contemporary anthropological data on Northwest Indian plant use plus his own historic research on the environment of Whidbey Island, White revived Cooper's argument that the prairies were shaped by Indian fire, and found a reason in the propagation of three useful plants. The paper, printed in *Arizona and the West* in 1975, was influential in the emerging field of environmental history. A third important regional paper, not reprinted here, was Helen H. Norton's 1979 "The Association between Anthropogenic Prairies and Important Food Plants in Western Washington." Norton, while acknowledging the precedents of Cooper and White, built on them. An ethnobotanist well versed in the growing regional descriptive school of Erna Gunther and Nancy Turner, she uncovered historical data on Indian fire use in the Nisqually Plains and analyzed Cooper's prairie plant list, making the discovery that an unusually large proportion of the prairie plants were utilized by the Indians for food, technology, and medicine. By 1979 the link between Indian fires, environmental modification, and useful plants had become clearer.

In the early 1980s, on the eastern margin of the Pacific Northwest, foresters Stephen Barrett and Stephen Arno produced several papers on the effects of Indian fires on Rocky Mountain forests. The precedent here was the growing literature on fire ecology, and the desire to—using methodologies from forestry—test the hypothesis drawn from the local body of historical and ethnographic sources that Indian fire as well as natural fire had important effects on the environment. Helen Norton, Robert Boyd, and Eugene Hunn's 1983 "Klikitat Trail of South-Central Washington" returned to the records of the Pacific Railroad Surveys, in this case the journal of George McClellan, to study prairies situated along an otherwise forested, cross-montane trail. The journals contained evidence for anthropogenic fire, following Cooper, and Norton's analysis of a species list again showed a significant proportion of useful species. Robert Boyd's 1986 "Strategies of Indian Burning in the Willamette Valley" drew on two precedents: Henry Lewis's "Patterns of Indian Burning in California" and Carl Johannessen *et al.*'s "Vegetation of the Willamette Valley." Adding to Johannessen's list of sources on Indian fire, Boyd, following Lewis, analyzed the data in both a cultural and ecological context, and reconstructed the role of fire in the local subsistence round. Estella Leopold's 1988 "Ecological History of Old Prairie Areas in Southwestern Washington" drew on yet another line of evidence, that of palynology, to investigate the role of anthropogenic fire in the maintenance of regional prairies. Regional pollen sequences dating back several thousand years revealed a warm, dry period when the prairies were formed, followed by a cooler period until the present when human fires prevented their invasion by coniferous forests. Historical and ethnographic data subsequently supplied by Robert Boyd demonstrated the connection of fire to Indian subsistence. Henry Lewis and Theresa Ferguson's "Yards, Corridors, and Mosaics: How to Burn a Boreal Forest" builds on the fieldwork of Lewis and his student Ferguson on fire in several different foraging cultures, primarily northern Alberta and Australia, but also California and the Northwest. Like a companion paper by Lewis,[50] it searches for cross-cultural similarities in how foraging people burn their environments.

"Time to Burn: Traditional Use of Fire to Enhance Resource Production by Aboriginal Peoples in British Columbia," by ethnobotanist Nancy Turner, draws on all previous regional papers for its inspiration, but, with field data and an emphasis that are particularly Turner's: extensive ethnographic interviews on the role of fire in the management of specific useful plant species native to British Columbia. William Robbins' 1993 "Landscape and Environment: Ecological Change in the Intermontane Northwest" returns to the broader concern of environmental historians with the effect of anthropogenic fire on the landscape itself: precedents are White, Cronon, and Sauer. Robbins' data for the Columbia Plateau come mostly from his own historical research, but are influenced by rangeland manager Dean Shinn's "Historical Perspectives on Range Burning in the Inland Pacific Northwest"[51] and Eugene Hunn and Robert Boyd's anthropological studies. Indian fire is one of several human-caused environmental influences in the Northwest since the last glaciation. Ethnobotanist Leslie Johnson's 1994 "Aboriginal Burning for Vegetation Management in Northwest British Columbia" is based upon several years of field work among the Gitxsan and Wet'suwet'en peoples and is firmly in the school of Turner and Lewis: emphasizing the role of fire in the management of particular useful plant species as well as in shaping local environments. Jeff LaLande and Reg Pullen's "Burning for a 'Fine and Beautiful Open Country': Native uses of fire in Southwestern Oregon" builds on the work of Lewis and Boyd in adjacent Northern California and the Willamette Valley, with data collected by Pullen from the unpublished fieldnotes of ethnographers such as John Harrington, plus a concern with historical change and management issues arising from LaLande's historical studies and work with the U.S. Forest Service. John Ross's "Protohistorical and Historical Spokan Prescribed Burning and Stewardship of Resource Areas" is based upon several decades of fieldwork with the Spokan people. Ross shares with Hunn and Turner a concern with "traditional ecological knowledge" concerning fire management of useful species, and offers a perspective on fire use among eastern Salishan peoples that complements the more experimental methods and scientific data of Barrett and Arno.

Notes

1. George Vancouver, *A Voyage of Discovery to the North Pacific Ocean and Round the World, 1791–1795*, vol. II. W. Kaye Lamb ed. (London, 1984), 568.
2. Whidbey's observations are recorded in Archibald Menzies, "Menzies' Journal of Vancouver's Voyage, April to October, 1792" (*Archives of British Columbia* Memoir V, 1923), 48. The list of berries comes from Edward Bell, "A New Vancouver Journal" (*Washington Historical Quarterly* 5 and 6 var.pp., 1914 and 1915), 222. The "onions" were most likely camas lilies (*Camassia quamash*), in flower at the time of Vancouver's visit, though species of *Allium* also are native to the Northwest.
3. Jay Miller, letter to Robert Boyd, May 28, 1996.
4. Upper Rogue, upper Umpqua, Willamette, and Cowlitz valleys; Puget Sound and Strait of Georgia islands.
5. E.g., Hunn, Turner, Johnson, and Ross.
6. This paragraph draws on several papers presented in the 1997 American Association for the Advancement of Science symposium, "Was the Northwest Coast 'Agricultural'?," particularly the title paper, by Douglas Deur;

"Anthropogenic Plant Communities on the Northwest Coast: An ethnobotanical perspective," by Nancy Turner; and "Coast Salish Resource Management: Incipient Agriculture?," by Wayne Suttles.

7. James K. Agee, *Fire Ecology of Pacific Northwest Forests* (Washington, D.C., 1993).

8. The definition is from James Omernik, "Ecoregions of the Coterminous United States" (*Annals of the Association of American Geographers* 77(1): 118–25, 1987), 123. The standard work on ecoregions in Washington, Oregon, and Idaho is by Omernik and Alisa Gallant, *Ecoregions of the Pacific Northwest* (Corvallis, 1986). For British Columbia, the best delineation of ecoregions is by Dennis Dimarchi *et al.*, in the "Environment" chapter of R. Wayne Campbell *et al.*'s *The Birds of British Columbia*, vol. 1: 55–144 (Vancouver, 1997). For Oregon, an equivalent detailed delineation is the Defenders of Wildlife's *Oregon's Living Landscape: Strategies and opportunities to conserve biodiversity* (Portland, 1998). On the related topic of vegetation cover, standard works are Jerry Franklin and C. T. Dyrness, *Natural Vegetation of Oregon and Washington* (Corvallis, 1988) and Del Meidinger and Jim Pojar's *Ecosystems of British Columbia* (Victoria, 1991).

9. There are several pertinent sources, but the best summaries appear in Wayne Suttles's "Introduction" to *Northwest Coast*, vol. 7 of the *Handbook of North American Indians* (pp. 1–15, Washington, D.C., 1990) and the equivalent chapter by Deward Walker in *Plateau*, vol. 12 of the *HNAI* (pp. 1–7, Washington, 1998).

10. John Hoskins, "Narrative...," pp. 161–289 in Voyages of the "Columbia" to the Northwest Coast, 1787–1790 and 1790–1793, F. W. Howay, ed. (*Massachusetts Historical Society Collections* 79, 1941), 243; and LaLande and Pullen (this volume).

11. LaLande and Pullen (this volume), Warren Vaughan, "Early History of Tillamook" (ms. in Multnomah County Library, Portland); Reagan in Lewis and Ferguson (this volume).

12. Elizabeth Jacobs, "Nehalem Tillamook Ethnographic Notes," William Seaburg, ed. (ms. in Seaburg's possession).

13. Agee, 192.

14. Helen H. Norton, "The Association between Anthropogenic Prairies and Important Food Plants in Western Washington" (*Northwest Anthropological Research Notes* 13(2): 175–200, 1979), Appendix 1.

15. Douglas Deur, "Was the Northwest Coast Agricultural?," paper presented at symposium of the same name, 1997 Meeting of the American Association for the Advancement of Science, Seattle.

16. Vaughan, "Early History of Tillamook."

17. In "wet Douglas-fir" forests such as the Coast Range, fire-return intervals are long and stand-replacement fires usual. In the Coast Range of Oregon, fire histories show marked differences (in fire frequency and type) between the relatively wet ocean-facing west versus the drier eastern Willamette Valley margin. It has been hypothesized that late summer/early fall Indian-set prairie fires, abetted by seasonal east winds, were a significant factor in these differences. (Peter Impara, "Spatial and Temporal Patterns of Fire in the Forests of the Central Oregon Coast Range," PhD dissertation, Oregon State University, 1997.)

18. Franklin and Dyrness, *Natural Vegetation of Oregon and Washington*, 88.

19. Two other important sources are Helen H. Norton, "The Association between Anthropogenic Prairies and Important Food Plants in Western Washington" (*Northwest Anthropological Research Notes* 13(2): 175–200, 1979) and Patrick Dunn

and Kern Ewing, eds. *Ecology and Conservation of the South Puget Sound Prairie Landscape* (Seattle: The Nature Conservancy of Washington, 1997).

20. See George Dickey. ed., *The Journal of Occurrences at Fort Nisqually, Commencing May 30, 1833; Ending September 29, 1859* (Fort Nisqually Association, 1993). See also Norton, "Association . . .," 180–81.

21. George Gibbs, "Tribes of Western Washington and Northwestern Oregon" (*Contributions to North American Ethnology* 1(2): 157–361, 1877), 193.

22. Joseph Clark, *Lights and Shadows of Sailor Life* (Boston, 1847), 222. Though Clark does not mention fire, it was an integral component of the sequence, as the Fort Nisqually Journal citations demonstrate.

23. Carl Johannessen *et al.,* "The Vegetation of the Willamette Valley" (*Annals of the Association of American Geographers* 61(2): 286–302, 1971). A later version is in *Oregon's Living Landscape*, 194. As of this writing, the Oregon Natural Heritage Program is preparing a detailed, large-scale map of pre-settlement Willamette Valley plant cover. The map in Boyd (this volume) is an early draft.

24. Leland Gilsen, Luckiamute Basin Survey (ms., 1989).

25. On the latter, see Henry Lewis's classic "Patterns of Indian Burning in California: Ecology and ethnohistory," pp. 27–54 in Blackburn and Anderson, *Before the Wilderness . . .* (1993).

26. See John Evans, "Journal, July 11, 1854–August 4, 1856" of a geological survey of the Rogue (typescript of ms. in Library of Congress, Oregon Historical Society, Portland). This pattern is described for northwestern California and other regions in Henry Lewis's "Patterns of Indian Burning in California" and Lewis and Ferguson's "Yards, Corridors, and Mosaics" (this volume). Evans's descriptions especially recall those in George Gibbs's contemporary journal from the neighboring Klamath Valley, "Journal of the Expedition of Colonel Redick M'Kee, United States Indian Agent, through North-Western California. Performed in the Summer and Fall of 1851.". pp. 99–177 in vol. 3 of Henry Schoolcraft, ed., *Historical and Statistical Information Respecting the History, Condition and Prospects of the Indian Tribes of the United States* (Philadelphia, 1853). Neither Evans nor Gibbs, however, specifically mention fire.

27. Pre-contact fire intervals in "dry Douglas-fir" forests were typically more closely spaced than those in "wet Douglas-fir" forests, individual fire extents were smaller, and the fires themselves were less severe. Forests in the western Cascades of Oregon at contact were apparently patchworks composed of mosaics of different-aged stands. There have been several studies of Cascade Range Douglas-fir fire histories; the best known is Peter Teensma's "Fire History and Fire Regimes of the Central Western Cascades of Oregon" (PhD dissertation, University of Oregon, 1987). See also Wallin *et al.* 1996 (fn. 7, conclusion).

28. Sahaptin-speaking peoples include most of the Warm Springs peoples, Yakama, Walla Walla, Palouse (all in the Columbia Basin ecoregion); and Taitnapam and Klikitat (in the Cascade ecoreion) (see Map 1).

29. See Eugene Hunn, *Nch'i-Wána, "The Big River": Mid-Columbia River Indians and Their Land* (Seattle, 1990), 119–34; and Alan Marshall, Nez Perce Social Groups: An ecological interpretation (Ph.D. dissertation, Washington State University, 1977).

30. The evidence consists of a body of fifteen citations, drawn from Robbins and this author's notes (1806–1858): four citations date from May 1 through June 15;

seven from August 2 through September 3, and four (all, unfortunately, from 1834) from the third week of August through September 1.

31. Verne Ray, "Culture Element Distributions XXII: Plateau" (*Anthropological Records* 8: 99–258, 1942), 117, 132.

32. Marshall, "Wild Horticulture: The Nez Perce subsistence base" (paper presented at the 1991 meeting of the American Anthropological Association, Chicago).

33. Cline, Walter *et al.*, "The Sinkaietk or Southern Okanogan of Washington" (*General Series in Anthropology* no. 6, 1938), 19.

34. See also Nancy Turner *et al.*, Thompson Ethnobotany: Knowledge and Usage of Plants by the Thompson Indian People of British Columbia (*Royal British Columbia Museum Memoir* No. 3, 1990) and N. Turner, "Plant Resources of the *Stl'atl'imx* (Fraser River Lillooet) People: A Window into the Past," pp. 405–69 in Brian Hayden, ed., *A Complex Culture of the British Columbia Plateau: Traditional Stl'atl'imx Resource Use* (Vancouver, 1992).

35. See Loren Eiseley, "Man the fire-maker" (*Scientific American* 191: 52–57), 1954; Kenneth Oakley, "On man's use of fire, with comments on tool-making and hunting," pp. 176–93 in Sherwood Washburn, ed., *The Social Life of Early Man* (New York, 1961); and Walter Hough, "Fire as an agent in human culture" (*U.S. National Museum Bulletin 139,* 1926).

36. Sauer's relevant works include "A Geographic Sketch of Early Man in America" (*Geographical Review* 34(4): 529–73, 1944); "Grassland Climax, Fire, and Man" (*Journal of Range Management* 3(10): 16–21, 1950); "Fire and Early Man" (*Paideuma* 7: 399–407, 1962); and "Man's Dominance by Use of Fire," (*Geoscience and Man* 10: 1–13, 1975).

37. Perhaps the most notable of Sauer's followers is William Denevan of the University of Wisconsin. See in particular his "The Pristine Myth: The Landscape of the Americas in 1492," in the special 1992 issue of the *Annals of the Association of American Geographers*, commemorating the Columbian quincentenary. William Dickinson's 1994 presidential address to the Geological Society of America, "The times are always changing: The Holocene saga" (*GSA Bulletin* 107(1): 1–7, 1995), is yet another example of how this theme has entered the scientific mainstream.

38. Stewart's important papers, noted in several of the contributions to this volume, include "Burning and Natural Vegetation in the United States" (*Geographical Review* 41(2): 317–20, 1951); "Why the Great Plains are treeless" (*Colorado Quarterly* 2: 40–50, 1953); "The Forgotten Side of Ethnogeography," pp. 221–48 in Robert Spencer, ed., *Method and Perspective in Anthropology* (Minneapolis, 1954); "Forest Fires with a Purpose," "Why Were the Prairies Treeless?" and "Forest and Grass Burning in the Mountain West," all in *Southwestern Lore,* 1954–1955; and "Fire as the First Great Force Employed by Man," pp. 115–33 in William Thomas, ed., *Man's Role in Changing the Face of the Earth* (Chicago, 1956). Stewart's recent biography, *Cannibalism is an acquired taste: and other notes from conversations with anthropologist Omer C. Stewart* (Carol Howell, ed.; Niwot, CO, 1998), contains a section on his work on anthropogenic fire written by Henry Lewis. As of this writing (1998), Stewart's "800 page" manuscript is being edited by Lewis and Kat Anderson, and will be published by the University of Oklahoma Press. For two other contributions on fire and the Great Plains (by an anthropologist and limnologist) see Waldo Wedel, "The

Central North American Grassland: Man-made or Natural?," pp. 39–69 in *Studies in Human Ecology* (Washington, 1957), and Philip Wells, "Historical Factors Controlling Vegetation Patterns and Floristic Distributions in the Central Plains Region of North America," pp. 211–21 in Wakefield Dordt and J. Knox Jones, eds., *Pleistocene and Recent Environments of the Central Great Plains* (Manhattan, KN, 1970).

39. Lewis's relevant papers include *Patterns of Indian Burning in California: Ecology and Ethnohistory* (orig. 1973; reprinted in 1993 as pp. 55–116 in Thomas Blackburn and Kat Anderson, "Before the Wilderness: Environmental Management by Native Californians" [*Ballena Press Anthropological Paper* #40]); "The Role of Fire in the Domestication of Plants and Animals in Southwest Asia: A Hypothesis" (*Man* 7(2): 195–222, 1977); "Maskuta: The ecology of Indian fires in Northern Alberta" (*Western Canadian Journal of Anthropology* 7(1): 15–52, 1977); "Fires of spring" (film, 1978) and "Indian fires of spring" (*Natural History* 89: 76–83, 1980); *A Time for Burning: Traditional Indian Uses of Fire in the Western Canadian Boreal Forest* (Edmonton, 1982); "Fire Technology and Resource Management in Aboriginal North America and Australia:, pp. 45–67 in Eugene Hunn and Nancy Williams, eds., Resource Managers: North American and Australian Hunter-Gatherers (*AAAS Selected Symposium* #67, 1982); "Yards, Corridors, and Mosaics: How to Burn a Boreal Forest" (with Theresa Ferguson; 1988 and this volume); "Non-Agricultural Management of Plants and Animals," pp. 54–74 in Robert Hudson, K. R. Drew, and Leonid Baskin, eds., *Wildlife Production Systems: Economic utilization of wild ungulates* (Cambridge, 1989); "Ecological Knowledge of Fire: Aborigines vs. Park Rangers in Northern Australia" (*American Anthropologist* 91(4): 940–61, 1989), "Technological Complexity, Ecological Diversity, and Fire Regimes in Northern Australia: Hunter-Gatherer, Cowboy, Ranger," pp. 261–88 in A. T. Rambo and K. Gillogly, eds., "Profiles in Cultural Evolution" (*University of Michigan Anthropological Paper* No. 85, 1991); and "Management Fires vs. Corrective Fires in Northern Australia: An Analogue for Environmental Change" (*Chemosphere* 29(5): 949–63, 1994).

40. Julian Steward's "Ethnography of the Owens Valley Paiute" (*University of California Publications in American Archaeology and Ethnography* 33(3), 1933) initiated the discussion on West Coast resource management without agriculture; James Downs, in "The Significance of Environmental Manipulation in Great Basin Cultural Devleopment," pp. 39–56 in Warren d'Azevedo *et al.*, *The Current Status of Anthropological Research in the Great Basin: 1964* (Reno, 1966) introduced the term "environmental manipulation." For an influential review of the California proto-agriculture issue, see Lowell Bean and Harry Lawton's "Some Explanations for the Rise of Cultural Complexity in Native California with Comments on Proto-Agriculture and Agriculture" (orig. 1973; reprinted in 1993 as pp. 27–54 in "Before the Wilderness . . ."). Representative and well-known examples of the early classificatory phase of West Coast ethnobotany include George Mead's "The Ethnobotany of the California Indians: A compendium of the plants, their users, and their uses" (*University of Northern Colorado Occasional Publications in Anthropology, Ethnology Series* no. 30, 1972) and Erna Gunther's "Ethnobotany of Western Washington" (*University of Washington Publications in Anthropology* 10, 1945; rev. ed. 1973, University of Washington Press).

41. The most thorough treatment of (Marion) Kat(harine) Anderson's research is her 1993 dissertation, "The Experimental Approach to Assessment of the Potential

Ecological Effects of Horticultural Practices by Indigenous Peoples of California Wildlands" (Ph.D. dissertation, Wildland Resource Science, University of California); pertinent published articles include "California Indian Horticulture: Management and Use of Redbud by Southern Sierra Miwok" (*Journal of Ethnobiology* 11(1): 145–51, 1991), and "The Ethnobotany of Deergrass, *Muhlenbergia rigens (P)oaceae)*: Its uses and fire management by California Indian tribes" (*Economic Botany* 50(4): 409–22, 1996) and "From Tillage to Table: The indigenous cultivation of geophytes for food in California" (*Journal of Ethnobiology* 17(2): 149–69, 1997) on utilized species; "Tending the Wilderness" (*Restoration and Management Notes* 14(2): 154–66, 1996), "California's Endangered Peoples and Endangered Ecosystems" (*American Indian Culture and Research Journal* 21(3): 7–31, 1997), and (with Michael Barbour and Valerie Whitworth) "A World of Balance and Plenty: Lands, Plants, Animals and Humans in a Pre-European California," pp. 12–47 in Ramon Gutierrez and Richard Orsi, eds., *Contested Eden: California before the Gold Rush* (Berkeley, 1997) on broader management and ecosystem issues. "Before the Wilderness: Environmental Management by Native Californians," edited by Thomas Blackburn and Kat Anderson, was published as *Ballena Press Anthropological Paper* no. 40 (Menlo Park, CA, 1993).
42. See also Deur's "Salmon, Sedentism, and Proto-Cultivation: Towards an Environmental Prehistory of the Northwest Coast," to appear in Paul Hirt and Dale Goble, eds., *Northwest Lands and Peoples: An Environmental Anthology.* (Seattle, in press).
43. Among the small body of regional palynological studies few (e.g. Leopold and Boyd, this volume) consider the human factor in pre-settlement vegetation change. Other researchers, however, recognize the need. See Richard Hebda and Cathy Whitlock, "Environmental History" (pp. 227–54 in Peter Schoonmaker, Bettina von Hagen, and Edward Wolf, *The Rainforests of Home: Portrait of a North American Bioregion.* Washington, 1997), 247–48.
44. See James Chatters, "Population Growth, Climatic Cooling, and the Development of Collector Strategies on the Southern Plateau, Western North America" (*Journal of World Prehistory* 9(3): 341–400, 1995).
45. For a second recent archaeological study that uses charcoal remains and palynology to determine past patterns of anthropogenic burning, see Paul Delcourt *et al.*, "Prehistoric Human Use of Fire, the Eastern Agricultural Complex" and "Applachian Oak-Chestnut forests: Paleoecology of Cliff Palace Pond, Kentucky" (*American Antiquity* 63(2); 263–78, 1998). Delcourt *et al.* hypothesize that a local vegetation shift from fire-intolerant cedars to fire-tolerant oak and chestnut (plus associated useful understory species) was due largely to purposive anthropogenic burning.
46. An early article, cited in the first paper of this volume, is Charles Cooper's 1961 "The Ecology of Fire" (*Scientific American*, April 1961: 150–60). A selection of papers from the early years of the Tall Timbers proceedings gives an idea of the breadth and significance of their contributions, e.g.: "Fire, a Tool Not a Blanket Rule in Douglas-fir Ecology" (Leo Isaac, vol. 1: 1–17, 1962), "Fire Ecology— Grasslands and Man" (Edwin V. Komarek, vol. 4: 169–220, 1965), "Fire and the Ecology of Man" (Komarek, 6: 142–170, 1967), "Fire and Animal Behavior" (Komarek, 8: 160–206, 1969), "Prescribed Burning for Elk in Northern Idaho" (Thomas Leege, 8: 235–53, 1968), "The Forest Primeval in the Northeast—A Great Myth?" (Daniel Thompson and Ralph Smith, 10: 255–65, 1970). Three

notable recent volumes arising from symposia, all edited by Johann Goldammer, are *Fire in the Tropical Biota: Ecosystem processes and global challenges, Fire in Ecosystem Dynamics: Mediterranean and Northern perspectives* (both 1990; The Hague and New York) and *Fire in the environment: The ecological, atmospheric, and climatic importance of vegetation fires* (New York, 1993). Stephen Pyne's books originally were published by Princeton and Holt; both were reprinted in 1997 by the University of Washington Press. Walstad *et al.'s* volume is from Oregon State University Press; Agee's from Island Press, Washington, D.C. A classic, yet older, regional study is Rexford Daubenmire's "Ecology of Fire in Grasslands," pp. 209–66 in J. B. Cragg, ed., *Advances in Ecological Research* vol. 5 (New York, 1968).

47. See Richard White's "American Environmental History: The Development of a New Historical Field" (*Pacific Historical Review* 54(3): 297–337, 1985). "Indians in the Land: A conversation between William Cronon and Richard White" (*American Heritage,* Aug–Sept 1986, 19–25) is a stimulating introduction to some of the ideas of the environmental historians about Indian land use. The quotation from White comes from his co-authored (with Cronon) "Ecological Change and Indian-White Relations," pp. 417–29 in Wilcomb Washburn, ed., *History of Indian-White Relations,* vol. 4 of the *Handbook of North American Indians* (Washington, 1988), 421. On the concept of ecological transition, see John Bennett, *The Ecological Transition: Cultural anthropology and human adaptation* (New York, 1976). Boag's *Environment and Experience* was published in 1992 by the University of California Press; Bunting's *The Pacific Raincoast* in 1997 by the University of Kansas, and Robbins's *Landscapes of Promise* in 1997 by the University of Washington Press.

48. Pp. 13–70 in volume 12 of *Report of Explorations and Surveys to Ascertain the Most Practicable and Economical Route for a Railroad from the Mississippi River to the Pacific Ocean . . .* 36th Cong., 1st Sess., House Executive Document 56 (Serial Set no. 1055).

49. The crucial passage from "Botany of the Route" is reproduced in Lewis and Ferguson (this volume).

50. "Fire Technology and Resource Management in Aboriginal North America and Australia," pp. 45–67 in Eugene Hunn and Nancy Williams, eds., Resource Managers: North American and Australian Hunter-Gatherers (*AAAS Selected Symposium* #67, 1982).

51. *Journal of Range Management* 33(6): 415-23, 1980.

Aboriginal Control of Huckleberry Yield
in the Northwest

David French

The use of fire by human beings, both in the intentional burning of grasslands and forests and as an agricultural and horticultural technique, has been a recent topic of research.[1] This paper adds new data on the use of fire as a plant control mechanism—specifically to increase yields of wild huckleberries—and explores the implications of this mechanism. The data are derived from field work with Chinookan and Sahaptin Indians living on the Warm Springs Reservation in Oregon and elsewhere in the Northwest.[2]

While the culture of the Chinookan-speaking Wascos and Wishrams sometimes has been classified as peripheral Northwest Coast, the economy differed only in emphasis, not in fundamental characteristics, from that of the adjacent Sahaptin-speakers along the Columbia River. The latter are easily classed with the Plateau. In both cases, the basic foods were roots, salmon, game, and berries. In the early 19th century the Wasco-Wishram spent more time near the Columbia River than did the Sahaptins and achieved greater exchangeable surpluses in salmon. Village as opposed to camp living patterns were correspondingly more important for the Chinookans.[3]

The move to the Warm Springs Reservation following the treaty of 1855 did not fundamentally change the annual cycle of resource exploitation. Salmon were caught from the spring through the fall, with a lull in mid-summer. Roots were dug during the spring and early summer. Although hunting occurred throughout the year, the most important season was the fall: in the Cascade Mountains it was undertaken concurrently with berry picking by the women.

More than a dozen species of berries and berry-like fruit were gathered by the Indians. Half of these belong to the genus *Vaccinium*, which includes huckleberries and blueberries. In northern Oregon and southern Washington the black mountain huckleberry (*Vaccinium membranaceum* Dougl. ex Hook.)[4] is by far the most important from the point of view of human exploitation, both in past times and today. The fruit is nearly black, sweet, and aromatic.

While *Vaccinium membranaceum* can survive in localities shaded by trees, the most favorable environment is an open one, including areas deforested by fires. Within a few years after a fire, these huckleberries are the dominant vegetation and are loaded with berries in favorable years. Subsequently, willows, alders and other deciduous growth begin to replace the huckleberries in most localities. Coniferous trees, such as firs and pines, eventually become the dominant vegetation. Early in this century, wide areas near Mt. Hood and Mt. Jefferson were open as a result of forest fires; older Indians, remembering this, now discuss these areas as if they had deteriorated. From the Indian point of view, the huckleberry patches have been overrun with "weeds" in the form of coniferous trees.

There is abundant evidence that the Sahaptin and Chinookan Indians had a thorough understanding of the ecological relationships sketched above. Their solution to the problem of declining huckleberry yields was to start fires under controlled conditions. The aim was to re-establish berry patches of proven value without burning whole regions. The method of control was simple: fires were started at the end of the huckleberry season in the late fall. By this time, winter rains already had started and further rain as well as snow followed. Forest fires burning under such conditions do not spread beyond limited areas before they are extinguished by the moisture. A common technique for increasing the probability that a fire would indeed occur was to leave a log burning that had served as a reflector during the course of the heat drying of huckleberries.[5]

Lena Waters (Yakama) drying huckleberries, Sawtooth berry fields (Mt. Adams), 1936. USDA Forest Service photo by Ray Filloon. Courtesy of Rick McClure, Gifford Pinchot National Forest (Vancouver WA).

Time does not permit the discussion of other plant control techniques in the area. The burning of grasslands occurred in both eastern Oregon and the Willamette Valley. A non-fire form of control mechanism was the practice (still carried on today) of leaving some of the plants in a root patch to permit perpetuation of the crop.

The settled, regular way of life in fishing villages would lead one to expect that the adoption of agricultural crops from Whites would not be a difficult step for Chinookans and Sahaptins. This was indeed the case, with the Wasco beginning to cultivate garden patches near the Columbia by 1845, soon after the arrival of missionaries in the area. Following the treaty, they became diligent farmers on the reservation. Although the Sahaptins evidently found gardening and farming in partial conflict with their more mobile way of life, they did not resist agriculture as such, and they added certain forms of farming to their economy far sooner than did, say, Plains Indians. In short, the data support the hypothesis that the adoption of agricultural techniques is not difficult for a people who: 1) are familiar with the idea of controlling plant growth, and 2) have a way of life involving at least some degree of stability of residence during the growing season. The rapid adoption of potatoes among the Coast Salish provides a comparable case.[6]

Assuming that a plant species was available which was valued by these Indians and which provides a better yield under cultivation than growing wild, it would not be surprising to learn that this plant had been cultivated in aboriginal times. There is strong evidence, which sometimes has been overlooked, that this was exactly the case along the Columbia River. The reference is to tobacco. Several anthropologists have discussed the evidence for the aboriginal cultivation of tobacco along the north Pacific Coast, but it seems worthwhile here to call attention to the fact that the best early data on tobacco come not from the coast itself, but from the explorations of the botanist David Douglas along the Columbia River, specifically from the area we have been discussing. Douglas not only reported seeing a plant (by implication cultivated) in the hands of an Indian at Celilo Falls, which was Sahaptin territory, but he also chanced upon a tobacco patch and collected specimens that are neither the wild tobacco now growing in the area nor a species cultivated by Europeans (*Nicotiana attenuata*[7] or *N. bigelovii* var.). The patch was located above Willamette Falls, in the territory of Kalapuyan Indians, neighbors of Chinookan peoples. Turn-of-the-century ethnographers explicitly attribute tobacco growing to the Wishram.[8]

The connection between tobacco-growing and berry patch burning is somewhat more specific than merely the general one of being two forms of plant control. The above sources all state that the tobacco was planted in ashes provided by the burning of dead trees, stumps, or logs. The growing of tobacco seems to have ceased soon after Douglas's 1825 report. It was supplanted by commercial tobacco, provided by White traders. Interestingly enough, however, modern Indians still retain the belief that a distinctly different wild species (that continues to be smoked in emergencies) grows best where there has been a fire.

The formal question of when horticulture was adopted and practiced is not of importance in this context. Whether or not tobacco was still being grown around 1840, when missionaries introduced garden crops, is of less significance than the fact that the Indians continued to appreciate the principle of plant control, e.g. berry patch burning, and that there was persistence of functional relationships in the economy which would facilitate the adoption of gardening.

To summarize: a method for the control of huckleberry crops has been described, and this has been interpreted in terms of 1) general understanding and control of plants; and 2) a specific technique of control, namely burning, which also was employed with tobacco (coupled with the idea of planting). The relatively rapid adoption of White crops and techniques was explained not only in terms of familiarity with ideas of plant control but also in terms of the relatively stable village life that had been associated with a fishing economy. The stability is necessary but not sufficient for agriculture to be invented or adopted.

Paper read at the American Anthropological Association meeting, Chicago, December 1957; not previously published

Notes

1. See Charles Cooper, "The Ecology of Fire" (*Scientific American* 204(4): 150–60, 1961); on fire in grasslands and forests see Omer Stewart, "The Forgotten Side of Ethnogeography," pp. 221–40 in Robert Spencer (ed.), *Method and Perspective in Anthropology* (Minneapolis, 1954) and "Fire as the First Great Force Employed by Man," pp. 115–33 in William Thomas (ed.), *Man's Role in Changing the Face of the Earth* (Chicago, 1956); for horticultural and agricultural fire see Harold Conklin, "An Ethnoecological Approach to Shifting Agriculture" (*Transactions of the New York Academy of Science* Series 2, 17: 133–42, 1954) and H. H. Bartlett, "Fire, Primitive Agriculture, and Grazing in the Tropics," pp. 692–720 in Thomas (ed.), *Man's Role in Changing the Face of the Earth.*
2. The research was supported by grants from the Wenner-Gren Foundation, the American Philosophical Society, Carl Reynolds, and the Social Science Research Council.
3. On classification in the Northwest Coast culture area see Alfred Kroeber, "Cultural and Natural Areas of Native North America" (*University of California Publications in Archaeology and Ethnology* vol. 38, 1939), 30 and Map 6; Philip

Drucker, *Indians of the Northwest Coast* (New York, 1955), 7; on the Plateau culture area see Verne Ray, *Cultural Relations in the Plateau of Northwestern America* (Los Angeles, 1939).

4. "Black mountain huckleberry" is the most common term, and will be used throughout this volume; *V. membranaceum* is called by several other names: "twin-leaved huckleberry," "mountain bilberry," and "blue huckleberry" among botanists alone.

5. Later research provides more detail on the post-harvest burn: "certain men were responsible for watching and maintaining the condition of the berry-picking areas"; ". . . one or two men were chosen specifically for the task of staying behind to burn the fields. These men were chosen for their knowledge, because not only did they have to burn the fields, they had to call on the rain and thunder to put the fire out." "The mountains provided signs of the coming weather which the old people could read, thus, for example, predicting rain, and individuals were available who could produce rain, if it became necessary." The first and last sentences are from Kathrine French *et al.*, "An Ethnographic Overview of the Mt. Hood National Forest, Oregon" (*Archaeological Investigations Northwest Report* No. 86, 1995); the middle two are from Cheryl Mack, "Past Human Uses—Watershed Analysis of the Eastern Portion of the Upper White Salmon River Drainage" (ms., 1994).

6. For a discussion of Coast Salish potato cultivation see Wayne Suttles, "The Early Diffusion of the Potato among the Coast Salish" (*Southwestern Journal of Anthropology* 7(3): 272–88, 1951).

7. *N. multivalvis* in the original. *Multivalvis* is an old name for *Nicotiana quadrivalvis*, one of two native tobaccos found in the Pacific Northwest. See James Hickman, ed., *The Jepson Maual of Higher Plants of California* (Berkeley, 1993), 1072. *Nicotiana attenuata*, however, is the only species reported to be used by the Indians of the Plateau culture area, of which the Wascos and Wishrams were marginal members. See Eugene Hunn, Nancy Turner, and David French, "Ethnobiology and Subsistence," pp. 525–45 in Deward Walker, ed., *Plateau*, vol. 12 of the *Handbook of North American Indians* (Washington, 1998), 535.

8. On West Coast tobacco cultivation, see John Harrington, "Tobacco Among the Karuk Indians of California" (*Bureau of American Ethnology Bulletin* 94, 1932), and Robert Heizer, "The Botanical Identification of Northwest Coast Tobacco" (*American Anthropologist* 42(4): 704–6, 1940). David Douglas's citations on tobacco may be found in his "Sketch of a Journey to the Northwest Part of the Continent of North America during the years 1824–25–26–27" (*Oregon Historical Quarterly* 5: 230–71, 325–69; 6: 76–97, 206–27, 1904–05), 249 and 269. A second version of Douglas's tobacco account from his *Journal of Travels in North America, 1823–1827* (New York, 1953) is cited in Boyd (this volume). Edward Curtis in "The Wishram," pp. 172–82 in *The North American Indian*, vol. 8 (Norwood, MA, 1911), 173; and Leslie Spier and Edward Sapir in "Wishram Ethnography" (*University of Washington Publicatons in Anthropology* 3(3), 1930), 269, note Wishram tobacco cultivation.

Indian Land Use and Environmental Change
Island County, Washington: A Case Study

Richard White[1]

The first Americans to settle in Island County, Washington Territory, in the late 1850s regarded the region as a virgin wilderness. Heavy coniferous forests and small prairies covered the several islands in Puget Sound that composed the county.

On these islands, Salish tribes followed age-old practices of fishing, hunting, and gathering, and Whites presumed that these people had adapted to the land, enjoying its abundance and suffering its scarcities. The prairies and forests seemed obviously the creation of unrestrained nature. Few observers were aware that the Indians inhabiting the area actually had played an active role in shaping their environments, not indirectly, as any population shapes the ecology of a region merely by occupying it, but consciously and purposefully to fit their own needs. Through the use of fire and a simple technology, the Indians over many generations had encouraged the growth of three dominant plants on the islands—bracken, camas, and nettles—to supplement their regular diet of fish and small game, and also had created the conditions that fostered immense forests of Douglas-fir. A study of the early Salish experience in Island County demonstrates salient features in the process by which hunting and gathering peoples profoundly altered their natural environment.[2]

At the arrival of White settlers, the Indian population in Island County, an area of approximately 206 square miles, lived wholly on two large islands, Whidbey and Camano. In size, Whidbey ranks second only to Long Island in the continental United States; Camano is about one-fifth the size of Whidbey. Small fertile prairies, located largely on the northern part of Whidbey Island, comprised about 5% of the county. The remaining terrain was hilly, forested, and infertile.[3]

Four Salish tribes—the Skagit, Kikialos, Snohomish, and (later) the Clallam—had lived on parts of these islands since about 1000 A.D. Each tribe was a loose aggregation of villages united by language and blood, rather than by a centralized political system. Anthropologists have classified all these tribes as saltwater or canoe Indians, who, despite differences in language and kinship, shared basically similar culture traits.[4]

The Salish viewed the land as being occupied not only by humans, plants, and animals, but also by a vast array of spirits associated with specific animals or natural phenomena. This added dimension gave nature an ambience and

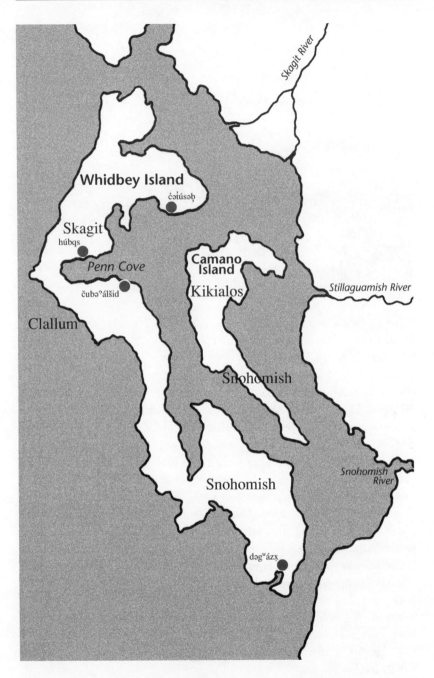

Whidbey and Camano Islands: ethnographically attested winter villages. Map by David Myhrum. Source: Wayne Suttles and Barbara Lane, "Southern Coast Salish," pp. 485-502 in Suttles, ed., Northwest Coast, vol. 7 of the Handbook of North American Indians (Washington, 1990), 486.

Penn Cove (above) and Cultus Bay (facing page) on Whidbey Island (Washington Territory) in the 1850s. Drawings from the Pacific Railroad Surveys, vol. 12, Book 1, opposite pp. 306, 288. OrHi #s 98636, 98637.

additional meaning. Plants and animals took on not only economic but also religious significance. Although the settlers dismissed these ideas as superstitions, the Salish possessed an acute knowledge of the natural world. Their understanding of plant life, for instance, was both thorough and refined. They named and classified plants, observing subtle differences in taxonomy and habitat. This knowledge was not solely utilitarian; the Indians observed and studied plants whether they were useful or not.[5]

The Salish quest for salmon (*Oncorhynchus* spp.)—the principal food staple for all Puget Sound Indians—largely determined the location of their villages on the islands. Salmon fishing oriented the tribes toward the rivers, and tribal boundaries in the county were the logical continuations of mainland river systems that lay opposite the islands. As a result, the people of the Snohomish River settled on southern parts of Whidbey and Camano islands, while the tribes on the Skagit River built villages on North Whidbey. The Kikialos were strictly an island tribe, living on North Camano, but their territory faced the Stillaguamish River and they crossed to the mainland each fall to fish its banks.[6]

At the peak of Salish population (before 1770), the Salish villages contained between 1,500 and 2,500 people, living in more than ninety-three places. Most of the sites were summer camping grounds inhabited seasonally for fishing, hunting, and berry or root gathering, but the Salish occupied as many

as fifteen permanent villages on the islands. Since the Indians sought safe and protected coves for canoe anchorages and a local supply of fish and shellfish, the selected village locations were principally on northeast Whidbey and Camano. Three large Skagit villages on Penn Cove, on North Whidbey, formed the population center of the islands. The Snohomish had villages on South Whidbey, while the Kikialos occupied permanent sites along the western and northern beaches of Camano. Most of the land on southern Whidbey and southern Camano had no permanent population.[7]

The large concentration of nonagricultural people on the islands called for a sensitive adjustment to the environment, and a willingness to use every available source of food. This adjustment was reflected in the Salish food cycle of hunting, gathering, and fishing. Although the cycle varied from tribe to tribe, the Salish moved periodically through their territories in Puget Sound following the annual pattern of abundance. From May to October, hundreds of mainland Indians joined permanent residents on the islands for root gathering and hunting. For all the Indians in the county, gathering vegetable products comprised a crucial element of their food cycle. At least fifty plants, exclusive of trees, were used by the Skagit alone.[8]

The Salish search for food plants ended in September, when the first salmon of the great fall runs started up the rivers, and the Indians moved off the islands and gathered on the riverbanks to take them. For two months, incredible numbers of fish crowded the streams. The large groups of Indians who fished and the immense quantities of fish caught led early settlers to regard salmon as their major food. Salmon were indeed of fundamental importance, but the Salish had other sources of sustenance and were prepared to survive the occasional failure of the salmon to appear.[9]

The Indian food cycle confused most early White observers. At times they saw the Indians as incurably nomadic, wandering across the land in search of food. But this was hard to reconcile with the strong Salish attachment to their permanent villages and their reverence for the graves of their ancestors. The tenacity of this devotion both impressed and bewildered the Americans when they sought to displace them. They found Salish devotion to their villages and lands as formidable as the huge cedar houses in which they lived. Actually the permanent villages and seasonal wandering in search of food formed the poles of the Salish's physical relation to the land. Both were basic.[10]

Even modern anthropologists have tended to view the Salish as moving easily over the land, adapting to natural abundance and leaving no trace, with the settlers inheriting the land much as the first Indians had found it. They described the Indians as living off the "spontaneous product of nature" for generations until they eventually were displaced. Both the settlers and scholars have presumed that the components of the Salish food cycle were gifts of virgin nature. But in the plant communities that existed at the time of early settlement, there was evidence of substantial Salish influence on the environment. Three plants in particular—bracken, camas, and nettles—found in abundance by surveyors and settlers, were closely tied to Salish cultural practices.[11]

Prolonged human occupation of a site usually led to a local enrichment of the soil. Succeeding generations of Indians living at the same village inevitably produced considerable amounts of waste. Shells and bones, plant refuse, ashes from fires, and excrement of humans and animals all gradually rotted and provided the soil with significant amounts of potash, phosphorous, and nitrogen. These accumulations of waste also provided seedbeds for many of the ancestors of human food crops.[12]

The nettle (*Urtica dioica*), for example, preferred rich soils and historically has been associated with human occupation. The nettle probably spread from the prairies, where it was a native plant, into the vicinity of the Salish villages. As with corn, constant proximity brought familiarity and, eventually, the discovery of uses for the plant. The Indians of Puget Sound made extensive use of the nettle. They extracted a medicine and a dye from it, and peeled, dried, and rolled the bark into a two-ply string for fishing and duck nets. Moreover, as a wild nettle patch generally indicated rich ground, the Indians later used the plant as a guide in starting potato patches. According to their own testimony, the Skagit Indians tended the nettles in a manner closely resembling cultivation. They kept the nettle patches free of weeds and burned the plant refuse in the fall after harvesting. The Salish clearly encouraged the nettle over other plant species of the prairies.[13]

The Salish not only burned nettle patches but also regularly burned entire prairies in mid-summer or early fall when the rains had stopped and grass was

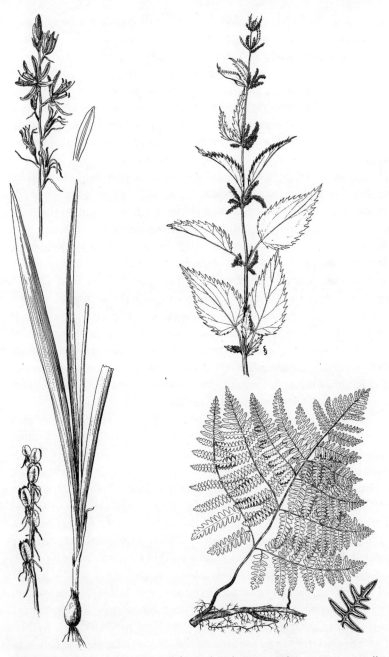

Bracken fern (lower right), camas (left), and nettle (upper right) were economically important plants for generations of Western Washington Salish Indians. Drawings of fern and nettle are from Helen Gilkey (comp.), Weeds of the Pacific Northwest, pp. 14 and 67. Camas appears in C. Leo Hitchcock, Vascular Plants of the Pacific Northwest, vol. 1, p. 783.

tall and tinder dry. The first settlers on Whidbey found these fires alarming, for they threatened their crops and houses. Because Whites refused to tolerate the occasional destruction of their property, the beginning of American settlement saw the cessation of Indian burning on the prairies.[14]

Few settlers gave much thought to the reasons behind these fires. One of the few who did was James G. Cooper, a botanist with the railroad expedition that reached western Washington in 1853. Cooper recognized that the Salish had definite and sensible reasons for burning, and concluded that if they ceased the practice the forest soon would encroach on the open lands. The Indians, he wrote, "burned to preserve their open grounds for game, and for the production of their important root, the camas." The introduction of the horse, according to Cooper, had provided a further inducement for firing the grasslands. Fresh pastures sprang up in burned-over country. Cooper's comments on Indian land use were insightful, but were largely ignored. Actually, they fit the inland Indians of southern Puget Sound better than they did the saltwater Salish of Whidbey.[15]

The Salish of Island County had no reason to burn to increase grazing areas, for they had no horses, nor were they dependent on large game animals for food. Even deer, a relatively minor source of food, were browsers that did not require extensive grasslands for feed. Undoubtedly, Indian burning encouraged game animals by enlarging their feeding areas, but this was not necessarily the rationale for burning. More likely, the initial impetus for fires was to increase vegetable production.[16]

The desire to encourage the growth of bracken (*Pteridium aquilinium*), a fern which reached heights of seven feet on the prairies, and camas (*Camassia quamash*)—which Cooper noticed dominating large expanses of open land— were the main reasons for setting fires. Both plants were staples of the Indian diet. The Salish ground dried bracken roots into flour, which they baked for bread. They boiled the fresh camas, eating them like potatoes, or dried and preserved the bulbs. The abundance of these plants on the prairies was not fortuitous. Rather than being major Indian food sources because they dominated the prairies, bracken and camas more likely dominated the prairies because they were major Indian food sources. According to Carl Sauer, the noted geographer, the very existence of people like the Salish depended on "acting intelligently within the range of their experience." Observing the changes that fire brought in its wake and using the altered landscape to their own advantage were "advantageous behavior" that enabled the Salish to survive.[17]

In the Puget Sound region, bracken was a pioneer invader of disturbed or burned-over lands. Burning facilitated the plant's spread over the prairies where the dense growth of native grasses often blocked its progress. Once established, the extensive root system of the fern, and the death of its topgrowth in the fall, protected it from fatal damage by fire and gave it an advantage over less resilient rivals. The encouragement of bracken would not have benefited a pastoral people seeking to enlarge their grazing lands. In fact, bracken was a poor feed after its first growth, and pastoral peoples lamented its increase. But the Salish were not herdsmen. They valued the fern as an important source of food, and sought to promote its growth.[18]

The camas plant benefited more indirectly from burning. Like bracken, its topgrowth died off in late summer, and fall prairie fires did it little harm. Unlike bracken, however, the mere destruction of competing plants did not contribute to its spread. Direct human or animal intervention was necessary for the plant to widen its range. The Skagit moved camas bulbs into fresh areas, at first perhaps unwittingly but later with zeal and care. Harvesting enabled the camas to increase; for dropped, split, and discarded bulbs spread the plant to new areas. Gathering the crop with a digging stick became a type of "unplanned tillage." According to Indian and White testimony, cultivation to ensure a better harvest eventually supplemented the digging and transplanting of mature bulbs. Such a technique approached true farming—as did other Salish practices. For example, they also worked in plant refuse around another food plant, the tiger lily (*Lilium columbianum*). The Indians of the upper Skagit, and probably the Whidbey Skagit, practiced a primitive cultivation of both the lily and the wild carrot (*Perideridia gairdneri*). When the potato was introduced into Puget Sound, the Salish quickly became adept at the cultivation of that crop without any direct instruction by the settlers.[19]

Indian modification of the vegetational community of the prairies was significant and purposeful. Salish practices involved a rational manipulation of the environment, and this manipulation had profound ecological effects. Burning destroyed conifer seedlings and shrubs that encroached on the prairies, while at the same time it encouraged bracken to become the dominant vegetation of the open lands. Other Salish practices helped spread camas and nettle plants. Unwanted trees or shrubs surviving the fires were pulled out by hand. When the Whites arrived, they regarded the prairies as wild. They damned bracken for making plowing difficult, cursed the painful sting of the nettle, and praised camas as pig food. In fulfilling the Biblical injunction of sinking plowshares into earth, they imagined that they were putting the stamp of man upon the land. But the stamp of man was already firmly present.[20]

Salish influence on the landscape extended beyond the limits of the prairies into the surrounding forests. Indians used wood extensively, especially red cedar (*Thuja plicata*), but also Douglas-fir (*Pseudotsuga menziesii*), hemlock (*Tsuga heterophylla*), and alder (*Alnus rubra*). Yet considering the abundance of the forests and the massive size of the towering trees, direct Salish use probably had little impact on forest ecology. The conifers of western Washington were so huge that it took the neighboring Makah Indians two

(above) Penn Cove circa 1900, showing prairies and forest. (facing page) House frames from the Skagit village at Snatelum Point. negs. no. UW 18307 & NA 696. Special Collections Division, University of Washington Libraries.

weeks to fell a Sitka spruce (*Picea sitchensis*) by fire and axe. To cut the fir and cedar of Island County would have demanded similar labor. The occasional felling of one of these giants would have made only a minuscule difference in the forest as a whole.[21]

For the Salish, the forest yielded other products besides wood. They searched among the trees for berries, fireweed (*Epilobium angustifolium*), and game, none of which favored deep forest but thrived in the clearings and young successional forests that followed fires. The upper river Indians, fearing the immediate destruction of existing game animals, were wary of fire, but the saltwater peoples of the lowlands apparently burned over berry fields without much hesitation. They particularly sought to promote the growth of fireweed and berries that formed part of the normal successional pattern on such lands. Berries were an important food, while fireweed, along with other materials, was used in the weaving of blankets. The very name "fireweed," given it by the settlers, showed the close connection between this plant and burning.[22]

The first United States surveyors to examine Whidbey and Camano islands in the late 1850s made significant comments on the condition of the forests at the time. There had not yet been a decade of settlement, and most of the islands were unoccupied and practically unexplored. The surveyors made two critical observations: 1) that Douglas-fir was the dominant forest species of the islands, closely followed by hemlock and Sitka spruce and cedar; and 2) that large areas in the forests had been burned.[23]

In the hemlock-cedar climax forests in Island County, Douglas-fir relied for propagation on the destruction not only of other trees but also of the mature fir itself. Fir not only thrived on catastrophe, it depended on it. Fir seedlings died in the dense shade of mature forests, while hemlock and cedar seedlings survived, spread, and eventually displaced the mature fir as they fell from age and disease. Without interference, the climax forest of the region would have been primarily cedar and hemlock. As Douglas-fir of all ages and sizes abounded on the islands, mature forests obviously had been destroyed. This destruction clearly did not result from harvesting, nor was there evidence of extensive kills by disease or insects. The surveyors blamed the destruction on fire.[24]

Normally, the fires that had destroyed the virgin forests of Island County could have been ascribed to lightning. However, few thunderstorms occurred in western Washington. Thunderstorms swept the mountains on the mainland, but they would have had to be of staggering proportions to reach Puget Sound. Furthermore, such fires never could have reached Island County, simply because Whidbey and Camano were islands. Yet fires were so extensive and common on the islands that, of the sixteen townships surveyed in the 1850s, six contained burned-over forests. In five of these, the damage was substantial. This burning gave the Douglas-fir its advantage and enabled the tree to dominate the forests of the islands.

Extensive forest burning in the county resulted either from prairie fires that accidentally spread to the woods, or from fires deliberately set to extend berry grounds. With the brisk winds that blew across the islands, a small fire could spread rapidly. As Indian fires were the main source of forest burning in Island County, and probably in the entire Puget Sound region, they played a critical role in determining the species composition of the forests. The result was a large stand of Douglas-fir in the lowland forests of Puget Sound, and a successional growth of groundsel (*Senecio sylvaticus*), fireweed, berries, and bracken; and fir, alder, and hemlock seedlings.[25]

In the northern coniferous forests, burning had shaped woodland ecology for centuries. Fire formed a crucial part of the forest environment. It not only liberated mineral nutrients accumulated in the litter, humus, wood, and foliage of the old forest, but it simultaneously prepared seedbeds and triggered the release of some seed supplies. The periodic destruction of old forests kept a significant proportion of each region in young trees and thus reduced the susceptibility of the forest to insects and disease. In a sense, fires were so common and critical that the species composition that would have developed without fire would have been unnatural. The only unusual aspect of the situation on Puget Sound was that such a large percentage of fires were of human origin.[26]

Fire not only shaped the forests but also the animal population that inhabited the woodlands. Both deer (*Odocoileus hemionus*) and elk (*Cervus canadensis*) were abundant in Island County when settlers first arrived, and according to Miron Heinselman, a forester who had studied forest fires, these animals were "best adapted to recent burns and early succession forests—not climax forests." Thus by setting fires, the Salish provided these animals with their habitat and increased their numbers—as well as the number of their predators, the wolves.[27]

The Salish accomplishment in creating and maintaining their ecosystem was impressive. Because of this, the Indian population of 1770 was larger than any human population on the islands before 1910. They populated their islands with spirits and powers, but did not restrict their manipulation to magic. Their technology was limited, but they used it effectively. Unlike the Indians of the upper rivers, the Salish rarely suffered seasonal scarcities or periodic famines. Indeed, in terms of camas, berries, bracken, deer, and elk, the islands were a food-exporting region. This had been brought about by Indians learning, through observation and tradition, to alter natural communities to fit their needs, without destroying in the process the ability of these communities to sustain the cultures that had created them. Far from being creatures of their environment, the Indians had shaped their world and made it what it was when the Whites arrived.[28]

Originally published in Arizona and the West 17(4): 327–36, 1975

Notes

1. The original version of this paper was read at the Pacific Northwest History Conference at Tacoma, Washington, in April of 1975. A second version of this article appeared as chapter 1, "Shaping the Face of the Land," in *Land Use, Environment and Social Change: The Shaping of Island County, Washington* (Seattle, 1980).

2. Aboriginally, the Salish had been a hunting, gathering, and fishing people. By the 1850s, they were raising potatoes and beans. The adoption of agriculture had not significantly altered older patterns of land use when Whites first settled. See Wayne Suttles, "The Early Diffusion of the Potato Among the Coast Salish" (*Southwestern Journal of Anthropology* 7(3): 272–88, 1951; reprinted in *Coast Salish Essays* [Seattle, 1987], 137–51).

3. *U.S. Soil Survey of Island County, Washington* (Washington, D.C.: USDA Soil Conservation Service, Series 1949, No. 6, 1958), 3, 5–6.

4. Marian Smith, "The Puyallup-Nisqually" (*Columbia University Contributions to Anthropology* 32, 1940), 28–32. See also George Gibbs, "Tribes of Western Washington and Northwestern Oregon" (*Contributions to North American Ethnology* 1(2): 157–361, 1877), 178. Indeed, tribal divisions did not differentiate the villages of the Puget Sound region as well as the cultural divisions of inland, river, and saltwater—divisions first mentioned by American settlers and later adopted by anthropologists.

5. *Ibid.*, 58–59. June Collins, *Valley of the Spirits: The Upper Skagit Indians of western Washington* (Seattle, 1974). Herman Haeberlin, "The Mythology of Puget Sound," *Journal of American Folklore,* 37:371-438, 1924, 378–79, 383–84, 391. Ella C. Clark, *Indian Legends of the Pacific Northwest* (Berkeley, 1969), 199–201. James Swan, *The Northwest Coast, or Three Years Residence in Washington Territory* (New edition, Berkeley, 1972), 316. Claude Levi-Strauss, *The Savage Mind* (Chicago, 1966), 3–10, makes the point of the exact knowledge of plant life possessed by hunting and gathering peoples in general.

6. The Clallam do not fit this pattern. They arrived in Island County after the introduction of the potato and seized a small area of fertile prairie land to grow that crop. *Pioneer and Democrat* (Olympia, Washington), April 9, 1853. Victor J. Farrar (ed.), "The Diary of Colonel and Mrs. I. N. Ebey," *Washington Historical Quarterly [WHQ],* 8(2):124-52, 1917, 139. Paul Kane, *Wanderings of an Artist among the Indians of North America . . .* (Toronto, 1925), 157–58.

7. The basic data on population and village sites is from Herbert C. Taylor, "Aboriginal Populations of the Lower Northwest Coast," *Pacific Northwest Quarterly,* 59(4):158-65, 1963, 160–63, and Alan Bryan, "Archaeological Survey of Northern Puget Sound" (*Idaho State University Museum Occasional Paper No. 11,* 1963), 12–13. See also Thomas T. Waterman, [Puget Sound Geography] (ms. No. 1864 in the National Anthropological Archives, Smithsonian Institution, 1920). I have modified the population estimates.

8. Erna Gunther, *Ethnobotany of Western Washington* (Seattle, 1973), *passim.* For information on the food cycle, see Herman Haeberlin and Erna Gunther, "The Indians of Puget Sound" (*University of Washington Publications in Anthropology* 4(1), 1930), 20–21, 26; June Collins, "John Fornsby: The Personal Document of a Coast Salish Indian," pp. 285-341 in Marian Smith (ed.), "Indians of the Urban Northwest" (*Columbia University Contributions to Anthropology* 36, 1949), 294–95,

302. *Duwamish et al. vs. United States of America*, United States Court of Claims, Seattle, 1932, docket F-275, collection of tribal briefs, two volumes, I, 314–15, Pacific Northwest Collection, University of Washington [UWash], Seattle. Bryan, *Survey*, appendix, 1–11.

9. Collins, "John Fornsby," in Smith (ed.), *Indians of the Urban Northwest*, 302–3.

10. E. A. Starling to Isaac I. Stevens, December 10, 1853, "Letters from agents assigned to Puget Sound District, Washington Superintendency, Bureau of Indian Affairs, Record Group 75," National Archives. Stevens to George W. Manypenny, December 26, 1853, "Indian Appropriations," *House Miscellaneous Document 38*, 33 Congress, 1 Session (Serial 741), 11.

11. Haeberlin and Gunther, *Indians of Puget Sound*, 20. For a more recent assertion of the same opinion by an ecologist, see Loye Miller, "Some Indian Midden Birds from the Puget Sound Region," *Wilson Bulletin* [Wilson Ornithological Society], 72(4): 392-97, 1960), 397.

12. Bruce Proudfoot, "Man's Occupance of the Soil," pp. 8–33 in Ronald Buchanan, Emrys Jones and Desmond McCourt (eds.), *Man and His Habitat: Essays presented to Emyr Estyn Evans* (London, 1971), 12.

13. *Ibid.*; Gunther, *Ethnobotany*, 28; *Duwamish et al.*, 1, 314–15. Swan, *Northwest Coast*, 77. Swan described the abundance of nettles around old village sites on Shoalwater Bay.

14. James G. Cooper, "Report upon the Botany of the Route," *Explorations and Surveys . . . for a Railroad . . . to the Pacific Ocean* (12 vols., Washington, 1855), 12, Book 2, 23. Farrar (ed.), "Ebey Diary," *WHQ*, 7(4): 307-21, 1916, 309, 321.

15. Cooper, "Botany," *Railroad Reports*, 12, Book 2, 22–23.

16. Bryan, *Survey*, appendix, 4.

17. Cooper, "Botany," *Railroad Reports,* XII, Book 2, 22–23. Winfield S. Ebey, Diary, July 1, 5, 1858, Ebey Collection, UWash. Walter Crockett to Harvey Black, October 15, 1853, Manuscript Collection, UWash. Francis Kautz (ed.), "Extracts from the Diary of A. V. Kautz," *Washington Historian*, 1(4):181-86, 1900, 184; *Land and Life: A selection from the writings of Carl Ortwin Sauer* (Berkeley, 1963), 178–79.

18. Gunther, *Ethnobotany*, 14–15; F. Fraser Darling, *West Highland Survey: An Essay in Human Ecology* (Oxford, 1955), 172; George Neville Jones, "A Botanical Survey of the Olympic Peninsula, Washington" (*University of Washington Publications in Biology* 5, 1936), 36–37. Jerry Franklin and C. T. Dyrness, *The Natural Vegetation of Oregon and Washington* (Portland: USDA Forest Service, General Technical Report PNW-8, 1973; reprinted Corvallis: Oregon State University Press, 1988), 89. Ecologists and shepherds in areas with climates similar to that of Island County have noted that continued burning and heavy grazing of open lands lead to immense increases in the amount of bracken.

19. Camas was widespread on the prairies, and Whidbey was especially noted for its huge yields. Farrar (ed.), "Ebey Diary," *WHQ*, 8(2), 134; "Message of the President," *Senate Executive Document 1, 33* Cong., 2 Sess., (Serial 746), 455. George Gibbs, "The Indian Tribes of Washington Territory," *Railroad Reports,* I, 432–33; Sauer, *Land and Life,* 180; *Duwamish et al.*, I, 314–15, 319–20; Gunther, *Ethnobotany*, 25; Collins, *Valley of the Spirits*, 55.

20. *Duwamish et al.*, I 319. Crockett to Black, October 15, 1853, Manuscripts Collection, UWash. Farrar (ed.), "Ebey Diary," *WHQ*, 8(2), 134.

21. James G. Swan, Diary, November 21, 1863, Swan Collection, UWash. For more information on Salish use of timber, see Gunther, *Ethnobotany, passim*; Haeberlin and Gunther, *Puget Sound*, 15, 32, 34; John Osmundson, "Man and His Natural Environment on Camano Island, Washington," (M.A. thesis, Washington State University, 1971), 41; and Joan Vastokas, Architecture of the Northwest Coast Indians of America (Ph.D. dissertation, Columbia University, 1966) and "Architecture and Environment: The Importance of the Forest to the Northwest Coast Indian," *Forest History*, 13(3):12-21, 1969.

22. Gunther, *Ethnobotany*, 41. Gunther here apparently rules out the possibility that the Salish procured fireweed by burning.

23. Book 1: 312, 333, 576, 585, 596, 603; Book 10: 486, 523, 534, 540, 562, 582; Book 11: 686; Book 12: 422, 426, 445, 488, 525, 526, 542, "Field Notes of the United States Surveyor," Bureau of Land Management, Portland, Oregon.

24. The ecology and successional patterns of the forests of the Pacific Northwest are in Thornton Munger, "The Cycle from Douglas Fir to Hemlock," *Ecology*, 21(4):451-59, 1940, 451–59; J. V. Hoffman, "The Establishment of a Douglas Fir Forest," *ibid.*, I(1):49-54, 1920, 49–54; Jones, *Botanical Survey*, 32; and Franklin and Dyrness, *Natural Vegetation*, 82–84.

25. For natural succession and plant growth following burns, see Franklin and Dyrness, *Natural Vegetation*, 64–67.

26. Miron L. Heinselman, "The Natural Role of Fire in Northern Conifer Forests," in Charles W. Slaughter, Richard J. Barney, and George M. Hansen (eds.), *Fire in the Northern Environment—A Symposium* (Portland: Pacific Northwest Forest and Range Experiment Station, 1971), 64–67.

27. *Ibid.;* George Vancouver, *A Voyage of Discovery to the North Pacific* (six vols., London, 1801), II, 167. Crockett to Black, October 15, 1853, Manuscript Collection, UWash. Bryan, *Survey*, 47, and appendix, 7–11. Joseph Perry Sanford, Journal, June 15, 16, 1842, Records of the U.S. Exploring Expedition...Charles Wilkes, 1838–1842, Records of the Hydrographic Office, Office of Naval Records, RG 76, NA. *Duwamish et al,* I, 319.

28. The population of Island County in 1910 was 4,704; in 1900 it was 1,807. *Thirteenth Census of the United States, Population*, I, 977. Collins, "John Fornsby," in Smith (ed.), *Indians of the Urban Northwest*, 294–95, 302.

Indian Fires in the Northern Rockies
Ethnohistory and Ecology

Stephen W. Barrett and Stephen F. Arno[1]

In Western North America, fire history information is important for implementing ecologically sound management for vast areas of publicly owned wildlands. Fire histories help elucidate the role of fire in maintaining diverse ecosystems. Many studies have shown that forests burned cyclically for thousands of years before settlement by Euro-Americans; in contrast, many areas have not burned in this century, in part because of efficient fire suppression. Ironically, by "protecting" areas from fire, we have inadvertently removed one of nature's primary rejuvenating processes.

Lightning is a major cause of forest fires, but it is relatively uncommon in lower-elevation forests and grasslands. Here, in both pre- and post-contact times, humans have been a potentially important source of ignitions. Until recent decades, however, little information existed on Indians' role in causing fires in the West. For example, were Indian-caused fires commonplace? If so, why were such fires ignited? Which forest types were affected, and to what extent? Besides being interesting anthropology, such information can help today's foresters refine their knowledge of ecosystem processes. Accordingly, the authors conducted a study of the role of Indian-caused fires in the Northern Rocky Mountains.[2]

The Salish (i.e., Flathead and Pend d'Oreille tribes) and Kootenai Indians were the principal inhabitants of western Montana for 6,000 to 10,000 years before settlement by Euro-Americans.[3] These tribes had a hunter-gatherer economy and may have numbered only a few thousand at any given time.[4] Increasing settlement after about 1860, however, greatly hampered the Indians' way of life, and the tribes eventually were moved to their present reservation north of Missoula, Montana. Before our study, evidence of Indian fire practices was sketchy. To document Indian influence in area fire history, we designed a two-phase study focusing on ethnohistory and forest fire ecology.

Ethnohistory of Indian Fires

The ethnohistorical phase of the project, conducted in 1980, consisted of a review of early written records and oral history interviews. We first searched the literature for old journals and other eyewitness accounts of Indian-caused fires. Then, with the aid of tribal culture committees and historical societies, we sought out and interviewed knowledgeable descendants of early-day Indians and settlers. Short oral history interviews helped ascertain whether Indians had used fire and, if so, why.[5] Of our fifty-eight informants, thirty-one were Indians and twenty-seven of European descent. When asked whether earlyday Indians purposely had ignited fires, 41% answered yes, 12% answered no, and the remaining 47% did not know. Thus only about half the informants claimed knowledge on the subject, and the high proportion of "don't know" answers reflects a dwindling knowledge of early history. However, the large proportion of "yes" versus "no" responses (77% vs. 23%) verified our initial impression from journals that Indians frequently had used fire to manipulate the landscape. One researcher's subsequent review of forty-four historical accounts suggested that Indians had caused as many as 41% of 145 observed fires between 1776 and 1900 in the Inland West.[6] Seven of the ten fires witnessed by explorers Lewis and Clark between 1805 and 1806 in the Northern Rockies, for instance, were attributed to Indian ignitions.[7]

Seven informants cited specific locations where Indians regularly burned valley bottoms. One elderly man's parents told him that they always knew when the seasons were about to change because every year during late fall, Flatheads set fires in the Ninemile Valley west of Missoula. A common practice was to ignite the valley bottom upon leaving for the main winter encampment in the nearby Bitterroot Valley. The parents of an elderly resident in the Swan Valley, northwestern Montana, gave virtually the same information about Kootenai Indians in that location.[8] On August 23, 1805, in the present-day Beaverhead Valley in southwestern Montana, Captain Meriwether Lewis submerged the expeditions' canoes under water to protect them from "the fire which is frequently kindled in these plains by the natives."[9]

Written records verified that fire was an important element of Indian subsistence technology. Fire facilitated hunting, was used in game drives and surrounds, stimulated forage, and helped influence game movements in general. During missionary work in the 1840s, Father Pierre deSmet witnessed a fire surround near Lake Coeur d'Alene in northern Idaho:

> On both ends of their line they light fires, some distance apart, which
> they feed with old garments and worn out moccasins . . . The
> frightened deer rush to right and left to escape. As soon as they smell
> the smoke of fires, they turn and run back. Having the fires on both
> sides of them and the hunters in the rear, they dash toward the lake,
> and soon they are so closely pressed that they jump into the water, as
> the only refuge left for them. Then everything is easy for the hunters;
> they let the animals get away from the shore, then pursue them in
> their light bark canoes and kill them without trouble or danger.[10]

An informant from an earlier study described a somewhat different technique:

The fire surround was held in some level region where deer were known to be abundant. The drive leader called the men of the camp together and asked them to prepare a quantity of pine-wood torches. The following morning the hunters assembled, and lighted torches were given out to a number of them. Carrying these, they then began to move out, in two directions, to form a large circle, setting fire to the brush and trees along the way. Others with bows and arrows were stationed at intervals around the fire circle, to shoot any animals that might try to escape through the flames. At the starting point a small area was left unfired. As the deer fled around the inside of the fire ring, they arrived at this opening where other bowmen were waiting for them. White tail and mule deer, as well as bears, were secured in the surround. Elk, ranging at higher altitudes during these months, were never taken in this way.[11]

Frequent burning promotes grass at the expense of shrubby forage,[12] and Indians used this knowledge to influence general game movements. By regularly burning certain areas, hunters knew that deer likely would frequent the nearby unburned stands.[13] A journal from July 1860 describes this use of fire near present-day Lookout Pass, on the Montana-Idaho border:

> In returning, the Indian set fire to the woods himself, and informed us that he did it with the view to destroy a certain kind of long moss which is a parasite to the pine trees in this region, and which the deer feed on in the winter season.[14] By burning this moss the deer are obliged to descend into the valleys for food, and thus (the Indians) have a chance to kill them.[15]

Fires also were used to improve grazing, particularly after horses were obtained in the early 1700s. Horse ownership was one measure of power and wealth, and Indians frequently kept large numbers. One informant said that 100 or more horses often accompanied small bands passing by his parents' homestead near the Ninemile Valley. To stimulate grass, Indians commonly burned ungrazed areas in early spring or fall. In 1860, U.S. Army Lt. John Mullan kept a detailed journal during a reconnaissance from Fort Benton, on the upper Missouri River, to Fort Walla Walla, Washington. Mullan noted five instances of Indians burning valley grasslands, and he repeatedly mentioned seeing many horses, as well as "luxuriant" grasses in many locales. In March 1860, near present-day Missoula, for example: "The grass had all been burnt by the Indians along the Bitter Root River . . ."[16] One recent Blackfeet Indian informant mentioned so-called "horseback lightning," or igniting the prairies using transported embers.

Several informants said that Indians used fire to maintain open campsites and trails. The small trees and brush killed by these fires simultaneously served as a future source of firewood. Open forests allowed much easier travel, a fact often noted by early settlers. Several informants and a journal said that Indian

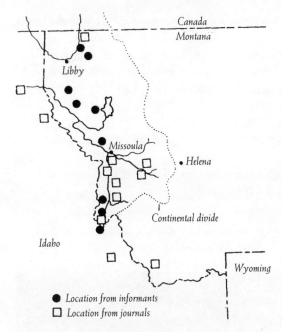

Locations of known Salish or Kootenai ignitions in western Montana and adjacent areas between approximately 1805 and 1920. Location references are listed in Barrett (1981, fig. 3).

women were responsible for conducting such burning, using wet blankets to control small strip fires. Concerning trails, 1890s forest surveyor Horace Ayres noted:

> There is no doubt that some of the fires, especially on the higher (mountain) ranges, are due to lightning, but most of those in the valley seem to have been set by Indians and other hunting parties or by prospectors. The trails most frequented by Indians, such as the Jocko and Pend d'Oreille, are noticeably burned especially about the camping places.[17]

Regular underburning in ponderosa pine (*Pinus ponderosa*) also made approaching enemies more readily visible, and essentially could fireproof a campsite by eliminating cured grasses. Grass fires occasionally were ignited for warfare. In 1858, a traveler in the Tobacco Valley (northwestern Montana–southeastern British Columbia) witnessed Kootenai Indians using fire to repel an attack:

> If the Blackfeet had any idea of the Kootenais setting the grass afire they would not have selected the grove . . . for the battle ground. Indians are careful in not (accidentally) setting fire to grass in the close vicinity of their villages, and the Blackfeet had no thought of fire being set out and afterwards extinguished by the squaws and their wet blankets.[18]

Grass fires commonly were used for communication.[19] In contrast to the sophisticated smoke signals often portrayed in Hollywood movies, however, Indians simply ignited entire valley bottoms, producing dense smoke visible for miles. Large grass fires thus served many other purposes simultaneously, as described above. On August 31, 1804, near the Lemhi River in eastern Idaho, members of the Lewis and Clark Expedition witnessed the following:

> This day warm and Sultrey, Prairies or open Valies on fire in Several places. The countrey is Set on fire for the purpose of collecting the different bands (of Pend d'Oreille Indians), and a Band of the Flatheads to go to the Missouri (River drainage) where They intend passing the winter near the Buffalow.[20]

Early-day trapper Warren Ferris observed several such fires:

> On the 13th (August 1833), we continued down this (Bitterroot) river, till evening and halted on it. The (Flathead) Indians with us,

Circa 1840 painting by Father Nicolas Point depicting an Indian fire surround near Lake Coeur d'Alene, Idaho. "Chasse d'automne aux chevreuils" (fall deer hunt) from Nicolas Point, S.J., Souvenirs des Montagnes Rocheuses, Livre 3, Chasses indiennes. Courtesy of the Archives de la Compagnie de Jésus, Province du Canada-français, St-Jérôme, Québec, #1603. The painting is interesting for several reasons. First, besides portraying an actual incident, it shows a unique fire surround in which a lake was used to entrap prey. Equally interesting, however, is that the painting shows a raging crown fire surrounding the camp—undoubtedly inaccurate because the Indians clearly were more interested in hunting than fleeing from a dangerous fire. (Father DeSmet's accompanying journal verifies that small surface fires were employed.) Point's abstract painting thus implies more than just artistic license—a deep-seated fear of wildfires.

announced our arrival in this country by firing the prairies. The flames ran over the neighboring hills with great violence, sweeping all before them, above the surface of the ground except the rocks, and filling the air with great clouds of smoke.[21]

From the summit of Cota's Defile (i.e., August 1832, present-day Bannock Pass) we saw a dense cloud of smoke rising from the plains to the southeastward, which we supposed to have been raised by the Flatheads, who accompanied Fontanelle to Cache Valley, and who were now in quest of the village to which they belong. The Indians with us answered the signal by firing a quantity of fallen pines on the summit of a high mountain.[22]

Ferris also saw an accidental blaze evolve into a worrisome "communication fire" near present-day Deer Lodge, Montana:

A careless (Flathead) boy scattered a few sparks in the prairies, which, the grass almost instantly igniting, was soon wrapped in a mantle of flame. A light breeze from the south carried it with great rapidity down the valley, sweeping everything before it, and filling the air with black clouds of smoke . . . (The fire) however occasioned us no inconsiderable degree of uneasiness as we were now on the borders of the Blackfeet country, who it was reasonably inferred might be collected by the smoke, which is their accustomed rallying signal, in sufficient force to attack us . . . Clouds of smoke were observed on the following day curling up from the summit of a mountain jutting into the east side of the valley, probably raised by the Blackfeet to gather their scattered bands, though the truth was never more clearly ascertained.[23]

Interestingly, descendants of settlers often seemed to have more detailed recollections of Indian fire practices than did Indian descendants. Lack of trust by Indian informants may be one factor. Some research on Indian burning (e.g., Ross, this volume), suggests that understanding of firing techniques and ecosystemic effects was specialized knowledge, possessed by only a few individuals, and therefore may not have survived. Indians may have considered fire a rather unremarkable, albeit necessary, tool, also reducing the likelihood that much oral history would be passed down through the generations. By contrast, because settlers often viewed fire as destructive and dangerous, anti-fire biases increase the likelihood that settlers would pass along recollections of Indian ignitions. Several Indian informants stressed that their forebears were careful not to ignite severe fires. In fact, early forest surveyor John Leiberg said that typical ponderosa pine stands were never conducive to severe crown fires:

The fires in the Bitterroot Basin were as extensive as elsewhere in the West, but have done far less damage to the merchantable timber. This is due to the resistance offered by the yellow pine and to the small quantity of litter and humus in the forest. The ground in this kind of growth is always covered with a thin layer of pine needles—never a proper humus—and is usually free from undergrowth, or has but a minimum. Grasses or sedges in bunches cover the ground thinly, hardly ever forming a continuous sod. In consequence fire runs through the forest rapidly.[24]

Regarding seasons of burning, the informants and journals suggested that most intentional burning occurred in fall or early spring—when old grasses were ignited easily without causing destructive forest fires.[25] Early-day Indians undoubtedly knew that summer fires could be hazardous, and only a few accounts mention Indians causing fires during that season. Nevertheless, early forest surveyors often attributed destructive forest fires to Indians and prospectors,[26] but they also rarely recognized lightning as a major cause:

> Most of the fires that can be traced to the period of Indian occupancy appear to have originated along the lines of trails (crossing the Bitterroot mountains) . . . The probability is that many fires spread from their camps and others were set purposely to destroy the forest and encourage grass growth. This latter seems to have been the case in the alpine fir type of forest along their trails, where now occur so many of the bald or grassy mountain slopes.[27]

Because of their European heritage, early foresters had a strong anti-fire bias. Fire was considered undesirable and destructive, rather than yielding any potentially beneficial effects. Leiberg wrote the prevailing sentiments of the day: "the after effects of fires in this region are various, but are always evil, without a single redeeming feature."[28] Leiberg also obtained the following misinformation from an old Indian in the late 1890s.

> An educated Nez Perce, with whom I conversed regarding the matter stated that forest fires were never started through design, but might have accidentally spread from signal fires kindled by different bands or individuals while on the hunt, that they might know the whereabouts of one another.[29]

At first glance, this statement appears to suggest Indians did not use fire to manipulate landscapes. But Leiberg had an anti-fire bias (typical of many Euro-Americans) and the informant might have mistrusted the interviewer's motives. Or, he may have been referring to destructive forest fires in the Bitterroot Mountains, rather than light grass fires in the Wallowa Valley.

Although fall grass fires occasionally might have developed into severe burns in the adjacent steep mountains, informants and journals yielded no evidence of purposeful burning in high mountain terrain, or in moist riparian forests. We found only three references to high-altitude fires started by Indians. Warren Ferris' journal twice notes mountaintop bonfires ignited for communication. And Lewis and Clark's journals cite an instance of Indians torching several dead fir trees at night along the Lolo Trail, for entertainment and spiritual reasons.[30] But, unlike people of European descent, Indians did not view forests as a source of saw timber in need of careful protection. Thus, if valley bottom fires sometimes burned high mountain forests, the post-fire communities might only benefit Indian economies. Some informants said that these fires would stimulate game browse and food plants such as blue huckleberries (*Vaccinium globulare*), which grow best in moist subalpine forests prone to infrequent severe fires. Purposeful burning in subalpine forests would be more difficult, because moist fuels can impede spreading fires during most fire seasons. And conflagrations can result on those infrequent occasions when ignitions coincide with fuels highly receptive to fire. In any case, extensive lightning fires appear to be sufficient to account for most of the fire history reported for subalpine terrain.[31]

We found little detailed information about methods of application. Evidence of highly technical burning practices was lacking in journals and oral history interviews, perhaps for several reasons. In lieu of technical knowledge possessed by the few specialized burners such as that reported for the neighboring Spokan (Ross, this volume), it appears that Salish and Kootenai burning was largely informal and opportunistic, rather than highly systematic, as has been reported for tribes in California and northern Alberta.[32] The data suggest that Indians in the Northern Rockies burned largely on an ad hoc basis. The principal exceptions might be highly localized fires: burning for game drives, clearing around campsites, and during warfare. Available evidence therefore suggests that these quasi-nomadic hunter-gatherers simply used fire informally as a tool to aid subsistence. Nonetheless, Indian fires clearly were frequent and widespread in certain environments, and benefited many elements of ecosystems besides humans.

Ecology of Indian Fires

We investigated fire history in Montana's dry lower elevation forests west of the Continental Divide.[33] Here, broad grassland and forested valleys are surrounded by steep, heavily forested mountains. During the presettlement era, most lower-elevation forests were dominated by old-growth ponderosa pine, western larch (*Larix occidentalis*), and interior Douglas-fir (*Pseudotsuga menziesii* var. *glauca*). Multiple fire scars on trees show that, although old trees are adapted to survive recurrent surface fires, pine and larch also depend on such fires to stimulate regeneration. Otherwise, stands develop understory thickets of Douglas-fir and grand fir (*Abies grandis*), reducing overall vigor. With continued fire exclusion, Douglas-fir- and grand fir-dominated stands eventually would replace native ponderosa pine-larch-Douglas-fir communities.

General distribution of the Pacific slope form of ponderosa pine, Pinus ponderosa var. ponderosa (after Little 1971); the map also shows the approximate distribution of mixed conifer-ponderosa pine types similar to those in western Montana. Lettered areas indicate locations where Indian burning has been implicated as an important ecological factor.

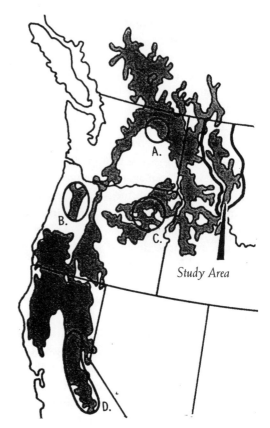

A.

B.

C.

D.

Study Area

The historical journals suggested that most Indian fires occurred in valley grasslands and adjacent dry forests.[34] By contrast, early travelers rarely noted Indian burning in less well-traveled mountain canyons. Therefore, we used a paired-stand approach to investigate whether measurable differences in fire frequency existed between such areas. We sampled 10 "heavy-use" stands at the edges of the broad intermountain valleys, and 10 comparable but "remote" ponderosa pine stands several miles up nearby canyons. Without frequent Indian-caused fires, both locales presumably would have similar fire frequencies (i.e., caused by lightning).

To estimate fire history, we sawed fire scar samples from old-growth trees, using the annual growth rings to identify specific fire years (see figure on facing page).[35] We used these samples to estimate fire frequency, first, for the presettlement era (pre-1860), then for the settlement (1861–1910) and fire exclusion (post-1910) periods. In the latter period, land management agencies tried, with considerable success, to exclude all fires.[36]

Between ca. 1500 and 1860, fire frequency was substantially shorter in nine of ten heavy-use stands than in their remote counterparts. Three heavy-use stands were in areas identified by informants as having been repeatedly

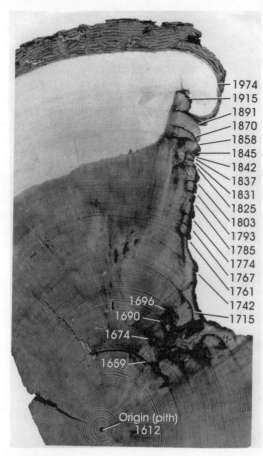

Cross-section of a ponderosa pine from the Bitterroot Valley, Montana, with scars from recurrent low-intensity fires. The tree recorded twenty-one fires between 1659 and 1915. Fire suppression interrupted the pattern of frequent fires after 1915. USDA Forest Service photo.

burned by Indians, and these stands had some of the shortest fire intervals, averaging about seven years each. In fact, pre-1860 fire intervals averaged less than ten years in most of the heavy-use stands. By comparison, fires averaged fifteen to twenty years on most remote sites. Statistically, the fire intervals for three heavy-use stands were significantly shorter (0.05 probability).[37] Also, the nine-year-long mean fire interval for all ten heavy-use stands combined was significantly shorter than the eighteen-year-long mean interval for all remote stands. The one "remote" stand not following the above pattern occurs in a canyon near hot springs well used by Indians. Therefore, poor sample site selection may have produced this result. Remote-stand fire intervals were more variable than in heavy-use stands, consistent with a regime of random lightning fires. By contrast, the heavy-use stands had comparatively uniform fire intervals, highly suggestive of a human-dominated (controlled) fire history.

We hypothesized that burning likely increased after the tribes acquired horses in the early 1700s. Horses greatly improved Indian mobility, and the tribes maintained very large herds, perhaps requiring more frequent or

Repeat photography near Sula, Montana. This area of the upper Bitterroot Valley, with many ancient Indian campsites, was visited by Lewis and Clark in 1805–06, Nez Perce Chief Joseph in 1877, and other early travelers. Circa 1895 photograph shows an open stand of ponderosa pines resulting from frequent fires. By 1980, in the absence of fires, the stand soon became dense (see facing page). The first photograph is courtesy of the Darby Historical Society; the second is by George Gruell of the USDA Forest Service. Photos no. 85-0031 & 0032, K. Ross Toole Archives, University of Montana.

widespread burning to rejuvenate grass and clear trail underbrush. We therefore compared pre-and post-1730 fire frequency, using data from nineteen of the oldest trees in the database. Post-1730 fire intervals were somewhat shorter than before 1730, but differences were not significant statistically, suggesting relatively uniform fire frequency from at least 1500 to 1860. The analysis yields several potential interpretations. First, Indian burning may not have changed substantially after acquisition of the horse. Or, Indians may have rotated grazing areas in such a way that burning occurred irregularly in some locales. Any chronic over-grazing would have reduced the ability and need for deliberate burning, by depleting grassy fuels.[38] Conversely, if increased burning had destroyed some fire scar evidence, we would have been unable to detect subtle changes in already high fire frequencies.

Fire patterns during the settlement period (1861–1910) were similar to those before 1860, but differences between heavy-use and remote stands were less pronounced. Nonetheless, overall fire frequency still was significantly

shorter in the heavy-use stands (i.e., twelve vs. fifteen years). Interestingly, mean fire intervals grew shorter in some remote stands, while increasing in some heavy-use stands. Given the short fifty-year period, such results simply might be due to chance. However, Indian burning was in decline by 1860, and prospectors, settlers, and others may have caused fires in both heavy use- and remote areas.[39]

During the fire exclusion period (post-1910), fire occurrence diminished markedly in most stands. Moreover, differences between heavy-use and remote stands were no longer significant. Fire intervals longer than 35 years were common in both types of locations, and several stands did not burn at all between 1910 and 1980. So consider the abrupt change in humankind's role in fire history: Euro-Americans reversed untold centuries of frequent Indian- and lightning-caused fires in grasslands and dry ponderosa pine forests.

Recently, Arno and others studied fire history in a cool, moist forest at Seeley Lake, northeast of Missoula, Montana.[40] Unlike in the drier valleys to the west, moist western larch forests often experienced comparatively long fire intervals (e.g., 35–200 years).[41] Yet the 600-year-old larch at Seeley Lake had many fire scars, leading the researchers to suspect Indian burning. In fact, artifacts revealed a major campsite for at least 3,500 years[42], and an earlier-cited quote about burning near trails and camps refers to this very locale.[43] Underburns averaging every twenty-four years maintained a park-like stand—highly unusual for such productive forests. Unfortunately, the thinning fires virtually ceased after the late 1800s and the old-growth trees now are heavily crowded by understory thickets.

Fire History: Lessons from the Past

Primeval fires throughout the Northern Rockies contributed to the high level of landscape diversity encountered by early-day settlers. Frequent surface fires in semi-arid valleys prevented heavy accumulations of forest fuels, tree crowding, and subsequent stand deterioration. The recurring underburns thus precluded highly destructive fires by promoting open stands of large fire-resistant trees. Conversely, lightning caused most fires higher in the mountains, and fire intervals and severities were more variable. This fire pattern produced a mosaic of different-aged stands, in contrast with the old, park-like pines in the lower valleys. The net result of thousands of years of that fire history was a complex of diverse and dynamic ecosystems that evolved with repeated disturbance.

After millennia of subsistence in the Northern Rockies, Indians were well accustomed to interacting with fire in the environment. But Euro-American civilization, challenged by this uncontrollable force of nature, had a cultural aversion to fire. Since 1900 we have tried to eliminate most forest fires, with varying success. But in just one century, settlement has changed the landscape, altering biodiversity, forest growth, wildlife habitat, and a host of other factors. In recent years, land managers have begun to move away from simple custodial management and total fire suppression. Instead, managers now are considering the aboriginal model of what has been termed "adapting to nature."[44] In the 1990s, foresters increasingly use prescribed fires and stand thinnings to return Western forests to a semblance of their historical condition and enhance long-term forest health.

Originally published in the Journal of Forestry 80(10): 647–51 (1982).
Substantially revised for this publication.

Notes

1. Authors are, respectively, Consulting Research Forester (995 Ranch Ln, Kalispell MT 59901) and Research Forester (USDA Forest Service Intermountain Fire Sciences Laboratory, Box 8089, Missoula MT 59807).

2. Stephen Barrett, "Relationship of Indian-caused fires to the ecology of Western Montana forests" (M.S. thesis, University of Montana, Missoula, 1980).

3. Carling Malouf, "The coniferous forests and their use through 9,000 years of prehistory" (pp. 271–90 *in Coniferous Forests of the Northern Rocky Mountains, Proceedings of the 1968 Symposium* (Missoula, 1969); Wayne Choquette, "Cultural resource overview of the Bonneville Power Administration proposed transmission line from Libby Dam, Montana, to Rathdrum, Idaho" (*Washington Archaeological Research Center Project Report* 100, Pullman, 1980).

4. James Teit, "The Salishan tribes of the western plateaus" (*Bureau of American Ethnology* 45th *Annual Report*, pp. 23–396, 1928).

5. Willa Baum, *Oral History for the local historical society* (Nashville, 1974).

6. George Gruell, "Fire on the early Western landscape: An annotated record of wildland fires, 1776–1900" (*Northwest Science* 59(2): 97–107, 1985). (The author reviewed journals of travelers in Montana, Idaho, Wyoming, Nevada, Utah, and eastern Oregon).

7. *Ibid.*

8. Personal communication with Gary McLean, Archaeologist, Flathead National Forest, Kalispell, MT.

9. Gary Moulton (ed.), *The Journals of the Lewis & Clark Expedition* Vol. 8, June 10–September 26, 1806. (Lincoln, NE, 1988), 148.

10. Hiram Chittenden and Alfred Richardson (eds.), *Life, letters, and travels of Father Pierre-Jean DeSmet, 1801–1873.* (New York, 1969), 1021–22.

11. Claude Schaeffer, "The subsistence quest of the Kootenai" (Ph.D.dissertation, University of Pennsylvania, 1940), 13. Northwest Plateau peoples used several varieties of deer drives. For a second example of a circle drive with fire from Coeur d'Alene, see deSmet in Boyd (this volume). Coeur d'Alene also drove deer in winter snow without benefit of fire.

12. Gruell, "Fire on the early Western landscape."

13. John Lieberg, 1899. "Bitterroot Forest Reserve." In *19th Annual Report of the U.S. Geological Survey* (1897–1898), Part V., Forest Reserves. pp. 253–82.

14. Members of the genus *Alectoria* are not mosses or parasites, but epiphytic lichens.

15. John Mullan, "Report of a reconnaissance from the Bitterroot Valley to Fort Hall." In *Explorations and surveys for a railroad route from the Mississippi River to the Pacific Ocean,* (U.S. War Dept., vol 12, Book I, 1853–1855. 36th Cong., 1st Sess., House Ex. Doc. 56, 1861), 151–52.

16. Mullan, *ibid.*, 37.

17. Horace Ayres, "Lewis and Clark Forest Reserve, Montana." (pp. 27–80 In *21st Annual Report of the U.S. Geological Survey* [1899–1900], Part V, Forest Reserves, pp. 72–103, 1900.)

18. William Hamilton, "A trading expedition among the Indians in 1858 from Fort Walla Walla to the Blackfoot country and return." (*Contributions to the Historical Society of Montana* . . . III, Helena, 1900), 110–11.

19. Gruell, "Fire on the early Western landscape."

20. Moulton *ibid.,* 179.

21. Warren Ferris, *Life in the Rocky Mountains: A diary of wanderings on the sources of the rivers Missouri . . .,* Paul Phillips, ed. (Denver, 1940), 215.

22. *Ibid.,* 103.

23. *Ibid.,* 106–7.

24. Leiberg, "Bitterroot Forest Reserve," 275.

25. Such statements might simply reflect bias if modern-day Indians were worried about inadvertently protraying their ancestors as arsonists, or conversely, as highly responsible "land stewards."

26. Leiberg 1899 *ibid.,* Ayres, "Lewis and Clark Forest Reserve," and Ayres, "Flathead Forest Reserve, Montana" (pp. 245–316 In *20th Annual Report of the U.S. Geological Survey* (1898–1899), Part V, Forest Reserves, 1900).

27. Leiberg 1899, 387.

28. Lieberg 1899, 388.

29. Lieberg 1899, 387.

30. Moulton, *The Journals of the Lewis and Clark Expedition,* 50.

31. Peter Mehringer, Stephen Arno, and Kenneth Peterson, "Postglacial History of Lost Trail Pass Bog, Bitterroot Mountains, Montana" (*Arctic and Alpine Research* 9: 345–68, l977).

32. Richard Reynolds, "Effect of natural fires and aboriginal burning upon the forests of the central Sierra Nevada" (M.A. thesis, University of California, Berkeley, 1959).

33. Stephen Barrett and Stephen Arno, "Indian fires as an ecological influence in the Northern Rockies" (*Journal of Forestry* 80(10): 647–51, 1982).

34. Gruell, "Fire on the early Western landscape."

35. Stephen Arno and Kathy Sneck, "A method for determining fire history in coniferous forests of the Mountain West" (USDA Forest Service General Technical Report INT-42, 1977).

36. Arno, "Forest Fire History in the Northern Rockies" (*Journal of Forestry* 78(8): 460-65, 1980); James K. Agee, *Fire ecology of Pacific Northwest forests* (Washington, 1993).

37. George Snedecor, *Statistical Methods* (Ames IA, 1967).

38. Agee, *Fire ecology of Pacific Northwest forests.*

39. Ayres, "Lewis and Clark Forest Reserve," "Flathead Forest Reserve"; Leiberg, "Bitterroot Forest Reserve."

40. Stephen Arno, Helen Smith, and Michael Krebs, "Old growth ponderosa pine and western larch stand structures: Influences of pre-1900 fires and fire exclusion" (USDA Forest Service Research Paper INT-495, 1997).

41. Stephen Barrett, Stephen Arno, and Carl Key, "Fire regimes of western larch-lodgepole pine forests in Glacier National Park, Montana" (*Canadian Journal of Forest Research* 21: 1711–20, 1991).

42. Personal communication with Milo McLeod, Archaeologist, Lolo National Forest, Missoula MT.

43. Ayres, "Lewis and Clark Forest Reserve," 257.

44. Colin Hardy and Stephen Arno, "The use of fire in forest restoration" (USDA Forest Service General Technical Report INT-341, 1996).

The Klikitat Trail of South-central Washington
A Reconstruction of Seasonally Used Resource Sites

Helen H. Norton, Robert Boyd, and Eugene Hunn

Introduction

Comment and Context

T he subsistence economy of the Northwest Coast has been described most frequently as one based on aquatic resources, especially the five species of anadromous salmon. In addition to aquatic foods, many of the more southerly and interior peoples of the Northwest Coast depended heavily on terrestrial resources. Throughout the Northwest Coast, important terrestrial resource sites were connected to settlement areas by well-used trails. The communication function of aboriginal trails has obscured their role in the subsistence economy.

Terrestrial resources crucial to native economies were concentrated in grasslands and prairies. Many of these open places were anthropogenic in nature and supplied food and medicinal plants as well as forage and grazing for game and horses. Several early observers commented on the singular appearance of these prairies, but few recognized their origin and fewer still acknowledged their importance to the native subsistence economy. The grasslands stood in sharp contrast to the densely forested surrounding country and became of immediate importance to the Euro-Americans as settlement sites and range land. Thus, many of the aboriginal prairies no longer are available for archaeological inspection.[1]

The Klikitat Trail of south-central Washington, an overland route from Fort Vancouver to The Dalles and Yakima (see maps), is one example of a trail that connected aboriginal settlement and subsistence areas. In this paper, we examine the various resource areas along the Klikitat Trail and make some suggestions about their archaeological significance based on linguistic, botanical, and related data. From an archaeological standpoint, our subject matter is non-traditional. There are few studies of aboriginal trails or resource areas that provide models for this kind of work.[2] With very little strictly archaeological data at hand,[3] we have relied on auxiliary sources of information for our reconstruction. Our data are primarily ethnohistorical. We have

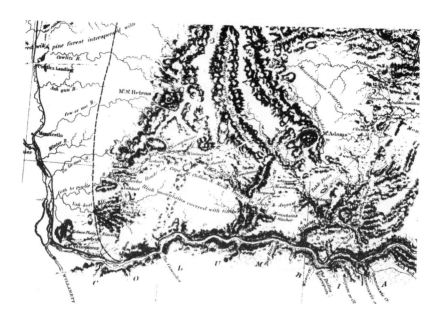

Map 1. Route of the McClellan party over the Klikitat Trail, 1853. Report of the Pacific Railroad Expedition, vol. 12, map no. 3 (cropped). OrHi #10438

organized and interpreted these data from an ethnobiological perspective and combined them with the limited ethnographic field data on aboriginal settlement and land use patterns to arrive at an approximation of the Klikitat subsistence pattern, seasonal round, and the role the Klikitat Trail played in that pattern.

Ethnographic Background[4]

The Klikitat (/xwa'lxaypaml/)[5] were the major ethnic group of the south-central Washington Cascades in the early historic period. They were closely associated with Upper Chinookan peoples of the north bank of the Columbia, sharing winter village and salmon fishing sites with them. Judging from the location of winter village sites and summer camps, the traditional Klikitat life-range included the drainages of the Wind, Little White Salmon, and White Salmon Rivers, and the lower reaches of the Klickitat River. The extent of Klikitat occupation of the Lewis River drainage before the demographic and economic dislocations caused by Euro-American intrusion is difficult to determine. By the mid-1800s, the Lewis River was occupied by close linguistic relatives of the Klikitat, the "Lewis River Cowlitz," /táytnapaml/ speakers, down to within 5 miles of its junction with the Columbia, where they were joined by the Klikitat sometime before 1850. Many sites along the Lewis

River had Sahaptin names by 1853 (Map 2), suggesting a respectable time depth for the occupation or regular use of the lower Lewis by Sahaptin speakers, whether Klikitat or /*táytnapaml*/.[6]

Klikitat Indians had a "prairie-oriented" subsistence strategy, which contrasts with the shoreline orientation of most Northwest Coast Indian societies. Like the Cowlitz to the north and west, they had no direct access to saltwater resources and only limited access to the Columbia River fisheries. The Klikitat Trail, a network of trails and prairies, linked their subsistence areas. Their country was well endowed with camas (*Camassia quamash*) and huckleberry (*Vaccinium* spp.), resources of open meadow or prairie habitats that the Indians maintained by periodic intentional burning. These prairie resources attracted visitors from Yakima Valley and Columbia River villages as well, some as much as 100 kilometers distant.[7]

The aboriginal relationship between Klikitats and their Chinookan neighbors poses an intriguing ecological puzzle. The two groups maintained linguistic and ethnic distinctiveness despite intermarriage and co-utilization of all major resources of the south-central Cascades and upper Columbia River Gorge. There is no record of conflict between them over resources. Available evidence suggests that the ethnic boundary was reflected in contrasting subsistence strategies. The Chinookans of the upper Columbia Gorge were aquatic in orientation and moved primarily east and west along the river by canoe in search of seasonal harvests. The Klikitat moved north to south with the seasons, up the tributary valleys—later on horseback—taking advantage of resources ripening at a range of elevations. They spent the better part of their subsistence effort in upland meadows. This is an example of two cultural groups sharing a territory by virtue of their contrasting niches.[8]

The Klikitat also were favorably situated to take advantage of trans-Cascade trade; a network of trails linked their camas and berry campsites to the lower Yakima Valley (via upstream tributaries of the Klickitat and Yakima Rivers), to winter villages and salmon fishing sites of the Columbia between the White Salmon River and The Dalles, and to Chinookan villages of the lower Columbia River via a trail down the Lewis. In the Chinookan villages, Klikitat traded "slaves, skins, deer meat, hazelnuts, huckleberries, and camas." The Klikitat were well known for their fine cedar root baskets, which still are made today. After 1800 they also traded horses to people west of the Cascades. Two widely renowned "Indian racetracks" are located in Klikitat country and were foci of large, ethnically diverse gatherings in the month of August coincident with the huckleberry harvest. These meetings provided an opportunity for socializing, gambling, and trading, and added to the significance of the Klikitat Trail.[9]

Ethnohistorical Data on the Klikitat Trail

Sources

With the exception of a questionable 1830 account,[10] there is no evidence of non-Native penetration of the mountainous region traversed by the Klikitat Trail prior to 1853. In that year, the Pacific Railroad Survey made a thorough examination of the route. The manuscript and printed documents of the expedition provide the only detailed source of information on aboriginal exploitation areas along the trail. Regular use of the western half of the trail declined significantly after the Indian Wars and removal of most of the local native people to the Yakama Reservation in the late 1850s. Documentary sources after that time are correspondingly scarce. Our primary sources were two manuscript daily journals of survey members George McClellan (1853) and James G. Cooper (1853, 1855). Parts of McClellan's journal have been cited previously, but Cooper's diary, to our knowledge, has not been used by Northwest researchers. We also have employed selected works from the official 1854–1855 Pacific Railroad Report.[11]

Aboriginal Prairies

Members of the Pacific Railroad Survey, like previous explorers, were impressed by the prairies that dotted the otherwise unbroken forest of western Washington. Cooper summarized their observations:

> . . . the prairies . . . form . . . the division most important to the
> settler, who, in the western section, finds the absence of trees
> . . . desirable. . . . From February to July they look like gardens such is
> the brilliancy and variety of the flowers with which they are adorned.
> The weary traveler, toiling through the forests, is sure to find in them
> game, or, at least, some life to relieve the gloomy silence of the
> woods.[12]

Cooper's interest in western Washington prairies led to numerous descriptions and hypotheses concerning their origin and maintenance. He classified the regional prairies into two major categories, wet and dry. The dry prairies are of particular concern in an examination of the Klikitat Trail. Regarding the origin and maintenance of dry prairies, Cooper wrote:

> It is certain that the Indians have always been in the habit of burning
> off these prairies annually to kill the young trees and cause a fresh
> growth of grass . . . . The first Indian immigrants may have found spots
> yet unwooded by the extending forests, which were and still are
> almost the only resort of game such as deer and elk. To keep these as
> hunting grounds they used the only means they knew . . . . they also
> derived one of their principal vegetables from these same prairies and

still, the whole tribe resorts to them and encamps during June and July to gather the kamass root. They do not however seem to have resided permanently on them except when open to the river banks. I cannot, otherwise than by this agency of man, account for the existence of many prairies whose outline is as sharply defined by the unbroken edge of forest as if carefully cleared for the farmer, every stump dug out, and the ground levelled—raked smooth, and sown with grass and flowers.[13]

Survival of aboriginal prairies into historic times was the result of one of two processes: regular inundation, which inhibits or retards tree growth during part of the year; or regular burning which destroys adventitious species. Without one or both of these processes, fast-growing trees eventually would have moved onto the prairies, overtopping and thus eliminating the unique prairie flora. Many prairie species are intolerant of even light shade. For example, oak (*Quercus garryana*), most huckleberries, and other berries all cease bearing when overtopped. Climate, particularly the amount of precipitation, has been argued as the cause for the continuance of western Washington prairies, but that argument must be discounted for two reasons: 1) prairies were found from sea level to 1,500 m in areas having from 250 to 2,280 mm of rain annually, and 2) survey maps document the disappearance of many prairies in the last 130 years due to lack of burning and the inevitable encroachment of forest, not to climatic change.[14]

There is strong ethnohistorical evidence of patterned burning by Indians to maintain grassy open areas in western Washington and Oregon. There is ample evidence of fire along the Klikitat Trail, but it is difficult to separate human causation from natural factors. There is ethnographic documentation of patterned aboriginal burning in sub-alpine huckleberry meadows, and many of the west-side prairies were of anthropogenic origin. But some of the burned forests encountered by the survey probably were caused by lightning strikes, then as now an important cause of forest fires in the southern Cascades. Volcanism, such as the 1842 eruption of Mount St. Helens, also caused forest fires.[15]

Prairie Foods

Cooper noted that of "360 species of plants . . . collected west of the Cascade range . . . , more than 150 are peculiar to these prairies." Analysis of Cooper's plant lists show that of the 148 native prairie species, over two-thirds are recorded in the literature as being important either for food, medicine, or artifacts. Of the sixty-five plants mentioned on the Klikitat Trail, fifty-eight were used in the material culture as medicines or especially as food (see Table 1 at end of chapter).[16]

Important food plants are camas, found in wet prairies and Garry oak and hazel (*Corylus cornuta*), found in dry open areas. The latter two provided nuts. Oregon grape (*Berberis* spp.), serviceberry (*Amelanchier alnifolia*), and various species of *Rubus*, all valued for their berries, are found in sunny microhabitats ranging from rocky areas to open woods. Bracken fern (*Pteridium aquilinum*) proliferates in open and edge environments, while strawberry (*Fragaria* spp.) and huckleberry abound in subalpine meadows. Many of these species are early succession plants, which favor burned-over areas.[17]

The prairies also attracted animals. With regard to elk, Cooper noted

> The Indians formerly killed them by enclosing a large space by a circle of men and then gradually narrowing it until they drive the game into an open spot where they were easily killed. The black tail deer also occurs rather sparingly about the borders of these prairies.

The prairies also supported rabbits and mountain beaver, from whose fur clothing was made, as well as several other mammals and birds.[18]

The Klikitat Trail

The Klikitat Trail passes through a highly variable terrain (Maps 1-3). Elevations range from near sea level at Vancouver to over 900 m on the high plateau south of Mount Adams; average annual precipitation varies from more than 2,500 mm on the upper Lewis River to 400 mm at Conboy Lake. The trail traverses five major vegetational zones listed by Franklin and Dyrness.[19] Four of these zones contained important native foods exploited by the Klikitat. Within each of these zones, many of the food sources were concentrated in prairie areas. The Klikitat Trail connected these seasonally utilized subsistence locations and also served as a trade and communcation route. The Trail filled a role in Klikitat culture not unlike that of the Columbia River among neighboring Chinookans. The accompanying maps show the location of major sites along the trail. Table 2 (at the end of the chapter) incorporates descriptions of each named site.

Low Prairies (Zone 1)

On the first part of the Klikitat Trail there was a series of prairies, numbered by the settlers "First" through "Fifth Plains." The corresponding Indian names, as recorded by J. F. Minter, were Wahwaikee, Pahpoopahpoo, Heowheow, Kolsas, and Simsik (see maps and Table 2). These qualify as typical "dry forest prairies" in Cooper's typology (though parts of Kolsas seem to have been wet).

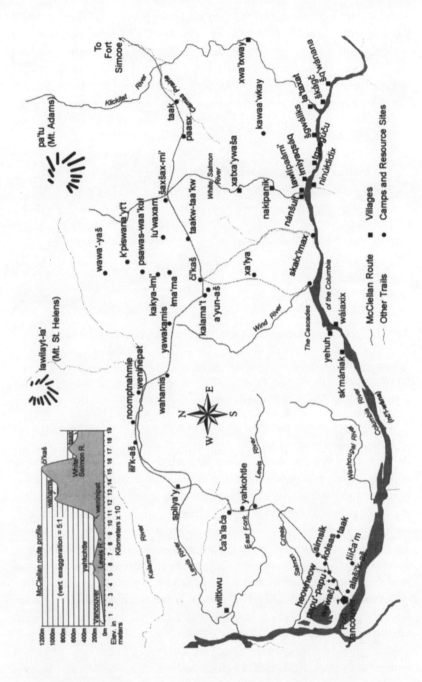

Map 2. *The Klikitat Trail: detail showing Indian place names (transcriptions by E. Hunn in Sahaptin orthography). Map by Ric Vrana. Inset is a vertical cross-section of the trail.*

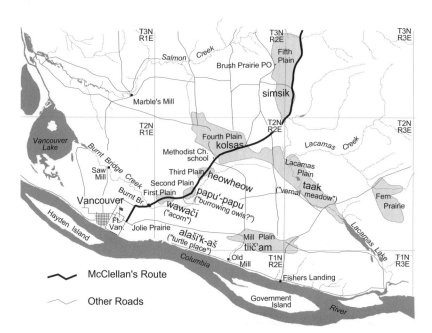

Map 3. Clark county prairies, mid-1800s. Map by Ric Vrana based on George Goethals's 1883 "A Map of the Country in the Vicinity of Vancouver Barracks, Washington Territory." Courtesy of the Clark County Historical Society, Vancouver. The locations of First, Second, Third, and Fifth Plains, as well as all Indian names, are from George McClellan's 1853 manuscript journal.

Plains one through five were covered in part with "good grass" acceptable to horses and were noted for their profusion of berries. Eight edible varieties are mentioned in the journals; of these, seven ripen in July and August, lending support to Cooper's contention that "berries form the chief food of the natives at this season (late summer)."[20] Plants gathered for their sprouts in the spring, including fireweed (*Epilobium angustifolium*), salmonberry (*Rubus spectablis*), and thimbleberry (*R. parviflorus*), were also common. Most of these species are early succession plants, which quickly invade burned-over areas. Frequent journal references to the prairies' "sharply defined borders" and circular or oval shapes suggest a controlled burning pattern, like that reported for fire-maintained fields elsewhere. This pattern is the result of firing vegetation from the peripheries of the field to the center to avoid setting fire to adjacent woodland.

On Simsik, the survey party found an "old Indian camp" at a "detached clump" of fir trees. No details are given, and we cannot be sure if this camp consisted merely of hearths and refuse, or if it included traces of temporary structures. The Klikitat utilized both the ramada and the rush mat lodge common to most Plateau peoples.[21]

Low Forests (Zone 2)

This region is covered by the typical coniferous forest [Douglas-fir (*Pseudotsuga menziesii*), western hemlock (*Tsuga heterophylla*), and western red-cedar (*Thuja plicata*)] of western Washington and Oregon. The economically useful flora in this area are transitional between that of the lower plains (Zone 1) and that of the high mountain zone (Zone 4). Berries remain of major importance, with serviceberry, dwarf huckleberry (*V. caespitosum*), and elderberry (*Sambucus* spp.) mentioned by the survey party, as well as acorns and hazelnuts. McClellan noted that Yahkohtl (now Yacolt) " . . . abounds with berries & is much visited by the Indians about a month later . . . "[22], that is, late August, the time the dwarf huckleberry ripens. Chalacha (/čaʾaˀlačaˀ/; "bracken fern," now Chelatchie) Prairie was noted for berries as well as its dense stands of bracken fern and a grove of oaks. Bracken fern rhizomes, dug in late fall, were an important source of carbohydrate throughout the southern Northwest Coast. Acorns, a vegetable protein source, were valued by the natives of western Washington.[23]

Fire is mentioned frequently in both McClellan and Cooper's journal entries for this region. Enroute from Simsik to Mankas Prairies, the survey party encountered a "Brulée" ["burn" in French] . . . covered by large snags; between Mankas and Yahkohtl they passed through a "forest" of uniform-sized fir seedlings "as if the ground had lately been a prairie & the trees had grown up

Fourth Plain, sketch by Paul Kane, 1847. Courtesy of the Royal Ontario Museum 80 ETH 193, 946.15.166

suddenly and all together." Cooper implicitly contrasts this "young forest" with Yahkohtl prairie, which " . . . seems to have been caused by fires as there are several mounds scattered over it, the remains of stumps & logs." Both areas were able to support trees, but on only one were they growing back. The obvious implication is that Yahkohtl prairie was being maintained by aboriginal firing.[24]

The railroad survey encountered small groups of natives in the Zone 2 prairies. A few "Tlikatat" families were camped at a falls on the Yahkohtl River (now the East Fork of the Lewis) fishing for steelhead. Gear used in fishing at such locations consisted not only of "traps," but also spears. These were Plateau-style mounted Indians. McClellan states "They had a double barrel shot gun etc—their saddles resemble those of the Comanches."[25]

At Chalacha, Indians were cultivating potatoes, introduced in the area by the Hudson's Bay Company. The Chelatchie area has very good soil. Because of its subsistence potential (as well as its isolation), the Indian Agent recommended in 1854 that Chalacha be made a reservation for the Vancouver Klikitat, Lewis River /táytnapam/, and Cowlitz. Cooper noted the abundance of serviceberries and huckleberries at Spilyeh (/spilya'y/, "mythological coyote"). Thirty years later huckleberries still were important here; an 1883 journal noted that Native Americans had " . . . lately took forty gallons of berries away. They pick them very rapidly by means of a wooden comb, raking it through the bush and holding a dish underneath."[26]

"Four archaeological sites" have been identified in the vicinity of Yacolt and Chelatchie.[27] To date, however, there has been no intensive archaeological work in the area.

Lewis River Camps (Zone 3)

The 28 miles of trail between Spilyeh and Wahamis Prairies passed through heavy forest along the Lewis River. There were no prairies or sizable open areas, and economically useful plants mentioned were limited to kinnikinnick (*Arctostaphylos uva-ursi*), an occasional source of berries and an Indian tobacco. This segment of the trail also lacked grass for horses. The survey party's mounts suffered, and were weak from lack of food after the third day.

In the early 1950s, an archaeological survey of this portion of the Klikitat Trail revealed

A total of 6 sites . . . Four were very small campsites probably used by travelers and hunting parties . . . one site was apparently used primarily as a chipping station. The most important site was an isolated semi-subterranean pit-house, located on the river near a spot which was excellent for fishing.[28]

Subalpine Prairies (Zone 4)

On August 5, the railroad survey left the dense forest of the Lewis River Valley and climbed to the thinly wooded mountain plateau southwest of Mount Adams. The three prairies visited in this subalpine area, Wahamis, Yawakamis, and Chequos, supported extensive tracts of huckleberry. Chequos (/čí ꞌkaš/), in particular, was a traditional huckleberrying ground. The primary species gathered was black mountain huckleberry (*V. membranaceum*), the largest native Northwest huckleberry and one of the most valued. Black mountain huckleberry is an early succession plant that grows best in recently burned-over areas. Burning not only removes competition from other species but serves to prune the bushes, stimulate sprouting, and destroy parasites.[29]

On August 9, McClellan recorded twenty Klikitat lodges at Chequos Prairie. The huckleberry season was called /wíwnumi/ ("of black mountain huckleberry") by Klikitat Sahaptins and was inaugurated by a first-fruits ceremony, one of several such rites observed annually by Sahaptin peoples. A quotation from missionary Henry Perkins describes a typical "berry month" (at the Mount Adams fields) in 1843:

> August 19 . . . People moving to the mountains for berries. They obtain at this season the large mountain huckleberry. The berry month is to the natives like one great holy-day. . . . The young, the

Indians playing the spear game in what appears to be a mountain clearing. Sketch by Joseph Drayton, 1841. Courtesy of the Oregon Historical Society, OrHi #46190.

middle-aged, & the aged share alike in the release which is thus
afforded them . . . .They are usually absent on these excursions from
four to six weeks; during which each family lays in, for winter use,
four or five pecks of nice dried berries. These they mix from time to
time with pounded salmon, & a good portion of salmon oil & thus is
prepared one of the best dishes which an Indian can make.[30]

George Gibbs noted that the Klikitat at Chequos were "using the sweat
lodge . . . a small oven-shaped affair heated with stones" as a means of ritual
purification after the death of a kinsman from smallpox, which was then
raging among the Indians seen on the Trail. Sweat lodges were still in use in
the area in 1980 by Indian berrying parties from the Yakama reservation.
David Douglas described sweat lodges of this type in the vicinity of Vancouver
in 1825. Such structures should leave distinctive archaeological remains.[31]

Prairies East of the Crest (Zone 5)

Descending eastward from the subalpine plateau, "the wood became very
open & of large pine trees [*Pinus ponderosa*] standing 20–30 yds. apart, the
ground below being covered with grass and small shrubs." Ponderosa pine is
widely recognized by ecologists as a fire dependent species. "Before fire control
was initiated about 1900, fires burned through Pinus ponderosa stands at
intervals variously reported as 8 to 20 years." The clearing effect of regular
burning would explain the open, grassy "ornamental" areas noted.[32]

The easternmost prairies are seasonally inundated.[33] At Hoolho-olse
(/šaxšax-miʔ/, Trout Lake) the horses grazed upon horse mint (*Agastache
occidentalis*) and the common bunch grass (*Festuca idahoensis*) of the plateau.
At Tahk (/taak/, Conboy Lake) Garry oak reappeared and the indigenous
roots, wapato (*Sagittaria latifolia*) and camas, were found in abundance. Camas
and wapato, as well as other vegetables and meats, were baked in earth ovens.
An early description from the 1820s noted:

the *Quamash* of the natives, who prepare its roots in the following
manner. A round hole is scraped in the ground, in which are placed a
number of stones and a fire is kept burning on them until they are red
hot, when it is removed and replaced by some brush-wood and straw,
on which the roots are laid (covered with leaves, moss, or straw, with
a layer of earth), and they remain there until they are baked or
roasted.

Contemporary Sahaptin peoples still use this type of oven. Processing camps
seem to have been situated on the borders of prairies.[34]

The Conboy Lake area also was the site of a late summer congregation of
Sahaptin peoples (and of Chinookans and Interior Salish), who gathered to
harvest camas, trade, and race horses. Gibbs said that the Klikitat met the

Yakama at the Conboy Lake "Tahk" in late August for horse racing, a report confirmed by the Indian Agent at the temporary White Salmon Reservation. Given the importance of this prairie as a subsistence area, like Chalacha in the west, the Columbia district Indian agent recommended, in 1854:

> that a large reservation should be made as soon as possible in the Camass prairie on White Salmon River [sic., actually in the Klickitat River drainage]. This prarie suplies sevral of the large tribes of the middle district, and some of the bands of the Southern with a great part of their winters' food.

The Klikitat Trail in the Context of the Klikitat Seasonal Round

Summary of Seasonal Round

Various lines of evidence, ethnohistorical, ethnobotanical, and ethnographic, suggest that the Klikitat seasonal round proceeded as follows: 1) winter villages on the middle and upper stretches of the Klickitat, White Salmon, and (perhaps) other rivers to the west (see map) occupied from October–November until early May, with visits to the Columbia by fishing parties. 2) Late winter–early spring harvest of suckers (*Catostomus* spp.)[35] and early "Indian celeries" (especially *Lomatium grayi*) using the winter village as a base camp. 3) Late April–early May gathering at the Columbia to harvest spring Chinook salmon.[36] 4) Late May–July harvesting and preparing of camas at middle-elevation prairies, with harvest of early-maturing fruits such as serviceberry, chokecherry (*Prunus virginiana*), kinnikinnick, and hawthorn (*Crataegus douglasii*), along with trout (as at Trout Lake). 5) the peak social concentration of the summer in "huckleberry month" (August) at subalpine meadows and burned clearings on the Cascade crest. Hunting and fishing was pursued at a distance from these camps by parties of men. Socializing, gambling, horse racing, and trading also were important activities. 6) Return to middle-elevation prairies to harvest later-maturing fruits, nuts, and camas, September–November. While November is cited as the peak acorn harvest month among the Wishram, hazelnuts could be harvested in late August or early September.[37] 7) Return to winter villages, reliance on dried stores of roots, bulbs, berries, nuts, and fish, while also hunting game driven out of the mountains by winter snows.

Winter Villages

In early contact times, the Klikitat occupied a string of winter villages on the north bank of the Columbia from a point midway between The Dalles and the Klickitat River to the mouth of the White Salmon. Most of these settlements were co-occupied with the Chinookan-speaking White Salmon people. Predominantly Klikitat winter villages were located on the middle and upper stretches of the Klickitat and White Salmon Rivers (Map 2).[38]

Twentieth-century Indian informants named two villages upriver from the mouth of the Klickitat, /šqʼwánana/ and /škágč/, "inhabited partially by Klickitat." /łaʼtaxat/ was located, downriver from /šqʼwánana/ and /škágč/, at the mouth of the Klickitat. Lewis and Clark visited a village of eleven lodges at this location on October 29, 1805, but considered its occupants culturally and linguistically identical to adjacent Chinookan villages. The standard Wishram Ethnography considers /łaʼtaxat/ a White Salmon settlement and the name an Upper Chinookan designation. On the return trip, however, the explorers found twenty lodges and "about 100 fighting men of several tribes from the plains to the north collected here waiting for Salmon," clearly a reference to Sahaptin speaking groups, most likely Klikitat and their Yakama relatives. Joint occupation also is suggested by the facts that the name "Klikitat" is derived from Upper Chinookan /łaʼtaxat/ and that contemporary descendants of Klikitat-speakers still fish for salmon and steelhead in the narrow gorge some 2 miles above the Klickitat River mouth.[39]

The next village downriver on the Columbia, called /šgwáliks/ in Upper Chinookan, is described in "Wishram Ethnography" as a Klikitat village of fifty individuals. Evidence in Lewis and Clark for a Klikitat or mixed White Salmon-Klikitat village near the mouth of the White Salmon River is ambiguous. The three closely spaced villages cited in "Wishram Ethnography" at this location probably include both the "Klikitat" settlement /lawli-pa-amiʼ/ and Lewis and Clark's "We-ock-sock Wil-la-cum" village. It was at the White Salmon mouth that the two explorers, on their 1806 ascent of the Columbia, first noted horses, "Nez Perce style" clothing, and Plateau style houses. Wishram Ethnography describes these populations as mixed White Salmon-Klikitat. Klikitat also are said to have had fishing sites at the mouths of the Little White Salmon and Wind Rivers, linked by trails to inland berry fields. Lewis and Clark, however, reported no villages, Klikitat or otherwise, between the White Salmon River and head of The Cascades 10 miles below the mouth of the Wind River.[40]

Lewis and Clark named the White Salmon River "Canoe Creek" for the several canoes noted at its mouth, and they commented that "in this creek the Indians above [perhaps those of the upriver Klikitat villages, /nakipanik/ and /xatxaʼywaša/] take their fish." Thus, the ethnographic claims that Klikitat had access to the Columbia River anadromous fish resources, though at odds on certain details, are supported by the earliest ethnohistorical records.[41]

Twentieth-century informants described three of these Klikitat winter villages as permanently occupied. It seems likely that a few people might have remained in the villages year round, or that villagers were never absent for extended periods, since the distance between the Columbia River and Klikitat root and berry grounds is but 30–60 km. James Selam, a John Day River, Sahaptin-speaking Indian, whose family camped at the subalpine site /a´yun-aš/ ("place of lovage, *Ligusticum canbyi*") while berry picking and racing horses at /kalama´t/ ("yellow pond lily," *Nuphar polysepalum*) during the late 1920s, reports that men would leave these high camps (occupied in August and September) to fish at the Columbia, presumably traveling down the Wind, Little White Salmon, or White Salmon rivers to the mouths. They would bring their catch back for the women to prepare. It is likely that there was a constant coming and going between high country camps and camas meadows and the fishing stations during the spring, summer, and fall, especially in view of the coincidence of salmon runs with these upland resource harvest periods. Whether these villages were occupied permanently or only in winter, stored dried foods would have been of great significance to survival during the winter months, the low point of anadromous fishing activity.[42]

Interior Resource Areas

Gibbs noted that the usual residence of the Klikitat Indians during the summer is "around Chequoss, one of the most elevated points on our trail from Fort Vancouver across the Cascades." The survey party's "Chequoss" is certainly the same site as the ethnographer's *te´ikwa´c* which has been located 3 km east of the Indian race track at /kalama´t/. Hunn visited /kalama´t/ with James Selam in late August 1981, and found abundant black mountain huckleberry and dwarf huckleberry with some grouseberry (*V. scoparium*), all three highly valued Sahaptin fruit resources. The meadow supported palatable forage grasses (e.g. *Calamagrostis purpurascens*) and the small temporary pond sported a few yellow pond lilies (*Nuphar polysepalum*) for which the site is named. In 1981, the race track meadow was being overgrown with lodgepole pine (*Pinus contorta*).[43]

Patterned burning of mountain huckleberry meadows by Sahaptin Indians is fairly well documented, for the practice persisted in sub-alpine areas around Mounts Adams, Hood, and Jefferson well into the early decades of this century. Indians allowed berry-drying fires (see below) to spread when the harvest was finished and they were departing from the fields. Autumn rains extinguished these fires. Fire as a mechanism in maintaining the productivity of these sites is highlighted by place names such as /lu'waxam/ ("burnt ground") and /taakw-taa'kw/ ("many [small] meadows"), such as might be produced by controlled Indian burning. In the absence of regular firing in the past half-century, many huckleberry fields have reverted to forest. The Twin Buttes (/wawa'-yaš/; "mosquito place") field near Mount Adams has diminished during this period to one-third of its original area.[44]

In 1936, the U.S. Forest Service sought to document the traditional Indian custom of "berrying" in the Mount Adams country (where the U.S. Forest Service has set aside huckleberry fields exclusively for Indian use). At that time, Indians from four Northwest states still traveled to this area to gather and process huckleberries for winter use. Women were the principal pickers and processors, while men engaged in hunting, fishing, and social and political activity. Berries were collected in traditional baskets as well as in disposable cedar bark baskets of two- to four-liter capacity made at the berrying grounds. Indian women could gather four liters in a single day. The Twin Buttes field has produced as much as 170 liters per hectare.[45]

An ancient method of drying with indirect heat prepared the berries as a raisin-like product for easy transport and storage. The women chose logs as fuel, then

> . . . scooped out the earth along one side of it, and from this trench
> built up a parallel ridge about three feet from the log. The slope of the
> ridge on the side facing the log would be approximately 45°. Upon
> this she would place a tule mat or some other suitable covering and
> put a row of stones along the lower edge.[46]

Berries were either spread on the mat and dried, or dried on long racks above smoldering logs. Trenches of this nature and stones, along with charred material, may remain in situ as archaeological evidence.[47]

Klikitats West of the Cascades

By the beginning of the 19th century, the Klikitat proper (/xwa'lxwaypam/) had split into two groups, one inland east of the Cascades in traditional Sahaptin territory, the other west of the Cascades between the Lewis and Columbia Rivers.[48] The occupation of the western lands was facilitated by several factors: 1) the adoption of the horse and the subsequent ease of transport over the Klikitat Trail; 2) the attraction of traditional subsistence resources (berries, deer, camas, etc.) and (after contact) White trade goods; and 3) the depopulation of the Chinookan villages by disease, which left a vacuum ready to be filled by newcomers.

Information on these western Klikitat is sparse. The various ethnohistorical sources point to a duplication, with some modification, of the subsistence round practiced east of the Cascade crest. The important foods of the western group were concentrated in anthropogenic prairies. Data suggest that the Klikitat maintained a winter village at or near LaCamas Plain (near Fort Vancouver), on the lower reaches of the Washougal River.[49] Many of the subsistence areas in the northwestern portion of Clark county were co-utilized with Lewis River /táytnapam/, a kindred Sahaptin group. All western Klikitat (along with the Lewis River /táytnapam/) were moved to the Yakama Reservation in the late 1850s.

Conclusion

The Klikitat Trail is an example of an aboriginal trail that served as a route of trade and communication, but more importantly, joined native settlement and subsistence sites. Using ethnohistorical and ethnographic sources, we have established that the Trail connected a series of interior resource areas. These resource areas were joined by feeder trails to settlement sites in the lower reaches of Columbia River tributaries. Most of these resource sites are non-forested, grassy prairies containing a wide range of economically useful plants and animals. Evidence has been presented that many of these prairies were maintained by patterned burning. Archaeological remains in such areas are limited to temporary structures, food gathering and processing apparatus, and scarred trees (either from cambium removal for food or bark removal for manufacturing purposes).[50] We suggest that further trail studies may provide insights in problems of culture contact, trade, and subsistence patterns, and that coordinated ethnohistorical, cultural, ecological, and archaeological research offers the greatest potential for isolating and identifying aboriginal subsistence strategies.

Originally published in Prehistoric Places on the Southern Northwest Coast, edited by Robert E. Greengo, pp. 121–52, Thomas Burke Memorial Washington State Museum Research Report Number 4, 1983. Revised and updated for this publication.

Table 1: Plants cited by McClellan and Cooper on the Klikitat Trail[51]

Polypodiaceae
Pteridium aquilinum (L.) Kuhn [*Pteris aquilinea* Linn.], bracken.

Taxaceae
Taxus brevifolia Nutt., western yew.

Cupressaceae
Chaemaecyparis nootkatensis (D. Don) Spach, yellow cedar.
Thuja plicata Donn. [*Thuja gigantea* Nutt.], western redcedar.

Pinaceae
Abies grandis (Dougl.) Forbes, grand fir.
[*A. Menziesii* Lambert] Now?
Picea englemanni Parry [*Abies canadensis* Michx.], Englemann spruce.
Picea sitchensis (Bong.) Carr., or *Pseudotsuga menziesii* (Mirabel) Franco [*A. taxifolia* Lambert], Sitka spruce or Douglas-fir.
Pinus contorta Dougl., lodgepole pine.
Pseudotsuga menziesii (Mirabel) Franco [*A. Douglasii* Sabine], Douglas-fir.

Alismataceae
Sagittaria latifolia Willd., wapato.

Cyperaceae
[*Carex* spp.] Both Cooper and McClellan mention *Carex*. Cooper published five species of this sedge.

Liliaceae
Camassia quamash (Pursh) Greene [*C. esculenta* Lindl.], camas.
Trillium chloropetalum (Torr.) Howell or *T. ovatum* Pursh [*T. grandiflorum* Salisb.], trillium.

Salicaceae
Populus tremuloides Mich., trembling aspen.
P. trichocarpa T. & G. [*P. angustifolia* Torr.], black cottonwood.

Betulaceae
Alnus rubra Bong. [*A. oregana* Nutt.], red alder.

Fagaceae
Corylus cornuta Marsh [*C. americana* Walter], hazelnut.
Quercus garryana Dougl., Garry oak.

Paeoniaceae
Paeonia brownii Dougl., Brown's peony.

Ranunculaceae
Aquilegia formosa Fisch. [*A. canadensis* (Linn.)], columbine.
Acteae rubra (Ait.) Willd. [*Actea arguta*], baneberry.

Berberidaceae
Berberis aquifolium Pursh, Oregon grape.
B. nervosa Pursh, Oregon grape.

Fumariaceae
[*Dicentra exima*] Now?

Grossulariaceae
Ribes bracteosum Dougl., stink currant.
R. divaricatum Dougl., straggly gooseberry.
R. lacustre (Pers.) Poir., swamp gooseberry.

Rosaceae
Amelanchier alnifolia Nutt. [*A. canadensis* Linn.], serviceberry.
Crataegus douglasii Lindl. [*C. sanguinium*], black hawthorn.
Fragaria vesca L., strawberry.
F. virginiana Duchesne, strawberry.
Oemleria cerasiformis (H. & A.) Landon [*Nutallia cerasiformis* T. D. & G. (G.)], Indian plum.
Prunus emarginata (Dougl.) Walp. [*Cerasus mollis* Dougl.], bittercherry.
Pyrus fusca Raf. [*P. rivularis* Dougl.], crabapple.
Rosa nutkana Presl. [*Rubus Nutkanus* Moc.], rose.
[*Rosa Sinnamous*] Now?
Rubus leucodermis Dougl., blackcap.
[*Rubus occidentalis*] Now?
R. spectablis Pursh, salmonberry.
R. ursinus Cham. & Schlecht. [*R. macropetalus* Dougl.], blackberry
[*Sorbus* spp.] Mountain ash.
Spiraea betulifolia Pall., spirea.
S. douglasii Hook., spirea.
[*S. tomentosa*] Now?

Aceraceae
Acer macrophyllum Pursh, big leaf maple.
A. glabrum Torr., maple.
A. circinatum Pursh, vine maple.

Rhamnaceae
Ceanothus sanguineus Pursh [*C. oreganus* Nutt.], buckbush.

Elaeagnaceae
Shepherdia canadensis (L.) Nutt., soapberry. Mentioned by McClellan and Cooper but no binomial given. In Cooper's published list he says it is found only in the Straits of Juan de Fuca.

Onagraceae
Clarkia quadrivulnera (Dougl.) Nels. & Macbr. [*Oneothera quadrivulnera (G.)* Dougl.], godetia.
[*O. apacos*] Now?
Epilobium angustifolium L., fireweed.

Araliaceae
Oplopanax horridum (J. E. Smith) Miq. [*Echinopanax horridum* Smith], devil's club.

Ericaceae
Arctostaphylos columbiana Piper [*A. tomentosa* Pursh], manzanita.
A. uva-ursi (L.) Spreng., kinnikinnick.
Gaultheria shallon Pursh, salal.
Vaccinium caespitosum Michx., blueberry
V. membranaceum Dougl. [*V. myrtilloides* Mich.], black mountain huckleberry.
V. ovalifolium Smith, early huckleberry.
V. ovatum Pursh, evergreen huckleberry.
V. parvifolium Smith, red huckleberry.

Caprifoliaceae
[*Sambucus* spp.]

Curcurbitaceae
Marah oreganus (T. & G.) Howell [*Megarrhiza Oregona* Torr. and Gray], manroot.

Compositae
[*Solidago elongata* Nutt.] Now? A goldenrod.

Table 2: Descriptions of the Klikitat Trail and campsites[52]

Descriptions are from Cooper (C) and McClellan (M). Dates, distances (from Vancouver) and site spellings are by Minter. Elevations are approximated from USGS maps.

7-18-1853 Wahwaikee (/wawačí/, "acorn") (First Plain). 61 meters. 2.25 miles from Vancouver

" . . . nearly circular in form . . . (Spruces) which form a very sharply defined border around it . . . noticed in the wood *Sicyos Oreganus* very common. It is said to be used by the Indians medicinally . . . .Also *Berberis aquifolium* . . . .*Rubus nutkanus occidentalis* & *spectabilis* are common and their fruit with other berries forms the chief food of the natives at this season. *Epilobium angustifolium, Spirea betulifolia* & *douglasii* are the most striking flowers now in bloom." (C)

"Hazel and maple are found along the road and on the stream—saw some small speckled trout in the stream. The 1st plain is a small prairie nearly circular and almost ¼m in diameter—the grass is good." (M)

Pahpoopahpoo and Heowheow (Second and Third Plains). 64 meters

" . . . small opening[s] dignified by the name of prairie; these are partially cultivated & have pretty good grass upon them." (M)

7-21 Kolsas (Fourth Plain). 70 meters. 7.25 miles

" . . . about 12 miles in circumference and nearly oval in form . . . on low swampy parts a coarse species of *Carex* is the chief grass and is eaten readily by horses. Scattered Spruce trees dispersed in groups over the dry portions give the appearance of old cultivated grounds. The *Oneothera apacos* and *O. quadrivulnera* with some *Solidagos* and other Composites are the only flowers I saw at this season." (C)

"The only water is a small stream about ¹/₄m from the Kolsas—it heads in a marsh at the SE border of the Prairie.The best grass is on the N edge, and in the marsh to the SE. The road today leaves the Kolsas plain . . . It was an old disused Indian trail . . . The undergrowth is of various kinds—we found an abundance of the black and red huckleberry (the latter a delightfully acid flavor),—the Sah-lal berry (growing on a species of low vine),—the Oregon grape (the leaf of which closely resembles the holly),—the blackberry,— dewberry,—thimbleberry etc. The arrow wood abounds . . . we found the white maple and willow . . . " (M)

7-22 Sunsic Prairie (Fifth Plain.) 79 meters. 13.25 miles

" . . . about 6 miles circumference . . . " (C)

"Sim-sik prairie is about ¹/₂m long & ¹/₄m wide—running nearly N & S. It is covered by a rather coarse grass, tufted and intermixed with a bush resembling the Chickasaw plum, a large fern, huckle-berries etc. It is surrounded by a dense fir forest, a circular clump of which forms one camp, & there is another detached clump in the center." (M)

7-23 Mesache ("bad"; Chinook Jargon) Camp. 183 meters. 19.75 miles

" . . . we entered a forest of more immense growth than any I have yet seen. Many trees of *Abies douglasii* and others being 10 to 12 ft. in diameter. The latter begins to be less common than hitherto. *A. Canadensis* replacing it. Saw also *Thuja gigantea* 30 to 40 ft. high and a species of *Vaccinium* with red acid berries resembling cherries in taste . . . " (C)

"Our camp was a poor one . . . for it was nothing but a succession of little openings among the huge dead firs—all blackened by the fires with a coarse marsh grass for the animals: a fine clear stream . . . " (M)

7-24 Mankas Prairie. 198 meters. 25.75 miles

"Noticed on the way quantities of berries of the different species of *Rubus, Uva Ursi, Amelanchiar* etc. Mankas prairie 4 miles in circumference covered thickly with *Spirea tomentosa* or *douglasii* . . . Also a shrub called "bear berry" in fruit, *Rosa sinnamous, Crateagus sanguineum* etc. The hills to the north rise steep from the plains and the lofty trees around it keep off the wind making the air hot . . . 18 ¹/₂m. from Calissis Prairie. The day was very hot and the atmosphere smoky from fires in the woods nearby . . . *Epilobium angustifolium* the "willow herb" colors the whole country with the hue of its purple flowers." (C)

" . . . the trail better cleared of brush. We found immense quantities of Blackberries, soapberries, thimbleberries, red huckleberries, Oregon grape, Salal berry etc . . . Mankas Prairie is about ¹/₈m wide & 1m long—good grass . . . It is, as usual, surrounded by the eternal fir . . . " (M)

7-25 Yahkohtl Prairie (Yacolt). 198 meters. 35.25 miles
"The route from this River [Yacolt] to the plains was through a young forest chiefly of trees from ¹/₂ to 1 ft. in diameter with a few large ones scattered among them as if the ground had lately been a prairie and the trees had grown up suddenly and all together. The ground [was] nearly level & little obstructed by logs or underbrush, it was the pleasantest part of our route so far . . . This prairie is four miles long extending toward the south and two miles wide. The Red fir is the most common tree about here and is scattered in groups over the surface. Along the border grows the *Pyrus rivularis*, *Amelanchier, Spirea douglasii*, which are now in fruit—*Cerasus mollis*, a bitter cherry not yet ripe. The gound is covered with *Vaccinium caespitosum* a species about 6 inches high with a blue berry from which the Indian name of the plain is derived . . . Saw on the way *Vaccinium ovalifolium* a blue acid berry growing near the red fruited species . . . .Along the border of this prairie & on every elevation is a thick growth of fern (*Pteris*) higher than a man's head . . . .On this prairie grows a species of Elder" (C)

"The trail [from Mankas] follows the length of the prairie & then plunges into the thicket—first passing thro' a dense growth of wild roses . . . the wild gooseberry occurs here, and at other places during today's march . . . On the rocky border of the stream . . . there was an Indian Camp—It is scarcely possible to imagine a more miserable sight—their tents do not deserve the name—consisting merely of 3 sticks propped together with a torn blanket thrown over. They were making their fish traps etc . . . . The atmosphere is very smoky—caused by fires in the mountains. . . . Indian squaws went off about 7 [am] for the traps they left at the falls . . . The prairie being in all some 2m long . . . They catch the Salmon trout here—the Salmon does not come up this far. . . . The grass is very fine (M)

7-31 Chalacha (/ča'a'lača/; "bracken fern") Plain. 180 meters. 41 miles
"This is of an oval form and about 5 miles long by 2 wide, surrounded by huge precipitous hills above which towers the snow-capped peak of St Helens in a direction nearly northerly from the prairie . . . On the end of this prairie is a grove of oaks, the only species I have seen here, peculiar from being always unmixed with evergreens which cover nearly the whole country." (C)

"Found a few Indians on the prairie—they have cultivated a patch of the prairie near the eastern end . . . Found the Indian potato patches to be very inconsiderable in extent . . . A creek clear & good . . . [the prairie] runs about ENE is some 1¹/₂m long by ¹/₃m wide . . . The n side of the prairie is confined by higher, but somewhat less bold hills—on the top of the highest is a bare cliff used by the Indians as a "watch-post."..upper end [of prairie] .

. . thro' a dense patch of fern . . . This patch of fern, as well as two or three others, was taller and denser than any I have ever seen—it is over the head of a man on horseback and so dense that it is scarcely possible to force a way through it . . . .The prairie of Chelacha takes its name from a long grass which grows there." (M 7-25-53)

8-1 Spilyeh (/*spilya´y*/; **"myth coyote") Prairie. 137 meters. 51 miles**
[enroute] "Noticed on the hillside a Taxus (Yew) in fruit." (C)

"Spil-yai is the Indian name of the bad ford (illegible) of the Cathlepootle . . . We saw wild cherry, hazel, oak, ash etc . . . this prairie runs about NE & SW, it is ³/4m long by ¹/4m wide; has water on either side, & is covered with fine grass and an abundance of service & Huckleberries . . . " (M)

8-2 Lakas (or Lacash) (/*ìlì´k-aš*/; **"kinnikinnick place") Camp. 152 meters. 57.5 miles**
[enroute] " . . . camped on the east side . . . of the Cathlapootle [River] . . . in a grove of young spruce trees the ground being covered with *Uva ursi* . . . and small poplars." (C)

"The La-cahs (*Uva-ursi*) abounds here, it is used by the Indians for kinnakanick . . . there is little or no grass . . . " (M)

8-3 Noomptnahmie Camp. 305 meters. 65.5 miles
[enroute] " . . . through a region mostly burnt over recently and with a young growth of trees covering it . . . Noticed a species of *Sorbus* in fruit, the berries being orange color and larger than those growing in the Eastern states." (C)

" . . . ash, maple, hazel, fir & cedar compose the growth—a few red huckleberries, oregon grapes & blackberries occur—the ground is covered by a large leafed sorrel and a plant resembling the may apple." (M)

8-4 Weinnepat Camp. 305 meters. 72 miles

8-5 Wahamis (Susuk) Camp (Two-by-Four Prairie?). 976 meters. 78.75 miles
"The hill was covered with a species of *Vaccinium* the fruit nearly as finely flavored as a grape, and the ground in many places carpeted by strawberry vines with ripe fruit of delicious flavor. Blue purple red yellow and white flowers adorned the hill side and altogether this was one of the pleasantest camps since leaving Vancouver...Two Pines & a species of dense leaved spruce . . . " (C)

"We have an abundance of excellent grass and the coldest possible water. Found quite large quantities of wild strawberries on the side of the mountain—their flavor was excellent . . . " (M)

8-6 Yawakamis (McClellan Meadow). 1037 meters. 88 miles
" . . . a small meadow full of excelient grass where we encamped. Most of the way led through a burnt forest with but little living vegetation . . . (C)

"a small pretty prairie where were a number of old Indian huts." (M)

8-8 Chequos (Chickwass)(/čiʼkaš/; "rough place"). 1189 meters. 93.75 miles

"Chiquass prairie a high plain mostly covered with young spruce. The hills around are almost all burnt over . . . " (C)

"There are two ponds of water for the animals & a well for drinking purposes . . . Some 20 lodges of Indians in the vicinity. One died yesterday of the small-pox—which disease is making great ravages among them. Those who buried him go thro' a course of 3 days steaming and bathing by way of purification . . . The prairie in which we now are, and those to E. seem to make up an old & immense crater . . . Strawberries very abundant now in this vicinity. The grass in the crater is good—timber very poor— water only in ponds . . . " (M)

8-9 Resumé by Cooper at the Summit

"In ascending a gradual disappearance of some plants is noticed and a substitution of others. *Aquilegia formosa* has continued common up to this point. The three species of *Abies* composing the lower forest are here replaced to an extent by two others and by two species of Pine. Oaks disappeared with the Cathlapootle river and the maples are now very rarely seen . . . " (C)

8-11 Hoolho-ose (Wilwilchelis) (at or near Trout Lake, /šaxšax-miʼ/, "kingfisher's"). 579 meters. 105.75 miles

"After passing the first two miles the wood became very open & of large pine trees standing 20 or 30 yds apart, the ground below being covered with grass and small shrubs. The scene resembled ornamental forest grounds more than wild uncultivated woods." (C)

"The circular valley of the lake is green & pretty—an abundance of horse mint grows there . . . While in the Conf ground we met 3 or 4 parties of Indians, who were suffering terribly from the small pox . . . fine pine timber, with some [illegible] oak . . . Grass good—found here the blue bunch grass of the plains." (M)

8-12 Tahk (/taak/; "vernal meadow")Prairie (near modern Glenwood). 549 meters. 114.25 miles

"Noticed the oak again at this place . . . Found a species of *Paeonia* (Brownie) around the prairie with ripe seed, the root is used by the Indians here to give their horses long wind. The prairie is about 10 miles in length and three wide containing a marshy lake and appears to be subject to overflowing." (C)

"An open country . . . white and yellow pine—oak, fir & spruce etc . . . Good grass & excellent water . . . The Camash root abounds, also the Wapatoo." (M)

Acknowledgments

We would like to express our appreciation to the National Science Foundation research grants (BNS 76-16914 and BNS 80-21476), E. Hunn, principal investigator, for funding of portions of this research. We also wish to express our gratitude to the Smithsonian Institution Archives for permission to cite or quote material from Cooper and Everette.

Notes

1. James G. Cooper, "Notes for 1855 . . ." [Northern Pacific Railroad Survey] (Smithsonian Archives, Record Unit 7067); F. C. Ugolini and A. K. Schlichte, "The effect of Holocene environmental changes on selected western Washington soils," *Soil Science* 116(3): 218–27, 1973); Richard White, "Indian land use and environmental change: Island County, Washington, a test case (1975 and this volume); and Helen H. Norton, "The association between anthropogenic prairies and important food plants in western Washington" (*Northwest Anthropological Research Notes* 13(2): 175–200, 1979).

2. For a West Coast precedent, see L. L. Sample, "Trade and Trails in Aboriginal California" (University of California Archaeological Survey, Report no. 8, 1950).

3. The only archaeological work of note published before 1983 is Jerry Jermann and Roger Mason's "Cultural resource overview of the Gifford Pinchot National Forest: South-Central Washington" (University of Washington Office of Public Archaeology, Institute for Environmental Studies Reconaissance Report No. 7, 1976). Since 1983, archaeologists have shown an increased interest in the area. See, for example, Cheryl Mack's "Prehistoric Upland Occupations in the Southern Washington Cascades" (*Archaeology in Washington* I: 49–57, 1989) and Dennis Lewarch and James Benson's "Long-Term Land Use Patterns in the Southern Washington Cascade Range" (*Archaeology in Washington* III: 27–40, 1991). Cheryl Mack's "In Pursuit of the Wild Vaccinium: Huckleberry Processing Sites in the Southern Washington Cascades" (*Archaeology in Washington* IV: 4–16, 1992) follows most closely the themes raised in our original 1983 publication.

4. The ethnographic record for the Klikitat is meager. A primary source is Verne Ray's "Native villages and groupings of the Columbia Basin" (*Pacific Northwest Quarterly* 27(2): 99–152, 1936), 148–50, which lists seventeen named Klikitat village and campsites; Edward Curtis's "The Klickitat" (pp. 37–40 in *The North American Indian*, vol. 7, 1911) is only four pages long. Some further information is found in reports of neighboring groups such as the Cowlitz (V. Ray, *Handbook of Cowlitz Indians,* Seattle, 1966); the Wasco-Wishram (Leslie Spier and Edward Sapir, "Wishram Ethnography" [*University of Washington Publications in Anthropology* 3(3), 1930]; and David French, "Wasco-Wishram" [pp. 337–429 in Edward Spicer, (ed.), *Perspectives in American Indian culture change,* Chicago, 1961]); and the Yakama and Columbia River Sahaptins (e.g. Helen Schuster, "Yakima Indian traditionalism: a study in continuity and change," Ph.D. dissertation, University of Washington, 1975; and Eugene Hunn, *Nch'i-Wána: the "Big River": Mid-Columbia Indians and their Land,* [Seattle, 1990]). Linguistic

analyses include Willis Everette, "Yakima vocabulary recorded at Simcoe mountains
. . ." (National Anthropological Archives Ms. #698, 1883); Melville Jacobs's
"Northwest Sahaptin texts" (UWPA 4(2): 85–292, 1931, *Columbia University
Contributions to Anthropology* 19, 1934), and "Historic perspectives in Indian
languages of Oregon and Washington" (*Pacific Northwest Quarterly* 28(1): 55–74,
1937); and Bruce Rigsby, "Linguistic relations in the southern plateau" (Ph.D.
dissertation, University of Oregon, 1965).
   5. /xwaʾtxaypam/ is the Klikitat self-designation in their own tongue, a dialect of
the Sahaptin language. /xwaʾtxaypam/ translates as "Steller's Jay people" (/xwaʾtxay/
"Steller's Jay" + /-pam/ "people of"). The Klikitat dialect is most closely allied with
Yakama (/mámačatpam/) and Upper Cowlitz (/táytnapam/), adjacent members of
the Northwest dialect group (NW) of the Sahaptin language. Klikitat speakers also
had frequent intercourse with speakers of the Columbia River dialect cluster of
Sahaptin, including the /wayamłáma/ of Celilo Falls area and the /tinaynułáma/ of
the village of Tenino. See Bruce Rigsby, "Linguistic relations in the southern
plateau," for details on linguistic classifications and orthography.
   6. See Spier and Sapir, "Wishram Ethnography," 167, on Klikitat/Chinookan
coocupation; Ray, "Native villages and groupings of the Columbia Basin" on
Klikitat settlements; and Ray, *Handbook of Cowlitz Indians*, A7–A8 on the
/táytnapam/ problem.
   7. Ray, *Handbook of Cowlitz Indians*, A12, identified the Klikitat as "prairie
oriented"; Eugene Hunn, in "Mobility as a factor limiting resource use in the
Columbia Plateau of North America" (pp. 17–43 in E. Hunn and Nancy Williams,
[eds.], *Resource managers: North American and Australian hunter-gatherers,* Boulder,
1982), discusses mobility and the subsistence round.
   8. Lewis and Clark noted Chinookan riverine movement in their *Journals*
(Moulton 1991 [v. 7] 38, 57). On the concept of ecological niche, see Thomas
Love, "Ecological niche theory in sociocultural anthropology: A conceptual
framework and application" (*American Ethnologist* 4(1): 27–41, 1977).
   9. Ray, *Handbook of Cowlitz Indians*, A9 on the Lewis River trail; Edward Curtis,
"The Chinookan Tribes" (pp. 85–156 in *The North American Indian*, vol. 8, 1911),
94 on trade with Chinookans; Nettie Kuneki, Elsie Thomas, and M. Slockish, *The
Heritage of Klickitat Basketry: A history and art preserved* (Portland, 1982) on
baskets; and George Gibbs, "Report of George Gibbs to Captain McClellan on the
Indian tribes of the Territory of Washington, 3/4/54" (pp. 419–55 in *Report of
exploration of a route for the Pacific Railroad from St. Paul to Puget Sound,* 33d Cong,
1st Sess, HExDoc 129, 1854), 421 on racetracks.
   10. The "Journal of John Work," (*Oregon Historical Quarterly* 10[ ]: 296–313,
1909) describes what apparently was an early traversal of the trail by a Hudson's
Bay Company trader.
   11. The sources are James G. Cooper's two "Notebooks," dated 1853 and 1855
(Smithsonian Institution Archives, Record Unit 7067); and George McClellan's
"Journal" (Microforms Collection A228, University of Washington Libraries,
5/20–12/11, 1853), previously cited by Jermann and Mason in "Cultural resource
overview of the Gifford Pinchot National Forest." The official *Report of exploration
of a route for the Pacific railroad from St. Paul to Puget Sound* (33d Cong, ist Sess,
HExDoc 129) includes George Gibbs's "Report . . . on the Indian Tribes of the
territory of Washington," and J. F. Minter's "Itinerary of Captain McClellan's
route," pp. 387–403.

12. J. G. Cooper, "Reports of explorations and surveys to . . . the Pacific Ocean in 1853—5" (Washington, 1860), 19, 23. A longer passage from this same source appears in Lewis and Ferguson (this volume).

13. Cooper, "Notes for 1855 . . .," 12–13. See also Cooper, "Reports of explorations . . .," 23, cited in Lewis and Ferguson (this volume).

14. See Cooper 1853 "Notebook . . .," 1855 "Notes . . .," and Reports of Explorations . . .; Norton, "The Association between Anthropogenic Prairies and Important Food Plants . . ."; and Ugolini and Schlicte, "The effect of Holocene environmental changes . . ."; Frank Lang, "A study of vegetation change on the gravelly prairies of Pierce and Thurston counties, western Washington" (M.A. thesis, University of Washington, 1961); and Don Minore, "The wild huckleberries of Oregon and Washington—a dwindling resource" (USDA Forest Service Research Paper PNW-143, Portland, 1972).

15. White and Boyd (orig. 1975 and 1986, and this volume); Norton, "The Association Between Anthropogenic Prairies and Important Food Plants in Western Washington"; Carl Johannessen *et al.*, "The vegetation of the Willamette Valley" (*Annals of the Association of American Geographers* 61(2): 286–306, 1971).

16. The Cooper quotation is from "Reports of explorations . . .," 23; his plant list appears in Cooper and George Suckley, *The Natural History of Western Washington . . . Plants and Animals Collected from 1853–57* (New York, 1859); an analysis appears in the appendix to Norton, "The Association Between Anthropogenic Prairies and Important Food Plants in Western Washington."

17. See Nancy Turner, *Food Plants of Coastal First Peoples*, Royal British Columbia Museum Handbook (Vancouver, 1995); and Minore, "The wild huckleberries of Oregon and Washington," on huckleberries.

18. The quotation is from Cooper's "Notes . . .," 6; the same manuscript, pp. 36–37, notes other prairie fauna.

19. As defined in Jerry Franklin and C. T. Dyrness, *Natural Vegetation of Oregon and Washington* (orig 1973; 1988 reprint by Oregon State University Press), 45.

20. Cooper 1853 "Notebook . . .," 4.

21. See Verne Ray, *Cultural Patterns in the plateau of northwestern America* (Los Angeles, 1939), 132–39.

22. McClellan 1853 "Journal," 18.

23. On bracken, see Helen H. Norton, "Evidence for bracken fern as a food for aboriginal peoples of western Washington" (*Economic Botany* 33(4): 384–96, 1980); on acorns, see Norton, "The Association Between Anthropogenic Prairies and Important Food Plants in Western Washington."

24. Both quotations are from Cooper's 1853 "Notebook . . .," 13.

25. The trap may be the "double funnel" trap noted in Verne Ray's "Culture Element Distributions 22: Plateau" (*Anthropological Records* 8(2), 1942), 107. Spears have been recovered archaeologically on the upper Cowlitz River: see David Rice, "Indian utilization of the Cascade Range in south central Washington" (*Washington Archaeologist* 8: 5-20, 1964), 14. The quote from McClellan is on p. 13 in his 1853 "Journal."

26. On the Chalacha Prairie Reservation recommendation, see William Tappan, "Annual Report, southern Indian district, Washington Territory, 1854" (Records of the Washington Superintendency of Indian Affairs, 1856-74 no. 5, roll 17: "Letters from employees assigned to the Columbia River or southern district . . .," National

Archives); huckleberry gathering is described by Emily Lindsley in "The 1883 ascent of Mt. St. Helens," (*Northwest Discovery* 1: 296–305, 1980), 299.

27. See Hal Kennedy and Jerry Jermann, "Report of an archaeological survey in the Mount St. Helens area, Gifford Pinchot National Forest" (University of Washington Office of Public Archaeology Reconnaissance Report, 1975), 26.

28. Alan Bryan, "Archaeology of Yale Reservoir, Lewis River, Washington" (*American Antiquity* 20: 281–83, 1955), 282.

29. Chequos appears in Ray's "Native villages and groupings of the Columbia Basin," 149; on fire and *V. membranaceum*, see Minore, "The wild huckleberries of Oregon and Washington," 6, 9; and Fred Hall, "Literature review of huckleberry" (USDA Forest Service memorandum, file #2210, Portland, 1964), 1–5.

30. The Sahaptin term for huckleberry season is from Everette's "Yakima vocabulary," 106; see E. Hunn and D. French, "Lomatium: a key resource for Columbia Plateau native subsistence" (*Northwest Science* 55(2): 87–94, 1981); the quote from Reverend Henry Perkins is from his "Wascopam mission journal" (pp. 271–303 in Robert Boyd, *People of The Dalles: the Indians of Wascopam Mission* (Lincoln, NE, 1996).

31. The Gibbs quotation is from his "Report . . . to Captain McClellan," 432; McClellan's "Journal," entry of 8/8/53, describes the smallpox; Hunn's *Nch'i-Wána*, 265–68 discusses contemporary Sahaptin sweatlodges, and Douglas's 1825 description is from the *Journal kept by David Douglas during his travels in North America, 1823–1827* (New York, 1959), 114-15.

32. Cooper, in his 1853 "Notebook . . .," 22, describes the open ponderosa stands; Franklin and Dyrness, in "Natural vegetation of Oregon and Washington," 180, are the authorities on fire frequency in ponderosa stands.

33. The same is true for those at the Trail's western extremity (e.g., Vancouver and LaCamas prairie [/alaší'k-aš/ ["turtle place"] and /taak/ ["vernal meadow"]); see map of Clark County on page 00.

34. The early description of the earth oven is from "The literary remains of David Douglas, botany of the Oregon Coast" (*Oregon Historical Quarterly* 5(3): 215–71, 1904), 244; Eugene Hunn's Sahaptin field notes (1976ff; in possession of author) contain data on contemporary earth ovens. Gibbs, in "Tribes of western Washington and northwestern Oregon" (*Contributions to North American Ethnology* 1(2): 157–361, 1877), 193, noted the location of processing stations.

35. On suckers, see Spier and Sapir's "Wishram Ethnography," 174; and E. Hunn, "Sahaptin fish classification" (*Northwest Anthropological Research Notes* 14: 1–19, 1979).

36. Lewis and Clark (Moulton 1991 [v. 7]), 121 note harvest of both "herbs" and spring salmon, on April 14, 1806.

37. Spier and Sapir, "Wishram Ethnography," 184; Hunn, Sahaptin field notes.

38. See Ray, "Native villages and groupings of the Columbia Basin," 148–150; Spier and Sapir, "Wishram Ethnography," 166–69; and Boyd, *People of the Dalles*, 40–44.

39. See Ray, "Native villages . . ."; Sapir and Spier, "Wishram Ethnography"; and Curtis, "The Klickitat," 37, and "The Chinookan Tribes," 181, on these villages. Lewis and Clark's description of /ła'taxat/ is in Moulton, *Journals* [v. 7], 121; Hunn, in *Nch'i-Wána*, 273, discusses contemporary Klikitat upstream fisheries.

40. See Spier and Sapir, "Wishram Ethnography," 167; Ray, "Native villages . . .," 148; and Lewis and Clark (*Journals*, [v. 5], 352; [v. 7], 119). Jermann and Mason,

"Cultural resource overview of the Gifford Pinchot National Forest," 63, note Little White Salmon and Wind River sites.

41. Lewis and Clark, *Journals* (Moulton 1988 [v. 5], 352); Ray, "Native villages . . ." on the upstream locations.

42. Ray, "Native villages . . .," Hunn, in *Nch'i-Wána*, 130–33, describes in some detail the historic late summer activity on the north bank of the Columbia Gorge.

43. See Gibbs, "Report . . .to Captain McClellan . . .," 421; Ray, "Native villages . . .," 149; and Hunn, *Nch'i-Wána*, 94, on a later (1983) visit to the race track.

44. French (1957 and this volume) is the source on berry-drying technology and the fires that resulted from it; Minore, "The wild huckleberries of Oregon and Washington . . .," 8, notes the historic contraction of the fields.

45. Ray Filloon's "Huckleberry pilgrimage" (*Pacific Discovery* 5: 4–13, 1952) is the published result of the 1936 Forest Service documentation; Minore, "The wild huckleberries of Oregon and Washington . . .," 1, is the source for the statistics on the Twin Buttes field productivity.

46. Filloon, "Huckleberry pilgrimage," 5. See French (this volume) for a 1936 photograph.

47. Since the 1983 publication of this paper, Cheryl Mack, in "Aboriginal Use of Log-fire Drying Trenches in the Southern Washington Cascades" (paper presented at the 42nd Annual Northwest Anthropological Conference, 1989) and "In Pursuit of the Wild Vaccinium: Huckleberry Processing Sites in the Southern Washington Cascades," has investigated the archaeological evidence for huckleberrying sites in the Indian Heaven Wilderness Area of the Gifford Pinchot National Forest.

48. Curtis, "The Klikitat," 46. The split is mentioned in several contemporary historical sources as well.

49. See *Reports and letters, 1836–1838, of Herbert Beaver . . .* (Portland, 1959), 58; Gibbs, "Report . . . to Captain McClellan," 420; and Tappan, Annual Report.

50. Since original publication of this paper, there has been more research on this topic. See, for example, Eric Bergland's "Historic Period Plateau Culture Tree Peeling in the Western Cascades of Oregon" (*Northwest Anthropological Research Notes* 25(2): 31–53, 1992). At Fort Nisqually, the Hudson's Bay Company paid Indians for bark used to roof buildings.

51. Synonymized from C. Leo Hitchcock *et al.*, *Vascular Plants of the Pacific Northwest* (Seattle, 1955–1969), with archaic name used by Cooper bracketed. Fifty-eight of the sixty-five plants noted in the journals are known to have been used for food, medicine, or in the material culture. Names marked with "Now?" are those for which the senior author could not connect Cooper's species name with the contemporary Latin binomial.

52. Since Cooper and McClellan often did not travel with each other, we have attempted to place their descriptions, which may have been made on another date and another site, in the proper locations. Sahaptin transcriptions of place names have been added where appropriate. Species binomials as given in the original journals have been italicized and corrected for spelling.

Strategies of Indian Burning
in the Willamette Valley[1]

Robert Boyd

Introduction

Previous Research

In 1971, geographer Carl Johannessen and colleagues at the University of Oregon published an article, "The Vegetation of the Willamette Valley," which proposed that, prior to European contact, the Willamette Valley, though surrounded by dense forests of Douglas-fir, was an open oak-savanna grassland. They also presented historical evidence to show that these prairie grasslands were maintained by annual fires set by the aboriginal inhabitants of the valley, the Kalapuya Indians. In 1979, geographer Jerry Towle, citing Johannessen *et al.*'s evidence, suggested that archaeologists and cultural anthropologists should incorporate the heretofore neglected historical information on anthropogenic burning and its relationship to Willamette Valley Indian subsistence. Building upon what has been established by previous researchers, the present paper attempts to reconstruct the role of man-made fires in the hunting-gathering practices of the Kalapuya Indians.[2]

This paper is organized in three parts: the first is an overview of pre-contact environment and Kalapuya culture; the second presents extant historical data (1826–1847) on Indian-caused fires in the Willamette Valley; and the third considers the relationships between burning and important aboriginal food sources, utilizing all known data on the Kalapuya as well as kindred and adjacent peoples of native Oregon, and from this suggests a reconstructed Kalapuya burning schedule.

Environmental Setting

The Willamette Valley is one of a series of north-south valleys found in the Pacific Coast states of California, Oregon, and Washington. Within the border formed by the Cascade and Coast ranges, the central valley floor is relatively level, interrupted here and there by low-lying hills. Because of its low gradient (rising from less than 30 meters at Champoeg to little over 120 at Eugene), the lower courses of the Willamette and its major western tributaries are slow and meandering. Prior to the establishment of agriculture and water diversion projects, the valley contained numerous seasonal lakes and marshes.[3]

In western Oregon, temperature range is not pronounced, with averages of 3 degrees centigrade in January and 18 degrees centigrade in July and August. There is marked seasonality in rainfall, with more than three-fourths of the average annual precipitation of 965 mm falling between October and March. July and August are the driest months, with an average of only 15 mm. Lightning storms are rare, occurring in significant numbers only in the higher elevations of the Cascade Range. As in California, natural fires are associated with summer storms, which influence upland coniferous forests far more than coastal or valley environments.[4]

Several researchers have attempted to reconstruct the pre-contact plant cover of the Willamette Valley. The most successful of these (Habeck 1961, Johannessen *et al.* 1971) used early 1850s land survey records, in association with early historical accounts of valley explorers and pioneers. These documents indicate that at the time of first settlement, most of the valley was open grassland with scattered concentrations of oaks in hilly areas, an environment that might best be termed an "oak savanna." Similar biotypes, differing only in higher frequencies of xeric plants, were found in other interior valleys to the south and in California.

Closer examination reveals that the Willamette Valley was subdivided into a number of microenvironments, each with its characteristic vegetation. The exact composition of some of these plant communities is difficult to reconstruct because of widespread disturbances associated with the introduction of agriculture and the rapid invasion of numerous exotics after the mid-1800s. In the grasslands, one of the most severely altered communities, two perennial grasses—*Festuca rubra* and *Deschampsia cespitosa*—appear to have been locally dominant, their occurrence depending upon availability of water. Oaks (*Quercus garryana*) originally were found dispersed over the savanna in concentrations free of underbrush (called "oak openings" by the surveyors). In the nearly 140 years since the cessation of regular burning, surviving openings have grown into closed oak forests with understories dominated by hazel (*Corylus cornuta*), poison oak (*Rhus diversiloba*), and serviceberry (*Amelanchier alnifolia*).[5]

A second microenvironment was especially important in the northern portion of the valley, where low elevations, high water tables, and seasonal flooding created marshy areas around low-lying lakes (such as the now-drained Wapato Lake, and Lake Labish), and in gullies containing feeders to the main rivers (known locally as "swales"). Dominant forms here were various species of *Glyceria*, *Juncus*, and bulbous plants such as camas (*Camassia quamash*), wapato (*Sagittaria latifolia*), and wild onion (*Allium* spp.), all favored foods

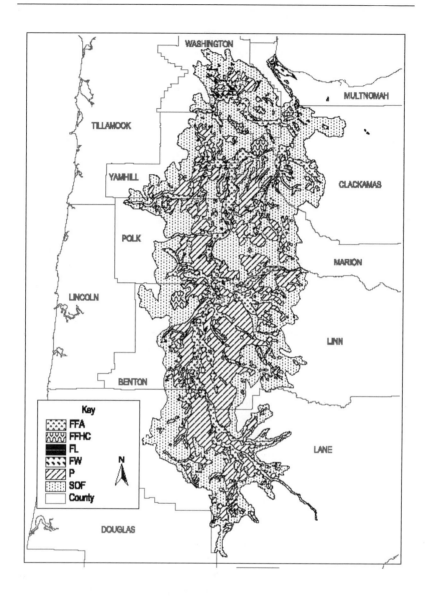

Map 1. Presettlement vegetation of Willamette Valley, based on General Land Office
plat maps, 1851-1865. FFA—Mixed deciduous riparian forest (Oregon ash, bigleaf
maple, black cottonwood, red alder, white oak, dogwood, willow). FFHC—Coniferous
forest (Douglas-fir, western hemlock, western red cedar, bigleaf maple, yew, vine maple).
FL—Red alder swamp. FW—Willow swamp. P—Prairie (wet and dry,
undifferentiated). SOF—Savanna and oak woodland (white oak and Douglas fir,
locally with ponderosa pine and black oak). Courtesy John A. Christy, Oregon
Natural Heritage Program. More detailed coverage at a scale of 1:24,000, based on
General Land Office survey notes, is currently under development.

of the aborigines. In the narrow corridor along major waterways, deciduous forests, composed chiefly of ash (*Fraxinus latifolia*) and alder (*Alnus rubra*), constituted a third microenvironment. The winter villages of the valley Indians were located in this zone.[6]

Finally, in the higher elevations of the surrounding Coast and Cascade mountains, dense coniferous forests dominated by Douglas-fir (*Pseudotsuga menziesii*) were found. Although the coniferous forests were exploited minimally by the Kalapuya, the ever-shifting forest edges, with their diverse flora (such as salal {*Gaultheria shallon*}, Oregon grape {*Berberis nervosa*}, and berries {*Rubus* and *Vaccinium* spp.}) were utilized seasonally by the Indians.[7]

The following eyewitness accounts, dating from 1841 and 1844, give some idea of the topography and vegetation of the pre-settlement valley.

> 8/7/41 . . . the Yamhills [Eola Hills] . . . are a little singular being the only hills of any magnitude that rise from the great Walamat Valley—in an extent of Prairie from 60 to (1)00 miles either way . . . from the top of these at an alt. of about 1,000 feet—had a grand panorama view . . . prairie to the south as far as the view extends—the streams being easily traced by a border of trees that grew up on either bank . . . white oak scattered about in all directions. (Emmons 1841)

> Productions Strawberries Rasp Berries Dew Berries Whortle berries service Berries and numerous other kinds so that fruit of that description is plenty from may until September the vallies abound in different kinds of edible roots, the most common of which is La Camas . . . resembles onions in shape and looks but has a sweetish taste and grows abundantly so much so that I am told that . . . when it is in bloom in many places hides almost every other sign of vegetation. The Wappatoo grows in swampland and resembles potatoes these two roots with the acorns that grow on the low scrubby White oaks which far surpass any thing of the kind that I have ever seen and form a range for hogs the best that could possibly be . . . grass of an excellent quality abounds on the high hills and in the vallies . . . the grass commences growing when the rains begin in the fall and continues to grow through the fall winter and spring and dies with the dry weather in summer. (Shaw 1844)[8]

Contemporary researchers agree that the oak savanna of the Willamette Valley was a seral community, maintained by frequent firing. In the nearly 140 years since initial agricultural settlement, with fire removed as an important ecological factor, forest cover (both Douglas-fir and Garry oak) has increased and now covers most areas not cultivated or grazed. Hypothetically, a continuation of current fire control will result in replacement of Garry oak in most areas by mixed stands of Douglas-fir and big-leafed maple (*Acer macrophyllum*), given the inability of the oak to reproduce in its own shade.[9]

Palynological studies indicate that the Willamette Valley has been dominated by oak savanna for more than 6,000 years. The origin of the valley biotype appears to data to the warmer and drier climate of the Hypsithermal period (8000–4000 B.P.) when natural conditions probably prevented the establishment of a closed canopy forest. Yet the Willamette Valley oak savanna has persisted throughout the millennia since that time, despite the appearance of a modern climate amenable to forest growth, and contrary to the pattern of forest spread characteristic of the last century.[10]

Natural fires do not occur frequently enough to account for the continuation of the subclimax vegetation. Some other force must have been responsible. It was this kind of evidence and this line of reasoning that led both James Habeck and Carl Johannessen *et al.* to consider the sizable historical literature on Indian burning in the Willamette Valley, and to hypothesize that regular aboriginal fires were the main cause of the perpetuation of the oak savanna.[11]

Native Inhabitants of the Willamette Valley
The Kalapuya

In pre-contact times, the Kalapuya Indians were the sole inhabitants of the prairies of the Willamette Valley.[12] To the north and west were peoples of the Northwest Coast culture area: Chinookans in the valley of the Columbia; Salishan Tillamook and various "coastal Penutian" peoples (Alsea, Siuslaw, Coos) along the Oregon Coast. To the east were members of the Plateau culture area: Molala on the western slopes of the Cascade Mountains; and various Sahaptin peoples to the east of the Cascade crest.

Although most anthropologists include the Kalapuya in the Northwest Coast culture area, some have been inclined to incorporate them into an expanded Plateau culture area. In 1951, archaeologist Lloyd Collins, utilizing a trait list of 31 items of Kalapuya material culture, found that 45% were shared with Northwest Coast cultures, while 87% also were characteristic of the Plateau culture area. Important Plateau culture traits include a diversified subsistence base with an emphasis on wild root crops, extensive use of earth ovens, seasonally occupied semi-subterranean houses and mat lodges, sweatlodges, buckskin clothing, first fruits ceremonies, rite of passage feasting, and an emphasis on individually obtained spirit power through spirit questing. More recently, anthropologist David French has gone a step further: emphasizing the underlying shared importance of "reliable ample harvests of {wild} plant foods," he suggests that "a Plateau-Valley-California area would have more unity than many writers have supposed. What features set off California from Takelma, Kalapuya, Sahaptin? . . . religious features perhaps

. . . there are no distinctive features." French's "Valley" subprovince includes Kalapuya (Willamette Valley), Umpqua (upper Umpqua Valley), and Takelma (upper Rogue Valley).[13]

Kalapuya economy was based on a diverse assemblage of wild plants, with a secondary emphasis on game. Unlike the Indians of the Northwest Coast culture area, salmon was relatively unimportant to the Kalapuya for the simple reason that the Willamette Falls blocked runs of most anadromous fish.[14] In the total inventory of wild foods, the bulb of the camas lily apparently was of major importance, and prominent mention is given to hazel nuts, acorns, tarweed (*Madia* spp.), wapato, and an assortment of berries (especially the native blackberry, *Rubus ursinus*). Game included two species of deer, white-tailed (*Odocoileus virginianus leucurus*) and the black-tailed (*O. columbianus*) (the former being of major importance), elk (*Cervus canadensis*), a variety of waterfowl, quail, and doves. Small animals and insects were "gathered." Salmon were obtained in barter with Chinookan peoples at Willamette Falls (in return for processed camas cakes and game). The majority of foods were processed and stored for winter use. All in all, it was a diversified resource base, with similarities to both the Plateau (camas, other roots, and berries), and native California (acorns, hazelnuts, tarweed, and grass seeds). As we will see, burning was an important tool in both the collection and management of most of these species.[15]

Lewis and Clark estimated 9,000 Kalapuyans in 1805–1806; a quarter century later, Hudson's Bay Company figures were given as either 7,785 or 8,870. Allowing for mortality from two earlier smallpox epidemics (circa 1775 and 1801–1802) yields a conservative aboriginal population of 14,760, or a density of about one person for every $2^{1}/_{4}$ square kilometers. These figures are compatible with those given for the Tualatin Kalapuya on the basis of winter-village lists, and with figures now generally accepted for hunting-gathering groups occupying similar resource areas in native California.[16]

Direct White contact with the Indians of the Willamette Valley began in 1812, with the exploring parties of Astorian Robert Stuart and Donald McKenzie. This was contact of an intermittent nature, however, limited to seasonal forays by trappers and traders, and for nearly twenty years the Kalapuya remained relatively untouched and unaffected by white influence.

Beginning in 1831 and for each summer thereafter, the Indians of the Willamette and lower Columbia Valleys were subjected to an annual attack of a disease that is now considered to have been malaria. The effect of this exotic disease on a "virgin soil" population that had no genetic or cultural means of coping with it was devastating; in 1841, the surviving population was estimated at 600. Documentary evidence for aboriginal burning of the Willamette prairies comes from both the pre- and post-malaria eras. Although the introduction of endemic malaria certainly caused a shift in subsistence strategies away from swampy areas where malarial mosquities had become established, and the abandonment of other regions due to gross population decline, large-scale burning by Indians continued over sizable segments of the valley until immigrant settlers forced an end to the practice in the mid 1840s.[17]

The Kalapuya, Umpqua, and Takelma Indians were removed to the Grand Ronde Reservation near the present town of Willamina in 1855. Anthropological field work among surviving Kalapuya was late and piecemeal, gathered in 1877, 1913–14, and the 1930s.[18] The surviving field notes on subsistence (for the best-documented Kalapuya group, the Tualatin) have been assembled in Henry Zenk's 1976 "Contributions to Tualatin Ethnography." Information on Kalapuya burning practices was not gathered by the early anthropologists, however, and there are no living natives who remember aboriginal burning practices (nor have there been for many years). Correspondingly, archaeological data gathered to date are devoid of useful information about the role of anthropogenic fire in aboriginal cultures.

Historical Evidence

Fortunately, there are numerous references in the written records of early explorers and settlers that document regular firing by Willamette Valley Indians. William Morris was the first researcher to use this historical evidence in his 1936 history of forest fires in the Pacific Northwest. Johannessen *et al.* (1971) quote a number of published historical works to support their thesis on the role of aboriginal firing in the maintenance of the oak savanna biotype of the valley, and their summary has been cited as proof of the aboriginal impact on the Oregon environment in many later works by geographers and foresters.[19] Morris and Johannessen *et al.*'s list of sources on burning are not, however, exhaustive, and neither study places the data in a wider ecological or cultural context. In this paper, all available information, both published and unpublished, is considered in order to determine the temporal and spatial patterns of burning in the Willamette Valley.[20] These data are then combined with what is known concerning aboriginal foraging practices, with a goal of infusing cultural meaning to the historical reports.

The first 12 years of White contact with the Kalapuya (1812–1824), when the fur trade was in the hands of the Northwest Company, are very poorly recorded.[21] There are no references to Indian burning practices for this period. With the 1825 initiation of the Hudson's Bay Company's annual southern trapping expedition to California, however, the documentary situation changes.

From the 1826 expedition two important documents, the journals of Alexander McLeod, leader of the party, and David Douglas, a botanist who traveled with him, survive.[22] Departing from Fort Vancouver in early September, the expedition passed through the Willamette Valley during the midst of the summer burning season. Upon entering what apparently was the Yamhill Valley on the 18th of September, McLeod noted "several Indian habitations" and a landscape "much overrun by fire." On the west bank of the Willamette River near the site of Salem, the party was obliged to ford the river in order to find food for their horses because the land was "burned and destitute of grass."[23]

Over the next few days, Douglas recorded:

9/27 Country undulating; soil rich, light with beautiful solitary oaks and pines interspersed through it and must have a fine effect, but being all burned and not a single blade of grass except on the margins of the rivulets to be seen.

9/30 (heading south) . . . Most parts of the country burned; only on little patches in the valleys and on the flats near the low hills that verdure is to be seen. Some of the natives tell me it is done for the purpose of urging the deer to frequent certain parts to feed, which they leave unburned and of course they are easily killed. Others say that it is done in order that they might better find honey and grasshoppers, which both serve as articles of winter food.[24]

The landscape continued as above until the party reached the foothills of the Calapooya Mountains.

10/2 (McLeod) Pasture is rarely found in the course of this day none has been seen, altho' we traveled good twenty miles and had to put up along a small river that our horses might have the pickings along the margin of the woods, elsewhere the fire destroyed all the grass.

(Douglas) . . . not yet a vestige of green herbage; all burned except in the deep ravines. Covered with *Pteris aquilina* [bracken fern], *Solidago* [goldenrod], and a strong species of *Carduus* [probably *Cirsium*, thistle] . . . My feet tonight are very painful and my toes cut with the burned stumps of a strong species of *Arundo* [probably reedgrass, *Calamagrostis*] and *Spiraea tomentosa* [probably ninebark, *Physocarpus*].[25]

The McLeod expedition spent the next three weeks in the Umpqua country before moving on to California. Douglas separated from the rest of the party and in early November backtracked to Fort Vancouver through what was now a completely altered landscape. Where formerly there had been scorched plains, he found "Country open, rich, level, and beautiful." Fall rains had caused a greening of the prairies. The food supply—deer on the way down—was replaced on the return trip by waterfowl that were stopping on their migration south at newly formed marshes and lakes. In March, when McLeod and the others returned to Fort Vancouver after spending the winter in California, they found that heavy winter precipitation had flooded large areas: "... made little progress owing to the country being inundated, every little brook or low place is full of water."[26]

McLeod's journal from a subsequent 1828 trapping expedition also has been preserved.[27] By this date, the annual burning of the prairies was a well-known phenomenon that the Hudson's Bay trappers considered an impediment to easy travel through the valley. In a letter to the company factor Dr. John McLoughlin at Fort Vancouver, dated September 8, 1828, McLeod complained, "our progress will be dilatory owing to the Country being entirely burnt, poor as our animals are just now in a short time hence they will be much more so."[28] Near the site of Salem, on the same day, McLeod noted "of late the fire had committed such ravages that Scarcely any feeding is left for our Animals." On September 15: "our route led southward, the Want of Grass made us go till 9 P.M. when we reached a small River where there is a little Picking for our Animals." South of the Santiam River, on September 30th, the journal provides a hint of the nature and size of Kalapuya seasonal foraging parties:

> ... delay was occasioned by the Indians being dispersed in detached Parties in various directions, remote from each other, and as the object of the Party was to obtain horses, as many as possible [from the Indians], much time was lost to visit the different Parties of Indians.[29]

For the next 12 years, despite the presence of numerous trapping expeditions in the Willamette Valley, accounts of Indian burning are relatively sparse. Three documents that do contain some information, however, are a Hudson's Bay Company journal of an 1834 trapping expedition, and the diaries of two Methodist missionaries from an 1840 trip to the mouth of the Umpqua. Along the Long Tom and Mary's Rivers, July 1st and 2nd, the H.B.C. journal noted:

> ... herbage getting dry & the ground has an arid appearance; on the lower spots grass luxuriant. The Indians set fire to the dry grass on the neighboring hill ... The plain is also on fire on the opposite side of the Willamette.

The Methodists experienced difficulties soon after leaving Willamette Mission (near modern Salem) on August 19, 1840. The plains south of the Santiam River "had been all overrun with fire a short time previous" which had "stripped them of their verdure, and we could not find grass enough for our horses."[30]

In the summer of 1841, Charles Wilkes, commander of the United States Exploring Expedition, a scientific party surveying the West Coast, sent a party of 28 men under George F. Emmons to explore the Hudson's Bay trail connecting Fort Vancouver with the Sacramento River. After the model of the Lewis and Clark Expedition, most of the party members kept their own journals of the trip. The longest and most informative of these documents are those of Emmons and his subordinate Henry Eld, both in manuscript; three journals of expedition members, all published, give fewer details. Wilkes himself summarized some of the main findings of the overland party in volumes four and five of the official journal of the Exploring Expedition. The following quotations on Indian burning are drawn from the writings of these six individuals.[31]

Wilkes himself did not participate in the overland expedition. He did, however, penetrate the Willamette Valley as far south as Willamette Mission (near modern Salem) where he witnessed the open prairies of the central valley. His observations are recorded in the June 9th entry from his diary:

> One of the most striking appearances of the Willamette Valley is the flatness of its Prairies in some instances a dead level for miles in extent—and it becomes a problem of some difficulty to solve how they have been produced. Fire is no doubt the cause of them but the way the forests are growing around them would almost preclude this supposition as but thin belt of wood frequently occurs between extensive ones. Since the country has been in the possession of the whites it is found that the wood is growing up rapidly a stop having been put to the fires so extensively lighted throughout the country every year by the Indians. They are generally lighted in Sept. for the purpose of drying the seeds of the [blank] (sunflower) which is then gathered and forms a large portion of their food.[32]

Emmons and the other members of the overland party were forced to wait until Henry Eld, on a survey of Gray's Harbor in the north, was able to join them. Hudson's Bay Company employees warned the Americans that they would have problems if they waited too long.

> an old Hunter at Fort Vancouver [said] that they would find it very difficult to provide grass for their horses on the route, the prairies having been burned by the Indians and that another great difficulty would be the danger of laming the horses, the small stems having been exposed on the surface by the burning of the grass.[33]

At Fort Vancouver on July 31 Emmons said, "the Indians were just commencing to burn the country, thereby interposing an obstacle that increases with my delay."

Emmons entered the Willamette Valley in early August, and waited at Willamette Mission for a full month before Eld finally appeared. Like Wilkes, he also ascended the "Yam Hills" (apparently the modern Eola Hills) for a view of the valley. Near the present town of Newberg, on August 7th, Emmons reported:

the country becoming smoky from the annual fires of the Indians—
who burn the Prairies to dry & partially cook a sunflower seed—which
abounds throughout this portion of the country & is afterwards
collected by them in considerable quantities & kept for their winter's
stock of food. The forests are also frequently burnt to aid them in
entrapping their game—these two burnings combined form the
greatest obstacle the travelers encountered in this country—one
blocking up the way—& the other destroying the food of the animals
[i.e., the expedition's horses].[34]

On August 8th, while camped on the west side of the Willamette across from
the Methodist mission:

Wind light and variable—very warm, clouding over after Mer[idian]
all the country west of us [present Amity area] apparently on fire from
the dense volums [sic] of smoke continually rising—it is fortunate for
the settlers that at this season these Prairies are not subject to heavy
winds—for if they were there would be no arresting the fires that are
so often kindled by the Indians.

Emmons was reporting from the fringes of White settlement in the
Willamette basin, which in 1841 were limited to the lowlands and river
bottoms extending from Champoeg south to what is now Salem. On August
10th he traveled the 8 miles from Willamette Mission to the southern terminus
of the settled area at the Mission Mill, moving between the wooded margin
of the river's floodplain and the grassy high prairie.

. . . part of our route lay over the low & part on the high prairie
bottom—through open and wood land . . . composed of a variety of
wood—the principal portion being Pine, Fir, Ash & Oak—with some
Cherry, Cotton, Willow etc.—the prairie had not yet been burnt on
this side of the river & the grass had all the appearance of made hay.

It was early September when Henry Eld and his men finally joined Emmons
and the overland journey began. Although the explorers spent only three
weeks traversing the interior valleys of western Oregon, it was during the
height of the native burning season, and all the journals are replete with
references to the aboriginal practice. On September 9th, near present-day
Independence, Eld made his first reference to fire.

Atmosphere filled with smoke consequently unable to see much of the
surrounding country. Country much burnt . . . Our route has been
through what might be called a hilly prairie country, the grass mostly
burnt off by recent fires, and the whole country sprinkled with oaks,
so regularly dispersed as to have the appearance of a continued
orchard of oak trees.

The following day, another of the party members noted his interpretation of
why the natives burned the plains.

Two views of Willamette Valley prairies from Chehalem Mountain. Champoeg is in the foreground; the French Prairie in the distance. Top: by Paul Kane, 1847. Courtesy of the Royal Ontario Museum, 77 ETH 201, 946.15.193. Below: by George Gibbs, 1851. Courtesy of the Peabody Museum, Harvard University.

Map 2. Overland route of the 1841 U.S. Exploring Expedition, with place names mentioned in the text.

The country continued level, but all the vegetation, except the trees, had been destroyed by fire, said to have been kindled by the Prairie Indians for the purpose of procuring a certain species of root, which forms a principle part of their food.[35]

On the 11th, when the party advanced as far as the Long Tom River, Emmons recorded:

Weather warm, quite smoky . . . Passed over a level prairie [south of Marys River]—perfectly barren having been burnt like most of the country—could not determine the extent owing to the smoke which confined our view within a space of about two miles round . . . came

> upon the banks of a small River called the Lum-tum-buff . . . the pack
> animals . . . having traveled all day over the burnt prairie without
> water . . . rushed headlong down the banks.

The Expedition's botanist found that burning was (to use the words of his
predecessor David Douglas) "highly unfavorable to botanizing."[36] The only
plant life he encountered was restricted to a narrow band alongside permanent
sources of water.

> On the banks [of the Long Tom] grew Dogwoods, *Spiraea*, Willows,
> Alder, and close by Clumps of a large *Pinus* . . . procured Seed of
> *Madia elegans* [tarweed], but rascally Indians by setting fire to the
> prairies had deprived us of many fine plants.[37]

Travel was difficult on the prairies. The days continued "hot and foggy"
and visibility, Emmons reported, was "confined . . . within a space of about
two miles around." The land was "burnt and parched" (Eld), "bands of wolves
were met with," and there was no water or grass for the horses. During the
night of the 12th, the animals escaped and were found the next day in a
"marshy place."[38] The night of the 13th was spent at the base of the Calapooya
Mountains.

> . . . encamped on a fine piece of prairie grounds of about a mile and a
> half in length and one half mile in width which being well clothed
> with grass was too valuable to be passed over without giving our
> horses a chance at it . . . it proved to be a thick smoky evening so as
> to preclude all possibility of getting the North Star (Eld).

Here the botanist was able to collect some plant specimens.

> Weather very hot and foggy, Plants: Gentians sp . . . *Glaucus* [saltwort]
> in marshes . . . *Eryngium* [wild carrot] sp . . . .*Madia elegans* in great
> abundance. *Madia*-looking annual. flos: small, yellow, dry banks.[39]

Passing out of the Willamette Valley (though still in Kalapuya territory)
the fires continued. The following three passages were written in the Yoncalla
area.

> 9/15 Calm, sultry & smoky as ever—the air from the prairies fanning
> past me—some thing like the heated air from [an] oven . . . (Emmons)

> 9/17 the weather continues thick and smoky the sun seen only
> occasionally and then of a dense blood red color and looking much
> larger than [illegible] . . . from daylight to ten A.M. hunting the
> horses in the smoke . . . through valleys . . . principally oak trees with
> grass growing under them . . . The prairies mostly today are on fire,
> winding its course slowly with the wind across the plains and up the
> hills . . . our route lay directly through where it was burning but the
> grass is not thick enough to render it very dangerous, and we crossed
> without injury; it is well the grass is not more than it is or our route

assumedly would be extremely perilous, it is probably owing to the
fact that the prairies are burned every year that the grass is so thin
(Eld).

9/18 . . . the flats between the rising ground is rich deep soil with
Clumps of Ash and dogwood, the grass had all been burnt up by a fire
which we saw rageing [sic] ahead of us and were compelled to urge
our horses through it. Campd. on Billys River. Atmosphere so dense
that we could not see more than ¹/₄ of a mile ahead.[40]

For the next 10 days, the overland party traveled through the territories of
two non-Kalapuyan peoples of southwestern Oregon: the Athapascan Umpqua
(of the middle Umpqua River) and Takelman-speaking Indians (of the South
Umpqua and middle Rogue Rivers). Throughout this region and into the
country of the Shasta Indians of northern California, the burning continued.[41]

Following the exceptionally well-documented year of 1841, there is a two-
year gap in the record of indigenous burning. In 1844, after two annual
migrations over the Oregon Trail had brought more than 2,000 settlers to the
Willamette Valley, the last documented occurrences of intentional burning
are described for the Indians. All three accounts for this year describe burning
or its effects in the Yamhill Valley. Jesse Applegate, a settler of 1843, established
a farm on the Rickreall Creek. His "Recollections" contains one of the most
graphic accounts of native burning extant.

. . . we did not yet know that the Indians were wont to baptise the
whole country with fire at the close of every summer; but very soon
we were to learn our first lesson. This season the fire was started
somewhere on the south Yamhill, and came sweeping up through the
Salt Creek gap. The sea breeze being quite strong that evening, the
flames leaped over the creek and came down upon us like an army
with banners. All our skill and perseverance were required to save our
camp. The flames swept by on both sides of the grove; then quickly
closing ranks, made a clean sweep of all the country south and east of
us. As the shades of night deepened, long lines of flame and smoke
could be seen retreating before the breeze across the hills and valleys.
The Indians continued to burn the grass every season until the
country was somewhat settled up and the whites prevented them, but
every fall, for a number of years, we were treated to the same grand
display of fireworks. On dark nights the sheets of flame and tongues
of fire and lurid clouds of smoke made a picture both awful and
sublime.[42]

The "sage of Yoncalla" (as Applegate was later known), by his dramatic
treatment of this episode, gives a probably exaggerated impression of the
normal intensity of the Indian fires.[43] Though certainly productive of great
clouds of smoke, they probably were usually more like the slow burn described
by the more matter-of-fact Henry Eld.[44]

Although Applegate gives no dates for the above incident other than "late summer," collateral information indicates that it may have been late September. An 1844 manuscript diary written at Willamette Mission, due east of the "Salt Creek Gap" across the Willamette, notes on September 28th and 30th "tended to watching the fire that was burning over the country . . . did chores and watched the fire."[45] Perhaps five weeks later another pioneer, James Clyman, viewed the same landscape described by Applegate, as recorded in the following quotations.

> 11/5/44 Crossed a range of high rounded hills [probably the Dundee Hills] and whare [sic] it had been burned 16 or 18 days it was now green and fair pasturage.<end extract>

Autumn rains, of course, were responsible for this quick revitalization of the vegetation.

> 11/9 . . . the valy [Yamhill] covered in a growth of green grass, the old haveing been burned off not exceeding Thirty days . . . the Wally of the wilhamet skirted with irregular Stripes of green Prairie lately burned off white not burned brown.

> 11/11 . . . greate Quantities of wild geese seen flying and feeding on the young grass of the lately Burned Prairies which are Quite Tame and easily approached on horseback.[46]

Clyman's diary covers almost an entire year in the Willamette Valley, until June of 1845. His very descriptive account of the natural vegetational sequence on the prairie lands will be quoted later.

Kalapuya Burning: The Subsistence Context

Omer Stewart was the first anthropologist to record in detail the phenomenon of aboriginal burning. In 1953, he had "completed the first draft" of an eight-hundred page manuscript, including tables and bibliography, presenting the evidence that aborigines the world over burned vegetation, and attempting to determine the effect such burning has had on the so-called "natural vegetation." This manuscript, unfortunately, has never been published. Stewart's approach was cross-cultural in nature; he was not concerned with reconstructing the patterning of anthropogenic fire in local cultural and ecological systems. But his classification of burning incidents by "reasons" lends itself to such reconstruction. In North America:

> Although fire is reported most frequently used to aid hunting—to encircle, to rouse, to stampede—fifteen other reasons for setting fires are given. These were as follows: to improve pasture, improve visibility, collect insects, increase yield of seeds, increase yield of

berries, increase other wild vegetable foods, make vegetable food available, remove or thin trees to allow other growth, clear land for planting, stimulate growth of wild tobacco, aid in warfare, produce a spectacle, and reduce danger from snakes, insects, etc. Sheer carelessness, of course, is often reported as a cause of fires.[47]

Fire obviously was a multipurpose tool in many pre-White-contact Indian cultures. Not all of the reasons listed here, of course, are reported for the Kalapuya, and only those that are related to subsistence pursuits will be discussed in this paper. It has been suggested that dividing Stewart's many aboriginal reasons for burning "into immediate effect and deferred effect sets is useful."[48] This division works particularly well for the Kalapuya, and will be used in this section of the paper. The "immediate effect set" includes instances where fire was used as a tool in the hunting and gathering process itself. The "deferred effect set" incorporates situations where fire was used to produce long-range future benefits (such as increased yields). Reasons in the first category were relatively obvious to early Euroamerican observers and are more or less well reported in the literature. The second category was subtler and not so apparent to early observers. Since early anthropologists did not conduct in-depth interviews with knowledgeable Kalapuya informants on ecological matters, we have virtually no hard data on burning for future effects. By ethnographic analogy with better-known neighboring Indian cultures, however, it is possible to make suggestive statements. When these probable uses of fire "fit" in with what we know about the Kalapuya subsistence strategy and the pre-White ecosystem of the Willamette Valley, the likelihood of their existence among the Kalapuya is strengthened.

The Circle Deer Hunt

For the Kalapuya, the sources indicate that there were two major direct uses of fire: in the circle hunt of deer and in the gathering of tarweed. The quotation from Emmons (8/7/41, above) states this in no uncertain terms; the following statement from a Salem pioneer of 1847 corroborates Emmons and adds some information of secondary uses of fire.

> The theory that I gained from the old settlers in regard to it [Indian burning] and my own observations is this; up to 1845 the Indians had a custom of burning off the country for the purpose of driving the game and also make the grass grow better, to keep down the undergrowth of timber, and collect seeds.[49]

The most common deer in the Willamette Valley in pre-White times was not the same species found in the forested areas of the valley today. The black-tailed deer (*Odocoileus hemoinus*) has supplanted the white-tailed deer (*O. virginianus leucurus*) over most of its range. The latter now is threatened (due basically to habitat loss)—and limited to two small herds in the lower Columbia near Rainier and the Umpqua Valley close to Roseburg.

The most frequently mentioned method in the anthropological and historical sources of hunting this small deer was stalking by a single hunter disguised in a partial hide of the animal. Burning might indirectly influence this method of deer hunting by producing restricted feeding areas (yards) where the animals would congregate and be more easily killed. I will discuss this usage in the next section.

Of immediate interest is the use of fire in the communal fall hunt of deer. The fire drive is widely reported throughout French's Plateau-Valley-California culture area. The University of California's areal "Culture Element Distribution" lists report it for 4 out of 10 Indian groups in the Plateau, 11 out of 16 in northeast California, and 10 out of 16 in northwest California.[50] I will discuss three examples: the Kalapuya, Coeur d'Alene (Plateau), and Shasta (Northeast California).

There are two references in the literature on the Kalapuya to a large-scale, communal circle drive of deer. The main source for both apparently was the Santiam Kalapuya, Joseph Hudson.[51] Hudson describes the practice as it existed in the pre-malaria period (before 1831) when the Santiam still had sufficient manpower to carry out the hunt. Hudson was interviewed sometime in the early reservation period (probably around the year 1880) by newspaperman Samuel Clarke and pioneer John Minto.

Samuel Clarke was noted as a writer of popular history, and the following excerpt is drawn from the article "The Great Fall Hunt of the Willamette," which originally appeared in *The Oregonian*, and was reprinted in *Pioneer Days of Oregon History* (1905).

> Old Quinaby[52] and Jo Hutchins [Joseph Hudson] who lived at Grand Ronde both told how their tribes prosecuted a great fall hunt for the purpose of laying in meat for the winter. The bands that occupied the region that included the east side of the valley, from the Molalla to the Santiam, all united in this annual roundup. It required a great force of men to carry out the programme. They formed a cordon around all the territory indicated. Men were placed in position along the rivers named and including the foothills of the Cascades. The great square encircled all Marion County (as constituted today) that is not rough mountainous country. To have placed men a quarter of a mile apart would have required fully 500. They called into active service boys able to draw a bow, and old men not incapable of duty.
>
> This annual hunt was conducted under the orders of the most famous war chief, and all others had to receive instructions and live up to them. There was considerable skill required to do this correctly and effectively . . . Possibilities were carefully calculated in advance and pains taken to plan operations early in the fall of the year, when

storms were not frequent and the game easily controlled . . . . At a given signal, made by a fire kindled at some point as agreed, they commenced burning off the whole face of the country and driving wild game to a common center . . . If badly managed, the game could break through and escape to the mountains . . . When the circle of fire became small enough to hunt to advantage, the best hunters went inside and shot the game.[53]

The second quotation, which does not mention the use of fire, but otherwise (in broad outline) corroborates Clarke, is from John Minto.

Joseph Hudson . . . pointed to a time when his people had numbered eight thousand, as he estimated, at which time and later, to the time of his grandfather, Chief San-de-am, his people used the circle hunt, driving the deer to a center agreed upon, by young men as runners, the point to drive to being selected as good cover to enable the bowmen to get close to the quarry.[54]

The chief problem with the Clarke account is that it is hard to believe that all of Marion County was involved in a single drive. Other than this criticism, the outline is similar to circle drives reported from other North American tribes, and probably is ethnographically sound. For instance, the following account from the Coeur d'Alene Indians of the Columbia Plateau in Idaho replicates much of what Samuel Clarke says for the Kalapuya.

The Indians watch for the proper time to go all together for a hunt or "surround" of deer . . . they determine the extent of the surround, according to the number of hunters of which the band is composed. A hunting-chief is chosen, and all his orders are thereafter executed promptly and punctually . . . When the "surround" is performed in a valley . . . the hunters form a complete circle, determining the size of it by their own number. Then they . . . burn their old rags in a hundred little fires round about, to prevent the deer from escaping from the circle. Pursued in every direction, the terrified animals flee from one clump of wood or brush to another, until finally enveloped on all sides and finding no issue, they fall into the hands of the hunters. It is seldom that a deer escapes them . . . They are easily killed with clubs, lances, and even knives . . . sometimes as many as 200 to 300 are killed in a single surround. Ordinarily, however, the number is less. After the hunt, the flesh of the deer is divided among all the families by the chief of the tribe, or by him who has managed the expedition. The portions are regulated according to the number of persons constituting the different families. The hunter who kills the animal has sole right to the skin.[55]

There are many similarities between the Coeur d'Alene and Kalapuya fire drives. In each case, a high degree of cooperation was necessary, coordinated by a special hunt leader. The communal drives could involve a large number of people and had the potential of producing considerable return in protein, of great importance in the yearly round of subsistence activities. The Coeur d'Alene quotation also describes the post-hunt distribution of meat, again similar in outline to that reported for other hunter-gatherers.

The fire drive also was common throughout adjacent portions of California; closer at hand, it was used by the Takelma of the middle stretches of the Rogue River. For the neighboring Shasta:

> . . . [when] the oak-leaves began to fall, men went out and set fires in circles of the hills. The ends of the curved lines forming the circles of fire did not meet, and in this opening the women stood rattling deer-bones, while men concealed in the brush were ready to shoot the deer as they rushed out.[56]

Deer, principally white-tailed, was the most important source of animal food for the Kalapuyans. It is mentioned more than any other animal in Jacobs' "Kalapuya Texts." Venison apparently was smoked and stored for winter use. The timing of the circle hunt makes sense in its closeness to the beginning of the five-month winter season and also because it was that time of the year when the animals themselves were fattest, having gorged themselves on newly fallen acorns in the oak openings. The documented pre-settlement presence of elk on the open prairies of the Willamette Valley raises the possibility that they, also, were hunted by the fire drive.[57]

Tarweed

A second major reason why the Kalapuya burned the prairies related to the harvesting of tarweed (*Madia* spp.), a major food source of the valley Indians. Tarweed also was an important wild crop of the Takelma, and was utilized by many California Indians as well.[58]

Burning is always mentioned as an integral part of the tarweed gathering process, but its specific function in this context has never been made clear. The following quotations from two of the three "interior valley" peoples (i.e., Kalapuya and Takelma) describe most of the particulars of tarweed gathering.

According to Jesse Applegate, from 1844 on the Yamhill:

> It was a custom of these Indians late in autumn, after the wild wheat, *lamoro sappolil* [Chinook Jargon] was fairly ripe, to burn off the whole country. The grass would burn away and leave the *sappolil* standing, with the pods well dried and bursting. Then the squaws, both young and old, would go with their baskets and bats and gather in the grain. The *sappolil* we now know as tarweed.[59]

George Riddle, a pioneer of 1851, describes tarweed gathering among the Takelma-speaking Cow Creek Indians.

During the summer months the squaws would gather various kinds of seeds of which the tar weed was the most prized. The tar weed was a plant about 30 inches high and was very abundant on the bench lands of the valley and was a great nuisance at maturity. It would be covered with globules of clear tarry substance that would coat the head and legs of stock as if they had been coated with tar. When the seeds were ripe the country was burned off. This left the plant standing with the tar burned off and the seeds left in the pods. Immediately after the fire there would be an army of squaws armed with an implement made of twigs shaped like a tennis racket with their basket slung in front they would beat the seeds from the pod into the basket. This seed gathering would last only a few days and every squaw in the tribe seemed to be doing her level best to make all the noise she could, beating her racket against the tip of her basket. All seeds were ground into meal with a mortar and pestle.[60]

Finally, the ethnographer of the Takelma said:

> . . . the stalks . . . of the yellow-flowered tarweed . . . were first burnt down to remove the pitchy substance they contained . . . the seeds were beaten out by a stick used for the purpose into a funnel-shaped deer-skin pouch with the mouth wider than the bottom . . . The seeds were parched and ground before consumption . . . [61]

The plants apparently were burned prior to harvesting to remove the sticky resin and facilitate gathering. If the tar was a hindrance to cattle browsing in the vicinity, it also must have been so for the Indian women who gathered tarweed seeds. The hairs on the seed case also are reported to have a disagreeable odor. Burning apparently was never intense enough to destroy the plants; most sources make a point of stating that the stalks remained standing erect. Firing also may have loosened the seeds in their cases and parched them slightly. Burning must have taken place before the seeds were fully ripe, at which time they fall naturally from the pod.

The implements of tarweed harvest were similar among all three interior valley groups. All used a variation on the seed beater "shaped like a tennis racket," and carried the seeds home in a soft, funnel-shaped basket carried by a burden-strap on the back. The seeds might first be beaten into a bucket or other container and then transferred to the back, or into the burden basket itself, held in front by the Indian women.

Once gathered, the seeds might be parched again with coals in a special ash-bark tray before being ground into a meal with stone mortar and pestle. A Salem settler stated that the meal "resembled pepper in appearance, but was sweet tasting." Jacobs' Santiam Kalapuya informant told him that ground hazelnuts and camas might be mixed with the tarweed meal. The processed seeds then were stored for winter use.[62]

The Indians apparently valued the tarweed highly. The 1877 Tualatin field notes state that tarweed patches were individually owned, and that each plot "might produce 10–20 bushels of seeds."[63] Tarweed therefore received an unusual amount of attention from the Kalapuya: unlike other utilized grass seeds, which simply were beaten off when ripe, *Madia* required burning; and given its high desirability and limited occurrence (at least in some areas) plots of wild tarweed, unlike other food plants, might be considered family or personal property. Elsewhere, species of *Madia* were likewise subject to intense attention.[64] In Chile, among the Araucanian Indians, *Madia sativa* (the major food species in the Pacific Northwest) was domesticated, both for its meal and as a source of oil.[65] The meal has a high protein content; the polyunsaturated oil, described "as clear as the best olive oil," is high in linoleic acid.[66]

Insects

A third direct reason for native grass burning was that it aided in the collection of grasshoppers. "Kalapuya Texts" notes:

> When it was summertime they burned over the land when they wanted to eat grasshoppers. When they burned the land, they burned the grasshoppers (too). And then they (women) gathered up the grasshoppers, and they ate those grasshoppers it is said.[67]

The method of capturing grasshoppers by field burning was widespread in Great Basin and interior valley regions. It also is reported ethnographically for the Takelma, Shasta, and Achumawi-Atsugewi.[68] A more descriptive account is the following, from the "Upper Columbia and the Interior of Oregon" (Sahaptin and/or Paiute) in the 1850s.

> . . . [the Indians] collect a great many large black crickets, and grasshoppers by the bushels . . . I have often seen them encircle the grasshoppers in a ring of fire by igniting the grass; their wings are scorched by the blaze, and they fall to the ground, when the Indians gather around, collect them and eat them . . . [or] they put [them] into a mortar with acorns or bread root, and pound into a mass which is then kneaded, placed on a board and baked for bread—the legs of the grasshoppers and crickets making a very rough crust.[69]

Although the Indians also used fire in the collection of yellow jacket larvae, it did not require burning of sizable areas. Jacobs' fieldnotes state that a fire was set atop the underground nest, driving out the adults and roasting the larvae. Douglas' statement that the Indians burned to get "honey" is a probable reference to this mode of collection. The Takelma had an identical practice.[70] Also reported from the basin and interior valley areas is the use of smoke to drive rodents (ground squirrels in the Willamette Valley) from their burrows.[71]

The above three types of burning yielded immediate rewards—venison, tarweed seeds, and roasted insects.[72] The Kalapuya also burned for reasons that did not produce instant results. The ground under oak trees was fired regularly to remove brush and facilitate future acorn gathering. Some areas were burned to make individual hunting of deer easier. Patches of ground in woody areas were burned prior to the broadcasting of tobacco seeds. And, by ethnographic analogy with the Shasta and others, it is likely that the Kalapuya burned to promote growth of desirable basket-making materials[73] and to create environments favorable to the growth of wild berry and root crops.

Acorn Gathering

Two wild nuts—hazel (*Corylus cornuta*) and acorn (*Quercus garryana*)—were utilized as food by the Kalapuya. Acorns, a staple crop in native California, were relatively less important to the Indians of the Willamette Valley. The Kalapuya lacked both the variety of oak species and the complex methods of acorn preparation used by California Indians.

Nevertheless, the descriptions of oak openings found in the journals of early explorers and settlers indicate that the Kalapuya were concerned enough about the acorn harvest to follow the California practice of burning underneath the trees. The following quotation by a pioneer of 1845 implies as much.

> Upon the slopes of these [Eola] hills are several thousand acres of white oak from six to twenty feet in height, some of them large diameter, and all with large bushy tops: the ground being covered with grass, at a distance they look like old orchards.

Also in 1845, Samuel Hancock commented on the unusual shape of the oak trees in the Willamette Valley: "very low with bushy tops . . . [that] reminded me of the apple trees at home." Regular low-intensity burning of the oak understory apparently produced standardized, well-groomed oak groves that resembled fruit and nut orchards cared for by the more complex techniques of arboriculture familiar to the American settlers.[74]

The ethnographic information on burning in oak groves by the Indians of northern California is relatively detailed and provides a model for the practice among the Kalapuya. The Karok reason for burning under the oaks was as follows:

> Mamie Offield says the trees are better if they are scorched by fire each year. This kills disease and pests. Fire also leaves the ground underneath the trees bare and clean and it is easier to pick up the acorns.[75]

The literature on the Tolowa states:

> Burning under trees to make acorns drop off; also to kill parasites on or underneath trees.

Before leaving an oak grove after the annual acorn collection, they burned the grass over the entire flat. Tolowa informants claim that this reduced underbrush and kept the grass from growing too high, so that the fallen acorns could easily be located during the next year's harvest.[76]

Although the expressed reason for burning given by native informants was to facilitate gathering, the removal of shrubby growth would have other effects as well. Henry Lewis notes that firing, by reducing competition from other plants, would cause an increase in acorn production. In the Willamette Valley, Samuel Hancock was so impressed with the heavy production of acorns in the oak openings that he stated, "such is the abundance that I have no doubt but that the Indians and bears chiefly subsist on the products of these trees." One emigrant recalled the "very heavy mast of acorns" in the oak openings around Salem in the late 1840s, which, in the absence of continued burning, sprouted and grew into oak forests.[77]

The acorns were not, of course, eaten by the Indians alone, as the passage from Hancock indicates. Bears and rodents favor acorns, but more importantly from the viewpoint of the Kalapuya, so do the deer *Odocoileus virginianus* and *O. columbianus*. In fact, many of the modern constituent understory species in valley oak groves are favored deer browse (including various berries [*Amelanchier* and *Rubus* spp.], vine maple [*Acer macrophyllum*], and hazel).[78]

"Wallammette" by Henry Warre, 1845. Showing oak savanna, with forested areas along waterways and in the distance. Courtesy of The Amon Carter Museum, Fort Worth, #1996.4.10, watercolor and graphite on paper.

Deer Habitat

Besides the communal fire drive, several references suggest that the Indians of the Willamette Valley and adjacent areas maintained, by controlled burning, a variety of microhabitats that simultaneously facilitated the hunt and were favored by deer. These microhabitats included prairie copses and fir groves, cleared forest understories, and burned-over grassy areas.

In reference to the first, it will be recalled that David Douglas said the prairies were burned "For the purpose of urging the deer to frequent certain parts to feed, which they leave unburned and of course they are easily killed." Similarly a Salem pioneer described isolated groves of Douglas-fir in the northern portion of the valley that were purposefully excluded from burning.

> These fir groves had been found necessary by the Indians to induce deer and other wild game to stay in the valley. The groves were undisturbed by fire . . . The Indians burned right up to imaginary lines, but never was the fire allowed to go past or get out of hand. So some authority must have existed among them because bienially the prairies were burned.[79]

Understory burning along forested riverbanks was reported by another emigrant as being important for maintaining elk and deer populations. A contrast was made between the appearance of previously burned and, in the absence of Indian practice, unburned areas in the Pudding River area during the mid-19th century.

> Elk once were very abundant along the placid stream and the ground was strewn with their cast antlers in every direction. Although well timbered this was all open woods when Mr. Cox first saw it [1846]. There was no underbrush. One might ride a horse anywhere and a deer might be seen and followed without impediment . . . The country was kept thus open by the Indians who were compelled by the whites to quit burning it over; then the brush sprung up . . . [80]

Ethnographic descriptions from neighboring peoples inhabiting forested environments emphasized the clearing of undergrowth to facilitate the hunting of deer. Thus the Coos-Kalawatset informant Frank Drew said, "The Inds. used to keep all the brush of all the Sius[law] country burned down so there was no retarding underbrush & deers were then visible from afar." A Klamath informant stated that brush was burned to facilitate hunting: "Now I just hear the deer running through the brush at places we used to kill many deer. When the brush got as thick as it is now, we would burn it off."[81]

Like the clearing of the oak openings to facilitate acorn gathering, the firing of certain environments to make hunting easier had less immediate consequences for local environments. Regular burning promoted the growth and regrowth of tender grasses and forbs favored by browsing animals. Recorded native accounts have emphasized the importance of fire to the hunt.

Others, however, indicate that the Indian had delayed returns in mind when they burned for deer. The following passages from the Tututni ("Ground burned over to produce a better drop of grass to attract wild game") and Tolowa ("Late spring . . . is said to have been the time for burning off the hillsides to improve the hunting grounds")[82] fall into this category, as does the following translated passage, for the Sahaptin Umatilla, recorded by a French traveler in 1853.

> At the end of summer they set fire with greater ease entire prairies; but there is only one useful goal: many weeks later, new grass, green and tasty, grows back, nutritiously richer and preferred by the beasts . . .[83]

One of the most profound effects of annual burning in the Willamette Valley was to encourage the regrowth and consequent year-round availability of grasses used for forage by deer and elk. Later, in a discussion of the seasonal round in the Willamette Valley, I will present documentary evidence for the year-round availability of pasture in pre-contact times. Deer often are described ecologically as being inhabitants of "edge" environments. Such "overlap" zones are characterized by a mixture and consequent diversity of species, both plant and animal. The Indian pattern of burning in the Willamette Valley produced an open prairie, interspersed with stands of oak and isolated fir groves, cut by riverine woods of ash and alder and bounded by mountain forests of Douglas-fir. This environmental mosaic was characterized by an unusual abundance of "edges," and consequently provided an optimum habitat for edge species such as the native white-tailed and black-tailed deer.

Tobacco Cultivation

Tobacco occupies a somewhat anomalous position in Kalapuya subsistence practices since it was the only species that was both planted and grown by "agricultural" methods. Burning was an invariable component of tobacco cultivation.

The basic source for tobacco growth in the Willamette Valley is David Douglas' journal. In late August 1825, near the "village of the Calapooie Indians . . . twenty-four miles above the [Willamette] falls" Douglas wrote:

> An open place in the wood is chosen where there is dead wood, which they burn, and sow the seed in the ashes . . . They do not cultivate it near their camps of lodges, lest it should be taken for use before maturity . . . fortunately I met with one of the little plantations and supplied myself with seeds and specimens without delay. On my way home I met the owner who, seeing it under my arm, appeared to be much displeased; but by presenting him with two finger-lengths of tobacco from Europe his wrath was appeased and we became good

friends. He then gave me the above description of cultivating it. He told me that wood ashes made it grow very large . . . .Thus we see that even the savages on the Columbia know the good effects produced on vegetation by the use of carbon.[84]

Marys River Kalapuya field notes collected in 1913 state:

> . . . Rotten logs burned up and tobacco-seeds put in with out spading. Occasionally place stirred up with stick. Each family planted for itself. When leaves ripe, they pull them out and dry them.

Nicotiana attenuata ("*N. rustica*" in Douglas) also was planted in burned-over areas by Upper Chinookans, all of the southwest Oregon Athapascans (i.e., Coquille, Tututni, Tolowa), and the Takelma and Shasta of the interior valleys to the south.[85]

Douglas' passage suggests that the Kalapuya were fully aware that ash acts as a fertilizer for planted seeds, and, it seems reasonable to assume, for seeds and rhizomes as well. This knowledge certainly was possessed by other West Coast hunters-gatherers who grew tobacco.[86]

As the above examples imply, the Willamette Valley Indians must have had some understanding of the long-range effects that periodic firing had on the health and productivity of selected species. Burning oak groves to remove brush and refuse to make acorn gathering easier also reduced competition from other plants, killed parasites, and encouraged a higher level of acorn production. Firing areas to shoot deer more easily resulted in increased browse and pasturage for larger numbers of deer and elk. And, according to David Douglas, the fertilizing effect of wood ash on future tobacco propagation and growth was understood fully by the Indians.

Despite a lack of direct documentary evidence for the Kalapuya, it is highly probable that Willamette Valley Indians intentionally burned limited areas to promote the growth and increase the yield of three additional classes of economically useful plants: hazel (*Corylus cornuta*), some species of berries, and many root crops. All of these species are early succession plants that colonize recently burned or disturbed areas. As a group they are characterized by rapid growth, and in the absence of periodic burning are at a competitive disadvantage with longer-lived woody species.

Hazel

The evidence that the Kalapuya burned to effect hazel growth is mostly suggestive. The plant is an early fire follower and was important to the Kalapuya both for its nuts and as a source of basketry material.[87]

Corylus cornuta in the Willamette Valley today is a common constituent of the understory vegetation in stands of *Quercus garryana*. It also is reported as being "Partial to well-drained hillsides, old fields, slashings, and burned over areas." Once established, hazel grows rapidly and produces a profusion of suckers. Nut-bearing ordinarily does not commence until the fifth or sixth year, and in cultivated varieties, suckers are removed to encourage nut production.[88]

In all of aboriginal western Oregon and northern California, hazel withes were an important material in basketry. Surviving accounts invariably describe the hazel as new growth, harvested from plots that had been burned over the year before. This is the case for the Karok, Shasta, Tolowa, and the polyglot coastal natives of the Siletz Reservation of Oregon. In recent years, Grand Ronde Reservation basket-makers used hazel shoots from burned-over areas, which suggests this was an aboriginal Kalapuya practice as well.[89]

Hazelnuts were gathered by the Kalapuya in August and stored for winter use. Ethnographic data do not indicate that burning was a part of hazelnut collection in the Willamette Valley, though it is reported from elsewhere in western Oregon. The unpublished "Tututni Ethnography" describes burning over hazel-growing areas prior to nut collection in order to roast the nuts. Evelyn Dickson's 1946 thesis, "Food Plants of Western Oregon Indians," mentions burning of hazel patches "after [nut] gathering" by "some Oregon Indians" (affiliation not given, though Dickson's informants included southwest Oregon Athapascans, Kalapuya, and Molala).[90] Burning after harvest may have served as a "cleaning-up" operation, not unlike its function in the oak openings. Whether performed before or after harvest, however, firing would have the secondary effect of removing refuse, competing plants, and smaller branches and suckers, resulting in greater production of hazelnuts in following years.

Berries

Like hazel, most of the berries utilized by the Kalapuya were early succession plants that favor recently burned-over areas. And like hazel, they grow more rapidly and bear more fruit when competing plants have been reduced. For the Kalapuya, important species included, in open areas, the wild blackberry (*Rubus ursinus*) and strawberry (*Fragaria* spp.); and in forest clearings, various species of huckleberry (*Vaccinium*), salal (*Gaultheria shallon*), blackcaps (*Rubus leucodermis*), thimbleberry (*R. parviflorus*), and salmonberry (*R. spectablis*).[91] Some of these berries (*Rubus ursinus* and *Vaccinium*) were dried and stored by the Kalapuya; others were eaten fresh off the vine.

Neighboring peoples burned limited areas to encourage growth of berries. The unpublished "Tillamook Ethnography" states:

> Every few years the berry pickers would burn over the salal or shot huckleberry patch. That meant no berries there next season, but a greatly improved crop the second year. This was done to improve

blackberry patches as well; these vines bore more lavishly the immediately following season.[92]

Upper Skagit informants in the northern part of Puget Sound recalled that forest clearings were burned over "in a carefully controlled way" to encourage the growth and increase the productivity of various species of berries. Upper Chehalis informants stated that prairie areas were burned for the express purpose of promoting the growth of blackberries. Burning to "increase yields of wild huckleberries" was practiced until recently in areas of the high Cascades of Oregon and Washington by Sahaptin peoples from the Columbia Plateau. Fires were started in October when the huckleberry harvest was complete. David French states that the "Indians had a thorough understanding of the ecological relationships" involved.[93]

Roots

By removing competing woody species, regular burning also favors the growth of several species of wild roots eaten by the Kalapuya. These include the liliaceous species camas (*Camassia quamash*) and wild onion (*Allium* spp.) as well as the tuber of the lupine (*Lupinus* spp.) and the rhizome of bracken fern (*Pteridium aquilinum*). From Whidbey Island, the San Juan Islands, and the Victoria area, there are ethnographic and historic accounts of burning open areas to encourage the growth of both camas and bracken fern.[94] In the Willamette Valley, the closest to a statement documenting that Indians burned to encourage growth of wild roots is the aforementioned 1841 U.S. Exploring Expedition suggestion that fire was necessary "for the purpose of procuring a certain species of root." John Minto's interpretive statement on the reason for burning might be useful here as well. According to him, "fire was the agency used by the Calapooia tribes to hold their camas grounds for game and [waterfowl]."[95]

The Seasonality of Burning

In order to provide a context for the stated and inferred reasons for aboriginal burning in the Willamette Valley, a temporal framework must be established. The context of time is examined in two ways: the yearly round of subsistence activities and the seasonal pattern of plant succession.

From the historical sources quoted above, it is clear that native burning in the Willamette Valley was a phenomenon of late summer and early fall. There is no record of it occurring at any other time of the year—and this may be as much of a climatic as a cultural factor. The earliest data on record is the second of July (from the H.B.C., 1834), and the latest is Clyman's (assumed, not witnessed) date of the 20th of October (1846). The Methodist missionaries and the members of the Wilkes Expedition encountered the most intense burning during late August and early September (of 1840 and 1841, respectively). The burning season was over by that time of year when the Douglas-McLeod expedition traveled through the valley in late September (of 1826).

Subsistence Round

There is no detailed eyewitness account of the Kalapuya subsistence round. What information we have is incomplete and inferential, and comes from two sources: ethnographic and archaeological. For the Tualatin Kalapuya, Zenk located a yearly calendar in the 1877 ethnographic field notes of Albert Gatschet. This calendar shows that the Tualatin year was divided into halves, corresponding to the dual division of wet and dry seasons. From November through April, the Tualatin resided in "winter villages" located in the wooded (and thereby sheltered) tier along the banks of important northwestern tributaries of the Willamette. Tualatin winter villages apparently were composed of multi-family plank houses, like those of their Chinookan neighbors to the north; however, the surviving evidence from the southern Kalapuya area does not allow us to specify winter-village house type. We are similarly in the dark as to the size of aboriginal social groups for either the winter village or summer foraging units.[96]

Archaeological research by John White (1975) has clarified the nature of local movements during the dry half of the year.[97] White classified recent archaeological sites in the upper Willamette Valley by activity, environment, and seasonality, and arrived at four distinct types. Wet season camps were located in the forested strands of the major river tributaries. For the dry half of the year, there apparently was considerable movement from one environmental setting to another to take advantage of seasonally and locally available wild foods.[98] Three environments and three site types are involved. On the low, wet prairies (White's "primary flood plain") are the multi-activity sites that White deems "base camps." Pits for roasting camas, an exceedingly important food gathered in May and June, are found here. Located along the margin between the grasslands and the forests are White's "valley edge" sites, where hunting seems to have been the most important activity. Poorly known are the dry prairie ("narrow valley plain") sites. It is here that grinding implements—mortars and pestles, implying seed and nut processing—are concentrated. The dry prairies and the grasses and oaks that were found on them were apparently subjected to the most frequent and widespread burning by the Indians.

Seasonal Succession

As mentioned earlier, James Clyman's 1845–46 diary is an exceptionally good source on the seasonal floral succession in the Willamette Valley before its ecology was altered significantly by Whites. By following his notes, it is possible to get an idea of the sequence of wild foods available to the Kalapuya throughout a typical year, and by considering the known facts about anthropogenic burning, to make some statements about the impact fire had on plant succession.

As the record shows, most burning occurred in late August and early September. Clyman's journal in the valley begins on November 2, when rain had already rejuvenated large portions of the landscape.

> (in the Yamhill Valley) I walked over the green hills which were here and there dotted with cattle and horses feeding on the young grass now about three inches high and thick and thrifty as the summer growth of the western Praries. Likewise greate Quantities of water fowl seen on the low ground such as geese duck Brants and Cranes making fine amusement for the Sportsman.[99]

The "young grass," of course, was fire induced, not seeded by Whites. One of the major environmental effects of summer burning was to produce this secondary late fall growth of wild grasses. Fertilized by ash, the fall grasses were tender and nutritious. This second-growth grass certainly was a major winter supply of food in aboriginal times for deer and elk, and probably helped support a larger year-round population of these herbivores than would be possible under natural, non-fire conditions. Most of the wild grass species assumed to have been common in pre-White times in the Willamette Valley have a tendency to become tough, unpalatable, or even dangerous (such as squirreltail) to grazing animals in the fall.[100] Annual firing, of course, would eliminate this disadvantage.

Because the autumn regrowth of grass also was beneficial to cattle, early valley settlers frequently noted it in their journals. Two other accounts, from the Dundee hills of Yamhill County in 1845 and the Cow Creek valley of the upper Umpqua drainage in 1851, follow.

> . . . the grasses on these hills are a species of red clover, that grows in the summer season about one foot high, and a fine grass, which after the clover disappears, keep them clad in green during the winter. They thus furnish a perpetual supply of food for cattle the whole year.

> It was near the first of November 1885 that we settled upon the land now known as Glenbrook Farms . . . At that time Cow Creek valley looked like a great wheat field. The Indians, according to their custom, had burned the grass during the summer, and early rains had caused a luxuriant crop of grass on which our immigrant cattle were fat by Christmas time.[101]

Clyman also mentions "great Quantities of water fowl . . . such as geese ducks Brants and Cranes." The Willamette Valley is part of the Pacific Flyway, traversed by birds flying south in October and north in March. Some of the most common varieties on the October flyway today are the mallard, pintail, wigeon, teal (two species), and the Canada goose.[102] In Clyman's time, other species, such as the whistling swan and sandhill crane, now rare, probably were more common. Many of these waterfowl also benefited indirectly from the practice of large-scale burning. Geese especially (as is obvious in an earlier Clyman quote) will feed on tender young shoots of grass favored by fall burning. Various studies have shown that the food supply and nesting habitat of many species of ducks improves as a result of thinning and removal of woody plants through burning.[103] In 1908, John Minto recalled:

> . . . the millions of geese, brants, cranes and swans which wintered in Western Oregon. To me it seems easily unbelievable by a person coming here now to state the quantity of waterfowl, cranes, curlew and snipe which wintered on the grasses and roots of the damp lands of valleys and the sloughs, ponds and streams sixty-four years ago.[104]

A second passage from Clyman (not dated) noted that migratory birds were equally common in the spring: "waterfowl is plenty Beyond all conception in the rainy season all the Lowlands being litterly covered they all move to the north and east during months of April and May."[105] Clyman's and Minto's descriptions both indicate a much larger duck and geese population than we have today. How much of the decrease is due to hunting and how much to loss of habitat is hard to say.

The spring sequence follows:

> 3/1/45 . . . the hills are now fast becoming dry, green, and pleasant the grass which spread itself so nicely over the surface of the earth last fall is now beginning to shoot up and lengthen out.

> 3/13 Noticed five different kinds of small vegitables in full Bloom to day.

> 3/18 the hills handsomely rounded smoothe and thickly coated with green grass.

> 3/21 Strawberries in bloom and the hills completely covered with small flowers mostly purple and yellow.[106]

These passages are notable for their description of the early regeneration of native prairie grasses. Other pioneers noted this phenomenon as well. On February 22, 1833, one of the first settlers of the Salem area recorded "Extensive plains, well covered with grass interspersed throughout with oaks crowned with mistletoe . . . in favorable spots the grass has grown six inches."[107]

Returning to Clyman's diary:

4/21 greate Quantities of Firr Grouse on the hills. These grouse are fine eating much resemble a Pheasant [ruffed grouse] in appearance but are nearly double the weight [these were probably blue grouse (*Dendrogapus obscurus*)].

5/6 the hills have been for some days completely red with the clover now in full bloom

5/10 I rode through the entire upper settlement of the East of the willhamet [Waldo Hills?] and was highly pleased with the beautiful veriaty of hill and vally so softly varied and intermingled with hill and dale as Likewis timber and Prarie all luxuriently clothed in a rich and heavy coat of vegetation and litterly clothed in Flowers the upland in yallow and the vallys in purple. The Quantity of small flowering vegittiles is verry remarkable and beyond all conception.

A phrase from Wilkes, describing the Eola Hills on June 6, 1841, should help in the identification of the upland plants. "The hills were covered with wall-flowers, lupine, scilla, and quantities of ripe strawberries."[108]

Despite the designation "purple" (blue is more likely), the flowers in the valleys were almost certainly camas, the Kalapuya "staple," the generation of which was favored by burning. In a later entry, Clyman gave details on its former abundance.

Ten or twelve acres of cammace in one marsh is quite common and in many insteances it will yeild 20 Bushel to the acre . . . these extensive fields are always on wet land and in many places no other vegitable is found to intermix with it.

The Tualatin calendar collected by Albert Gatschet shows that camas was harvested from the beginning of March, when the first shoots appeared, throughout the summer. The most intense activity apparently was in late May, when the plant was in flower. By late summer, when gathering was completed, many camas marshes would be dry and susceptible to burning.[109]

By early June, another sort of flora had reached maturity, according to Clyman:

6/6 . . . observed quantities of wild pigeons feeding on the grass seeds several kinds of which are fully ripe.

6/8 (on the Long Tom?) Passed over a fine undulating country handsomely and thickly coated with grass some haveing the appearance of rye and timothy all kinds However covered in seed which [is] rather remarkable for it is well Known to all the western states that but few of Prarie grasses are laden down with seed and those grown in the oak Hills the more certain.[110]

Although the band-tailed pigeon definitely fed on grass seed, we have no direct documentary evidence that the Kalapuya utilized any seeds other than tarweed and wild sunflower, both available later in the year. Indirect evidence, however, exists in the form of Kalapuya seed-gathering equipment and locally abundant native grasses whose seeds were widely gathered in California. The seed-beater and conical burden basket that the Kalapuya used in the gathering of tarweed (above) are identical in form to those used to collect a wide variety of seeds by native Californians. At least two genera of native grasses—the bromes (*Bromus*) and wild ryes (*Elymus*), which are common to the Willamette Valley—were important food plants of California Indians. Wild barley (*Hordeum*) and needlegrass (*Stipa*), sometimes collected in California, also were present in the pre-White Willamette Valley. The bromes seed in July and others assumedly do as well.[111]

It was early in July that the 1834 Hudson's Bay Company journal first reported "herbage getting dry," and a few days later "the Indians set fire to the dry area on the neighboring hill." The implication is that there was selective burning at this early date of at least some of the grasses that had outlived their utility. In contrast, the burning of tarweed plots occurred only after that seed had ripened in early September. The extensive burns associated with communal deer hunts took place after the fawns had been weaned and the animals had fattened on acorns, and before the start of the fall rains—that is, late October.[112]

Reconstructed Burning Schedule

Given the above ethnohistoric and ethnographic information, we can reconstruct a probable burning schedule for the Kalapuya. In late spring and early summer, the Indians likely were concentrated at "primary flood plain" sites in the wet prairies, where root crops such as camas were collected and processed. There was no burning at this time. During mid-summer (July and August), the focus shifted to the dry prairies, and "narrow valley plain" sites were occupied more intensively. Burning in July and August apparently was sporadic, most likely occurring after the harvesting of seasonally and locally available wild foods (grass seeds, sunflower seeds, hazelnuts, and blackberries), in limited areas. The immediate effect of the early burns would be a "cleaning up" process; the long-term result would be to facilitate the re-growth, in future seasons, of the plants involved. In late summer, fire was used on the high prairies as a direct tool in the gathering of tarweed and insects. This was followed in October by firing of the oak openings, after acorns had been collected. Finally, from the "valley edge" sites, some Kalapuya initiated large-scale communal drives for deer, which provided a winter's supply of venison. The sequence ended as they returned to their sheltered winter villages along the river banks.

Conclusions

Omer Stewart stated that "Historical and anthropological records indicate that nearly every American Indian tribe set fire to the grass and woody vegetation in the area it occupied." In the Northwest Coast and Plateau culture areas south of the 49th parallel, available records indicate that, out of a total of forty identifiable ethnolinguistic units, twenty-six (65%) practiced some kind of patterned burning (exclusive of burning as a part of tobacco cultivation). The total number that actively managed plant and animal resources with fire probably is larger, since historical and ethnographic data on some groups in this region are exceedingly sparse.

Patterned burning is reported from the Rocky Mountains, Columbia Plateau, Middle Fraser, northern British Columbia, Pacific Coast, and Western Washington (see introduction). Some of the most impressive evidence for the aboriginal use of fire in the Northwest, however, comes from that special cultural subdivision which David French called the "Interior Valley Province." The historic records for the Kalapuya and the ethnographic data on the Karok, in particular, suggest that fire was important in a wide range of subsistence-related activities. The research of Johannessen *et al.* (1971) demonstrates that the Indian use of fire in the Willamette Valley was so frequent and widespread that it maintained what ecologists would call a "fire climax" biotype.

Clearly, fire was an important component in both the cultural and ecological systems of the prehistoric Willamette Valley. The Kalapuya Indians used fire in a wide range of subsistence activities, and fire was essential for maintaining a fire climax biotype. The link between the two systems was the natives' use of fire as a tool—a tool that simultaneously improved the subsistence quest while maintaining ecological diversity. With control over and knowledge of the ecosystemic effects of fire, the Indians established an important symbiotic relationship with their environment. Put in other words, the Kalapuya, like other Native North Americans, became an environmentally selective force, acting through their agent, fire.

Originally published in the Canadian Journal of Anthropology 5(1): 65–86 (Fall 1986) revised and updated for this publication

Notes

1. This paper originally was prepared for a reading and conference class with Dr. Wayne Suttles at Portland State University, in the fall of 1976. An abbreviated version was read at the Oregon Museum of Science and Industry in Portland, on January 15, 1977. Later drafts of this paper have benefited from the comments and suggestions of Pamela Amoss, Donald Grayson, Eugene Hunn, Brien Meilleur, Helen H. Norton, and Henry Zenk. I owe a special debt to Henry Lewis, who provided critical comment and encouragement, and shepherded this paper to publication.

2. The original sources, all from geographers at the University of Oregon, are Carl Johannessen *et al.*, "The vegetation of the Willamette Valley" (*Annals of the Association of American Geographers* 61(2): 286–306, 1971); Jerry Towle, Woodland in the Willamette Valley: An historical geography (Ph.D. dissertation, University of Oregon, 1974) and "Settlement and subsistence in the Willamette Valley: Some additional considerations" (*Northwest Anthropological Research Notes* 13(1): 12–21, 1979). The first researcher to assemble historical data on the use of fire by Willamette Valley Indians was forester William Morris, in "Forest fires in western Oregon and Washington" (*Oregon Historical Quarterly* 35(4): 313–39, 1936).

3. Jerry Franklin and C.T. Dyrness, *Natural Vegetation of Oregon and Washington* (orig. 1973; reprinted by Oregon State University Press in 1988), 12.

4. Data on climate come from the National Oceanic and Atmospheric Administration's (NOAA) *Climates of the States* (Washington, 1978), 814; on lightning fire distribution and frequency see William Morris, *Lightning Storms and Fires of Oregon and Washington* (Portland, 1938).

5. On species composition of the grasslands, see J. C. Nelson, "The grasses of Salem Oregon and vicinity" (*Torreya* 19(11); 216–27, 1919), and Franklin and Dyrness, *Natural Vegetation . . .*, 122. John Thilenius's "The *Quercus garryana* forest of the Willamette Valley" (*Ecology* 49(6): 1124–33, 1968) is the source for oak understory composition. Since 1985, there has been important new work on Willamette Valley native vegetation. See in particular the species lists in the appendix to Ed Alverson's "Use of a County Soil Survey to Locate Remnants of Native Grassland in the Willamette Valley Oregon" (pp. 107–12 in Richard Mitchell, Charles Sheviak, and Donald Leopold, eds., *Ecosystem Management: Rare Species and Significant Habitats,* Albany NY, 1990) and in Kathy Pendergrass's "Vegetation Composition and Response to Fire of Native Willamette Valley Wetland Prairies" (M.S. thesis, Oregon State University, 1995).

6. Seasonal flooding may have maintained the open nature of these low-lying areas. Before channelization, drainage, flood control, and other modifications, floods were more frequent and water regularly covered much of this land. See Patricia Benner and James Sedell, "Upper Willamette River Landscape: A Historic Perspective," pp. 23–46 in Antonius Laenen and David Dunnette, eds. *River Quality Dynamics and Restoration* (New York, 1997).

7. The basic source for species composition of these various communities is Franklin and Dyrness, *Natural Vegetation of Oregon and Washington.*

8. The first quotation is from George F. Emmons's "Journal kept while attached to the [U.S.] Exploring Expedition . . . No. 3" (WA MS 166, Western Americana Collection, Beinecke Library, Yale University, New Haven, 1841); the second from Alva Shaw, letter of 1844 (Oregon Historical Society Ms 941, Portland).

Other first-hand descriptions of pre-settlement topography and plant cover include John Work, "Journey from Fort Vancouver to the Umpqua River and return in 1834" (*Oregon Historical Quarterly* 24(3): 238–68); Charles Wilkes, *Narrative of the U.S. Exploring Expedition of 1838–1842* (Philadelphia, 1845); Joel Palmer, *Journal of Travels Over the Rocky Mountains . . .* (Cincinnati, 1847); and A. Shaw, Letter of March 3, 1848 (OHS Mss 941). An excellent description of seasonal changes in vegetation, *James Clyman, Frontiersman: The adventures of a trapper and covered wagon emigrant as told in his own reminiscences and diaries*, Charles Camp, ed. (Portland, 1960) is cited later in this paper.

9. Habeck, "The original vegetation of the mid-Willamette Valley"; Thilenius, "The *Quercus garryana* forest of the Willamette Valley"; Johannessen *et al.*, "The Vegetation of the Willamette Valley"; and Towle, "Woodland in the Willamette Valley." Habeck, "The original vegetation . . .," 16, discusses Garry oak to Douglas-fir transition.

10. The pioneering palynological studies are Henry Hanson's "Pollen study of lake sediments in the lower Willamette Valley of Western Oregon" (*Bulletin of the Torrey Botanical Club* 69(4): 262–80, 1942) and Calvin Heusser's *Late Pleistocene environments of North Pacific North America* (New York, 1960). A more recent overview of the palynological record is Cathy Whitlock's "Vegetational and Climatic History of the Pacific Northwest during the Last 20,000 Years: Implications for Understanding Present-day Biodiversity" (*The Northwest Environmental Journal* 8: 5–28, 1992). See also Estella Leopold and Robert Boyd's "An Ecological History of Old Prairie Areas in Southwestern Washington" (this volume).

11. An interesting sidelight to this history is that prescribed burning, after a hiatus of over a century, re-emerged as an important tool of environmental manipulation in the Willamette Valley. In the decade following the Second World War, an important grass seed industry became established in the south and central valley counties of Lane, Linn, and Marion. Seed growers discovered that annual fall burning was an excellent technique for removing litter and destroying various grass pathogens. Unfortunately, however, large-scale burning produces a great deal of smoke, which becomes trapped in the upper Willamette basin around the city of Eugene. Because of the pollution problem, field burning now is restricted by legislative decree. See Larry Svart, "Field Burning in the Willamette Valley: A case study of environmental quality control" (M.A. thesis, University of Washington, 1970).

12. After the "fever and ague" epidemics of the early 1830s, there was a significant influx of equestrian Sahaptin Klikitats from the Columbia Plateau into the Willamette Valley. These people were forcibly removed to their former homes in the early 1850s, and their descendants reside on the Yakama Reservation.

13. For a summary of the defining traits of the Northwest Coast culture area, see Philip Drucker, "Sources of Northwest Coast Culture," pp. 59–81 in *New Interpretations of Aboriginal American Culture History* (Washington, 1955); and Wayne Suttles, "Introduction," pp. 1–15 in *Northwest Coast*, vol. 7 of the *Handbook of North American Indians* (Washington, 1990). The list of Plateau culture area traits is summarized from Verne Ray, "Culture element distributions XXII: Plateau" (*Anthropological Records* 8(2), 1942). Lloyd Collins's analysis is in his University of Oregon M.A. thesis, "The Cultural Position of the Kalapuya in the Pacific Northwest"; David French's position was stated in "The Columbia-Fraser

Plateau: A little-known part of the world (talk given at the 32d annual Northwest Anthropological Conference, 1979).

14. From Henry Zenk's "Contributions to Tualatin ethnography: Subsistence and ethnobiology" (M.A. thesis, Portland State University, 1976), 69–70: "There is evidence that Willamette Falls presented an insurmountable obstruction to migratory fish during seasonal low-flow conditions. The spring chinook run, which ascended the falls during high water in the spring, was probably the only significant salmon run in the Willamette drainage in aboriginal times. Moreover, spring chinook ran only in the larger tributaries heading in the Cascades (notably in the North and South Santiam, McKenzie, and Middle Fork tributaries), and apparently were non-existent in the smaller and warmer western tributaries such as the Tualatin and Yamhill Rivers."

An intriguing (though unproven) possibility is that, in the lower-gradient tributaries of the western valley, aboriginal burning may have caused erosion and consequent silting of the rivers to the extent that they could not meet the requirements of water clarity and oxygenaton necessary for successful salmon spawning: "While the cultivation of crops is the major cause of indirect depletion, fires set for hunting drives, or for clearings in which wild grasses or other plants may be encouraged to grow are sometimes locally effective agents in the alteration of aquatic environments." (Gordon Hewes, "Aboriginal use of fishery resources in northwestern North America" [Ph.D. dissertation, University of California, 1947], 17). If true, this would indicate an interesting, but certainly unconscious, trade-off on the part of the Kalapuya Indians—promoting an increased prairie plant resource to the detriment of the existence of an anadromous fish resource.

15. The most thorough coverage of Kalapuyan subsistence is still Henry Zenk's 1976 "Contributions to Tualatin Ethnography"; a second major source is Melville Jacobs's "Kalapuya Texts" (*University of Washington Publications in Anthropology* 11, 1945).

16. All these estimates are discussed in detail in Robert Boyd, "Kalapuya Disease and Depopulation," in *What Price Eden?: The Willamette Valley in Transition, 1812–1855* (Salem, 1995). Lewis and Clark's Kalapuyan estimates ("Callahpoewah" and "Shoshones resident on the Multnomah") appear in their "Estimate of the Western Indians," pp. 473–89 in Gary Moulton, ed., *The Journals of Lewis & Clark* vol. 6 (Lincoln, NE, 1990). The Hudson's Bay Company figures are printed in Samuel Parker's "Report of a tour west of the Rocky Mountains in 1835–7," pp. 90–138 in Archer and Dorothy Hulbert, eds.; *Marcus Whitman, Crusader* (Denver, 1936), 123; and *Journal of an Exploring tour Beyond the Rocky Mountains, under the direction of the A.B.C.F.M . . . 1835–7* (Ithaca, 1838), 264.

17. On the "fever and ague" epidemics, see Sherburne Cook, "The Epidemic of 1830–33 in California and Oregon" (*University of California Publications in American Archaeology and Ethnology* 43(3): 303–26, 1955) and Robert Boyd, *The Coming of the Spirit of Pestilence: Introduced diseases and population decline among Northwest Coast Indians, 1774–1874* (Seattle, 1999), chap. 4. The 600 1841 estimate is from the "Diary of [Charles] Wilkes in the Northwest" (*Washington Historical Quarterly* 16(4): 290–301, 1926), 292.

18. Researchers included Albert Gatschet, Leo Frachtenberg, and Melville Jacobs. Melville Jacobs's "Kalapuya Texts" incorporates the most important myth and ethnographic elicitations collected by all three fieldworkers. Unpublished fieldnotes from all three are in the National Anthropological Archives at the Smithsonian

Institution and the Melville Jacobs Collection in the University of Washington Archives; notable documents include Frachtenberg's "Kalapuya Ethnology" (NAA Ms 1923-C, 1913) and Jacobs's "Kalapuya Element List" (undated manuscript at the Bancroft Library, University of California). For more recent ethnographic summaries based on these materials, see Henry Zenk's 1990 "The Kalapuyans," pp. 547–53 in Suttles, *Northwest Coast*; and 1995 "Describing a Vanished Culture: The Aboriginal Kalapuyans," in *What Price Eden?*

19. For instance, Franklin and Dyrness, *Natural Vegetation of Oregon and Washington* (1973); Jerry Towle, "Woodland in the Willamette Valley" and "Settlement and Subsistence in the Willamette Valley" (1974 and 1979); and Samuel Dicken, "Oregon geography before White settlement, 1770–1846 . . .," pp. 1–27 in Thomas Vaughan, ed., *The Western shore: Oregon country essays honoring the American Revolution* (Portland, 1975). More recently, environmental historians have begun citing this literature. See in particular Peter Boag, *Environment and experience: settlement culture in nineteenth-century Oregon* (Berkeley, 1992); and Robert Bunting, *The Pacific Raincoast: environment and culture in an American Eden, 1778–1900* (Lawrence, KAN, 1997).

20. Most of the passages quoted below are first-hand observations preserved in the daily journals and diaries of explorers, traders, and early settlers. In these accounts, references to aboriginal burning generally appear as notational asides to the writer's main purpose. For instance, smoke and fire sometimes were mentioned as part of a daily weather report or as a hindrance to travel. Taken by themselves, such passages have little meaning. Considered in the context of what we know from the field of fire ecology, however, they gain substance. The journals almost always give a date and frequently mention the location or environmental setting of the observation. The picture that emerges shows that Indian burning practices in the Willamette Valley were highly patterned, occurring year after year at regular times and in particular kinds of environments.

21. The only two surviving documents that contain any first-hand information on the valley and its inhabitants are "Robert Stuart's Narratives," pp. 2–263 in Philip Rollins, ed., *The Discovery of the Oregon Trail* (New York, 1935); and *The Journal of Alexander Henry the Younger, 1799–1814,* vol. 2: *The Saskatchewan and Columbia Rivers*, Barry Gough, ed. (Toronto, 1992).

22. Alexander McLeod, "Journal of a hunting expedition to the southward of the Umpqua," pp. 175–219 in Kenneth Davies, ed., *Peter Skene Ogden's Snake Country Journal, 1826–27* (London, 1961) and *Journal kept by David Douglas during his travels in North America, 1823–1827* (New York, 1959).

23. McLeod *"Journal"* (Davies), 175.

24. Douglas *Journal*, 213–14. The first quotation originally was cited in Johannessen *et al.,* "The vegetation of the Willamette Valley," 288; the second in Morris, "Forest Fires in Western Oregon and Washington," 316.

25. The quotations are from McLeod, *"Journal"* (Davies), 179; and Douglas *Journal*, 217 (the latter first cited by Johannessen *et al.*, 289). Similar entries to the above for October 2 follow in Douglas's journal: on the 5th the expedition again camped alongside a "woody stream" where there was fodder for the horses; on the 6th Douglas again reported "my feet are very sore from the burned stumps of the low brushwood and strong grasses." (*ibid.*)

26. Douglas *Journal*, 237; McLeod, *"Journal"* (Davies), 218.

27. Alexander McLeod, "Journal of occurrences on an expedition to the southward of the Columbia," pp. 112–27 in Maurice Sullivan, ed., *Travels of Jedediah Smith* (1934 orig.; 1992 reprint by University of Nebraska Press).

28. P. 11 in *The Hudson's Bay Company's First Fur Brigade to the Sacramento Valley: Alexander McLeod's 1829 Hunt*, Doyce Nunis ed. (Fair Oaks CA, 1968).

29. The quotations are from McLeod's "Journal" (Sullivan), 113 and 119.

30. See Work, "Journey from Fort Vancouver to the Umpqua River," 264; Gustavus Hines, *Oregon; Its History, Condition and Prospects* . . . (Chicago, 1852), 264; and Jason Lee, "Journal of an 1840 trip to the Umpqua" (*The Christian Advocate*, August 25, 1841).

31. The Emmons and Eld journals are held in the Western Americana Collection of the Beinecke Library at Yale University; the full citations are George F. Emmons, "Journal kept while attached to the Exploring Expedition . . . No. 3" (WA MS 166, 1841) and Henry Eld, "Journal. Statistics etc. in Oregon and California . . . Sept. 6th to Oct 29th inclusive" (WA MS 161, 1841). Microfilm copies of both are available locally. The others are *The Brackenridge Journal for the Oregon Country*, O. B. Sperlin, ed. (Seattle, 1931, orig. in the *Washington Historical Quarterly* vols. 21 and 22: var. pp., 1930 and 1931); "Titian Ramsay Peale, 1799–1885, and his journals of the Wilkes Expedition," Jessie Poesch, ed. (*American Philosophical Society Memoir* 52, 1961); George Colvocoresses, *Four Years in a Government Exploring Expedition* . . . (New York, 1852); and Wilkes, *Narrative of the U.S. Exploring Expedition.* The Peale diary is incomplete; that portion covering the Willamette Valley was lost on the expedition during an upset while crossing the south fork of the Umpqua River. A sixth journal of the overland trek apparently was kept by the official artist of the expedition, Alfred Agate. Charles Pickering's *The Races of Man, and their geographical distribution.* (United States Exploring Expedition, vol. 9, Philadelphia, 1848), 39, refers to such a manuscript, in addition to reproducing two of Agate's watercolors of Kalapuya Indians. I do not know the whereabouts of the Agate journal if, indeed, it still exists.

32. "Diary of Wilkes in the Northwest," 53–54.

33. George Sinclair, "Journal on the Porpoise" (Microforms, University of Washington Libraries), entry for October 18, 1841.

34. These comments are similar to those recorded by Wilkes two months earlier, and apparently arise from a shared pool of information.

35. Colvocoresses, *Four Years in a Government Exploring Expedition* . . ., 277.

36. "Letters of David Douglas" (*Oregon Historical Quarterly* 6(1): 76–97, 1904), 78.

37. *The Brackenridge Journal*, 57 (cited by Johannessen *et al.*, 290).

38. Wilkes, *Narrative* vol. 5, 222–23.

39. *The Brackenridge Journal*, 58.

40. *Ibid.*, 216.

41. Documentation for southwestern Oregon from the Wilkes Expedition journals appears in Jeff LaLande and Reg Pullen, "Burning for a 'Fine and Beautiful Open Country': Native Uses of Fire in Southwestern Oregon," this volume. For Indian burning in northern California, see Henry Lewis, "Patterns of Indian Burning in California: Ecology and ethnohistory" (orig. 1973; 1993 revision pp. 55–116 in Thomas Blackburn and Kat Anderson, *Before the Wilderness: Environmental management by native Californians* (Menlo Park, CA).

42. Jesse Applegate, *Recollections of my Boyhood* (Roseburg OR, 1914), 69 (cited by Morris, "Forest Fires," 317 and Johannessen *et al.*, 219).

43. Applegate's account, though certainly based on fact, is suspiciously similar in style to a passage in Washington Irving's *Adventures of Captain Bonneville* (1977 Twayne edition edited by Robert Rees and Alan Sandy, Boston, 245–46), describing burning of prairies by Cayuse Indians in the valley of the Grande Ronde in eastern Oregon. Applegate was a popular writer who modified and retold various boyhood experiences from the pioneer period of the 1840s in such a way as to make them more salable to the reading public of turn-of-the-century Oregon.

44. Eld "Journal," entry of September 17.

45. Alvin T. Smith, "Diary," (Ms 8, Oregon Historical Society).

46. *James Clyman, Frontiersman . . .*, 120–21. The first and third quotations originally were cited by Johannessen *et al.*, 290–91.

47. Stewart's relevant publications are "Why the Great Plains are Treeless" (*Colorado Quarterly* 2(1): 40–50, 1953); "The forgotten side of ethnogeography," pp. 221–49 in Robert Spencer, ed., *Method and Perspective in Anthropology* (Minneapolis, 1954), and "Fire as the first great force employed by man," pp. 115–33 in William Thomas, ed., *Man's Role in Changing the Face of the Earth* (Chicago, 1956). The excerpt on "reasons" comes from "Why the Great Plains are Treeless," 43. As of this writing (spring 1999), Stewart's magnum opus on Indian burning is being prepared, posthumously, for publication. The publisher is University of Oklahoma Press; the editors are Kat Anderson and Henry Lewis.

48. Homer Aschmann, "Aboriginal use of fire" pp. 132–41 in *Proceedings of the Symposium on the Environmental Consequences of Fire and Fuel Management in Mediterranean Ecosystems* (USDA Forest Service General Technical Report WO-3, 1977), 135.

49. Joseph Henry Brown, statement to Hubert Howe Bancroft, 1878 (manuscript, Bancroft Library, University of California).

50. See Verne Ray, "Culture element distributions XXII: Plateau" (*Anthropological Records* 8(2): 95–262, 1942); Erminie Wheeler-Voegelin, "Culture element distributions XX: northeast California" (*AR* 7(2), 1942); and Harold Driver, "Culture element distributions X: northwest California" (*AR* 1(6): 297–433, 1939).

51. Not to be confused with *John* Hudson, Melville Jacobs' main informant for his Santiam "Kalapuya Texts" (1945), who died in 1954. Joseph Hudson was John Hudson's father's brother. Henry Zenk has supplied me with the following information on Joseph Hudson. Under the name of "Al-qe-ma" or "Yelkma," he was a signer of both the Champoeg (1851) and Palmer (1855) treaties. He was sketched by George Gibbs around 1850 (David Bushnell, "Drawings by George Gibbs in the far Northwest, 1849–51" [*Smithsonian Miscellaneous Collections* 97(8)], 1938). Under the name of "Jo Hutchins" he is cited in at least two published works on the Grand Ronde reservation from the 1870s.

52. Quinaby was another well-known native of the early reservation period. See "Twilight of a Chief" by Oswald West in *The Oregonian* 10/22, 1950, magazine p. 12 for a popularized account of him in the late 1880s.

53. Samuel Clarke, *Pioneer days of Oregon history*, vol. 1 (Portland, 1905), 89–90 (reorganized by the author for clarity). Originally cited in Morris, "Forest fires . . .," 317.

54. John Minto, "The number and condition of the native race in Oregon when first seen by the white man" (*Oregon Historical Quarterly* 1(3): 296–315, 1900), 306–7. Originally cited by Zenk, "Contributions to Tualatin ethnography," 68.

55. *Life, Letters, and Travels of Father Pierre-Jean deSmet, S.J., 1801–1873* . . .vol. III, Hiram Chittenden and Alfred Richardson, eds. (New York, 1905), 1021–22. Another Coeur d'Alene account from deSmet appears in Stephen Barrett and Stephen Arno, "Indian Fires in the Northern Rockies: Ethnohistory and Ecology," this volume. See also John Ross, "Proto-historical and Historical Spokan Prescribed Burning and Stewardship of Utilitarian and Food Resource Areas," this volume, on the Spokan fire surround.

56. Wheeler-Voegelin, "Culture element distributions XX: northeast California"; Driver, "Culture element distributions X: northwest California." See LaLande and Pullen, "Burning for a 'Fine and Beautiful Open Country,'" this volume, on Takelma. The Shasta quotation comes from Roland Dixon, "The Shasta" (*Bulletin of the American Museum of Natural History* 17(5): 381–498, 1907), 431. The Shasta and Takelma also used another communal method involving brush or rope fences, but without fire.

57. On venison processing, see M. Jacobs, "Kalapuya Texts," 103, 251, 366, 369; on the autumn fattening of deer, Walter Taylor, ed., *The Deer of North America* (Harrisburg, PA, 1956), 82. "Robert Stuart's Narratives," 32; and Alexander Ross, *Adventures of the First Settlers on the Oregon or Columbia River* . . . (London, 1849), 36; are the authorities on elk in the Willamette Valley.

58. The basic information of Kalapuya use of tarweed appears in Zenk, "Contributions to Tualatin ethnography," 57–59. On tarweed use by California Indians, see George Mead, "The Ethnobotany of the California Indians: A compendium of the plants, their users, and their uses" (University *of Northern Colorado Occasional Publications in Anthropology, Ethnology Series* No. 30, 1972).

59. Applegate, *Recollections of My Boyhood*, 68. Originally cited in Zenk, "Contributions to Tualatin ethnology," 230.

60. George Riddle, *History of Early Days in Oregon* (Riddle, OR, 1920), 45–46. Cited in Zenk, "Contributions . . .," 59.

61. Edward Sapir, "Notes on the Takelma Indians of southwestern Oregon" (*American Anthropologist* 9(2): 251–75, 1907), 259. See also LaLande and Pullen, "Burning for a 'Fine and Beautiful Open Country'," this volume, for tarweed gathering among the Coquille Indians.

62. On the various implements of tarweed gathering and processing, see the *Indian Journal of Rev. R[obert]. W. Summers*, Martinus Cowley, ed. (Lafayette OR, 1994), 38–39, 78, 102. Zenk, in "Describing a Vanished Culture," gives Tualatin Kalapuya names for the implements, as well as the special verbs used for beating, pounding, and parching tarweed seeds. On the taste of the meal, see Horace Lyman, "Indian Names" (*Oregon Historical Quarterly* 1(3): 316–26, 1900), 325; on Santiam Kalapuya tarweed preparations, Jacobs, "Kalapuya Texts," 20.

   Another seed known to have been collected by the Kalapuya came from sundry species of *Balsamorhiza*, the western "sunflower." Other than the requisite burning in the case of tarweed, the gathering and preparation of sunflower and tarweed seeds was similar. Both were knocked off the plant with a beater into a small basket or bucket and then transferred to a larger soft burden basket on the back (M. Jacobs, "Kalapuya Texts," 37; Sapir, "Notes on the Takelma," 259). The sunflower seeds then were parched and ground into a paste. This similarity in collection may account partially for the frequent confusion of the two varieties in the early accounts (e.g., Wilkes and Emmons, above). A second significant difference was in the *time* of harvest. *Balsamorhiza* seeds were ripe in July; tarweed in September. See Zenk, "Contributions to Tualatin ethnography," 23, for a discussion of this identification problem.

63. Zenk, "Contributions to Tualatin ethnography," 58.

64. Six species of *Madia* are native to western Oregon. *Madia gracilis* and *M. exigua* were first reported from the West Coast by Vancouver's lieutenant, Archibald Menzies, in 1792. *Madia elegans* was first listed by David Douglas in 1825. Thomas Nuttall recorded the remainder, *M. glomerata, M. madiodes,* and *M. sativa* (though usually under obsolete scientific names), in 1834. *Madia sativa,* the species domesticated by the Chilean Indians, was collected on Sauvie Island, next to Fort Vancouver. C. Leo Hitchcock *et al., Vascular Plants of the Pacific Northwest* (Seattle, 1955) vol. 5, 261.

65. On Araucanian tarweed see Carl Sauer, "Cultivated Plants of South and Central America," pp. 487–543 in Julian Steward, ed., "Handbook of South American Indians" (*Bureau of American Ethnology Bulletin* 143, vol. 6, 1950), 495. The unusual disjunct distribution of *Madia sativa,* on both the West Coast of the United States and in Chile south of the Atacama Desert, is almost certainly the result of "direct, long distance dispersal by migratory birds." See Elsa Zardini, "*Madia sativa* Mol. (*Asteraceae-Heliantheae-Madinae*): An Ethnobotanical and Geographical Disjunct" (*Economic Botany* 46(1): 34–44, 1992), 38.

66. The quotation is from Giovanni Molina, *The Geographical, Natural and Civil History of Chile* (Middletown, CONN, 1808), 95; on protein content see Zardini, "*Madia sativa* Mol.," 40; on the characteristics of tarweed oil, Guillermo Schmeda-Hirschmann, "*Madia sativa,* a Potential Oil Crop of Central Chile" (*Economic Botany* 49(3): 257–59, 1995).

67. Jacobs, "Kalapuya Texts," 26; cited by Zenk, "Contributions to Tualatin ethnography," 131.

68. On the Takelma, see Edward Sapir in LaLande and Pullen, "Burning for a 'Fine and Beautiful Open Country'," this volume; for northern California, Wheeler-Voegelin, "Culture element distributions XX: northeast California," 53.

69. A. N. Armstrong, *Oregon* (Chicago, 1857), 119.

70. Douglas, *Journal,* 213–14; Zenk, "Contributions to Tualatin ethnography," 134.

71. Melville Jacobs, "Kalapuya Element List" (manuscript, Bancroft Library, n.d.); Omer Stewart, "Culture element distributions XIV: Northern Paiute" (*Anthropological Records* 4(3): 361–446, 1941), 369; Wheeler-Voegelin, "Culture element distributions XX: northeast California," 53.

72. Parenthetically, although it is not recorded for the Kalapuya, we might mention here the practice, reported from the Central Valley of California, of burning a species of grass to obtain salt. See Alfred Kroeber, "Salt, Dogs, Tobacco" (*Anthropological Records* 6(1), 1941), 4. The species in question is salt-grass, *Distichlis spicata,* also found in the Willamette Valley.

73. George James, *Indian Basketry* (New York, 1903), 79.

74. The quotations are from Joel Palmer, *Journal of Travels,* 173; and *The Narrative of Samuel Hancock: 1845–1860* (New York, 1927), 46, 48.

75. Sara Schenck and Edward Gifford, "Karok Ethnobotany" (*Anthropological Records* 13(6), 1952), 382. Cited in Lewis, "Patterns of Indian Burning in California," 103.

76. Harold Driver, "Culture element distributions X: northwest California," 381; Richard Gould, "Comparative ecology of food-sharing in Australia and Northwest California," pp. 422–53 in Robert Harding and Geza Telecki, eds., *Omnivorous Primates: gathering and hunting in human evolution* (New York, 1981), 442.

77. Lewis, "Patterns of Indian Burning in California"; *The Narrative of Samuel Hancock*, 48; Joseph Henry Brown, "Statement to Hubert Howe Bancroft," 2.

78. Taylor, *The Deer of North America*, 202, 554–55; Thilenius, "The *Quercus garryana* forest of the Willamette Valley."

79. Douglas *Journal*, 214; George Strozut, "Remembrances of Lewis Judson" (*Marion County History* 1: 21–29, 1955), 21.

80. J. Cox, "Reminiscences." In "Horace Lyman Papers" (Oregon Historical Society Ms. 722).

81. The Coos statement was collected by John Harrington, and was provided to the author by Henry Zenk; the Klamath quotation comes from Omer Stewart's "The forgotten side of ethnogeography," 119.

82. From Cora DuBois's "Ethnological Document No. 6" [Tututni fieldnotes] (Bancroft Library, 1934) and Philip Drucker, "The Tolowa and Their Southwest Oregon Kin" (*University of California Publications in American Archaeology and Ethnology* 35(4), 1937), 232–33. Both are cited in LaLande and Pullen, "Burning for a 'Fine and Beautiful Open Country'," this volume; and by Lewis, "Patterns of Indian Burning in California," 98.

83. Pierre Saint-Amant, *Voyages en Californie et dans l'Oregon* (Paris, 1854), 264. Translation by the author.

84. *Journal kept by David Douglas*, 59 (location), 141 (planting).

85. The Marys River citation is from Frachtenberg, "Kalapuya Ethnology"; French, "Aboriginal Control of Huckleberry Yield" for Upper Chinookans; Homer Barnett, "Culture element distributions VII: Oregon Coast" (*Anthropological Records* 1(3): 155–204, 1937), 175 for southwest Oregon Athapascans; Sapir, "Notes on the Takelma Indians," 259 for Takelma; and Wheeler-Voegelin, "Culture element distributions XX: northeast California," 92 for Shasta. See also LaLande and Pullen, "Burning for a 'Fine and Beautiful Open Country'," this volume.

86. David French, in "Aboriginal Control of Huckleberry Yield in the Northwest" (1957 and this volume) was the first to recognize the significance of Douglas's passage: it shows the ecological understanding that underlaid the Indian practice. There is some confusion over the exact identity of western Oregon native tobacco. French suggests it may have been *Nicotiana quadrivalvis*, a second native West Coast species, not the *N. attenuata* attested from the Plateau.

87. On Kalapuya uses of hazel, see Zenk, "Contributions to Tualatin ethnography," 89.

88. Thilenius, "The *Quercus garryana* forest of the Willamette Valley;" George Sudworth, *Forest Trees of the Pacific Slope* (Washington, 1908), 384; Lloyd Baron, *Growing filberts in Oregon* (Oregon State University Extension Bulletin No. 628, 1978), 20.

89. Schenck and Gifford, "Karok Ethnobotany," 386; James, *Indian Basketry*, and Richard Gould, personal communication, both cited in Lewis, "Patterns of Indian Burning in California," 97 and 99; Leone Kasner, *Siletz: Survival for an Artifact* (Dallas OR, 1976), 40–41; and Henry Zenk, personal communication, 1986.

90. DuBois, ["Tututni Ethnography"]; Evelyn Dickson, "Food Plants of Western Oregon Indians . . ." (M.A. thesis, Stanford University, 1946).

91. M. Jacobs, "Kalapuya Texts."

92. Elizabeth Jacobs, "Tillamook Ethnography" (unpublished manuscript).

93. June Collins, *Valley of the Spirits: the Upper Skagit Indians of western Washington* (Seattle, 1974), 57; Thelma Adamson, "Unarranged Sources of Chehalis Ethnology" (Melville Jacobs Collection, Box 77, University of Washington Archives, 1926–1927); French, "Aboriginal Control of Huckleberry Yield."

94. See in particular Richard White, "Indian land use and environmental change: Island County," 1975 and this volume; Wayne Suttles, "The Economic Life of the Coast Salish of Haro and Rosario Straits" (Ph.D. dissertation, University of Washington, 1951); Helen H. Norton, "Evidence for Bracken Fern as a Food for Aboriginal Peoples of Western Washington" (*Economic Botany* 33(4): 384–96, 1979); Nancy Turner and Marcus Bell, "The Ethnobotany of the Coast Salish Indians of Vancouver Island" (*Economic Botany* 25(1): 63–104, 1971); and Turner and Harriet Kuhnlein, "Camas (*Camassia* spp.) and Riceroot (*Fritillaria* spp.): Two Liliaceous 'Root' Foods of the Northwest Coast Indians" (*Ecology of Food and Nutrition* 13(4): 199–219, 1983).

95. John Minto, "From youth to age as an American" (*Oregon Historical Quarterly* 9(2): 127–72, 1908), 152.

96. Zenk, "Contributions to Tualatin ethnography," 40–41 (calendar); 140 (winter houses).

97. John White, "A proposed typology of Willamette Valley sites," pp. 17–140 in C. Melvin Aikens, ed., "Archaeological Studies in the Willamette Valley, Oregon" (*University of Oregon Anthropological Paper* No. 8, 1975).

98. It might be noted that most early White contact with unacculturated Kalapuya took place during the spring and summer months, when trapping expeditions were undertaken and when the natives were dispersed over the land.

99. *James Clyman, Frontiersman . . .,* 122.

100. USDA Forest Service, *Range Plant Handbook* (Washington, 1937), var. pp.

101. The first quotation is from Joel Palmer's *Journal,* 170; the second from George Riddle's *History of Early Days in Oregon,* 37.

102. Joseph Linduska, ed., *Waterfowl Tomorrow* (USDI Fish and Wildlife Service, 1964), 238.

103. See, for example, Estella Leopold and Nina Bradley, "Fire and productivity," pp. 27–37 in Martin Alexander, ed., *Let the Forests Burn?* (Fort Collins, CO, 1974).

104. Minto, "From youth to age as an American," 152.

105. *James Clyman, Frontiersman . . .,* 136.

106. *Ibid.,* 138–39.

107. John Ball, letter of February 22, 1833 (Oregon Historical Society Ms. 195; published and unpublished versions).

108. *James Clyman, Frontiersman . . .,* 143 Wilkes, *Narrative,* vol. 4, 358.

109. *James Clyman, Frontiersman . . .,* 152; the Tualatin calendar is in Henry Zenk, "Contributions to Tualatin ethnography," 40–42.

110. *James Clyman, Frontiersman . . .,* 154 and 157.

111. On wild seeds gathered by California Indians, see especially Schenck and Gifford, "Karok Ethnobotany," 379—80; and Victor Chesnut, "Plants Used by the Indians of Mendocino County, California" (*Contributions from the U.S. National Herbarium* 7(3), 1902).

112. Work, "Journey from Fort Vancouver to the Umpqua River," 264; *The Brackenridge Journal,* 57; Taylor, *The Deer of North America,* 75 and 82.

An Ecological History of Old Prairie Areas in Southwestern Washington

Estella B. Leopold and Robert Boyd

Mud layers read like pages in a book to students of fossil pollen, and every proper lake is a local library of information on past vegetation. In southwestern Washington, fossil pollen tells the story of vegetation development and climate change since the time when continental glaciers stood 3,000 feet thick near Olympia. The romance of a lost biome dominated by ice-age mastodons, and a warmer time when prairie Indian cultures were in their heyday, can be inferred from fossil evidence, and can be read between the lines of the pollen story. The sediment record of plant pollen and macrofossils tells a tale about past vegetation that cannot be obtained in any other way. Such a fossil record has particular relevance when it is combined with historical data.

Using the palynological record, this chapter reconstructs the vegetation history and post-glacial environments of southwestern Washington and relates these to historical accounts from Cowlitz and other Salishan Indian cultures that occupied the area. We seek evidence for possible interactions between Native Americans and their prairie landscapes. Salishan peoples appear to have shaped the environment to suit their own needs just as Whites have reshaped theirs. In their own different ways, each influenced the general character of the dominant forest and prairie vegetation of southwestern Washington.

The prairies of southwestern Washington and in the rain shadow of the Olympic Range resulted in part from a xeric summer-dry climate. They occurred in a mosaic of prairie patches; those between Chehalis and Seattle were chiefly on flat, gravelly terraces of glacial outwash, while farther south toward the Columbia River the prairie soils were fine-grained and the topography was more undulating. They were known for the great diversity of their herbaceous species, and stood in marked contrast to the less diverse flora of the surrounding coniferous forests.

Reading the Pollen Record

In the Pacific Northwest, botanist Henry Hansen at Oregon State University was the first to explore the composition of post-glacial pollen preserved in bog and marsh sediments. Armed with his peat corer, he found a forest sequence faithfully repeated in coastal lowland sites: the earliest post-glacial pollen seemed to be dominated by lodgepole pine (*Pinus contorta*), followed by Douglas-fir (*Pseudotsuga menziesii*) and more recently by western hemlock (*Tsuga heterophylla*). The work of Calvin and Linda Heusser (New York University) and Cathy Barnosky (now Whitlock) and others at the University of Washington extended this record and provided new details. By penetrating old explosion craters north of Vancouver, Washington, these researchers have described long pollen sequences of prairie development. A particularly detailed record comes from a 15-meter sediment core at Battleground Lake (Lewis River drainage) where Barnosky identified fossil bracts and needles to complement the pollen data. Three sites to the north provide additional information: Mineral Lake south of the Nisqually River (Lewis County), Nisqually Lake (Pierce County) in the gravelly prairies, and Cranberry Lake (also Pierce County) along the prairie fringe.[1]

Battleground Lake: The Chronology of Vegetation Change
In western Washington, when ice of the last glaciation draped the landscape north of Olympia (about 18–15,000 years ago), an odd mixture of herbs, shrubs, and conifers comprised an open type of vegetation near Vancouver: abundant grasses with snakeweed (*Polygonum bistortoides*), corn-salad (*Valerianella*), and Sitka berry (*Sanguisorba*) suggest mountain tundra-like habitats. But sagebrush (*Artemisia*), which was fairly abundant, implies summer-dry, perhaps steppe-like conditions. Lodgepole pine, that cosmopolitan tree which invades disturbed areas, was associated with spruces, probably including Engelmann and Sitka spruce (*Picea engelmanii* and *P. sitchensis*), and firs (Pacific silver fir and/or grand fir; *Abies amablis* and *A. grandis*). The dominance of diverse herbs and shrubs suggest a steppic parkland tundra with spruce as a major tree species. Initial vegetation might have resembled modern high-altitude communities east of the Cascade crest, according to Barnosky's interpretation.

As continental ice began to melt in the lowlands (15–11,200 years ago), some temperate plants appeared and tundra types were gone. Mountain hemlock (*Tsuga mertensiana*), Sitka alder (*Alnus sinuata*), lodgepole, and perhaps ponderosa pine (*Pinus ponderosa*) appeared and increased; vegetation became more luxuriant (based on increased pollen abundance), and diverse

Map 1. Location of Pollen Sites of Southwestern Washington cited in the text: Battle Ground, Cranberry, and Davis Lakes.

herbs and sagebrush still were present. Barnosky interprets this as parkland with little evidence of tundra plants. The vegetation cover suggests cool and more humid conditions south of the retreating ice sheet.

Early humans saw this landscape; a broken spear point (made of bone) embedded in the rib of a mastodon bears witness to humans' probable hunting activities near Sequim, Washington, some 12,000 years ago. There the pollen mix was similar to that at Battleground Lake. Other extinct megafauna are recorded at Sequim (bison, caribou) and in the coastal region, i.e., at Beacon Hill, Seattle (mastodon), and Hillsboro/Portland, Oregon (tapir, mastodon).[2]

Western hemlock and red alder arrived in the Vancouver area by 11,000 years ago, and according to Barnosky's data were followed within 500 years by many temperate types including Douglas-fir. The earlier absence of Douglas-fir in southern Washington has led to discussions of where this tree was during the full glaciation. Barnosky feels it probably was eliminated from the area north of the Columbia River, but the tree came back about 16,000 years ago just after the full glacial period. Then there is no record of it until

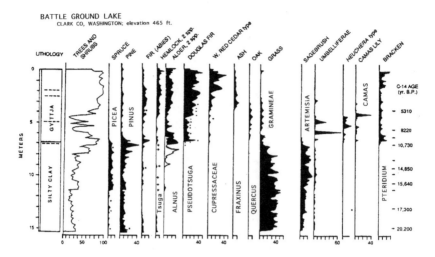

Pollen percentage diagram, Battleground Lake State Park, Clark County WA, selected taxa (after Barnosky, 1985). + indicates mountain hemlock pollen. Dots show position of macrofossils identified. Not all C-14 dates are shown. Several volcanic ash layers are found in this section (horizontal dotted lines in core).

ca. 11,000 years before present (B.P.). Within 1,000 years it spread virtually all the way to the Canadian border.[3]

Douglas-fir quickly became the dominant tree in the western Washington lowlands, where it was associated with an abundance of two successional species, red alder (*Alnus rubra*) and bracken fern (*Pteridium aquilinum*). These forests also contained western hemlock, probably grand fir, poplar (*Populus*), and white pine (*Pinus monticola*). The successional plants connote frequent fires and suggest open forests or forest in a mosaic with prairie patches.[4]

In southwestern Washington at Battleground Lake, however, the vegetation was more savanna-like, particularly between 9500–4500 years B.P.; Douglas-fir and oak (*Quercus garryana*) were the main trees associated with prairie and meadow grasses, camas lily (*Camassia quamash*), *Polygonum*, and various Compositae. Sporadic pollen peaks of camas lily, Umbelliferae, and alumroot (*Heuchera*) type suggest prairie plants flourishing periodically, perhaps after local fires. Bracken was widespread and abundant. During this warm, dry interval chinkapin (*Chrysolepis* or *Castanopsis*), which has schlerophyll leaves adapted to drought, expanded its range as far north as Seattle, and it became abundant in the southwestern part of the state. (At present, chinkapin is endemic along the Columbia Gorge and has only one outlying relict stand on the eastern side of the Olympics.) Between 9500–4500 B.P., the rich black prairie soils of southwestern Washington began to form. Associated with the prairie biome were the developing Indian cultures of southwestern Washington.

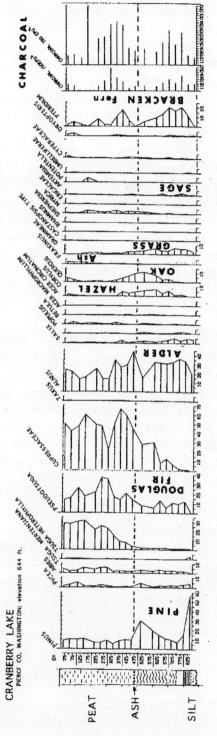

Pollen percentage diagram, Cranberry Lake, Pierce County WA, selected taxa. The volcanic ash layer (dashed line) is considered to be that of the Mazama Ash fall, dated at ~6800 yrs B.P. Based on this and the pollen zones, the sediment record starts at about 11,200 yrs B.P. Pollen diagram by Debbie Newman.

Between 4500 years B.P. and the present, a climatic cooling brought an increase in pollen of many conifers near Vancouver—Cupressaceae (probably western red cedar), Douglas-fir, western hemlock, ash, and others—while oak and prairie herbs and grasses declined. These data show that conifer forest expanded at the expense of grasslands in southwestern Washington; in the northern Puget Lowlands, forest composition shifted toward an increase in moisture-loving trees; especially notable was the rising importance of western red cedar (*Thuja plicata*).

Historical records come from the upper 16 cm of sediment at Battleground Lake; here pollen suggests at least two intervals of disturbance following settlement by Europeans. The first may have reflected logging outside the crater; weeds such as dock (*Rumex*), ragweed (*Ambrosia*), and also bracken fern increase to about 17% of the pollen/spore count. A second episode at 12 cm below the top of the profile records a drop in total tree pollen, particularly of Douglas-fir, while grass, bracken fern, and plantain increase. This change may reflect logging or deforestation that took place on the crater rim in the first part of the 1900s.

Cranberry Lake: Development of the Prairie Community

Pollen records can tell us not only the sequence of vegetational change but how and when the chief taxa of various plant communities came together. After the vegetation switched from cool late-glacial to warm Holocene plants, when chronologically did the prairie community appear in southwest Washington? Did the main types all appear together at once or did they "wander" into the area one at a time? Answers should reveal important details on the process of historic and modern prairie and savanna formation.

Cranberry Lake (Map 1) provides us with a broadly sampled pollen sequence from the margin of the prairie area along the Nisqually River east of Yelm in Pierce County. Though the core is not radiocarbon dated, it clearly shows the vegetation shifts at the chief zone boundaries recorded at Davis and Mineral Lake in the central Western Washington lowlands: from late glacial through early, middle, and late Holocene. Near the mid point in the core (depth 5.25 m) there is a layer of volcanic ash that undoubtedly records the explosion of Mount Mazama (circa 6800 years B.P.).

At the base of the core, the late-glacial zone is represented by silty mineral sediments and a single pollen sample at a depth of 8.00 m. As is characteristic in a wide number of sections in Washington, the pollen is dominated by pine, in part by lodgepole pine.[5] Associated with this is abundant pollen of alder (*Alnus*), some willow (*Salix*), spruce (*Picea*), and mountain hemlock. Above 8.00 m, the Holocene transition at Cranberry Lake is marked by a major change. Pine is replaced by a mix of alder, bracken fern, and Douglas-fir. Mountain hemlock shifts to western hemlock. This is the typical pollen assemblage of the early Holocene in western Washington.

But at Cranberry Lake, unlike the more northerly sites, we also see a prairie signal: grass pollen rises to 5—8%, and sagebrush is present. By the middle Holocene phase, hazel (*Corylus*) appears, and then Garry oak rises to an important 10% of the pollen count. At this point we have most of the main pollen indicators of savanna and prairie present together. While these are the chief prairie signals using pollen, one savanna element, Oregon ash (*Fraxinus pennsylvanica*), so far is absent.

In the last phase above the Mazama ash, the late Holocene pollen assemblage records a cooling somewhat like that at Battleground. Cranberry Lake shows a surprising *increase* of Douglas-fir, concomitant with rises in fir (*Abies*) and birch (*Betula*). Cupressaceae (either juniper or cedar [*Thuja*]) remains dominant, while alder continues at a moderately high level (>20%). In the non-tree fraction, there are small rises of cinquefoil (*Potentilla*) and Dryopteris fern. Oregon ash is the last identifiable member of the prairie savanna to appear in the Cranberry Lake pollen sequence. At Battleground Lake a similar pollen sequence occurs, but there the herbs are more prominent and some make extraordinary peaks.

The pollen evidence clearly indicates that the peak abundance of the prairie elements (grass, hazel, and oak) occurred in the early Holocene, before the Mazama Ash (6800 B.P.). Bracken fern can be considered a member of that assemblage too, as some of the historical and ethnographic accounts speak of bracken prairies. But the pollen evidence from a wide number of sites also clearly indicates a moderate cooling and perhaps moister time after the Mazama explosion. One wonders how the prairies continued to flourish during this less-than-optimal climatic period.

To find out how the prairies persisted until the present, we must turn to the historic and ethnographic records. The earliest historical records provide snapshots of what the prairies looked like before they were altered by agriculture and invasive species; the ethnographic record describes the cultural practices of indigenous peoples that modified the local vegetation.

Indians and Prairies

Historical Evidence

The journals of the first Euro-American explorers who passed through southwest Washington are invaluable sources on indigenous prairies: they not only give locations and point out major topographic features, but invariably describe plant cover as well. Lewis and Clark, for instance, during March and April 1806, encountered several small alluvial prairies along the lower

Columbia: at Deer Island, Quathlapootle (mouth of Lewis River), on Image Canoe (Hayden) Island, and opposite the mouth of the Quicksand (Sandy) River. Astonishingly, some of these prairies were composed almost wholly of camas lily, while others were of nearly pure onion (*Allium* or *Brodiaea*), as if they were vegetable gardens. The implications are that the digging stick methods of harvest and use of fire were selectively capable of encouraging certain species to an abundance no one has seen since.

In February 1814, Nor'wester Alexander Henry described the plain on which, 10 years later, Fort Vancouver would be established:

> February 6, Point Vancouver The Land adjoining the river is low and most overflown at high water; it is a meadow extending about 3 miles in length and at the widest part about $3/4$ mile in breadth to the foot of a beautiful range of high Prairie ground rising about 30 feet. On the top of this Hill is a most delightful situation for a Fort on a Prairie of about 2 Miles long, and 2 miles broad, good Soil and excellent Pine in abundance in the rear . . . Biche [black-tail deer] are apparently very numerous here and Chevreuil [white-tails] also. Their tracks, dung &c are to be seen in every direction. The fire seems to have passed through the lower Prairie last Fall, and the green grass is already sprouted up about four inches in height.[6]

At Fort Vancouver, in April 1825, in the "extensive natural meadows and plains of deep fertile alluvial deposit covered with a rich sward of grass and a profusion of flowering plants," Scottish botanist David Douglas collected specimens:

> my labour in the neighbourhood of this place was well rewarded by *Ribes sanguineum* [currant], *Berberis aquilifolium* [tall Oregon Grape], *B. glumacea* [*B. nervosa*, Oregon Grape], *Acer macrophyllum* [bigleaf maple], *Scilla esculenta* [*Camassia quamash*, camas], *Pyrola aphylla* [leafless pyrola], *Caprifolium cilosium* [honeysuckle], and a multitude of other plants[7]

Douglas's co-traveler, Dr. John Scouler, commented on the changes that had occurred on the prairie since construction of the fort:

> Ft. Vancouver . . . is situated in the middle of a beautifull prairie, containing about 300 acres of excellent land, on which potatoes & other vegetables are cultivated; while a large plain between the fort and river affords abundance of pasture to 120 horses besides other cattle. The forests around the fort consist chiefly of *Pinus balsamea* & *P. canadensis*.[8]

The visiting governor-general of the Hudson's Bay's Columbia District added:

> the pasture is good and innumerable herds of Swine can fatten . . . on nutricious Roots that are found here in any quantity . . . .the country [is] so open that from the Establishment there is good traveling on Horseback to any part of the interior[9]

Not mentioned in these early accounts, but described in later records, were the "dry prairies" of the interior of present-day Clark county.[10]

Further to the north, in the lands of Salishan Cowlitz-, Upper Chehalis- and southern Lushootseed- (Puget Salish) speaking peoples were, as one explorer described them, "a string of prairies which skirt the mountains from the Columbia at least as far as the Skywhamish [Skykomish]."[11] The largest of these were located along the regular route from the Columbia to Puget Sound (just to the east of the path of present-day I-5), and so were frequently described by early travelers. In 1811—12, a Northwest Company fur trader ascended the "Cow-lit-sick," where he found savannas: "beautiful high Prairies . . . occasionally interspersed with a few Oaks & pines &c and are the feeding ground of a great many Elk & deer."[12] Two years later, four Iroquois traders employed by the Company reported a

> pleasant Country, open and frequently intersected by small Prairies and Deer very numerous, the natives are also numerous, and have a great many Horses which they use in hunting the Deer.[13]

The most explicit description of the Chehalis and Cowlitz prairies comes from the pen of a Hudson's Bay Company doctor, trained in botany in his native Scotland, who passed through the "Cowlitz corridor" on his way from Fort Vancouver to Fort Nisqually in late May 1833:

> 5/25 arrived at a beautiful prairie extending NE & SW at least 4 miles—nearly a mile broad & very level, for two thirds of its breadth.—the brow of a gently sloping & winding elevation, appearing throughout whole extent, as the face, or rather flank of the remaining & western third . . . . The soil of prairie seemed fertile, it was covered with a luxuriant but not rank grass, & adorned with a much greater variety of flowers than either Cattlepootle or Jolifie plains[14], & much fewer trees, only single rows in some spots. Found ripe strawberries, on a sunny brae with an eastern exposure . . . .The prairie now seemed encircled with trees which rose a bristling serrated wall around.
>
> 5/27 Disturbed two deer as we ascended the gentle slope forming the eastern boundary of upper prairie of Cowlitz. Our course lay through rich & level prairies & prairions or smaller plains, separated from each other by belts of wood from 100 paces to $^1/_2$ a mile broad . . . .at first stage of portage 20 miles from Cowlitz & encamped in a long narrow prairie extending S. & N. of different elevations marked by winding slopes dotted with many wooden knools & its surface enamelled with a profusion of blue flowered kamass & yellow ranunchilus [buttercup]—a few Indian hovels were scattered along the margins of a lazy stream & in the hollow formed between two long winding woody elevations about 12 horses were feeding.

5/28 Encampment on Grand Prairie . . . from the brow of a hill
flanking prairie to N. had an extensive view—the broad flat plain of
green & yellow hues spread out beneath, encircled with wood . . .
Passed several beautiful prairies, the two latter of which have been of
a more sandy soil . . . a round eminence, a fairy knowl at NW side,
which perhaps was formerly an island in the lake which from the
sandy soil & profusion of rounded stones of boulders on the surface—I
suppose to have occupied plain."[15]

Dr. William Tolmie (who wrote the above passages) made several significant
observations: on the topography of the prairies—described as generally flat
or rolling with "few trees," in "single rows" or "woody knools," bounded by
ridges or trees (in one case a "serrated wall") or separated by "belts of wood";
on the diversity of plant cover—"luxuriant but not rank grass," with a "great
variety of flowers" and edible plants including areas "enamelled with a
profusion of blue-flowered kamass" and strawberries; and on edaphic prairie
types: in the Cowlitz/Chehalis area "fertile soil"; and the "sandy soil &
profusions of rounded stones" of the gravelly prairies of the southern Sound.
In a later letter from Fort Nisqually, Tolmie said the Cowlitz and Chehalis
prairies "In beauty . . . far surpass any thing of the sort I have ever beheld."[16]
Like Lewis & Clark, he has described an astonishing density of blue camas
lily, a feature no longer seen on any western Washington prairies!

*Mount Rainier from "La Grande Prairie," watercolor by Henry Warre, September 21,
1845. Note the flat prairie surface and rows of conifers along the margins. Courtesy of
the National Archives of Canada; Inventory No. I-62; Negative No. C-26341.*

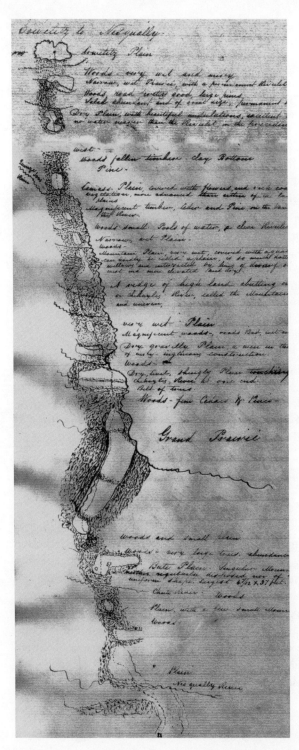

Map 2. Hudson's Bay Company route between the Cowlitz Plain and Nisqually River, showing outlines of plains and prairies. From James Douglas's manuscript "Diary" for April 22–October 2, 1840. Courtesy of Information Management Services (BC Archives), Victoria. Call # A B40 D75.2A.

In spring 1840, James Douglas, later the founder of Victoria and first governor of British Columbia, passed through the "Cowlitz corridor" and mapped the prairies he encountered along the way. His manuscript map, never before published, is reprinted here (Map 2).[17] Douglas also was struck by the edaphic difference between the south and north: the first "a rich clay" where "woods and Prairie predominate almost equally"; the second "poor rocky shingle," "three-fourths" of which was "level or undulating Prairies." The northern gravelly prairies are those on glacial outwash terraces; some of these occur at distinctly different levels, as on "Upper" and "Lower" Weir Prairie at Fort Lewis. Douglas contrasts these to the clay-rich soils in a more undulating terrain to the south of the glacial outwash train.

The plant cover was different too:

> There is a very marked distinction, in the indigenous product of the Prairies; those of the Cowlitz section are covered with an astonishing abundance of Camas, other bulbous roots, with a few humble flowers, while grass of a coarse quality appears more sparingly; the Prairies of the other section, on the contrary, exhibit less fecundity, having few or no Camas bulbs, but is rather thinly covered with a few short tender grass [sic], greatly relished by every variety of gramniverous quadruped, and whose nutritive qualities are in high repute.[18]

Douglas said the northern prairies "offer superior pasturage"; a year later an American explorer said of the Cowlitz and Chehalis prairies "here the ground is ready for the plough and nature seems as it were to invite the husbandman to his labour."[19] And so it was to be: in the 1850s, donation land claims blanketed both areas, and the prairies were converted rapidly to non-indigenous uses.

Ethnographic Evidence

But what of the indigenous inhabitants? How did they utilize and "husband" the southwest Washington prairies before being removed to reservations in the 1850s? Palynology helps reconstruct how the prairies originated; history tells us what they must have looked like throughout the pre-White era, and ethnography tells us how they were used.

No in-depth monograph on the Cowlitz or Upper Chehalis Indians has ever been published. But there is a wealth of information gathered from native informants in the late 1920s and 1930s by ethnographer Thelma Adamson, preserved in her fieldnotes in the University of Washington Archives, as well as an important collection of myth texts, also collected by Adamson, published in 1934.[20]

The Cowlitz Indians, despite their occupation of an area best known for its tree cover, have been termed a "prairie people."[21] Their lives centered on the open prairies depicted in Douglas's map: here their most important food plants were found; here was pasturage for their horses; their winter villages and summer camps were near or on the prairies; much of the action in their myths took place on prairies.

One of Adamson's informants, Mrs. Youckton, born at Cowlitz Prairie about 1865, said, "there used to be prairie all the way from Olympia to Tenino and Centralia." The Indians had names for every prairie along the way. Many of these names are preserved in Adamson's notes or in the myth texts. Provided with more up-to-date and precise transcriptions (and sometimes translations) by linguist M. Dale Kinkade, who interviewed some of the last Upper Chehalis and Cowlitz speakers, the names appear in Table I.

Table I: Prairies along or near the Hudson's Bay Company's track between Cowlitz (Toledo) and Fort Nisqually
(listed from south to north)
Indian names from M. Dale Kinkade[22]

Cowlitz names[23]

1. *ʔəwí-lkəˀnˀ* ("red-ochre place"): the prairie at Cowlitz Landing
Now-ok ("Big Prairie"): Cowlitz prairie, Hudson's Bay Co. farms on Cowlitz River; Cowlitz Mission
məx̣kanˀ ("horn, antlers?"): (lower) Lacamas and/or Mill Creek and prairie
2. *nixk'wâ-nəxtʼən* ("stretching a hide"): prairie with lots of camas; Lacamas Prairie
ləkəmós ílìˀ:prairie and creek close to Cowlitz [Chinook Jargon ("camas land") for above?]
3. *kuluˀln (kʼu-lu-łənˀ*, UpChe): Jackson Prairie

Upper Chehalis names[24]

4. *la tcʼt*: a prairie just NW of Napavine
5. *náwaqʷm* ("big prairie"): Newaukum River & Prairie [carrots and camas gathered here]
6. *suq̓ʷóh*: prairie across the river from Chehalis
7. *nsšəʔúmš* ("weeping prairie"): prairie north of Chehalis
8. *laik ! ut*: prairie south of Centralia
9. *Pawakʼ mstaleon*: little prairie on RR south of Centralia
10. *tá-łnʼcʼšnʼ* ("resting place"): Ford's Prairie
11. *náčʼałt*: Lincoln Creek; little prairie near Lincoln Creek
máqʷmaqʷm ("prairies"): Galvin on Lincoln Creek
12. *wəx̣é-uws*: prairie where community of Grand Mound is situated
ʔiłtálʼs: northern part of preceding prairie; Little Rochester Prairie
13. *ƛ'aqá-yqł* ("little long prairie"): Mound Prairie, west part
ƛ'aqáyqł ("long prairie"): Mound Prairie, east part; Rochester
14. *nisáyʼəqł*: prairie SW of Tenino (Rock Prairie?)
15. *nspístlʼš*: "Scatter Creek Prairie" (Violet Prairie?)
16. *taw somix*: prairie between Tenino and Olympia (Rocky Prairie?)

The Cowlitz and Upper Chehalis prairies were managed by fire. Explicit statements in Adamson's notes say so:

> Prairies were burned in early spring, when dry, so that a new growth would come in. The grass was bunch grass. This would be used for pasture ground." (Peter Heck, p. 297)

> Chiefs make Inds. burn prairies in Aug.; to make grass, strawberries, & black berries grow. (Jonas Secena, p. 348)

> Burn a spot and black berries would grow. Berry patches good for two or three years, and then weeds and no good. burn it, camp there, stay there, until berries all gone. (Pike Ben & wife)

The citations note prairie burning either in very early spring or fall, probably for different reasons. Burning in the fall may have been chiefly for pasture, though annuals and forbs such as strawberries and camas would benefit as well. The August burning would allow autumn regrowth of grass, which would last into winter, as in the Willamette Valley. A less frequent burning schedule (circa three years) is best for berry production, and may have been either in spring or fall.

Cowlitz "had to travel far in the hills for blackberries" (*Rubus ursinus*), huckleberries (*Vaccinium membranaceum*), and blueberries (*V. caespitosum*), where they also hunted deer, bear, and other game. The texts name other early succession berry species that "grow on Cowlitz Prairie": black-caps (*Rubus leucodermis*), salmonberries (*R. spectablis*), red huckleberry (*Vaccinium parvifolium*), gooseberries (*Ribes divaricatum*), and "June" (service) berries (*Amelanchier alnifolia*).[25]

As elsewhere in western Washington, the prairies were foci of economically important plants.[26] Among greens, dock (wild rhubarb; *Rumex occidentalis*), cow parsnip (*Heracleum lanatum*), and *yalp*, an unidentified 2½-foot-tall plant with white flowers, grew at the prairie's edge; the stalks of all were eaten.[27] Roots, including two species of camas (*Camassia quamash* and *C. leichtlinii*) and "wild carrot" (*Perideridia gairdneri*), were collected with digging sticks in late spring and baked. Some camas bulbs were huge—and up to two feet deep! Small tiger lily (*Lilium columbianum*) of the prairie has nutritious bulbs that were gathered in fall and boiled in water. Wild yellow sunflower roots (*Balsamorhiza deltoidea*) were eaten in summer and fall. From under the white oak trees at the prairie edge, the Indians gathered acorns in fall; they cooked these all night on hot rocks in a pit. The texts also note strawberries (*Fragaria vesca*) and state that grasshoppers were gathered by burning grassy areas.[28] The Cowlitz economy depended on this diverse productivity of prairies, and they enhanced the abundance of prairie plants by the use of fire.[29]

In the late 1700s, horses were introduced across the Cascades by eastern Washington Indians, and the Cowlitz, Upper Chehalis, and Nisqually became

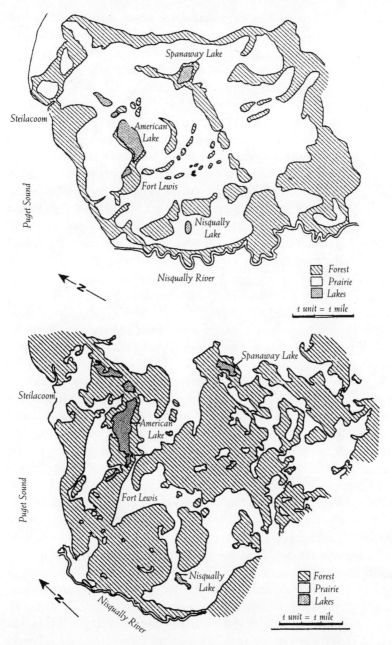

Maps 3 and 4. Change in areal extent of the Nisqually prairies over the past 150 years. Top: prairies in the 1850s, reconstructed from land use and other historical records. Bottom: shrinking of prairie area by the late twentieth century. From Arthur Kruckeberg, Natural History of Puget Sound, 287. Reproduced by permission, University of Washington Press.

equestrians.[30] These peoples were exceptional among Coast Salish Indians not only in the possession of horses but in the enhanced mobility associated with their possession. The presence of extensive prairies, modified by fire so that pasture was available year-round, may have served as a "preadaptation" to horse culture that other peoples west of the Cascades did not have and could not share.

Passages in the historical and ethnographic texts provide hints on the technology of burning. Jonas Secena stated that "chiefs" directed at least some of the burning. "Red (Douglas) fir" bark was "used for making fire." Sharp prairie borders with forests and boundaries on ridge tops suggest control; one myth ("The Boy and the Fire") implies that trails might serve as fire breaks. In this myth, a boy, fleeing fire, sought safety with Tree, Rock, Creek, Prairie, Rotten Log, and Trail. Tree and Rotten Log burned, Rock got "very hot," Creek boiled, and the grass on Prairie burned, but "Trail said 'Sometimes I burn, but only along the sides. Lie down on me.' He lay down on Trail and the fire passed over him."[31]

The Chehalis myth "Bluejay and his sister Yo'i"[32] shows that burning prairies had a role in native cosmology as well. Bluejay's sister Yo'i (perhaps magpie) married Fog, who turned out to be a ghost and who took Yo'i to the Land of the Dead. Bluejay wanted to visit his sister but had to pass through "five prairies, always burning" to get there. Yo'i told him he must carry five buckets of water to douse the fires in each prairie. On the way to the Land of the Dead, Bluejay first passed through five prairies "so full of beautiful flowers that [they] seemed to be on fire."[33] Then Bluejay entered the five blazing prairies ("*Słəts, słəts,* Fire Prairie"), each hotter than the last. He visited his sister in the Land of the Dead, where he had more adventures, but then had to return to the land of the living. Now, however, the order of the prairies was reversed. The flower prairies came first, and Bluejay, improvident or just plain foolish, used up a bucket and a half of precious water on them. Entering the fire prairies, he managed to stretch three buckets over the first four, but had only half a bucket to get through the last and largest. Bluejay ran through the flames, but near the end he ran out of water. He used his five bearskin robes to stifle the fire; he spat on it. "He had only a few steps left to go, when he began to shrivel up and roast. Suddenly he died, his claws drawn up together." Being a spirit-person, Bluejay did not really die, of course, but his foolish behavior made it impossible for the living to visit the dead any longer. The dead (as ghosts) can still visit us, but like Bluejay, they fall just before they get here and forget how to speak.

The Fort Lewis Prairies: Modern Remnants

The floral composition of native prairie communities has been studied systematically by several botanists.[34] On the Thurston County prairies, common species include bunch grasses (*Agrostis tenuis, Festuca idahoensis, Poa pratensis*), violet (*Viola adunca*), camas, *Brodiaea coronaria*, shooting star (*Dodecatheon hendersonii*), sedge (*Carex pennsylvanica*), kinnikinnick (*Arctostaphylos uva-ursi*), and mosses (*Polytrichium*) and lichens (*Rhacomitrium cladonia*). Bracken fern and salal (*Gaultheria shallon*) occur in dense stands in small areas.

The prairie flora and vegetation are best preserved in the military base at Fort Lewis, where frequent burning occurs as a result of military practices. These modern prairie remnants appear on Map 5. Typically in the Fort Lewis region, the prairies are surrounded by patches of oak savanna along the forest/

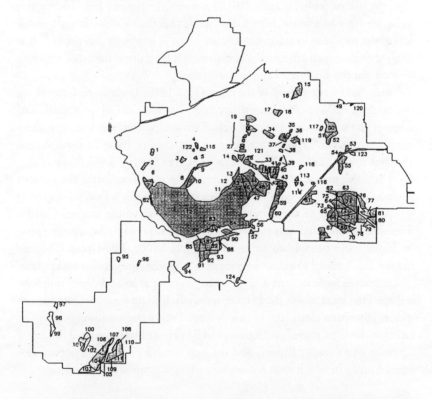

Map 5. Contemporary prairie units within the boundary of the US Army's Fort Lewis, Pierce County, WA. The largest prairie (6 miles long) is Ninety Six Division Prairie, along the north side of Nisqually River. Prairies shown are under active prescribed burn management by the Army, which maintains them well, though there are (non-native) weed infestations in some areas.

prairie ecotone. Members of the oak savanna are service berry, hazel, and Oregon Ash (which also typifies the moist creek sides). Spring ephemerals and bunch grasses characteristic of the prairie also occur under the open-structured oak savanna: shooting star, chocolate lily (*Fritillaria lanceolata*), and wheat grass (*Agropyron idahoense*).

The original forest in the Fort Lewis area was dominated by Douglas-fir, with western red cedar occurring in wet areas.[35] Historical stand data indicate that lowland Douglas-fir woods burned with low-intensity ground fires with a fire return interval measured at around fifty years.[36] Forests in the lowlands of King County observed and measured in 1907 show that Douglas-fir represented around 80—85% of the forest biomass (measured in board feet), with old-growth trees (called "red fir" for mature specimens and "yellow fir" for giant trees that were scaley barked). Their diameters commonly were eight feet dbh (diameter at breast height), and their stumps show that they were typically placed fairly far apart (10–25 meters). Testimony from old loggers living on Tiger Mountain, King County, said that the Douglas-fir old-growth forest was very easy to walk through, and that it was fairly fire-proof.[37] It is likely that this open structure was maintained by ground fires that regularly cleaned out the small trees and underbrush.

Forest has invaded much of the prairie area. In the Douglas-fir forest along the margins of Weir and Johnson prairies, the trees are all even aged, and none of them exceeds 12 inches dbh. Prairie-type soils are found in these peripheral forests.[38] Forest encroachment can be seen today in the scattered Douglas-firs on the 91st Division Prairie at Fort Lewis.

While the prairie at Nisqually survives in modified form, the present landscape of the Battleground Lake area is agricultural; a Douglas-fir forest grows on the rim of the crater, but it is nearly all young timber. Conifer forests have expanded into many former prairies, probably because burning by Indians was brought to an end in the late 1800s. The Upper Chehalis Indians are confined to a small reservation at Oakville; the Cowlitz are landless.

Europeans have written a new message across this landscape, and have reshaped the biota to suit their changing needs; it is unfortunate that so many species have been extirpated in this process. Prairie communities now are so rare that they badly need protection as well as prescribed burning. The Upper Chehalis and Cowlitz Indians and the new Washingtonians are a part of a linear history in which each has consciously restructured their landscape.

Originally published (in part) in the University of Washington Arboretum Bulletin 50(3): 14–17 (Fall 1987). Revised and expanded for this publication

Notes

1. See Henry Hansen, "Postglacial forest succession, climate and chronology in the Pacific Northwest" (*Transactions of the American Philsophical Society* 37, 1947); Calvin and Linda Heusser, "Sequence of pumaceous tephra layers and late Quaternary environmental record near Mt. St. Helens" (*Science* 210: 1007–9, 1980); and Estella B. Leopold *et al.*, "Pollen and lignin records of late Quaternary vegetation, Lake Washington" (*Science* 218: 1305–7, 1982). Southwest Washington pollen sites are discussed in Dennis Hibbert, "Pollen analysis of late-Quaternary sediments from two lakes in the southern Puget lowland, Washington" (M.S. thesis, University of Washington, 1979); Matsuo Tsukada, "*Pseudotsuga menziesii*: its pollen dispersal and late Quaternary history in the Pacific Northwest" (*Japanese Journal of Ecology* 32: 159–87, 1982); Cathy Barnosky, "Late Quaternary vegetation near Battle Ground Lake, Southern Puget trough, Washington" (*Geological Society of America Bulletin* 96(2): 263–71, 1985); and M. Tsukada, S. Sugita, and D. Hibbert, "Paleoecology in the Pacific Northwest I. Late Quaternary vegetation and climate" (*Verhand Internationale Vereinigung für Theoretiche und Angewandte Limnologie* 21: 730–37. 1981).

2. See K. Peterson, P. Mehringer, and C. Gustafson, "Late Quaternary vegetation and climate at the Manis Mastodon Site, Olympic Peninsula, Washington" (*Quaternary Research* 20(2): 215–31, 1983). On the Sequim megafauna, Carl Gustafson and Claire Manis, *The Manis Mastodon Site: An Adventure in Prehistory* (Sequim, 1984); the Beacon Hill and Hillsboro fauna are unpublished (D. Mullineaux; A. Barnosky).

3. Barnosky, "Late Quaternary vegetation near Battle Ground Lake"; M. Tsukada, "*Pseudotsuga menziesii*: its pollen dispersal and late Quaternary history in the Pacific Northwest" (*Japanese Journal of Ecology* 32: 159–87, 1982).

4. See Les Cwynar, "Fire and the forest history of the north Cascade Range" (*Ecology* 68(4): 791–802, 1987).

5. Hansen, "Postglacial forest succession . . ."; Cwynar, "Fire and the forest history of the North Cascade Range"; and Barnosky, "A record of late-Quaternary vegetation from Davis Lake, southern Puget Lowland, Washington" (*Quaternary Research* 16(1): 221–39, 1981).

6. Alexander Henry, *The journal of Alexander Henry the younger*, vol. 2, *The Saskatchewan and Columbia*, Barry Gough, ed. (Toronto, 1992), 675.

7. *Journal Kept by David Douglas During His Travels in North America, 1823–1827* (New York, 1959), 56. Honeysuckle is now *Lonicera ciliosa*.

8. "Dr. John Scouler's Journal of a Voyage to N.W. America," F. G. Young, ed. (*Oregon Historical Quarterly* 6, var. pp., 1905), 174. The two tree species probably are Douglas-fir and lodgepole pine; Scouler's names are not in current use.

9. *Fur Trade and Empire: George Simpson's Journal . . . 1824–1825* [etc.]. Frederick Merk, ed. (Cambridge MASS, 1931), 87.

10. See Helen H. Norton, Robert Boyd, and Eugene Hunn, "The Klikitat Trail of south-central Washington: A reconstruction of seasonally used resource sites," this volume.

11. George McClellan, "Journal," 5/20–12/11, 1853. Microforms Collection A228, University of Washington Libraries.

12. *The Discovery of the Oregon Trail: Robert Stuart's narratives of his overland trip eastward from Astoria in 1812–13*, Philip Rollins, ed. (New York, 1935), 30.

13. *The journal of Alexander Henry the younger,* 684.

14. At the mouth of the Lewis River and site of Fort Vancouver, respectively.

15. *The Journals of William Fraser Tolmie, physician and fur trader* (Vancouver, 1963), 191–93.

16. Letter of 9/20/33, William Tolmie Letter Book, Kew Garden Herbarium Library, Kew, England.

17. A copy of the map, made by Sir George Simpson a year later, *has* been published, in *London Correspondence Inward from Sir George Simpson,* Publications of the Hudson's Bay Record Society 29 (London, 1973), between pp. 76 and 77.

18. James Douglas, "Douglas Expeditions, 1840–41," Herman Leader, ed. (*Oregon Historical Quarterly* 32: var. pp., 1931), 11.

19. Charles Wilkes, "Diary of Wilkes in the Northwest," Edmund Meany, ed. (*Washington Historical Quarterly* 16 and 17 var. pp., 1925–26), 145.

20. Thelma Adamson, "Unarranged Sources of Chehalis Ethnology," Parts I and II, Melville Jacobs Collection, Box 77 (University of Washington Archives, 1926–27); "Folk-tales of the coast Salish" (*Memoirs of the American folk-lore society,* vol. 27, 1934).

21. Verne Ray, *Handbook of Cowlitz Indians* (Seattle, 1966).

22. Personal communication to authors, June 10, 1997. M. Dale Kinkade is professor of linguistics at the University of British Columbia. Most of the prairie names were reheard and retranscribed by Kinkade before the passing of the last speakers; names not reheard retain earlier (and less reliable) transcriptions.

23. M. Dale Kinkade, *Cowlitz (Salish) Dictionary.* Ms. in Kinkade's possession.

24. Kinkade, "Upper Chehalis Dictionary" (*University of Montana Occasional Papers in Linguistics* No. 7, 1991).

25. From "*X̣wə'ni* Travels," p. 258.

26. Helen H. Norton, "The association between anthropogenic prairies and important food plants in western Washington" (*Northwest Anthropological Research Notes* 13(2): 175–200, 1979).

27. The Chehalis myth, "Moon" (pp. 158–72), describes the mythological origin of these prairie plants.

28. "*Nəx̣ə'ntci* Boy," 231.

29. See also Erna Gunther, *Ethnobotany of western Washington: the knowledge and use of indigenous plants by native Americans* (orig. 1945; rev. ed. Seattle 1973).

30. Daniel Boxberger, "The Introduction of Horses to the Southern Puget Sound Salish," pp. 103–19 in *Western Washington Indian Socio-Economics: Papers in Honor of Angelo S. Anastasio* (Bellingham, 1984).

31. "The Boy and the Fire," p. 223.

32. Adamson, "Folk-tales," pp. 293–303. This is the Humptulips version; there is an Upper Chehalis equivalent on pp. 21–23.

33. The flowers may have been the red spear-flowers mentioned in "Moon"; here they are said to "produce an effect like the glow from phosphorous wood."

34. See Frank Lang, "A study of vegetation change on the gravelly prairies of Pierce and Thurston Counties, Western Washington" (M.A. thesis, botany, University of Washington, 1961); Reid Schuller, "Native Flora and Vegetation of Glacial Outwash Prairies in the Puget Trough Lowland (6 pp. unpublished report, Washington Natural Heritage Program, 1983); and Roger DelMoral and David Deardorff, "Vegetation of the Mima Mounds, Washington State" (*Ecology* 57(3): 520–30, 1976). Several papers in the volume *Ecology and Conservation of the South*

Puget Sound Prairie Landscape (Patrick Dunn and Kern Ewing, eds., The Nature Conservancy of Washington, 1997) discuss native species, species composition, and preservation/restoration efforts of native prairies in central Western Washington.
35. County Tax Records.
36. Leopold and class 1985 historical stand data; Peter Morrison and Frederick Swanson, "Fire history and pattern in a Cascade Range landscape" (USFS PNW General Technical Report 254, 1990).
37. Leopold, personal interview, 1980.
38. Frank Ugolini and A. K. Schlichte, "The Effect of Holocene Environmental Changes on Selected Western Washington Soils. (*Soil Science* 116(3): 218–27, 1973)

Appendix

In "The Association Between Anthropogenic Prairies and Important Food Plants in Western Washington" (1979),[1] Helen H. Norton made the important discovery that a large proportion of the plants native to the fire-managed prairies of western Washington were useful in the economy of the local Native Americans, either as food, in the technology, or as medicines. This insight came from her analysis of the prairie plants in James G. Cooper's list of "Plants collected West of the Cascade Mountains during 1854–55."[2] Following Norton's precedent, we here analyze a more recently compiled native species list, Reid Schuller's and James Barrett's 1983 "Native Flora of Glacial Outwash Prairies in the Vicinity of Pierce and Thurston Counties, Washington—A Hypothetical Reconstruction." Only plants with documented economic uses are listed below; they comprise something over 30% of Schuller's and Barrett's 180 total.

Economically Useful Plants of the Native Prairies of Pierce and Thurston Counties[3]

	Cooper[4]	Chappell[5]	Native Use[6]
Trees			
Alnus rubra, red alder			T, F
Picea sitchensis, Sitka spruce			T
Pinus monticola, white pine			t, m
P. ponderosa, Ponderosa pine	x		F
Pseudotsuga menziesii, Douglas-fir			T, f
Pyrus fusca, western crabapple	x		F, t
Quercus garryana, Oregon oak	x		F

	Cooper[4]	Chappell[5]	Native Use[6]
Shrubs			
Amelanchier alnifolia, Saskatoon	x		T, F
Berberis aquifolium, tall Oregon grape	x		F, T
Cornus nuttallii, Pacific dogwood			T
Corylus cornuta, California hazel			F, T
Holodiscus discolor, creambush oceanspray			T
Lonicera ciliosa, orange honeysuckle	sp.		t
Prunus virginiana, chokecherry	sp.		F, t
Rhamnus purshiana, cascara			M
Ribes sanguineum, red currant			f
Rosa pisocarpa, clustered wildrose	sp.		f
Rubus ursinus, trailing blackberry			F, C
Salix scouleriana, Scouler's willow			t
Symphoricarpus albus, common snowberry			t, M
Herbs			
Achillea millefolium, yarrow	x	x	M
Agrostis spp. (four), bentgrasses			C
Allium amplectens, slim-leafed onion			F
Apocynum androsaemifolium, spreading dogbane			T
Arctostaphylos uva-ursi, kinnikinnick	x		F
Balsamorhiza deltoidea, Puget balsamroot	x	x	F
Brodiaea coronaria, harvest brodiaea	x		F
B. hyacinthina, hyacinth brodiaea	x		F
Bromus carinatus, California brome	x		C
B. sitchensis, Alaska brome			T, C
Camassia leichtlinii, Leichtlin's camas			F
C. quamash, common camas (some spp.)	x	x	F
Carex spp. (nine), sedges		x	C, T
Danthonia californica, California danthonia		x	C
Delphinium menziesii, Menzies' larkspur	x		t, m
D. nuttallii, Nuttall's larkspur	sp.		t, m
Deschampsia caespitosa, tufted hairgrass			t
Dodecatheon hendersonii, Henderson's shooting-star	sp.	x	t
Elymus glaucus, blue wildrye		x	t
Epilobium angustifolium, fireweed	x		F
Festuca idahoensis, Idaho fescue		x	C
Fescue occidentalis, rubra western, red fescue	sp.		c

	Cooper[4]	Chappell[5]	Native Use[6]
Fragaria virginiana	x	x	F
broad-petalled strawberry			
Fritillaria lanceolata, chocolate lily	x	x	F
Goodyeara oblongifolia, rattlesnake plantain			M
Heuchera chlorantha, meadow alumroot			M
Hieracium cynoglossoides	sp.	x	f
houndstongue hawkweed			
Juncus effusus, common rush			t
Koeleria cristata, prairie junegrass	x	x	C
Lilium columbianum, tiger lily	x		F
Lomatium triternatum, nine-leaf lomatium	x		F
L. utriculatum, pomo-celery lomatium	x	x	f?
Madia exigua, minima, tarweeds	sp.		f?
Mentha arvensis, field mint	x		f
Perideridia gairdneri, Gairdner's yampah	x		F
Poa pratensis (2 more spp.), bluegrasses	sp.	x	C
Polypodium glycyrrhiza, licorise fern			m
Polystichum munitum, sword fern			T, f, m
Potentilla glandulosa, gland cinquefoil	sp.		f
Prunella vulgaris, self-heal	x	x	f
Pteridium aquilinum, bracken fern	x	x	F, t
Satureja douglasii,[7] yerba buena			f
Trifolium (four spp.), clovers	x		C
Trillium ovatum, white trillium			m
Viola adunca, early blue violet	x	x	m

Native use: C = forage foods of Cervids (deer and elk);F = food; M = medicine; T = technology. More important use given first; lower-case letters indicate that the species was relatively unimportant.

Additional Economically Useful Prairie Plants listed by James G. Cooper (1860)[4]

	Use	Environment
Trees		
Pinus contorta, lodgepole pine	T, F, m	DP
Taxus brevifolia, Pacific yew	T, M	B
Shrubs		
Ceanothus sanguineus, redstem ceanothus	C	B (Vancouver)
Lonicera involucrata, bearberry	t, C	WP
Philadelphus lewisii, mockorange	T, m	DP
Prunus emarginata, bittercherry	T, F	B

	Use	Environment
Ribes divaricatum, straggly gooseberry	F, M, t	B
Rosa gymnocarpa, dwarf wild rose	f	B
R. nutkana, common wild rose	F, M,t	DW
Rubus leucodermis, blackcap	F, t, c	DP, W
Sambucus cerulea, blue elderberry	F, t, m, c	DP
Spiraea douglasii, hardhack	t	WP
Vaccinium caespitosum, dwarf blueberry	F	P

Herbs

	Use	Environment
Agoseris glauca, mountain carrot	f	DP
Aquilegia formosa, columbine	f, m	DP
Chimaphila umbellata, common pipsissewa	m	DW
Cirsium undulatum, wavy-leaved thistle	F	DG (Columbia)
Conioselinum pacificum Pacific hemlock-parsley	f	WP
Disporum hookerii, Hooker's fairybell	f	P
Erythronium grandiflorum, avalanche lily	F	P
Fragaria vesca, woods strawberry	F	P
Galium triflorum, bedstraw	p	B
Geum triflorum, prairie smoke-avens	m	Whidbey Island
Heracleum lanatum, cow parsnip	F	WP (coast)
Hieracium scouleri, wooly-weed	f	BW
Osmorhiza occidentalis, western sweet-cicely	f	P
Plantago (two spp.), plantain	C, m	P (Chehalis)
Psoralea physodes, California tea	m	P
Stachys cooleyae, hedge nettle	f	"wet grounds"
Trifolium wormskjoldii, springbank clover	F	P
Vicea gigantea, giant vetch	f	"sand" (Steilacoom)

Use: C = forage foods of Cervids (deer and elk); F = food; M = medicine; P = perfume; T = technology. More important use given first; lower-case letters indicate that the species was relatively unimportant. Environment: B = borders; BW = burnt woods; DG = dry ground; DP = dry prairies; DW = dry woods; P = prairies; W = woods; WP = wet prairies.

Notes to Appendix

1. *Northwest Anthropological Research Notes* 13(2): 175–200.
2. Pp. 55–70 in "Report of the Botany of the Route," pp. 13–70 in vol. 12 of *Reports of Explorations and Surveys to Ascertain the Most Practicable and Economical Route for a Railroad from the Mississippi River to the Pacific Ocean . . ."* (36th Cong. 1st Sess., House Executive Document 56) (Serial Set no. 1055).
3. The base list is from Reid Schuller and James Barrett's "Native Flora of Glacial Outwash Prairies in the Vicinity of Pierce and Thurston Counties, Washington: A Hypothetical Reconstruction" (The Washington Natural Heritage Program, 1983). Schuller and Barrett compiled their list from several sources, both published and unpublished, dating between 1961 and 1982. Common names are from C. Leo Hitchcock's *Flora of the Pacific Northwest: an illustrated manual* (Seattle, 1973).
4. From James G. Cooper's "Plants Collected West of the Cascade Mountains during 1854–'55," pp. 55–70 in his "Report on the Botany of the Route." Only those plants listed as found on "prairie," "dry prairie," "wet prairie," "dry woods," and in a few cases geographically (Whidbey Island or Steilacoom; places outside Puget Sound if known locally as well) are included. Cooper's binomials are not always identifiable with modern scientific names. In some cases his originals have been identified successfully by Norton (1979), and are used here. "sp." in the Cooper column indicates that either unidentifiable species, or species other than those listed by Schuller and Barrett, are given on his list.
5. From Christopher Chappell and Rex Crawford, "Native Vegetation of the South Puget Sound Prairie Landscape," pp. 107–22 in Patrick Dunn and Kern Ewing, eds., *Ecology and Conservation of the South Puget Sound Prairie Landscape*, Seattle: the Nature Conservancy of Washington, 1997. Chappell and Crawford's list includes eighty species, both native and introduced, found in "contemporary prairie and oak woodland communities." Only those species occurring in the "Idaho fescue/White-top aster," "Oregon white oak/Long-stolon sedge-Camas," and "Oregon white oak/Snowberry/ Long-stolon sedge" communities are listed.
6. Standard ethnobotanical sources are used here. They include Erna Gunther's *Ethnobotany of Western Washington* (Seattle, 1973); Nancy Turner's *Plants in British Columbia Indian technology* (Victoria, 1979), *Food Plants of Coastal First Peoples* (Vancouver, 1995), and *Food Plants of Interior First Peoples* (Vancouver, 1997); and the "Environment" and "Ethnobiology and Subsistence" chapters of the *Northwest Coast* and *Plateau* volumes of the *Handbook of North American Indians* (1990, 1998). A notation indicates that the specific species was used by some, but not necessarily all, of the peoples of the two culture areas.
7. Listed as a prairie component only by Chappell and Crawford; not listed by Schuller and Barrett or Cooper.

Yards, Corridors, and Mosaics
How to Burn a Boreal Forest

Henry T. Lewis and Theresa A. Ferguson[1]

Introduction

Until shortly after World War II, Indians in northern Alberta regularly and systematically fired habitats to influence the local distribution and relative abundance of plant and animal resources. These habitat fires contributed to an overall fire mosaic that formerly characterized northern boreal forests. Cross-cultural comparisons of hunter-gatherer pyrotechnology in widely separated and different kinds of biological zones in North America and Australia reveal functionally parallel strategies in how habitat fires were employed, specifically in the maintenance of "fire yards" and "fire corridors."

The conifer forests of boreal Canada and Alaska, as well as those of the Rockies, Pacific Northwest, and Sierra Nevadas, have been termed "fire dependent ecosystems." In these forests, fire was a primary influence in determining both succession patterns and species composition, floral and faunal. And fire produced a clear pattern on the land, the "fire mosaic."

> The primeval landscape was a vast mosaic of stands in various age classes and successional stages following fires, interspersed with recently burned areas.[2]

Fire mosaics are shaped and structured by a complex set of variables including seasonality of burning, the frequency and intensity of individual fires, topography, fuel types and fuel diversity, the size of areas burned, the build-up of fuels, the conditions and fire histories of adjacent stands, and even the ecology of animals in affected areas. Studies in fire ecology can have considerable significance for anthropologists. They reveal how fire-influenced environments are especially well suited to hunting and gathering, and show that periodic fires can have important short- and long-term benefits.

> . . . any influence tending toward diversifying the landscape at large and small scales will *increase the diversity of the fauna as well as the population density of some species.* By maintaining a mosaic pattern in the boreal forest, fire assists in the maintenance of diverse wildlife populations. . . . The pattern and scale of burned and unburned patches is probably critical in determining the suitability of habitat for many species.[3]

Fires and the resulting fire mosaics are caused by both natural events (almost always lightning) and (to varying degrees) scheduled human activities. There is, however, an important difference in magnitude between natural and anthropogenic mosaics, specifically (as quoted above) in the "pattern and scale of burned and unburned patches." Natural fire mosaics are characterized by larger, less frequent, but usually hotter burned stands of vegetation; human-made fire mosaics (at least those fire-maintained by hunter-gatherers) entail smaller, more frequently, and more lightly burned patches of growth. These dissimilar characteristics result from the fact that natural and hunter-gatherer fires are set at different seasons and with different frequencies, and hunter-gatherer fires are set under essentially safer, managed conditions.[4]

In previous studies on northern Alberta,[5] our working assumption about Indian burning in the boreal forest region was that it represented an essentially small-scale, albeit more complex and intensified version of a natural fire mosaic. Our thinking was very much influenced by the interpretations of fire ecologists from such works as the Canadian Wildlife Service's 1977 compendium, *The Effects of Fire on the Ecology of the Boreal Forest*.[6] This and other more specifically focused studies provided us the biological background for our ethnographic inquiries and subsequent interpretations.

However, as a result of our more recent research in Australia and Wood Buffalo National Park, Alberta,[7] it appears that our working assumption of viewing human-made fire mosaics in northern Alberta as merely a more complex and intensified version of natural mosaics was far too simple.

A more appropriate model for Alberta's boreal forests comes from examples of how foragers used habitat burning in other parts of the world, particularly in more-or-less marginal environments in which primary productivity is relatively low. The Coast Range of northern California is one area of limited natural resources where indigenous burning practices have been studied.[8] The characteristic burning strategies found within this region involved the maintenance of what we call *fire yards* and *fire corridors*.

. . . *the most consistent pattern to emerge is that of summer burns in the higher elevation grasslands* [fire corridors] *of the coastal coniferous forest,* particularly in the inland areas away from the heaviest concentrations of redwoods. *Almost as consistent and certainly the most dramatic pattern to appear is that of opened grass "prairies"* [fire yards], *apparently within all elevations of the redwood and pine-fir sub-types in the northern Coast Range.* What these two patterns strongly indicate is the fact that the *Indians of this region had made a use of fire which involved a technologically sophisticated control of natural resources in a region in which the particular resources of forest plants and animals which they sought were not in great abundance.*[9]

As this paper will show, similar patterns are (or were) maintained by culturally unrelated groups of hunter-gatherers in quite disparate environmental settings, and all in areas of resource scarcity. In reassessing our work on the Indian fire regimes of northern Alberta, we feel that the following examples of hunter-gatherer uses of "fire yards" and "fire corridors" provide a sound comparative basis for constructing a more realistic model for interpreting indigenous burning practices in boreal forests and other regions of limited natural resources.

Prescribed Burning and the "Forest Primeval"

Although sounding somewhat contradictory, it is now accepted wisdom among fire ecologists that *prescribed* fires should be used to establish *natural* fire mosaics, at least in wilderness areas and in national parks where management can be practiced. The desirability of fire management in the northern boreal forests has been discussed in a number of published studies.[10] We must recognize that much of what is designated today as "wilderness" once was exploited and manipulated with fire by North American Indians.

The "virgin lands" first observed by Europeans in the sixteenth and seventeenth centuries were not an untouched wilderness. As several writers have noted, the "forest primeval" was a later, romanticized creation of the Euroamerican imagination. The forests, parklands, and prairies of North America already had been greatly influenced and actively managed by aboriginal peoples' widespread uses of fire.[11] The goals of Indian uses of habitat fires were predominantly technological, with the added awareness that fire is a tool of enormous potential and that it has complex and important ecological consequences.[12]

In addition to a number of ethnographic and ethnohistoric interpretations of North American Indian uses of fire, there is a significant body of comparable data on Australian Aborigines. Though the tropical and temperate rainforests, monsoon savannas, spinifex deserts, mulga scrubs, and eucalypt woodlands of the Australian continent are markedly different from North American biomes, the similarity of ways in which culturally and geographically distinct peoples have fire-managed these habitats is most impressive. Thus, though the boreal forests of northern Alberta could not be much farther removed from the temperate rainforests of southwestern Tasmania, the respective strategies in fire management are remarkably parallel.[13]

"Fire Yards" and "Fire Corridors"

The meanings implied in the terms *fire yards* and *fire corridors* are self-evident: fire yards are the openings or clearings (meadows, swales,[14] and lakeshores) within a forested area that are maintained by burning, while fire corridors are areas similarly maintained that make up the grass fringes of streams, sloughs, ridges, and trails. Our interviews revealed that both yards and corridors can be created by selected uses of fire if plant and edaphic conditions are appropriate, and that both types of areas are places in which animals alternately collect or traverse. For foraging peoples, the existence of fire yards and fire corridors provides both a greater abundance of plant-animal resources and a higher measure of hunting predictability.

Northwest California

As noted above, northwest California as a whole is a region of relative resource scarcity with a lower level of primary productivity. The Indian inhabitants of northwest California followed a pattern of firing both open areas within the forest and along grass-covered ridges. Fire simultaneously broke up the monotony of the forests and created economically useful areas. These "anthropogenic prairies"[15] were regularly burned in order to attract game from surrounding mature forest stands that were left purposefully unburned. Throughout the redwood forest belt, fires maintained fire yards and fire corridors and the economically useful plants that were found on them, preventing the open areas from being invaded by brush and trees. The resulting pattern was described by an early ethnographer of the Wiyot Indians in what is now Humboldt County:

> *Within the forests, at all elevations from sea level to the top of the ridges, there were* small open patches, known locally as *"prairies,"* producing grass, ferns, and various small plants. These prairies are too numerous to mention in detail . . . .*Most of these patches if left to themselves would doubtless soon have produced forests, but the Indians were accustomed to burn them annually* so as to gather various seeds, especially a species of sunflower . . . .The statement of Professor Jepson that "there is today more wooded area in Humboldt County than when the white man came over a half a century since," was confirmed by reports made to the writer that some of the old prairies had come up to young growth of forest. *These prairies were of incalculable value to the Indians, not alone for their vegetable products, but also for the game found upon them. A sharp contrast is drawn between the animal life in the forests and on these prairies* . . . ."[16]

This pattern of "prairies" (fire yards) and ridge tops (fire corridors) is strikingly different from what was carried out by some of the same Indians in drier, more resource-productive Douglas-fir-ponderosa pine forests on the inland side of the coastal ranges. It also differs significantly from the overall strategies of burning employed by Indians in the interior coniferous forests of the Sierra Nevada and Cascade Ranges, where understory burning was employed and a more characteristic mosaic pattern was maintained.[17]

Traditional burning practices were still recalled by a few northwest California Indians as recently as the early 1970s. A personal communication from ethnographer Richard A. Gould noted that the Tolowa and other Indians of the Klamath and Rogue River valleys burned selected areas and employed practices similar to those described for the 1800s and early 1900s:

> The term, "prairies," for the clearings in the redwood forest areas of northern California is really inappropriate, since most of these clearings are very small (the largest one I ever saw was only about ¼-mile long, and most are much smaller than that) . . . . *The Indians* (here I include Tolowa, Tututni, Yurok, Karok, and Wiyot) *did burn these areas over fairly often, and I think it would be fair to suggest that this burning helped to maintain these areas by inhibiting the growth of brush and trees.* These "prairies"—in all cases I have seen—did not contain any village or habitation sites, *since they lie within a zone of extremely poor natural resources for that region. However, these clearings are frequented by elk and deer, which the Indians there hunted whenever they could.*[18]

Finally, a forestry account from the 1930s notes the pattern for the region as a whole:

> The stories of old residents of the redwood region concerning the acts of the Indians are conflicting. Some believe that the Indians set the woods afire every season that there was a sufficient accumulation of litter to support a fire—every four or five years—and that *the course of an Indian traveling through the woods could be charted from a distance by the succession of smokes as he set fires.* Others say that the Indian was afraid of fire and set it only to drive game or to burn out his enemies, or that his prairie fires escaped into the woods.[19]

Western Washington

A similar situation has been described for western Washington by Helen H. Norton (1979) who, though working with a more limited number of historical accounts, includes supporting archaeological and botanical materials as well. Norton's thesis that the prairies and grasslands of western Washington were largely "anthropogenic" (shaped by man) is convincing and is supported by the functionally equivalent examples presented in this paper. In a later article (1983 and this volume), Norton and her colleagues describe a variety of what we call fire corridors, along a transmontane trail in south-central Washington.[20]

Norton includes an example for the Quileute Indians of the Olympic Peninsula for what it says about the frequency of burning and the kinds of areas involved.

> The burning of the fern year by year was what kept up the "prairies" of the peninsula and extended these areas. The Indians burned the ferns for the purpose of clearing out the prairies so they could shoot the deer and elk when they came to feed on young "fern sprouts."[21]

More impressive is the description provided by a mid-19th-century observer in the Puget Sound area:

> A few remarks are necessary upon the origin of the dry prairies so singularly scattered throughout the forest region. *Their most striking feature is the abruptness of the forests which surround them giving them the appearance of lands which have been cleared and cultivated for hundreds of years . . . .*The Indians, in order to preserve their open grounds for game, and for the production of their important root, the camas, soon found the advantage of burning . . . .On some prairies near Vancouver and Nisqually, where this burning has been prevented for twenty years past, young spruces are found to be growing up rapidly, and Indians have told me that they can remember when some other prairies were much larger than at present.[22]

Another historical reference to Indian fire in western Washington refers to large-scale burning on Whidbey Island northwest of Seattle. This involved the annual firing of the "greater portion" of the island's some 40,470 ha. Though effectively grasslands, Whidbey Island was rapidly taken over by Douglas-fir after the Indians were driven out by white settlers between 1850 and 1860:

> Whidbey Island, once largely deforested by the Indians' repeated "light burning," is now well forested with second growth Douglas-fir. It is a striking example of the ability of Douglas-fir quickly to reclaim lands long scourged by fire, after the periodic burning ceased . . . . Many of the Puget Sound Indians used the island for a hunting ground . . . . Deer were plentiful and large portions of the island were burned over annually to make better hunting. [My informant] recalls the time when areas now forested were treeless grass plains.[23]

Australia

Sylvia Hallam's 1985 paper, "The History of Aboriginal Firing," is a comprehensive critique of traditional aboriginal burning practices in Australia. Hallam's main concern is to refute several earlier studies that maintain that aboriginal fires had little or no effect upon the Australian landscape or differed little, in terms of results, from natural conflagrations.[24] She presents numerous examples from various parts of the continent of how Aborigines used habitat fires,[25] in order to demonstrate the considerable impact of aboriginal burning technology on natural environments, producing what she calls a "fine-grain mosaic" effect.

Hallam points out that fires were set in a variety of ways related to an overall set of climatic and environmental factors. She demonstrates that, in spite of important differences in the vegetational zones of Australia, as well as local differences in habitat types, there are basic similarities in the ways in which Aborigines fired "marginal places":

> Fire, then, could be most effective in marginal places—near the margin of the tropical rainforest (as at Lynch's Crater [Queensland]), or the eastern margin of the jarrah forest, as in Western Australian ethnohistorical sources, [and] in creating sclerophyll woodland in northwest Tasmania. *Firing could not and did not bring about major change in the core of the* [northern] *Queensland rainforest, the heart of the karri* [Western Australia], *the depths of the wet Tasmanian southwest . . . .It could and did create "clear patches" on the Bunya Mountains* [southern Queensland], *grassland corridor along valleys through the jarrah (e.g., the Chittering Valley or the Wooroloo Brook* [Western Australia]), *or maintain sedgeland corridors from the Cradle Mountain uplands to the coast in Tasmania.*[26]

Tasmania

Using a number of sources, the Australian historian Geoffrey Blainey (1976) described the overall impact of aboriginal fire technologies in Tasmania:

> The rainforest and its tangled undergrowth on the west coast is sometimes called "primeval," and the grassy valleys in the midlands are sometimes likened to an unchanged Garden of Eden . . . but it can scarcely be called primeval [since] in aboriginal times it was relatively open country and sufficiently grassed to attract game. *Other parts of the thick rainforest of the west coast were dissected in aboriginal times by tracks kept open by repeated burning;* when the Tasmanian aboriginals vanished the forest closed in, and ironically the tourist literature now describes it as impenetrable forest, parts of which have never been explored. There is strong evidence that some of the button grass plains and the sedgeland on the west coast, some of *the grassy patches at the headwaters of the north-flowing rivers,* and the parkland or grassland of the midlands were the result of the persistent burning by the Tasmanian aboriginals.[27]

Throughout the environmental zones of Tasmania, aboriginal burning resulted in a combination of yards, corridors, mosaics, and open grasslands. Like the temperate rainforests of northwestern America and western Canada, much of Tasmania is a poor region for hunting-gathering under natural conditions. Here again, fire was of singular importance in facilitating the growth of grasslands and increasing the abundance of animal life:

> *The regeneration after fires provides the conditions for rapid increases in animal populations* and the sclerophyll communities which they engender provide the niches for a wide spectrum of organisms. *Without fires this region of high rainfall would be almost destitute of animals.* Mature rainforest supports very little higher animal life and has virtually no forms which are specifically adapted to life within it. On the other hand, the sclerophyll communities carry a wide variety of crustaceans, insects, birds, reptiles, monotremes and marsupials.[28]

New South Wales

In other parts of Australia, Aborigines seasonally traversed a mix of habitat types which, when taken together, involved burning a combination of yards, corridors, mosaics, and open grasslands. As in Tasmania, but on a much smaller scale, the maintenance of yards and corridors appears to have been related directly to the relative abundance of natural resources in particular habitats. For instance, from the narrow coastal belt of wet sclerophyll forest between Norton Bay (Brisbane) and Port Jackson (Sydney), a mid-1840s explorer described yet another pattern of burning yards and corridors within a less-productive habitat type:

> The natives seem to have burnt the grass systematically along every watercourse and around every waterhole in order to have them surrounded with young grass as soon as the rain sets in . . . .Long strips of lately burnt grass are frequently observed, extending for many miles along the creeks. The banks of small, isolated waterholes in the forest were equally attended to . . . It is no doubt connected with the systematic management of their runs, to attract game to particular spots.[29]

Inland from the coastal belt, the country was a mix of habitat types: open forest, "impenetrable thickets," grassy woodlands, and treeless areas maintained by Aboriginal burning. In the Sydney area itself: "the trees were up to 30 m high, the forest or woodland lacked underwood and there was abundant tufted grass." These comments indicate that at the time of contact, the Sydney area was a parkland where Aborigines burned understory grasses. The parkland areas were adjacent to the coastal sclerophyll forest where fire yards and fire corridors also were maintained by Aboriginal burning.[30]

In 1836, long after the Aborigines had been eliminated from the Sydney area, another explorer noted:

> The omission of the annual periodical burning by natives, of the grass and young saplings, has already produced in the open forest lands

nearest to Sydney, thick forests of young trees, where, formerly, a man might gallop without impediment, and see whole miles before him. Kangaroos are no longer to be seen there; the grass is choked by underwood; neither are there natives to burn the grass, nor is fire longer desirable there amongst the fences of the settler.[31]

Northern Territory

Hallam's portrayal of a "fine-grain mosaic" applies most aptly to the environmental effects of hunter-gatherer practices in the monsoon savannas of the Northern Territory. Here, every three to four years, Aborigines burned almost all floodplains (90% and more), large sections of eucalypt woodlands (50% and more), tall open forests (30—35%), and escarpment vegetation (highly variable), all of which truly constitute a regional fire mosaic.[32] The only areas not burned were the small (usually no more than a few hectares in size) stands of tropical rainforest, paperbark swamps, and mangrove tidal flats. These areas of less fire-adapted vegetation are productively different from surrounding habitat types. Given their importance and their susceptibility to damage, they are fire-protected and left unburned. In the Northern Territory, whether monsoon tropics or central deserts, there is little aboriginal burning that fits the pattern of fire yards and fire corridors.

Aborigines did, and in some remote areas still do, create corridors in desert regions through which they passed, leaving more remote areas unburned. However, the scale of the burned areas is much greater and they are not created or maintained in the same way or for the same purposes as are the fire yards and corridors in temperate rainforest areas. Various researchers in the central deserts have stated that Aborigines show little concern with whether or not fires carry into old-growth unburned areas within their own territory. This apparent casualness contrasts markedly with the protection of small rainforest stands in the north.

From an examination of ethnographic and ethnohistoric data on North America and Australia, it seems evident that hunter-gatherers, whether living in marginal environments or only visiting less productive habitats, have developed parallel strategies for managing the relative abundance and regional distribution of plants and animals.

Northwestern Alberta[33]

The vegetation of northwestern Alberta changes progressively from where the Peace River enters the northwestern part of the province west of the small farm town of Hythe (55° 20N) to where it empties into Lake Athabasca and the Slave River near Fort Chipewyan (58° 46N) in the northeast. Along its course are several large prairies and aspen parklands that were, at the time of contact, kept open by Indian practices of burning.

Today, most of these areas include the prairie farmlands surrounding the towns of Grande Prairie, Valleyview, High Prairie, Spirit River, Fairview, Grimshaw, Peace River, and others. Further north, the prairies are smaller and more intermittent at such places as Manning, Paddle Prairie, Carcajou, La Crete, and Fort Vermilion. All of these prairies are associated primarily with solonetzic soils that have a high content of exchangeable sodium or magnesium. In many places the soils have become less saline due to leaching, a process known as "solodization." Current speculation suggests that the initial salinization of these soils dates to the period immediately following deglaciation. Solodization came later, proceeding at a rate dependent on both local and regional factors such as the height of the water table, the development of an integrated drainage, etc. With loss of soil salinity, fire would have become an important factor in maintaining these prairies.[34]

Among the few historical references to Indian burning on the prairies of the Upper Peace area of Alberta, the most extensive is by George M. Dawson, a biologist with the 1879 Canadian Pacific Railway survey party:

> Whatever theory be adopted, and many have been advanced, to account for the wide prairies of the western portion of America further to the south, the origin of the prairies of the Peace River is sufficiently obvious. There can be no doubt that they have been produced and are maintained by fires. The country is naturally a wooded one, and where fires have not run for a few years, young trees begin rapidly to spring up. The fires are, of course, ultimately attributable to human agency, and it is probable that before the country was inhabited by the Indians it was everywhere densely forest-clad.[35]

Ethnographic data support Dawson's theory on the maintenance of the prairies, but pedological data suggest he was wrong about their origins.

From the British Columbia border to Fort Vermilion, Indian burning practices seem to have differed primarily in the total area burned, largely a function of the amounts of prairie grasslands and parklands. In the west, at the time of contact, this probably ranged from 30 to 40% of the Grande Prairie-Peace River region to a much smaller total in the Fort Vermilion area of 2 to 3%.[36] Away from the Peace River and its major tributaries, and in all of the region east of Fort Vermilion, the "prairies" are little more than large meadows, usually adjacent to native settlements, and the soils are those characteristic of the northern boreal forest. Within the boreal forest itself are still smaller, more widely scattered meadows.

In the boreal forest of the far north, Indians continued to burn as recently as the early 1950s. The places most frequently mentioned as being fired were meadows: "hay meadows" near settlement areas and smaller meadows and swales scattered throughout hunting and gathering territories. In addition to these, fires were set along traplines and trails, around lakes and ponds, and within windfall or deadfall forests. A Beaver (Dunne-za) woman described the general patterns of burning in northernmost Alberta in some detail:

> They use to burn places where they think it was very useful. Like, for instance, the places where the horses used to winter in order to have plenty of good feed for them on grass; and then where there's lakes, around lakes, where there's muskrats, so that [the muskrats] could always have real fresh roots. Places where there's moose and where the moose usually like to roam around; they burn the brushes there so that they'll have good green leaves and things to live on in summer.
>
> They used to start burning when there was still snow, here and there, and some of the youngsters just ride on horses and they set matches, you know. That's how they burnt. They don't wait until its really dry because its dangerous. And, lighting [the grasses on] traplines there will be just about two of them and yet the fire's not dangerous. They just burn the areas they want. And, places where the Indians live close to, there'll be brushes like you see around, poplars growing in one place, eh. That's where they used to burn.
>
> Sloughs, where there's muskrats, that's where they used to burn. And where there's heavy brush, like a windfall and things like that, all of the young trees would grow, to attract the animals like moose. Where there's timber and moss they don't burn, of course, because the fire lasts and lasts and it's not good for fur bearing animals like pine martens and mink and lynx; that's where they mostly stay in winter, so they don't want to destroy that. They must be very wise, eh? Those people? That time?

In the more southern and western parts of the Peace River Basin, the overall fire mosaic at the time of contact would have been composed of large areas of prairies and parklands, fringed to the north, south, and east by large, variously aged stands of boreal forests. Toward the north and as far east as Fort Vermilion, the pattern would have changed gradually to more limited areas of smaller prairies and large meadows. Throughout the whole region, surrounding the prairies and parklands in the south and the meadows and forest openings in the north, there would have been a mosaic of forest stands primarily caused by natural fires.

Away from the small prairies and meadows, Indians fire-managed the plant and animal resources associated with trapping and trapline hunting. Traplines generally follow the meandering courses of creeks and sloughs where grasses provide food for herbivores, animals as disparate in size as mice and moose. The abundance and variety of these species directly influences the numbers of fur-bearing predators, and fires were used throughout the drainage areas of the boreal forest to affect the relative abundance of both. As an elderly Slavey (Dene-thah) trapper from the Hay Lakes region described it:

> In times past, people knew where to trap animals—mink, weasel, marten, lynx, lots of kinds. It makes a lot of difference for the trapper if an area was once burned. People know where to hunt. Our people have a name for those burned places in the forest called *go-ley-day*. They tell one another about those places and when to hunt there.

The timing of these burns was related to the return of fur trappers in the early spring, when the grassy areas were sufficiently dry and the surrounding forests were still too wet to burn. In some cases, where grasses had not sufficiently dried, Indians would set and leave campfires with one or more smoldering logs extending into the grasses; these delayed fuses later would ignite the area, sometimes days after their departure. As one Indian trapper noted:

> When we'd come off trapline it might be too wet to burn the sloughs or creeks (creekbeds). So we'd just build a big campfire and leave it. Maybe couple weeks later even, when the grass is really dry, the grasses would all get burned up, but the fire couldn't go anywhere because it was still damp in the bush.

Trapline fires left meandering lines of smokes as individual trappers fired streamside grasses on their way out to the larger streams and rivers, where trails joined. An Oblate priest described seeing trappers' fires in the Fort Vermilion are in the 1930s.

> From (Fort Vermilion) you could see the slopes of the Caribous (Caribou Mountains) and you could see the smokes, a string of fires, that the Indian trappers were setting as they came in the spring. You knew they were on their way home then. It was a grand sight!

An elderly Slavey from Meander River Reserve mentioned the trapper pattern of burning and the results of fire exclusion practices.

> Trappers burned when they were on their way home from spring hunting. At that time of year it was safe and they burned because it made it better for them in the winter with more animals to hunt and trap for. Nowadays you can't burn on the trapline because it's against the law, and it's not so good as before.

The regular firing of trapline corridors and yards was recognized as an integral, necessary feature of a hunting-trapping strategy. As has been shown for hunter-gatherers elsewhere in the world, the Indians of northern Alberta understood, and many still understand, the complex networks of plant-herbivore-predator relationships. The comments by informants often reflected the broader understandings about the connections between fire, plants, animals, and human practices. The following statements by older Slavey

Indians in the Hay Lakes-Meander River areas concern the systematic relationships between grasslands and forests.

> We made fire there by small creeks. All the grass burns. Then its good for the beaver. New white poplar would come out and the beavers like to eat that.

> A burn attracts all kinds of animals, especially the moose. In three years time the trees grow really fast and the moose like that too. If you burn in spring, the moose will be there in fall. When they burned, the people say, "I will hunt there." And they argue about it because they all know it will be good hunting.

> I did that burning by my trapline where the grass is growing. It's good for fox and lynx. They like eating rabbits and mice and they are in grassy places.

> Lots of animals that live in the forest come to the meadows and sloughs to hunt. Marten, like, they live in the woods but they hunt lots in the grassy places—specially mice. So you don't want to burn the woods, just the sloughs and meadows. Now, course, we don't burn any of it.

> Burning sloughs was also good for foxes. When you get thick grass all bent over it's hard for the fox to dig down to get the mice, and the foxes are really hungry that time of year (spring). When you burn it off, well sure you kill lots of mice—maybe hundreds; you can hear them in the fire but they come back by the thousands. Then it's easy for the fox to get the mice and we get lots of foxes too.

> Do you know that wolves hunt mice? I saw this one (wolf). Real funny. He was jump'n up and down, crazy like. He was catch'n mice. It was so funny I forgot to shoot'm. I laughed so loud he saw me and run away. He was catch'n mice along a creek we'd burned that year.

Within the surrounding boreal forest and areas of muskeg, small openings were maintained, in some cases "created." Sites were selected on the basis of existing vegetation, an indication of appropriate soils for the growth of desired grasses and shrubs.

> You could make a little grassy area some places in the muskeg. When you were on trapline in the winter you go (back) there and look for moose, cause they find those places and they like'm. It gotta be the right kind of place or the grass and brushes don't grow. The little white mosses grow there.

The apparent casualness with which people approached spring burning belied their understanding of how fires are controlled. "We didn't watch over the fire. Every time (in the spring) we came to a prairie in the bush, we made a fire there."

The only sections of forest intentionally burned were deadfall or windfall areas. These all but impenetrable areas were fired for essentially two reasons: they are devoid of game (except for some game birds that are all but impossible to shoot or retrieve), and they pose a serious danger to surrounding live forest if ignited by late summer lightning storms. As with meadows, deadfall areas could be burned under safer conditions in the spring and well before the onset of more dangerous burning conditions in summer. If the plant-soil associations were appropriate, deadfalls might be maintained as additional yarding areas through repeated spring burning.

When you burn the deadfall places it burns for a long time, not like the meadows—they burn out fast. Because there's all those dead trees. Maybe the next year you come back, burn it some more and then pretty soon it's all open and the moose really like those places.

In addition to the maintenance of traplines, fire was used to keep trails open. A former employee of the Alberta Forest Service described his observations of Indians burning along trails during the late 1920s.

I realized that those (trailside) fires weren't going to go anywhere. They (the Indians) only did it in the spring and the fire burned to the wetter stuff and went out . . . and that's the way they kept trails open through the muskeg areas.

Indian informants described similar examples of maintaining trails.

On a trail you set a fire and the following year, when you return to the same trail and there's new growth, that's where all the moose are. As I burned there in the fall, I would return in the spring—maybe five moose.

We used to make fire where there is too much brush to walk easily. After we burn, we could walk. Then, in fall time, we would go there to hunt moose.

Finally, marshes and lakeshores were fired to maintain them in stages of productive new growth as the preferred habitats of muskrats and water fowl, all important as a source of protein, the muskrat having an added attraction as a prime source of furs. Burning was carried out before nesting began.

We always burned just before all of the snow melted, before the ducks had started to nest. But we didn't burn after the ducks had nested; we knew when to burn and when not to burn. The spring fires made things good for the ducks, and it was good for all kinds of other animals too.

A lot of the burning was around the lakes, especially to make it better for the ducks. The ducks like the fresh roots that come in after a fire. They get, like, little potato-things, real sweet, that they like to eat.

There's still lots of ducks around, but not like they were before. There was lots more of them then.

Muskrats like to eat the grass roots, like the reeds that grow round a lake or pond. When you burn them the roots grow more and it makes it good for the muskrats. If it don't burn regular then it don't grow—it gets all choked up, dead stuff—and not so many muskrats.

Conclusion

At the time of contact, the overall mosaic of fire in northernmost Alberta included a combination of natural and human-made patterns. The pattern deriving from natural fires included large to very large "patches" of varying aged forests, which were primarily the consequence of lightning fires.[37]

In the same areas, standing out in contrast to the pattern of natural fire mosaics, were the Indian patterns of burning fire yards ("hay meadows" and small forest openings) and fire corridors (traplines, trails, streams, and lakesides). The Indian practice of burning windfall forests was similar to the natural patterning of fires, but only in that it involved relatively large areas of forest.

The combined natural and human-made boreal forest mosaics of Alberta were different from the more pronounced human-made mosaics described for temperate zones in Northeastern North America, California, and the Plains. Boreal Alberta burning most resembled the patterns of hunter-gatherer burning in the temperate rainforest zones of the Pacific Northwest and Australia.[38]

Our discussion of the pattern of yards and corridors has been at the most general level, without consideration of variations that occur within such a pattern. The spatial and temporal dimensions of variability include climate, fire, vegetation history, and even economic and socio-political factors. Given the variability within the Canadian boreal forest zone, specific patterns of burning must have varied from one boreal forest subtype to another as well.

In this respect, our research in northwestern Alberta may be considered as a "type site" for how fires have been used in the western boreal forest region. References for the more northern boreal forest support the concept of a yard-and-corridor pattern of burning,[39] but these do not provide the detailed regional information necessary for detailed comparison. Unfortunately, little research has been done to document the native use of prescribed burning elsewhere in the boreal forest, and historic references are sketchy and difficult to evaluate.

Viewed cross-culturally, the employment of functionally parallel solutions to similar problems in biologically different and geographically distant settings appears to represent a significant techno-ecological development by that category of people we classify as hunter-gatherers. An earlier study found parallels in the ways that North American Indians and Australian Aboriginal hunter-gatherers managed and manipulated the seasonality, frequency, intensity, and selectivity of habitat fires.[40] The cross-cultural similarities in "fire yards" and "fire corridors" we have noted here represent additional parallels in the human technology of fire, what anthropologist Julian Steward might have seen as examples of "multilinear evolution." That such cross-cultural parallels should exist, however, is perhaps less surprising than how long it has taken anthropologists to recognize them.

Beyond the broad similarities in the patterns of burning of the boreal forest region of northwestern Alberta and those of northwest California, western Washington, Tasmania, and a coastal portion of New South Wales, there also are important differences in the ways that the Alberta Indians came to terms with and manipulated boreal forests. Among the more important is the fact that northern forests, unlike temperate rainforests, are subjected to a much greater impact from natural fires. Fire ecologists have noted that

> Fire is an integral feature of the northern forest environment . . . (and) the widely distributed boreal broad leaf trees and conifers are well adapted to it.
>
> In the North, where there are still large uninhabited landscapes, lightning tends to ignite a greater proportion of fires than in more densely inhabited temperate regions. Lightning-ignited fires in remote areas under very dry conditions may quickly reach a large size, and suppression techniques are generally not effective, even if equipment and personnel are available.[41]

The boreal forests of Alberta also are similar to the forest areas of temperate regions in that primary production rates are relatively low. However, the distinctive pattern of natural fires and the corresponding adaptations of plants in the boreal forests have meant that the indigenous peoples of the Canadian north have had to develop a somewhat different burning strategy from that of hunter-gatherers in temperate forests. An important feature of hunting-gathering-trapping technologies in the Canadian north has been the employment of yards and corridors *alongside* the pattern of a natural fire mosaic, as a technique for attracting relatively scarce game to fire-maintained areas. In forested areas themselves, boreal Indian fires had relatively little effect other than burning windfalls and limiting the encroachment of trees into grasslands.

Our view is that lightning-caused fires, given their distribution and frequency, would have provided both advantages and disadvantages: advantages in terms of a regular forest recycling (perhaps every 80–90 years[42]), but disadvantages (in human terms) considering their unpredictability, intensity, and extent. Because of the essentially closed cover of boreal forests, understory burning (such as that carried out in the ponderosa pine forests of California or interior southeast British Columbia) was not possible, and (except in areas of windfall) they were precluded from management. Thus, the utilization and maintenance of yards and corridors in meadows, streamsides, sloughs, swales, lakeshores, and trails was an effective compromise within a region where, given a hunting-gathering technology, an overall man-made mosaic was not possible.

The role of fire in the wide range of geographical settings from around the world is infinitely variable and complex. Nevertheless, our data show important cross-cultural and intergeographical parallels in the ways in which hunter-gatherers use habitat fires. The use of fire to maintain corridors and yards in regions of low primary production clearly is a feature shared by hunter-gatherers in distinct regions and different parts of the world. It recalls the parallel patterns in hunter-gatherer use of fire seasonality, frequency, selectivity, and intensity of fires noted in an earlier paper.[43] In northern Canada (as elsewhere), native peoples have adapted the burning of fire corridors and fire yards to an environment in which natural fire is a continuing and integral factor.

Originally published in Human Ecology 16(1): 57–77 (1988)

Notes

1. We would like to thank Ross Wein for his comments and suggestions on this paper, especially his ideas about the characteristics of fire mosaics as they would occur under natural conditions in boreal forests. We also are indebted to several granting agencies for funds that supported our earlier research. They include the Social Sciences and Humanities Research Council; the Museum of Man, Fire Science Center (University of New Brunswick); the Boreal Institute for Northern Studies (University of Alberta); the Australian Institute for Aboriginal Studies; and the Northern Australian Research Unit (Australian National University).
2. Miron Heinselman, "The natural role of fire in northern conifer forests," pp. 61–72 in Charles Slaughter, Richard Barney, and George Hansen, eds., *Fire in the Northern Environment—A Symposium* (Portland, 1971), 61.
3. J. S. Rowe and G. W. Scotter, "Fire in the Boreal Forest" (*Quaternary Research* 3(3): 444–61, 1973), 458.
4. Henry Lewis, "A Time for Burning" (*Boreal Institute for Northern Studies Occasional Publication* No. 17, 1982b).
5. Theresa Ferguson, Productivity and Predictability of Resource Yield: Aboriginal Controlled Burning in the Boreal Forest (M.A. thesis, University of Alberta, 1979); Henry Lewis, "Maskuta: the ecology of Indian fires in northern Alberta" (*Western*

Canadian Journal of Anthropology 7(1): 15–52, 1977), "Indian fires of spring" (*Natural History* 89: 76–83, 1980), and "A Time for Burning."

6. John Kelsall, E. S. Telfer, and Thomas Wright, eds., "The Effects of Fire on the Ecology of the Boreal Forest, with Particular Reference to the Canadian North: A Review and Selected Bibliography" (*Canadian Wildlife Serivce Occasional Paper* No. 32, 1977).

7. Henry Lewis, "Fire technology and resource management in aboriginal North American and Australia," pp. 45–67 in Nancy Williams and Eugene Hunn, eds., "Resource Managers: North American and Australian Hunter-Gatherers" (*AAAS Selected Symposium* No. 67, 1982a); and "Burning the 'top end': Kangaroos and cattle," pp. 21–32 in Julian Ford, ed., "Fire Ecology and Management in Western Wilderness Australian Ecosystems" (*Western Australian Institute of Technology [WAIT] Environmental Studies Group Report* No. 14, 1985b); Theresa Ferguson, "Progress report to the Boreal Institute for Northern Studies" (ms., 1986). Since the original publication of this paper, Henry Lewis also has authored "Ecological and Technological Knowledge of Fire: Aborigines versus park rangers in Northern Australia" (*American Anthropologist* 91(4): 940–61, 1989).

8. See Henry Lewis, "Patterns of Indian Burning in California: Ecology and Ethnohistory" (orig. 1973; reprinted as pp. 55–116 of Thomas Blackburn and Kat Anderson, eds., *Before the Wilderness: Environmental Management by Native Californians* (Menlo Park, CA, 1993); on the primary productivity of the area see Martin Baumhoff, "Ecological determinants of aboriginal California populations" (*University of California Publications in American Archaeology and Ethnology* 49(2): 155–236, 1963).

9. Lewis, "Patterns of Indian Burning in California," 70.

10. See James Lotan *et al.*, "Proceedings, Symposium and Workshop on Wilderness Fire" (*USDA Forest Serivce General Technical Report* INT 182, 1985). For a review and evaluation of fire management studies up to 1983, see Martin Alexander and Dennis Dube, "Fire Management in Wilderness Areas, Parks, and Other Nature Reserves," pp. 273–97 in Ross Wein and David MacLean, eds., *The Role of Fire in Northern Circumpolar Ecosystems* (New York, 1983).

11. On the definition of "wilderness" and the effect of Indian fire on pre-White environments, see Gordon Day, "The Indian as an ecological factor in the northeastern forest" (*Ecology* 34(2): 329–46, 1953); Omer Stewart, "The forgotten side of ethnogeography," pp. 221–48 in Robert Spencer, ed., *Method and Perspective in Anthropology* (Minneapolis, 1954); and Stephen Pyne, *Fire in America: A Cultural History of Wildland and Rural Fire* (orig. 1982; Seattle, 1997), and "Vestal fires and virgin lands: a historical perspective on fire and wilderness," pp. 254–62 in James Lotan, "Proceedings, Symposium and Workshop on Wilderness Fire."

12. Henry Lewis, "Why Indians burned: specific versus general reasons," pp. 75–86 in James Lotan (*ibid.*). Whether or not Indian uses of habitat management were "ecologically sound" or "environmentally destructive" is not at issue here, and there certainly is no reason to assume that all Indians employed fire equally or effectively, however one defines "equally" or "effectively." Nonetheless, most of what North American Indians did with respect to affecting local environments appears to have worked effectively, over long periods of time, for hunting and gathering adaptations.

13. The list of studies on indigenous uses of fire in Australia is too long to detail here, but for most references the reader can consult Sylvia Hallam, "The history of

aboriginal firing," pp. 7–20 in Julian Ford, *Fire Ecology and Management in Western Australian Ecosystems* (1985); and Henry Lewis, "Burning the 'top end': kangaroos and cattle," also in Ford (*ibid.*, pp. 21–32). For a comparison of indigenous North American and Australian burning regimes, see Lewis, "Fire technology and resource management in aboriginal North America and Australia," pp. 45–67 in Williams and Hunn, *Resource Managers.*

14. The word "swale" derives from the Old English *swelan*, to burn.

15. The term is from Helen H. Norton, "The Association between Anthropogenic Prairies and Important Food Plants in Western Washington" (*Northwest Anthropological Research Notes* 13(2): 175–200, 1979).

16. Llewellyn Loud, "Ethnogeography and archaeology of the Wiyot territory" (*University of California Publications in American Archaeology and Ethnology* 14(3): 221–423, 1918) (emphasis added).

17. Lewis, "Patterns of Indian Burning in California," 60–70.

18. Quoted in Lewis (*ibid.*), 69; emphasis added.

19. Emanuel Fritz, "The role of fire in the redwood region" (*Journal of Forestry* 29(6): 939–50, 1931); emphasis added.

20. The two papers are Helen H. Norton, "The Association between Anthropogenic Prairies and Important Food Plants in Western Washington" (1979); and Helen Norton, Robert Boyd, and Eugene Hunn, "The Klikitat Trail of South-Central Washington: A reconstruction of seasonally used resource sites" (1983 and [revised], this volume).

21. From Albert Reagan, "Plants Used by the Hoh and Quileute Indians" (*Transactions of the Kansas Academy of Science* 37: 55–70, 1934), as quoted in Norton 1979, p. 178. Norton notes that the observer's comment about "fern sprouts" probably was wrong, as they can be toxic to game. Probably another species was intended.

22. James G. Cooper, partially quoted from Norton 1979, 179. The original citation is in James G. Cooper, *Reports of explorations and surveys to . . . the Pacific Ocean in 1853–55* (Washington, 1860), 23. Emphasis added in this excerpt.

23. Floyd Moravets, "Second Growth Douglas Fir Follows Cessation of Indian Fires" (*USDA Forest Service, Service Bulletin* 16(20): 3, 1932). I am grateful to Martin E. Alexander, Northern Forest Research Center, Canadian Forestry Service, Edmonton, for bringing this reference to my attention. See also Richard White, "Indian land use and environmental change: Island County Washington" (1975 and this volume) on the Whidbey Island prairies.

24. The complete citation for "The History of Aboriginal Firing" is in footnote 13 above. Among the earlier studies are Robin Clark, "Bushfires and vegetation before European settlement," pp. 61–73 in Peter Stanbury, ed., *Bushfires: Their Effect on Australian Life and Landscape* (Sydney, 1981) and "Pollen and charcoal evidence for the effects of Aboriginal burning on the vegetation of Australia (*Archaeology in Oceania* 18: 32–37, 1983); P. H. Nicholson, "Fire and the Australian Aborigine: an enigma," pp. 55–76 in Arthur Gill, ed., *Fire and the Australian Biota* (Canberra, 1981); and D. R. Horton, "The burning question: The Aborigines, fire and Australian ecosystems" (*Mankind* 13: 237–57, 1982a), and "Water and woodland: The peopling of Australia" (*Australian Institute of Aboriginal Studies Newsletter* 16: 21–27, 1982b).

25. Including her own *Fire and Hearth: a study of Aboriginal usage and European usurpation in southwestern Australia* (Canberra, 1975); Rhys Jones, "Fire stick

farming" (*Australian Natural History* 16: 224–28, 1969), and "The Neolithic, Paleolithic and the hunting garderners: Man and land in the antipodes," pp. 21–34 in Richard Suggate and M. M. Cresswell, eds., *Quaternary Studies: Selected papers from the IX INQUA Congress, Christchurch . . . 1973* (Wellington, 1975); Kevin Kiernan, Rhys Jones, and Don Ransom, "New evidence from Fraser Cave for Glacial Age of Man in south-west Tasmania (*Nature* 301: 28–32, 1983); Lewis, "Fire technology and resource management..." and "A Time for Burning"; Harry Lourandos, "10,000 years in the Tasmanian Highlands" (*Australian Archeologist* 16: 39–47, 1983); and Norman Tindale, "Ecology of primitive Aboriginal man in Australia," pp. 36–51 in Allen Keast, ed., "Biogeography and Ecology in Australia" (*Monographiae Biologicae* 8, 1959).

26. Hallam, "The history of aboriginal firing," 15 (emphasis added).

27. Geoffrey Blainey, *Triumph of the Nomads: A History of Aboriginal Australia* (Woodstock NY, 1976), 79 (emphasis added).

28. W. D. Jackson, "Fire, air, water and earth: An elemental ecology of Tasmania" (*Proceedings, Ecological Society of Australia* 3: 9–16, 1968), 9 (emphasis added).

29. Ludwig Leichardt, *Journal of an Overland Expedition in Australia, from Moreton Bay to Port Essington . . . during the Years 1844–1845* (London, 1847).

30. On the natural vegetation of Sydney, see J. A. Burrell, "Vegetation of the Sydney area: 1788 and 1961" (*Proceedings, Ecological Society of Australia* 17: 71–78, 1980).

31. Thomas Mitchell, *Three Expeditions into the Interior of Eastern Australia* (London, 1838), 413.

32. C. D. Haynes, "Man's firestick and God's lightning: Bushfire in Arnhemland" (paper presented to the ANZAAS 52nd Congress, Sydney, 1982) and "The pattern and ecology of Munway: Traditional Aboriginal fire regimes in North Central Arnhemland (paper presented at the wet-Dry tropics Symposium, Darwin, 1983); Lewis, "Fire technology and resource management . . ." (1982a), "Burning the 'top end'" (1985b), and "Ecological and Technological Knowledge of Fire . . ." (1988)

33. References for this section are drawn from Lewis, "Maskuta" (1977), and "A Time for Burning" (1982b); and Ferguson, "Productivity and Predictability of Resource Yield . . ." (1979).

34. S. W. Reeder and W. Odnysky, "Morphological and chemical characteristics of the solonetzic soils of northwestern Alberta" (*Canadian Journal of Soil Science* 44: 22–33, 1964); S. Pawluk (personal communication).

35. Dawson as quoted in John Macoun, *Manitoba and the Great North-West* (Guelph, 1882), 125.

36. These estimates are based roughly on the amounts of grassland and farmlands in the two areas.

37. Given this combination of natural and man-made fires and the overall reduction of fuels, it is probable that past fires were somewhat smaller, more frequent, and consequently less intense. Older Indian informants maintain that, largely because of fire exclusion practices and the build-up of fuel levels, fires (natural or caused by human activities) are now much larger and more dangerous than they were in the past.

38. Day, "The Indian as ecological factor in the north-eastern forest"; Lewis, "Patterns of Indian Burning in California"; Omer Stewart, "Forest-fires with a purpose" (*Southwestern Lore* 20(5): 42–46, 1954a) and "Why were the prairies treeless?" (*Southwestern Lore* 20(11): 59–64, 1954b); Norton "The Association

between Anthropogenic Prairies and Important Food Plants . . ."; Blainey, *Triumph of the Nomads*; Hallam, *Fire and Hearth,* and *"The history of aboriginal firing"*; Jackson, "Fire, air, water and earth . . ."; and Jones, "Fire stick farming."

39. See Charles Camsell and Wyatt Malcolm, "The Mackenzie River Basin" (*Geological Survey of Canada Memoir* 108, No. 92, 1919), 49; and Jean Michea, "Les Chitra-Gottineke: Essai de Monographie d'un Groupe Athapascan des Montagnes Rocheuses" (*National Museum of Canada Bulletin* no. 190, *Anthropological Series* no. 60, *Contributions to Anthropology,* Part 2, 1960), 60.

40. Lewis, "Fire technology and resource management in aboriginal North America and Australia" (1982a).

41. The first quotation is from J. S. Rowe, "Spruce and fire in northwest Canada and Alaska" (*Annual Proceedings, Tall Timbers Fire Ecology Conference* 10: 245–55, 1970), 245; the second appears in Wein and Maclean, *The Role of Fire in Northern Circumpolar Ecosystems,* 10.

42. Ongoing studies in Wood Buffalo National Park in Alberta show that fire frequencies in an area near Fort Smith have ranged from one fire every 35 to 55 years (*Annual Report of Research and Activities, Fire Science Center* [Fredericton, NB, 1985], 11.)

43. Lewis, "Fire technology and resource management in aboriginal North America and Australia."

"Time to Burn"
Traditional Use of Fire to Enhance Resource Production by Aboriginal Peoples in British Columbia

Nancy J. Turner[1]

Introduction

When they used to burn that grass above timberline they used to say
the Indian Potatoes [*Claytonia lanceolata*] were as big as your fist. Now
they are only that big [i.e., small], because they are not cultivated."
(Baptiste Ritchie, Mount Currie Stl'atl'imx speaker, May 1977).[2]

T he use of fire to maintain certain habitat conditions and enhance
the production of important resource plants and animals has been
practiced widely in human societies. One authority states, "All human
groups know fire, and most use it to clear the land for food production or
similar purposes." In Native North America, landscape fire was used to clear
vegetation and enhance the growth of certain plant and animal species, as
well as for various other purposes, and is well documented for many regions
of the continent, including the northeastern forests, the northern plains; the
boreal forest, particularly northern Alberta and Alaska; the interior west; and
western and central Washington and Oregon to California.[3]

In British Columbia, aboriginal burning practices are less well known,
although it is recognized that forest and meadowland fires were common and
widespread in prehistoric times, and that at least some fires were intentionally
set by indigenous peoples. The early aboriginal peoples and white settlers of
British Columbia, for example, have been called "the first game managers
. . . for they discovered that openings in the forest cover very often resulted
not only in a better crop of berries but also in the presence of a larger population
of deer." An 1859 surveyor in the upper Skagit area (now Manning Provincial
Park) noticed that Indian hunting groups deliberately set fire to the forest "to
clear the woods from underbrush and make travel easier." More recently, an
archaeologist contemplated the role of intentional landscape burning in the
vegetation of the Stl'atl'imx (Lillooet) area:

A striking feature of the regeneration of this burn (on Fountain Ridge
in 1931) is the dominance of evenly-spaced *Amelanchier alnifolia*

[saskatoon] in the shrub stratum. The abundance of this species is greater here than that observed elsewhere in the study area. It is interesting to speculate on the potential importance of such burns as berry gathering areas to the Stl'atl'imx people, and to the possibility that fires may have been deliberately set in order to create them.[4]

In this paper, various written reports and oral accounts of traditional burning practices from different regions of the province are compiled to show the physical and cultural extent of vegetation burning in British Columbia and to give some indication of the effects such burning may have had on the vegetation, particularly on the productivity of wild plant food resources. The term "landscape burning" is used here to distinguish large-scale intentional vegetation burning from the small, restricted fires used by aboriginal peoples for warmth, cooking, drying and smoking foods, smoke-tanning hides, preparing medicines, felling trees, or wood working.

Setting

British Columbia is vast and extremely diverse ecologically. Fourteen biogeoclimatic zones have been described on the basis of vegetation, climate, and geographical features. The indigenous peoples of the province, whose homelands fall within these zones, are culturally and linguistically complex. There are about 190 bands of first peoples within at least thirty distinct indigenous language groups, which are in turn classified within seven language families. Three major cultural divisions are recognized—Pacific Coast, Plateau, and Mackenzie River—and within these divisions there is a tremendous richness and variety of cultural features.[5]

Given this great environmental and cultural complexity, it must be stressed that firm records of aboriginal landscape burning as reported here are scattered and sparse, and do not necessarily prove that controlled burning of vegetation was a universal practice in British Columbia. Nevertheless, the range and extent of the records indicate more than just casual or sporadic use of fire to enhance resources.

Since organized fire suppression began in the northwestern United States and Canada in the early 1900s[6] and has continued to the present, most of the recollections of traditional landscape burning practices are from older records, or from elders of indigenous communities who participated in vegetation burning as youngsters, witnessed their relatives or others practicing it, or were told about it by their own elders.

Causes of Landscape Fires

There are many records of prehistoric and early historic landscape fires, as shown by dendrochronological studies, charcoal in soil profiles, and eyewitness accounts from early travelers and land surveyors.[7] Of course, not all nor even most of these fires were intentionally set. Lightning starts many fires each year, and accidental forest fires caused by unextinguished campfires or untended signal fires also have occurred regularly in the historic period. One can assume that they also occurred prehistorically. Historical references from western Montana indicate that haphazard ignitions were common and that aboriginal landscape fires often were set arbitrarily.[8]

Sometimes, too, intentional landscape fires were set by aboriginal peoples for purposes other than direct resource enhancement. For example, during a hunting expedition in the Cassiar Mountains of northwestern British Columbia in the early part of the century, the Tahltan guide set several grass fires in order to approach a herd of caribou downwind under the cover of the smoke. He claimed that his people always used this tactic under those circumstances.[9] Driving off mosquitoes and other insect pests, eliminating unwanted snakes, driving game in hunting, obtaining edible insects, clearing campsites and village sites of brush, clearing trails, improving communication, improving visibility, offense and defense in war, protecting forests from crown fires, and creating future supplies of dry fuelwood are other reasons given for intentional landscape burning by aboriginal peoples in British Columbia and neighboring areas.[10]

Evidence suggests that the frequency of landscape fires increased dramatically within the historic period. White explorers, travelers, prospectors, miners, ranchers, and settlers had their own reasons for landscape burning. Deliberately set fires were used by non-native people for hunting, eliminating insect pests, and creating supplies of dry fuelwood. Fire clearing of land also was practiced on a vast scale to facilitate mineral exploration, to allow agriculture, and to promote the growth of grass for domestic livestock.[11] To demonstrate the effect of non-natives on the landscape, geologist and naturalist George M. Dawson (1886) compared Crows Nest Pass, which at the time of his writing had been used for a few years by White travelers, with "North Kootanie" Pass, running parallel to the Crows Nest and " . . . scarcely used, except by the Indians." Whereas the former was "entirely destroyed" by fire, the woods of the latter were "generally unburnt."[12] It is estimated that 75% of interior forests of British Columbia have been burned over within the past century. This is despite the policy of active fire suppression as expressed as early as 1918 in *Forests of British Columbia*: "In the development of a forest administration, such as that in British Columbia, the first efforts, as is natural, are directed towards protection against fire and towards the collection of revenue . . . ."[13]

During his travels through British Columbia in the 1870s, George Dawson recounted his personal observations of the extent of landscape burning that had taken place. In more than fifteen different locations, he noted the landscape being extensively burned, with entries such as " . . . smoke from burning woods"; "The ground has been recently burnt over"; "Country passed over almost entirely burnt"; "following open, burnt ground covered with low bushes." This pattern was evident from southern Vancouver Island to the Chilcotin, to the Queen Charlotte Islands (Haida Gwaii), to the Skagit Valley, Coquihalla River, Vernon, and the Shuswap River area. It should be noted, however, that Dawson made no direct connection between aboriginal landscape burning and the burnt areas he observed. In general, it seems that he condoned most of the burning, and several times suggested that burning, followed by introduction of exotic feed grasses and hay species, would be advantageous for ranchers and travelers.[14]

Specific Records of Aboriginal Landscape Burning in British Columbia

Table 1 lists the peoples among whom landscape burning has been reported in British Columbia, plus reference sources. Table 2 lists the types of plants and plant species whose production has been reported to be enhanced by periodic landscape burning. (Both tables can be found at the end of the paper). In all, at least nineteen species of plants, including eleven fruiting shrubs, one herbaceous fruit (strawberry) and seven herbaceous "edible root" species, have been identified by various sources as having their production enhanced by periodic burning.

Interior Plateau

The most detailed aural account of aboriginal landscape burning is from the Pemberton Valley region within Stl'atl'imx (Lillooet) territory. This account, given originally in Stl'atl'imx in December 1969 by the late Baptiste Ritchie of Mount Currie, was translated by him for Salishan linguist Leo Swoboda, and later for Salishan linguist Randy Bouchard. Ritchie's general translation is provided here in its entirety.

Burning Mountainsides for Better Crops

I am telling you about the doings of our forefathers, why they always did well wherever they went for the purpose of picking all the berries and roots like potatoes [sk'am'c—Erythronium grandiflorum, yellow avalanche lily] that they ate. They used to burn one hill and use the other. When there were a lot of bushes ["sticks"; i.e. "when it got bushy"] then the ripe berries disappear and the roots like potatoes [Erythronium], skimuta [Lilium columbianum, tiger lily], skwenkwina [Claytonia lanceolata, spring beauty or mountain potato], disappear, when it gets too bushy. Then they burned. It was marked out and there one did his own burning. That is what they did so that they could go here and there to pick berries. Each one watched that it was really burnt. All the other bushes were removed. Then the berry bushes grew again. The roots like potatoes [Erythronium], the skimuta [Lilium], the skwenkwina [Claytonia], all those that were eaten by us, that is where they grow.

It was a few years, I guess it was almost around three years, before those things grew there again. Then there were really lots of berries. Everything was all really fertile. They rarely burnt the big trees. Only the small ones, only around the bushes was burned. It was the same with one hill as with another. That is why we see, we who are grown-up Indians, that all the hills seem to be burnt, because that was what they did to their own hills. They burned them so that they would get good crops there. They told others who went there, "do the same at your place, do the same at your place." Their own hills were just like a garden.

But now, because the white man really watches us, we don't burn anything. We realize already, it seems the things that were eaten by our forefathers have disappeared from the places where they burned. It seems that already almost everything has disappeared. Maybe it is because it's weedy. All kinds of things grow and they don't burn. If you go to burn then you get into trouble because the white men want to grow trees. Because they changed our ways they do good for us and we eat the food that the white men use. Then we forget the good

Spring beauty
(Claytonia
lanceolata)

food of our earliest forefathers. The roots like potatoes [*Erythronium*], the *skimuta* [*Lilium*] the *skwenkwina* [*Claytonia*], all of those were good to eat.

Now they have disappeared because the hills grew weedy and no-one seems to tend them, no one clears there as our forefathers did so thoroughly.

That is another story for you folks. Why our forefathers burnt. Now you must do it again. Now you know why everything that was near here just disappeared. There we used to go berry picking. There we went berry picking long ago. Now nothing. The food plants have now all gone. They have disappeared. It seems that everything grows on the hills. It has become covered with bushes all over.

Where we used to pick berries, oh, they were really plentiful! Right here where our house is situated now [in Mount Currie], that is where we used to come to pick berries. Like gooseberries [*sxniz'—Ribes divaricatum*]. Now there are no gooseberries near us. Now the other berries are the same. They have all disappeared. We named other grounds of ours around here, called them "The Picking Places" because that is where we went to pick berries. Now you will not find one single berry there.

That is my story to you about how those things which our forefathers ate have disappeared. That is all. You will still know, now that I am reminding you folks, what the old fashioned ways were like. I am Baptiste Ritchie here in Mount Currie.

I am *En Chinemquen*. That is all.[15]

There are other oral accounts of burning. Baptiste Ritchie (BR) and two other Stl'atl'imx elders, the late Charlie Mack Seymour (CM) of Mount Currie and the late Sam Mitchell (SM) of Fountain (*xaxl'ip*), were interviewed jointly in May 1977 by ethnographer Dorothy Kennedy. Their conversation, taped and transcribed by Kennedy, reveals further details of landscape burning:

CM: The only time they got a big fire is when they dig the roots.

BR: They burn the side of the mountain for berry places.

CM: Some time the burned hillsides burned until the snow went. To renew the roots and berries.

SM: Huckleberries [*Vaccinium membranaceum:*], raspberries [*Rubus idaeus*] and roots.

CM: Indian potatoes [*Claytonia*] are the roots.

BR: The ground gets soft.

SM: At higher places, up Pavilion Mountain. [Wild] potatoes grow better if it's burnt.

BR: When they used to burn that grass above timber line they used to say the Indian potatoes were as big as your fist. Now they are only

*Black mountain
huckleberry
(Vaccinium
membranaceum)*

that big [much smaller], cause they are not cultivated. They would burn every five or six years. The ground can only support so much. Now it's only timber grows. It takes away from the other.

SM: They burned at Lillooet to make the raspberries and west of Lillooet for huckleberries.

Another contemporary Stl'atl'imx speaker of Mount Currie, Alec Peters (personal communication, June 15, 1984; August 1986) also spoke of burning in a taped interview: "Well, they do that [burn] every few years, you know. Burn it . . . After a few years, the berry patches, they're not very good. And they burn it, and you get a new patch of berries." He said the areas were burned over every four to five years, " . . . when the bushes grew too old and stopped getting good crops." He also regretted that people are not allowed to do that any more: "the white people don't allow it." However, Mr. Peters said that now, people pick berries on logging sites—those logged one or two years ago. Mount Currie elder Margaret Lester (personal communication, June 15, 1984) echoed Alec Peters' recollections of burning practices, and his concern that plant resources were deteriorating from the cessation of controlled burning.

The late Annie York, Nlaka'pamux elder of Spuzzum in the Fraser Canyon, often recalled the practice of landscape burning from her early childhood, between seventy and eighty years ago.

They wait until close to fall. They know just when to burn. And then two or three years after, lots of huckleberries, lots of blueberries . . . And the *skamec* [*Erythronium grandiflorum*], that's when it grows, when you burn. I've seen it, when the old people used to do it. I was just a little girl. I'd go up the mountain with granny. After we'd pick berries, my uncle would say. "It's going to rain pretty soon; time to burn [so the fire will not spread too much]." He stays up [after we finished].

Then, we go back the next year, it's all burned. Now, it turns into bush. That's why we don't get many berries any more. We're not allowed to burn. [We get] some, but not the same as it used to be. They [berries] do [grow] after logging, but its not the right kind . . . .

Annie York noted that Frozen Lake near Yale used to be a prime huckleberry picking spot, but it is not as good as it used to be. "Before, it was plentiful, [when] they used to burn. Now, nobody burns." Botanie Mountain near Lytton was another area where burning was practiced, but now, according to Annie York, the *skamec* [*Erythronium*] is not as good, not as plentiful (Annie York, personal communication, January 24, 1991).[16] She also blamed trampling and overgrazing of the plants by cattle and horses in places such as Botanie Valley for causing a decline in the quantity and quality of *Erythronium* corms.

Annie York also recalled that individual bushes of hazelnut (*Corylus cornuta*) were burned in the Spuzzum area: " . . . If they can get hazelnuts, they eat that for their refreshments . . . they trade with that . . . because that used to be plentiful here [at Spuzzum] . . . They come down here for it [from further up the Fraser Canyon]. And then they [were] always burning them . . . those bushes, here and there, but not all of them [at once], and that's what makes them grow and makes them plentiful . . . " Hazel bushes also were burned by the Kalapuya of the Willamette Valley in Oregon. Hazel is an early fire follower, which seems to do well on burned over sites, presumably if the fire was of low intensity.[17]

Nlaka'pamux elder Hilda Austin of Lytton also recalled burning (personal communication, October 20, 1982):

Yes, he burns it. So the *mecekw* [*Rubus leucodermis*—blackcap] can grow there, the *c'elc'ala* [*Vaccinium membranaceum*—black mountain huckleberry] can grow there . . . He looks at the place [to see if] it's good to burn it, and he burns it . . . [NT: he would carefully choose

Hazelnuts (Corylus cornuta)

what the best place to burn was?] Yes. If it's going to burn too much
he just stops it [implying a fire of low intensity, easily extinguished].
[He would] just watch it. [NT: what other plants would grow well
after they burned it?] I guess, those onions, *qwelewe7* [*Allium cernuum*],
they grow there. *caw'ak* [*Lilium columbianum*—tiger lily], he grows
good, after it's burned, he grows in that. . . . There's places, you know,
are burned a lot. Sometimes, you know, it'll be burn and burn, and
now the *c'elc'ala* [black mountain huckleberry] grows good in there,
caw'ak [tiger lily] grows good in there, after they burning . . . That's
where I was picking the *c'elc'ala* this year. Up at Thompson Mountain
. . . In the olden days, there was hardly any bushes, trees. The people
burns, so the huckleberries can grow, blackcaps can grow. Nowadays,
the place is so bushy, just like it burns itself. Have to have men go out
and fight fires. Puts out itself . . .

Mabel Joe, Nlaka'pamux elder of Shulus in the Nicola Valley, also confirmed
the practice of landscape burning (personal communication, October 1984).
She said that in the old days they would do that every few years, when a place
started to get "too bushy." Now, she says, Coquahilla Pass, for example, is all
grown over and not as good as it used to be for huckleberries [*Vaccinium
membranaceum*]. She mentioned blackcaps [*Rubus leucodermis*] and wild
raspberries [*R. idaeus*] as two other types of berries that grow well after a
burn. She said the sidehill at Botanie Valley must have been burned over a
short while ago because the blackcaps there are really thick and good. Now,
people are not allowed to burn. "You just start a fire, and right away they put
it out." Nora Jimmie, another Nlaka'pamux speaker (personal communication,
August 8, 1984) recalled that burning the mountainsides promoted the growth
of nodding onions, wild raspberries, blackcaps, and probably huckleberries.

Secwepemc elder Mary Thomas (personal communication, 1994) also
recalled traditional burning by her parents and grandparents:

A lot of people couldn't believe that our people deliberately burned a
mountainside when it got so thick, nothing else would grow in it.
They deliberately burned it, at a certain time of the year when they
knew there was rains coming, they'd burn that, and two years, three
years after the burn there'd be huckleberries galore and different
vegetations would come up that were edible [roots, berries] . . . .[18]

Mary Thomas also noted that morel mushrooms (*Morchella* spp.) also flourish
after burns, but said that she did not recall her people eating those in the old
days. She learned about their edibility more recently. Nellie Taylor, Secwepemc
elder from Skeetchestn (personal communication, 1996) remembered from
the time she was a girl that the older people in the community worried about
the decline of berries from places where they were no longer allowed to burn.

Yellow avalanche lily [*Erythronium grandiflorum*], one of the root vegetables mentioned by Baptiste Ritchie and Annie York, also is mentioned in connection with burning in a Nlaka'pamux (Thompson) narrative, "The Grizzly Bear and the Hunters." In the text, it was mentioned that a sister had four brothers who had "burned a piece of the mountain side so that the *skamitch* root should yield a better crop, and it was here that the little sister went to dig roots."[19] Other references to landscape burning in the interior are provided in Tables 1 and 2.

Southeast Vancouver Island

In the early 1800s, several travelers and settlers on southern Vancouver Island commented on the landscape burning practices of the Straits Salish people. For instance, an anonymous 1849 newspaper article, "Colonization of Vancouver Island," noted

> Miles of the ground were burnt and smoky, and miles were still burning. The Indians burn the country in order to [promote] ... more especially, the roots which they eat. The fire runs along at a great pace, and it is the custom here if you are caught to gallop right

Blue camas (Camassia leichtlinii)

Bulbs of edible camas
(Camassia leichtlinii
[left] and C. quamash
[right])

through it; the grass being short, the flame is very little; and you are through in a second . . .

"The roots which they eat" undoubtedly pertains to the edible blue camas (*Camassia quamash* and *C. leichtlinii*), whose bulbs were a staple carbohydrate source for the aboriginal peoples of southeast Vancouver Island.[20] The suggestion that one could simply run through the fire implies a burn of low intensity, apparently within a garry oak savanna-type landscape. There is convincing evidence for aboriginal landscape burning of camas prairies in western Washington and large-scale burning by aboriginal people on Whidbey Island, Washington, in the latter case specifically to improve deer habitat and, hence, hunting.[21]

Many others also were impressed with the park-like qualities of the landscape. As early as 1790, Captain George Vancouver wrote about the islands in the vicinity of the future site of Fort Victoria, "I could not possibly believe any uncultivated country had ever been discovered exhibiting so rich a picture. Stately forests . . . pleasingly clothed its eminences and chequered its vallies; presenting in many places, extensive spaces that wore the appearance of having been cleared by art." Vancouver apparently never realized how the "delightful meadow[s]" he observed were maintained.[22]

The Hudson's Bay Company's "Fort Victoria Journal" records many days from July through September 1846–49 that were "very hazy" or "very smoky and hazy." On September 12, 1847, for example, is the notation, "Weather very hazy as yesterday with dense smoke." On August 23, 1849: "Fine dry weather . . . favourable to the spreading of the Fires which are burning fiercely in all the forests around the place destroying in the short space of a few hours more timber than half a century will replace." The fires were regarded as "very alarming" and unwelcome. It is unclear whether they were linked to the activities of the local Salish in this case, but it is likely that at least some of these summer fires were set by the aboriginal people. It is ironic that the landscapes so appreciated by the early explorers and colonists actually were created by the very fires they feared and disliked. In his official report in 1842 on the suitability of southeastern Vancouver Island for relocation of Hudson's Bay Company headquarters from Fort Vancouver, at the mouth of the Columbia, James Douglas described "a range of plains nearly six miles square containing a great extent of valuable tillage and pasture land equally well adapted for the plough or feeding stock." In a letter the following year, he portrayed this area as "a perfect 'Eden'"[23]

Wayne Suttles's Straits Salish consultants provide information on the growing and harvesting of camas, including post-harvest burning practices. Suttles notes that after settlers began encroaching on the "mainland" (southern Vancouver Island) camas prairies ("these were usually the first places to be settled"), the offshore islands around Victoria and the Saanich Peninsula became the only source of bulbs. Some of these islands were open to anyone for digging, whereas others, especially some with prime camas beds, were owned and tended by individual Straits Salish people. For example, Mandarte Island in Haro Strait belonged to three people, and an islet south of Sidney to another. Each summer, after the plants had flowered, the owners came with their families and relatives (and sometimes, their slaves). The men would go off fishing early in the morning while the women dug camas bulbs. The bulbs

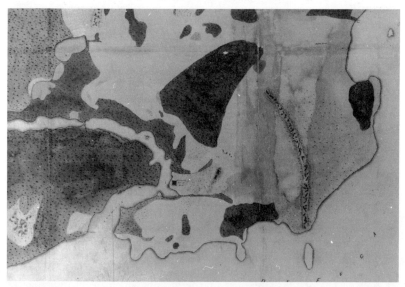

Victoria area, 1842, showing prairie extent. Lightly shaded areas were prairies; darker areas were forested. "Ground Plan of Portion of Vancouver Island Selected for New Establishment taken by James Douglas Esqr. Drawn by A Lee Lewes, L.S., 1842." HBCA Map collection G. 2/25 (N11761). Courtesy of the Hudson's Bay Company Archives, Provincial Archives of Manitoba.

were steamed in underground pits. "After they were through digging for the season, they burned off the island so that it would be more fertile the next year." Other beds on other offshore islets, whether privately owned or open to anyone for digging, also were burned off at the end of the digging. It is possible that the dense smoke noted around the Gulf Islands by George Dawson on August 10, 1876 came from post-harvest burning of camas beds, since it would have been in mid-summer, when the bulbs generally were harvested.[24]

An 1863 account from the Tsolum River area north of Courtenay describes "miles of beautiful prairie land" and "beautiful rolling prairie," and may be evidence of fire-maintained landscapes of the Comox Salish. Nick Page (personal communication, 1991) has surveyed a site in the Tsolum River drainage that shows evidence of landscape burning by the Comox. It is the northernmost location for garry oak (*Quercus garryana*) and because, unlike other garry oak sites, it falls within the moist coastal Western Hemlock Biogeoclimatic Zone, Page is convinced that the oaklands here are anthropogenic in origin and were maintained in the past by periodic burning. Further studies of this site are ongoing.[25]

W. Colquhon Grant's 1857 description of the Sooke area of southern Vancouver Island included the following statement pertaining to landscape burning along the coast:

> Although the thermometer sometimes reaches a height of 90 and 92 degrees [Fahrenheit], that is, only during the few hottest days in August; the usual thermometrical range during the dry season is from 60 to 80 degrees. *The natives all along the coast have a custom of setting fire to the woods in summer* [emphasis added], which doubtless adds to the density of the fogs, and increases the temperature of the atmosphere.[26]

Those who did recognize that aboriginal people set fires intentionally either did not understand the purposes of burning or did not appreciate the significance or the necessity of it. Grant, in his report to Governor James Douglas, complained of the practice and described his efforts to stop the fires that were

> . . . kindled promiscuously by the natives both in wood and prairie between the months of August and October. Their object is to clear away the thick fern and underwood in order that the roots and fruits on which they in a great measure subsist may grow the more freely and be the more easily dug up. I have endeavored in the neighbourhood of Mullachard [Grant's home in Sooke] to check these fires by giving neither potlache [gifts] or employment to any Indians so long as a fire was blazing in sight of my house.

To Grant, the habit of burning was "abominable" and destructive.[27]

Grant's successor, surveyor Joseph Pemberton, however, seemed more appreciative of the results of burning. He noted, "The open grounds also grow berries of many kinds, and roots such as onions, kamas, etc. on which the Indian, to a great extent, subsists." About the same time, a visiting naval officer, Edward du Verney, likewise noted the richness of the region's berries: "The forest is as full of wild strawberries as possible, and it abounds with other fruit bearing shrubs: last summer the officers of the 'Grappler' made enough preserves from the wild berries to last them all through the winter." These last observations undoubtedly reflect the effects of intentional landscape burning by local First Nations on southern Vancouver Island.[28]

Coastal Peoples

Evidence for aboriginal landscape burning within the central and north coastal region of British Columbia is more sporadic, but indications are that it was practiced at least to some extent. Franz Boas recorded a Kwakwakaw'akw (Southern Kwakiutl) prayer to berries, spoken by a woman before she picks the berries:

> I have come, Supernatural Ones, you, Long-Life-Makers, that I may take you, for that is the reason why you have come, brought by your creator, that you may come and satisfy me; you Supernatural Ones; *and this, that you do not blame me for what I do to you when I set fire to you the way it is done by my root (ancestor) who set fire to you in his manner when you get old on the ground that you may bear much fruit.*[emphasis added]. Look! I come now dressed with my large basket and my small basket that you may go into it, Healing-Women; you Supernatural Ones. I mean this, that you may not be evilly disposed towards me, friends. That you may only treat me well . . . .[29]

On the west coast of Vancouver Island, in the Nuu-chah-nulth homeland, a small area in Clayoquot Sound was said by George Louie (Manhousaht/Ahousaht) to have been burned deliberately to stimulate the growth of berries. This area, called *iihatis* (lit. "sudden flooding of the river"), is around a small creek on the east side of Herbert Inlet, south from Gibson Cove. It originally was part of the territory of the Otsosaht, one of the Clayoquot Sound tribes, but later, through warfare, became part of Ahousaht territory. The burning of this area was confirmed by Stanley Sam (Ahousaht/Clayoquot), who noted that Alaska blueberries (*Vaccinium alaskaense*), red huckleberries (*V. parvifolium*), and salal berries (*Gaultheria shallon*) grow particularly well after an area has been burned over.[30]

Another intriguing reference to fire in the region is a statement from the 1860s by pioneer businessman Gilbert Sproat:

Here and there in the forest are open spaces where the trees burnt by a fire—caused perhaps by the careless Indians—lie blackened on the ground, or where they appear lying white and withered, as if destroyed by some blast or circle of wind that left the surrounding trees uninjured.[31]

Larry Paul (personal communication, 1994) recalled that his mother, Alice Paul, told him they used to burn the meadowlands behind Hesquiaht village in order to kill the trees and create ready sources of firewood, which could be gathered as needed. Perhaps this is the same type of burning as that described by Sproat.

Nuxalk elders of the Bella Coola area also recalled landscape burning. When he was a boy, Willie Hans of Bella Coola (personal communication, May 1981) asked his father why there were so many burned trees around the Bella Coola valley, and his father explained that they burned to encourage the berries, especially raspberries (*Rubus idaeus*) and blackcaps (*R. leucodermis*). The late Felicity Walkus, who originally was from South Bentinck Arm, recalled that they "burned lots" around that area, and the late Dr. Margaret Siwallace, born at Kimsquit, said they also used to burn there to promote berry growth (both personal communications, May 1981).

The Haisla also burned areas within their territory in the vicinity of Kitimaat, to encourage the growth of berries, which were an important element in their diet.[32]

On Haida Gwaii (Queen Charlotte Islands) there is further evidence of burning. Haida elder Hazel Stevens of Skidegate said that one of the small offshore islands off Queen Charlotte City, Guden Island (the Haida name translates as "diarrhea island" because of its appearance) used to be burned, and was well known as a prime berry site for salal (*Gaultheria shallon*) and red huckleberries (*Vaccinium parvifolium*). People often stopped there to pick berries. Mrs. Stevens' implication was that the burning had enhanced the growth of berries, although she did not state this directly. In interviews dating

Salal (Gaultheria shallon)

from the 1970s, the late Solomon Wilson of Skidegate also alluded to burning berry patches. He mentioned a small camp called _hwt'uu_ on the south side of Maude Island in Skidegate inlet, where in historic times people grew potatoes and had a smokehouse. Salal berries and huckleberries were abundant around this camp, and, again, the implication was that this was because the area was burned frequently. The late Charlie Williams of Skidegate said in 1973 that large areas behind the villages of Skidegate and Tanu formerly were burned "so berries could be found afterward."[33]

The food plant species of indigenous peoples of British Columbia mentioned in this paper are described and illustrated in Nancy Turner, _Food Plants of Coastal First Peoples_ (1995) and _Food Plants of Interior First Peoples_ (1997); and in Harriet Kuhnlein and Nancy Turner, _Traditional Plant Foods of Canadian Indigenous Peoples: Nutrition, Botany and Use._[34] Aside from the direct production increase in plant food resources, First Nations peoples recognized that landscape burning also resulted in enhanced forage for deer and other game.[35] Later, production of forage for horses and cattle, as mentioned by George Dawson in his journals, also must have been a factor in decisions about landscape burning by aboriginal peoples of British Columbia, as it was in neighboring areas.[36] Furthermore, although no direct mention has been made of landscape burning enhancing the growth of medicinal plants or species used as materials in traditional technologies, this also may have occurred. One Lower Kootenai (Ktunaxa) man interviewed by Barrett said fire also was used to protect medicine plants, in particular the important ceremonial plant _7ayut_ (_Ligusticum_ sp.).[37]

Controlled Burning Techniques

Techniques of controlled burning are little known, since most of the elders who recalled the practice remembered only observing it from their younger days, not actually participating in it. From available evidence, mainly the accounts cited earlier, specific sites were preselected for burning over, and from all indications, the times for burning and the conditions also were selected, as they were by other peoples such as the Slavey (Dene-thah) of northern Alberta and the Salishan and Kootenai (Ktunaxa) peoples of western Montana. Annie York's (Nlaka'pamux) recollections of her uncle waiting until huckleberry picking was finished, then choosing a time just before a rainfall to carry out the burning, is in keeping with this suggestion. The Gitxsan and Wet-suwet'en peoples to the north practiced similar timing, with the addition of some types of burning in the spring. On southern Vancouver Island burning was carried out in the summer, after the camas harvest. This would have been a dry period, but since, at least in historic times, burning was carried out mainly on small islets, it would have been easier to control.[38]

Factors determining the nature of landscape burning for indigenous peoples of Montana and Alberta include seasonality (fires usually were set in fall or early spring when the ground was wet and hence control was better), time of day, relative humidity of certain fuel types, knowledge of winds, slope, size of areas burned, and frequency of burning. To further control set fires, the Slavey employed natural and human-made fire breaks, backfires, and active use of wetted conifer boughs to extinguish or direct the fire.[39] It can be assumed that these factors also were important to indigenous peoples of British Columbia.

Controlled landscape burning required a detailed and in-depth knowledge of natural systems, especially the ecological characteristics of vegetation and the successional nature of plant communities, as well as of various geographical and climatic features of the landscape. This knowledge, acquired through centuries and generations of careful observation and experimentation, seldom has been acknowledged by non-Native people. In fact, foresters and rangers often have regarded aboriginal landscape burning as nothing more than "carelessness."[40]

Resource Species Enhanced by Burning

Nineteen plant species (within two general categories—berries and roots) were reported by indigenous peoples to be enhanced by periodic landscape burning (Table 2). Of the species mentioned, eleven are shrubby fruiting species, one is the herbaceous wild strawberry, and the remaining seven are herbaceous plants with edible underground parts. All of the species have the capacity to regenerate from underground rhizomes or buried storage organs. A recent study has demonstrated that fruiting shrub species such as *Sambucus racemosa* (red elderberry), *Ribes laxiflorum* (white-flowered currant), *Ribes lacustre* (swamp gooseberry), and *Rubus parviflorus* (thimbleberry) readily re-establish through resprouting from underground rhizomes after clearcutting and burning, although *Vaccinium membranaceum* (black mountain huckleberry) was slow to re-grow.[41]

In general, it appears that many of the species whose growth and productivity are increased following landscape burning are successional species requiring clearings or open canopy for optimum growth, or are at least somewhat tolerant of open conditions. For example, Don Minore summarizes the situation for huckleberries and blueberries:

> Most huckleberry fields originated from the uncontrolled wildfires
> that were common in the Northwest before modern fire protection
> and control techniques were applied. Ecologically, these fields are
> seral—temporary stages in the natural succession from treeless burn to
> climax forest. Without fire or other radical disturbance, huckleberries

gradually are crowded out by invading trees and brush. A few years after establishment they produce a maximum amount of berries; then production gradually declines as other shrubs and trees dominate the site . . . . The acreage occupied by thin-leaved huckleberry fields is declining rapidly as old burns become reforested and new burns become increasingly rare. Many formerly productive huckleberry areas now produce no berries at all. Others are shrinking as trees and brush invade along their edges.[42]

From the testimonies of the native elders, such as Baptiste Ritchie and the late Julia Kilroy of Coldwater in the Nicola Valley, re-growth of the "root" plants after burning is accompanied by a notable increase in the size of the edible portion. Julia Kilroy, for example, recalled having seen some bulbs of tiger lily [*Lilium columbianum*] the size of tennis balls from a place where the area had been burned over the previous year, and attributed the immense size to the burning. Possibly increased growth would result from an increased supply of available nutrients near the surface of the ground following burning. Fire increases the pH of the soil through release of alkaline ions such as phosphorus, potassium, calcium, and magnesium, and studies show that these nutrients are more readily accessible to plants after a fire. The amount of nutrients released varies with the type of soil and intensity of the burn. Burning also would be expected to reduce competition from fire-intolerant species.[43]

Landscape Burning Today

Many aboriginal people in British Columbia still rely on wild foods for a substantial portion of their diet. The use of wild foods and traditional medicines, considered an important part of the cultural heritage of first peoples, is being promoted in native communities. In general, the traditional diet of indigenous peoples of Canada is considered to be a healthy one, and continuing and increasing use of wild foods is desirable from many perspectives. Given this situation, the enhancement of habitat for the growth of wild plant and animal foods should be given priority.[44]

Fire ecologists and wildlife biologists in western North America are rethinking the strategy of total forest fire suppression, which has dominated forest management practices in the present century. For example, a recent review notes that, as well as fire control, " . . . the skilled application of fire as a forest land management tool" may be undertaken in some situations.[45]

It might be argued that the present forest management policies of extensive clearcutting followed by slashburning in both coastal and interior forests is imitative of previous aboriginal landscape burning in the province. Indeed, several of the elders quoted in this study, including Alec Peters of Mount

Currie and Hilda Austin of Lytton, said that logged areas were where people now go to gather berries, and also to hunt. Hilda Austin (personal communication, 1982) discussed going to pick huckleberries on Thompson Mountain, about 20 km south of Spences Bridge, on Nicomen Creek:

> We were climbing, right to the other side of the mountain. The guys logs it, cuts that, and *c'elc'ala* [*Vaccinium membranaceum*] grows on that, that's where we were picking it . . . I guess there's lots of snow when he logs it, and that's why the stumps are long. Yes, that's where we were picking the huckleberries . . . .But it's just starting to grow, I guess. It's short . . . ..I see the boys, he went and hunts over there. They didn't cut the whole thing, you know, just certain places. Still, there're deer . . .

On the other hand, others do not consider these areas to be as good for berries as the traditionally burned places. Annie York (personal communication, January 1991) said, "They [berries] do come after logging but it's not the right kind; it's not as good." Intensive burning can be detrimental because it can result in decreased organic matter in the soil and increased erosion. Furthermore, aboriginal people say that access often is cut off to them when they try to go into logged areas of powerline rights-of-way. Additionally, with many areas now being sprayed with Roundup and other herbicides to eliminate brush and species such as alder (*Alnus rubra*) that might compete with commercial forest trees, people fear contamination. In 1986, for example, the Lillooet Tribal Council appealed six permits authorizing the forests ministry to apply Roundup in the Cayoosh, Texas, and Lillooet drainages, and a highways permit for application of Tordon 22K on a spot basis. The Haida also have expressed grave concerns about pesticides and other pollutants contaminating their wild foods and medicines.[46]

Another problem complicates the picture of traditional landscape burning and aboriginal resource use. Many aggressive exotic species have been introduced within the past century and before. Some of these, such as Scot's broom (*Cytisus scoparius*) on southern Vancouver Island, invade large tracts of land formerly occupied by indigenous plants. Broom and other weedy species do not seem to be harmed by burning, and can become established quickly in burned or logged areas once the original cover is removed.[47] Introduced species such as thistles (*Cirsium vulgare* and *C. arvense*), burdock (*Arctium minus*), knapweed (*Centaurea diffusa* and *C. maculosa*), mustards (*Brassica* spp., *Sisymbrium* spp. and related species), and foxglove (*Digitalis purpurea*) are taking over large tracts of logged, burned, or otherwise disturbed lands in British Columbia. These species, and the livestock they often accompany on range and meadow lands both in coastal and interior areas, pose an increasing threat to the productivity of traditional resource species. Trampling and overgrazing of pigs and sheep on southern Vancouver Island

Top: Vegetation immediately after burn. Below: Same place, one year after burn. Facing page: Same burn four years after fire

and the small islands of Haro and Rosario Straits, and undoubtedly the weedy species that accompanied them, spoiled the once-productive camas beds of the Straits Salish people in many places. Botanie Valley, by historical account one of the most productive traditional root-digging grounds of the entire province, has been changed irrevocably by trampling, grazing livestock, and the weedy plants accompanying them.[48]

Mary Thomas, Secwepemc (Shuswap) elder from the Salmon Arm area, has observed during the course of her own lifetime both a decline in burning practices and a marked deterioration in the size and abundance of traditional root vegetables such as yellow avalanche lily (*Erythronium grandiflorum*), and she believes this is due to the invasion of couch grass (*Agropyron repens*), knapweed and other weeds, and to trampling and overgrazing by livestock (Mary Thomas, personal communication, October and December 1991). In one intentionally burned area of grazing land on the Skeetchestn Reserve (Secwepemc) in Deadman's Creek valley near Savona, although there was a dramatic reduction of knapweed in the first year following the burn, the entire

area was repopulated by a dense growth of another weed, hedge mustard (*Sisymbrium loeselii*) (personal observation, 1990, 1991).

Thus, even if aboriginal landscape burning practices were reinstated, the resulting vegetation would not have the same composition as it had prehistorically. The situation is similar in California and elsewhere. The authors of a study of Chumash (Ventura County, California) burning note " . . . the effects and frequency of grass fires today are not necessarily comparable with those in aboriginal times before introduced weeds and heavy grazing destroyed native grasslands . . . ."[49]

If landscape burning to increase production of traditional plant resources were to be reincorporated into forest management strategies of the future, it would have to be done with caution and with careful monitoring of effects on native plant communities. Simple mimicking of past burning techniques may not produce the same enhancement of resource species. Minimal soil disturbance obviously is desirable to avoid damage to the underground reproductive parts of berry and other resource plants, and to avoid creating areas that are easily invaded by weeds. Soil temperatures that are too high might imperil the survivability of some resource species. Forest ecologists have been accumulating data on ecological effects of fire for the past quarter century and already know much on the variable effects of burning. But we must keep in mind that aboriginal peoples used different landscape burning strategies for different objectives and on different sites. Additionally, the effects of fire on each ecosystem and site can vary significantly; some sites might be affected detrimentally by fire. Nevertheless, with caution, it may well be worthwhile to attempt burning over certain restricted sites in traditional ways. Careful attention to season, weather, and other factors can reduce potentially adverse effects traditionally associated with fire. Hand pruning and mechanical brushcutting also might be investigated as alternatives to landscape burning.[50]

Conclusions

Oral accounts by contemporary indigenous people in British Columbia, especially those of the grandparent generation, provide many records of the practice of intentional landscape burning. Although such burning has not been done for many years because of government fire suppression policies dominant in the present century, records indicate that the practice once was widespread. The main purpose of landscape burning was to enhance the growth and production of plant food resources, especially certain types of berries and "root" vegetables, as well as to create good forage for deer and other game.

Burning generally was done at the end of the harvest season, and optimum productivity of berries and "root crops" was said to occur after about three years. Rotation of burning areas was practiced to achieve continual production in an overall area.

The importance of wild plant resources that are noncommercial and therefore do not feature in the mainstream economy also has been generally overlooked in resource planning and management in British Columbia and elsewhere. Perhaps it is time to reevaluate the directions of forest management. New forestry should both be more accommodating of the needs and traditional practices of indigenous peoples and give more recognition to the values of traditional resources.

Originally published in Archaeology in Montana 32(2): 57–73, 1991. Revised and updated for this publication.

Table 1. Summary of Oral and Literature Records of Aboriginal Landscape Burning in British Columbia

Language Group	References and Notes
1. Straits Salish	Anonymous 1849; Grant 1857; Suttles 1951a (meadows burned to enhance camas production; summertime)
2a. Upriver Halkomelem (Sto:lo)	Coqualeetza Education Training Centre 1981 (some patches of different kinds of blueberries were burned each year "to make more berries grow"); Butler and Campbell 1987 (note burning to enhance "blueberries")
2b. Cowichan Halkomelem (Quwutsun')	Elders recall that the wild strawberry patches "on the outside [waters]" (apparently West Coast, beyond Sooke) were fired every few years (Arvid Charlie, personal communication, 1996, from his great grandfather, Luschiim)
3. Comox	Garry oak woodland in Comox Valley said to have been anthropogenic (discussed in text; Nick Page, personal communication 1991).
4. Nlaka'pamux (Thompson)	Annie York, Hilda Austin, Mabel Joe, Julia Kilroy, Nora Jimmie, personal communication 1975–1991 cf. Turner *et al.* 1990: 123, 137, 191; Kennedy and Bouchard 1986: 128; Teit 1898: 72–74 (late summer; fall)
5. Stl'atl'imx (Lillooet)	Baptiste Ritchie, Sam Mitchell, Charlie Mack Seymour, Alec Peters, Nellie Wallace, Margaret Lester, personal communication 1977–1985 (see also quotations in text; Swoboda 1971)
6. Secwepemc (Shuswap)	Nellie Taylor, Mary Thomas, Ron Ignace, personal communication, 1995, 1996
7. Okanagan-Colville	Martin Louie, in Turner *et al.* 1980: 103; Kennedy and Bouchard 1986: 128
8. Ktunaxa (Kootenai)	Barrett 1980a (Montana Kootenai people suggested berry production was enhanced by landscape burning: this knowledge may also pertain to British Columbia Ktunaxa)

Language Group	References and Notes
9. Dakelhne (Carrier) and Wet'suwet'en	Johnson (this volume)—several accounts of burning; Rhea Joseph, personal communication, May 1981 (her father told her they used to burn off mountainsides in the Terrace area until the 1940s.)
10. Nisga'a (Nishga, Niska)	HMcM, cited by McNeary (1974: 38).
11. Gitxsan	Johnson (this volume) records numerous accounts of traditional burning around village and in montane areas of Gitxsan territory
12. Haida	David Ellis, personal communication, January 1991, 1992 (burning off areas on islands in Skidegate Inlet and behind Skidegate and Tanu; discussed in text)
13. Nuxalk (Bella Coola)	Margaret Siwallace, Willie Hans, Felicity Walkus, personal communication, 1981-84 (hillsides burned around South Bentinck Arm, Kimsquit, and Bella Coola Valley to encourage growth of raspberries, blackcaps, and soapberries)
14. Haisla	Berry production said to be improved by burning (Lopatin 1945)
15. Kwakwaka'wakw (Southern Kwakiutl)	Boas (1930) (berry picker's prayer quoted in text)
16. Nuu-chah-nulth (Nootka, West Coast)	Bouchard and Kennedy (1990) (Clayoquot Sound; see discussion in text)

Table 2. Types of Plants and Plant Species Whose Production Is Reported to be Enhanced by Periodic Landscape Burning (within British Columbia and Neighboring Areas).

Berries (general)	Landscape burning to enhance berry growth mentioned for Kwakwaka'wakw, Haida, Haisla, Ktunaxa, Stl'atl'imx, Nlaka'pamux, Secwepemc, Nuu-chah-hulth, Nuxalk, Wet'suwet'en, Gitxsan, Nisga'a (see Table 1 for reference citations)

Edible Roots	Landscape burning to enhance growth of edible (general) underground parts mentioned for Nlaka'pamux, Stl'atl'imx, Secwepemc (see Table 1 for reference citations)
Forage plants for deer	Mentioned for Okanagan-Colville, Nlaka'pamux, possibly Gitxsan, possibly Wet'suwet'en, Straits Salish, Ktunaxa (Moravets 1932; Barrett 1980a; Kennedy and Bouchard 1986: 128; Hilda Austin, personal communication, 1984; Johnson (this volume).
Allium cernuum (nodding wild onion)	Growth enhancement noted by Nlaka'pamux elders (Hilda Austin, Nora Jimmie, personal communication, 1984); large nodding onions recorded following burns in Gitxsan territory (Leslie Johnson, personal communication, 1990)
Amelanchier alnifolia (saskatoon or serviceberry)	Growth enhancement suggested after fires in Lillooet area by Mathewes (1978: 77)
Camassia quamash and *C. leichtlinii* (blue camas)	Patches burned over in summer in southern Vancouver Island and the Gulf Islands (Suttles 1951a)
Claytonia lanceolata (spring beauty)	Enhanced size and productivity noted by Stl'atl'imx and Secwepemc elders (see Table 1 for reference citations)
Corylus cornuta (hazelnut)	Individual bushes burned around Spuzzum to enhance production (Annie York, in Turner *et al.* 1990: 191)
Erythronium grandiflorum (avalanche lily)	Enhanced production noted by Teit (1898: 72–74), Annie York, in Turner *et al.* (1990: 123), Baptiste Ritchie (Swoboda 1971)
Fragaria chiloensis (?) (seaside strawberry)	Enhanced production noted for Cowichan Halkomelem (Quwutsun') (see Table 1 for reference citations) (species of strawberry implied by coastal habitat, but not confirmed)
Fritillaria camschatensis (rice root)	Possible enhancement of growth from burning of floodplain garden sites (Gitxsan—Johnson this volume)

Gaultheria shallon (salal)	Enhanced production suggested for Nuu-chah-nulth and Haida areas (see Table 1 for reference citations)
Lilium columbianum (tiger lily)	Enhanced size and productivity noted by Baptiste Ritchie (Swoboda 1971) and Julia Kilroy (Turner *et al.* 1990: 123)
Ribes divaricatum (wild gooseberry)	Enhanced production noted by Baptiste Ritchie (Swoboda 1971)
Rubus idaeus (wild raspberry)	Enhanced productivity noted by Willie Hans, Sam Mitchell, Mabel Joe, Nora Jimmie (all personal communication, 1977–84; SM to Dorothy Kennedy, 1977)
Rubus leucodermis (blackcap)	Enhanced productivity noted by Willie Hans, Mabel Joe, Hilda Austin (all personal communications, cf Turner *et al.* 1990: 279)
Shepherdia canadensis (soapberry)	Enhanced productivity noted by Margaret Siwallace (from Sandy Moody, personal communication, 1984); and Johnson (this volume).
Vaccinium alaskaense (Alaska blueberry)	Enhanced productivity noted by Stanley Sam (Bouchard and Kennedy 1990: 345)
Vaccinium caespitosum (dwarf huckleberry)	Enhanced productivity noted for Nlaka'pamux by Mabel Joe, Julia Kilroy, and Annie York (Turner *et al.* 1990: 218); for Gitxsan and Wet'suwet'en (Johnson this volume)
Vaccinium membranaceum (black mountain huckleberry)	Enhanced productivity noted by Stl'atl'imx, Nlaka'pamux, Gitxsan, Wet'suwet'en, and Okanagan-Colville elders (references cited in Table 1)
Vaccinium parvifolium (red huckleberry)	Enhanced productivity noted for Nuu-chah-nulth and Haida (Bouchard and Kennedy 1990: 345; David Ellis, personal communication,1991)
Vaccinium spp. (wild blueberries)	Enhanced productivity noted by Nlaka'pamux, Okanagan-Colville, and Sto:lo elders (Turner *et al.* 1980: 103; Coqualeetza Education Training Centre 1981; Turner *et al.* 1990: 218); and Butler and Campbell (1987)

Sources for Tables 1 and 2

Anonymous
1849 Colonization of Vancouver Island.
The Times May 4, 1849, pp. 18–19. London.

Barrett, Stephen
1980 Indian Fires in the Pre-Settlement Forests of Western Montana. pp. 35–41 in
*Proceedings of the Fire History Workshop, October 20–24, 1980, Tucson,
Arizona.* Coordinated by Marvin Stokes and John Dieterick. USDA Forest
Service General Technical Report RM-881. Fort Collins.

Boas, Franz
1930 The Religion of the Kwakiutl Indians.
Columbia University Contributions to Anthropology 10.

Bouchard, Randy and Dorothy Kennedy
1990 Clayoquot Sound Indian Land Use. Report Prepared for MacMillan Bloedel
Limited, Fletcher Challenge Canada, and the British Columbia Ministry of
Forests. Victoria.

Butler, R.W. and R.W. Campbell
1987 *The Birds of the Fraser River Delta: Populations, Ecology and International
Significance.* Canadian Wildlife Service Occasional Paper No. 65.
British Columbia Ministry of the Environment, Victoria.

Coqualeetza Education Training Centre
1981 *Upper Sto:lo* (Fraser Valley) *Plant Gathering.*
Sardis: British Columbia.

Grant, W. Colquhoun
1857 Description of Vancouver Island.
Journal of the Royal Geographical Society 27: 268–320.

Kennedy, Dorothy and Randy Bouchard
1986 Indian History and Knowledge of the Aspen Grove to Peachland Corridor of
the Coquihalla Highway. In *Coquihalla Highway Project, Merritt to
Peachland, B.C. Detailed Heritage Resource Inventory and Impact Assessment,
Appendix II* by Arcas Associates. Report prepared for the Heritage
Conservation Branch, Ministry of Tourism and Design and Survey Branch,
Ministry of Transportation and Highways, Victoria.

Lopatin, Ivan
1945 Social Life and Religion of the Indians of Kitimat,
British Columbia. *University of Southern California, Social Science Series* 26.
Los Angeles.

Mathewes, Rolf
1978 The Environment and Biotic Resources of the Lillooet Area. pp. 68–99 In
Reports of the Lillooet Archaeological Project No. 1: Introduction and
Setting. Edited by Arnoud Stryd and Stephen Lawhead. *National Museum of
Man, Mercury Series, Archaeological Survey Paper* No. 73. Ottawa.

McNeary, Steven
1974 *The Traditional Economic and Social Life of the Niska of British Columbia.*
Unpublished Report to the National Museum of Canada, Ottawa.

Moravets, Floyd
1932 Second Growth Douglas Fir Follows Cessaion of Indian Fires. *USDA Forest Service Bulletin* 16(20): 3.

Suttles, Wayne
1951 The Economic Life of the Coast Salish of Haro and Rosario Straits. Ph.D. dissertation, anthropology, University of Washington. Seattle.

Swoboda, Leo
1971 Lillooet Phonology, Texts and Dictionary. MA thesis, Linguistics, University of British Columbia. Vancouver.

Teit, James
1898 Traditions of the Thompson River Indians of British Columbia. *Memoirs of the American Folk-Lore Society* 6. New York.

Turner, Nancy, Randy Bouchard, and Dorothy Kennedy
1980 Ethnobotany of the Okanagan-Colville Indians of British Columbia and Washington. *British Columbia Provincial Museum Occasional Paper* No. 21. Victoria.

Turner, Nancy *et al.*
1990 Thompson Ethnobotany: Knowledge and Usage of Plants by the Thompson Indians of British Columbia. *Royal British Columbia Museum Memoir* 3. Victoria.

Acknowledgments

I am indebted to the knowledgeable indigenous people who provided the information included here, especially: the late Hilda Austin (Lytton), Arvid Charlie (Halkomelem, Cowichan), the late Willie Hans (Nuxalk, Bella Coola), Nora Jimmy (Nlaka'pamux, Fourteen Mile), Mabel Joe (Nlaka'pamux, Shulus), Rhea Joseph (Terrace area), the late Julia Kilroy and the late Bernadette Antoine (Nlaka'pamux, Coldwater), Margaret Lester (Stl'atl'imx, Mount Currie), the late Dr. George Louie (Nuu-chah-nulth, Manhousaht/Ahousaht; interviewed by Randy Bouchard and Dorothy Kennedy), Larry Paul and the late Alice Paul (Nuu-chah-nulth, Hesquiaht), Martin Louie (Okanagan, Penticton; interviewed by RB and DK); the late Charlie Mack Seymour (Stl'atl'imx, Mount Currie) and the late Sam Mitchell (Stl'atl'imx, *xaxl'ip* [Fountain]; both interviewed by DK), Alec Peters (Stl'atl'imx, Mount Currie), the late Baptiste Ritchie (Stl'atl'imx, Mount Currie; interviewed by Leo Swoboda, RB and DK), Stanley Sam (Nuu-chah-nulth, Ahousaht; interviewed by RB and DK), the late Dr. Margaret Siwallace (Nuxalk, Bella Coola, formerly of Kimsquit), Hazel Stevens (Haida, Skidegate, interviewed by David Ellis) Nellie Taylor (Secwepemc, Skeetchestn), Mary Thomas (Secwepemc, Enderby), the late Felicity Walkus (Nuxalk, Bella Coola, formerly of south Bentinck Arm), the late Charlie Williams (Haida, Skidegate; interviewed by DE), the late Solomon Wilson (Haida, Skidegate; interviewed by DE), and the late Annie York (Nlaka'pamux, Spuzzum).

Randy Bouchard and Dorothy Kennedy, of the British Columbia Indian Language Project, Victoria, have been extremely helpful in sharing their own research information with me and in pointing out additional sources of information. John Parminter, Fire Ecologist with the Protection Branch, British Columbia Ministry of Forests, Victoria, provided me with many important references, as did Ruth Kirk of Tacoma, Washington. Others who helped me in this project include: Dr. Marianne Boelscher Ignace, Secwepemc Cultural Education Society, Kamloops, British Columbia; Dr. Brian Compton, Department of Botany, the University of British Columbia; Alison Davis, Environmental Studies Program, University of Victoria; Leslie M. Johnson, Department of Anthropology, University of Alberta, Edmonton; Dr. Andrea Laforet and Dr. Gordon M. Day, National Museum of Civilization, Ottawa; Dana Lepofsky, Department of Archaeology, Simon Fraser University, Burnaby, British Columbia; Dr. John Lutz, Department of History, University of Victoria; Dr. Helen H. Norton of Anacortes, Washington; Dr. Eugene Hunn, Department of Anthropology, University of Washington, Seattle; Dr. Brent Ingram, Plant Science Department, University of British Columbia; David Ellis of Vancouver; Dr. Richard J. Hebda, Botany Unit, Royal British Columbia Museum, Victoria; Dr. Henry T. Lewis, formerly Department of Anthropology, University of Alberta, Edmonton; Nick Page, Department of Forestry, The University of British Columbia, Vancouver; Karen Golinski, Environmental Studies, University of Victoria; Dr. Gerry Allen and Dr. Joe Antos, Department of Biology, University of Victoria; Dr. Duncan Taylor, Environmental Studies Program, University of Victoria; R. Yorke Edwards of Victoria, and Robert D. Turner of Victoria.

An earlier version of this work was published in a special issue of *Archaeology in Montana* (Volume 32, number 2) as "Burning Mountain Sides for Better Crops, Aboriginal Landscape Burning in British Columbia" (1991). I am particularly grateful to Kenneth Cannon, editor of that issue, for his help in developing the paper. I appreciate the opportunity provided by Robert Boyd to revise and update this work and include it among many others to help complete a better picture of aboriginal burning practices in the Northwest.

My interviews with Stl'atl'imx and Nlaka'pamux people in 1984 and 1985, and with the Secwepemc people from 1991 to 1996, were funded through research grants from the Social Sciences and Humanities Research Council of Canada.

Notes

1. Author is professor, Environmental Studies Program, University of Victoria, Victoria, British Columbia, Canada V8W 2Y2.
2. Transcribed from a taped interview with Dorothy Kennedy.
3. The quotation is from Eugene Anderson, *The Food of China* (New Haven, 1988), 11. Regional works on Native North American fire use include 1) northeast: Gordon Day, "The Indian as an Ecological Factor in the Northeastern Forest" (*Ecology* 64(1): 78–88. 1983); 2) northern Plains: Mavis Loscheider, "Use of Fire in Interethnic and Intraethnic Relations on the Northern Plains" (*Western Canadian Journal of Anthropology* 7(4): 82–96, 1977); 3) boreal forest: Dennis Dube, "Fire Ecology in Resource Management: workshop proceedings: December 6–7, 1977" (*Canadian Forestry Service Information Report* NOR-X-210, Edmonton, 1978); Harold Lutz, "Aboriginal Man and White Man as Historical Causes of Fires in the Boreal Forest, with particular reference to Alaska" (*Yale University School of Forestry*

Bulletin No. 65, 1959); Henry Lewis, "Maskuta: The Ecology of Indian Fires in
Northern Alberta" (*Western Canada Journal of Anthropology* 7(1): 15–52, 1977),
"Traditional Uses of Fire by Indians in Northern Alberta (*Current Anthropology* 19:
401–2, 1978), "Hunter-Gatherers and Problems for Fire History" (pp. 115–19 in
Marvin Stokes and John Dieterich, "Proceedings of the Fire History Workshop,
October 20–24, 1980, Tucson" (*USDA Forest Service General Technical Report* RM-
81, Publication No. 17, Edmonton, 1982), and Lewis and Ferguson (this volume);
4) interior west: Stephen Barrett, "Relationship of Indian-caused Fires to the
Ecology of Western Montana Forests" (M.S. thesis, University of Montana, 1980a),
"Indians and Fire" (*Western Wildlands* 6(3): 17–21, 1980b), "Indian Fires in the
Pre-Settlement forests of Western Montana" (pp. 35–41 in Stokes and Dieterich,
"Proceedings of the Fire History Workshop . . .," 1980); Barrett and Arno (1982
and this volume); and George Gruell, "Indian Fires in the Interior West: A
Widespread Influence," pp. 68–80 in James Lotan *et al.* "Proceedings—
Symposium and Workshop on Wilderness Fire, Missoula, November 15–18, 1983"
(*USDA Forest Service General Technical Report* INT-182, Ogden, 1985); 5) western
and central Washington and Oregon: Helen H. Norton, "The Association between
Anthropogenic Prairies and Important Food Plants in Western Washington"
(*Northwest Anthropological Research Notes* 13(2): 175–200, 1979); French; Norton,
Boyd, and Hunn; Boyd; and Robbins (all this volume); 6) California: Henry Lewis,
"Patterns of Indian Burning in California: Ecology and Ethnohistory" (pp. 55–116
in Thomas Blackburn and Kat Anderson, *Before the Wilderness: Environmental
management by native Californians* (Ballena Press anthropological paper no 40,
1993 [orig. 1973]); and Jan Timbrook, John Johnson, and David Earle,
"Vegetation Burning by the Chumash," pp. 117–49 in Blackburn and Anderson
(*ibid.*; orig. 1982). For North America in general, see Lewis, "Why Indians
Burned: Specific versus General Reasons," pp. 75–80 in Lotan *et al.*,
"Proceedings—Symposium and Workshop on Wilderness Fire"; Barbara Mills,
"Prescribed Burning and Hunter-Gatherer Subsistence Systems" (*Haliksa'i: UNM
Contributions to Anthropology* 5: 1–26, 1986); Stephen Pyne, *Fire in America: A
Cultural History of Wildland and Rural Fire* (Princeton, 1982) and "Indian Fires"
(*Natural History* 2(83): 6–11, 1983); and Omer Stewart, "Burning and Natural
Vegetation in the United States" (*Geographical Review* 41(2): 317–20, 1951), "The
Forgotten Side of Ethnogeography," pp. 221–48 in Robert Spencer, ed., *Method
and Perspective in Anthropology* (Minneapolis, 1954), and "Fire as the First Great
Force Employed by Man," pp. 115–33 in William Thomas, ed., *Man's Role in
Changing the Face of the Earth* (Chicago, 1956).
4. See John Parminter, "An Historical Review of Forest Fire Management in British
Columbia" (M.F. thesis, University of British Columbia, 1978); James Hatter,
"Wildlife and People in Interior British Columbia" (*Transcations of the Thirteenth
British Columbia Natural Resources Conference, Victoria,* 1961); Robert Mierendorf,
"An Archaeologist's View," pp. 15–19 in Vicki Haberl, ed., *Reflections of the Past:
Manning Park Memories* (Victoria, 1991); and Rolf Mathewes, "The Environment
and Biotic Resources of the Lillooet Area," pp. 68–99 in Arnoud Stryd and
Stephen Lawhead, eds., "Reports of the Lillooet Archaeological Project No. 1:
Introduction and Setting" (*National Museum of Man Mercury Series, Archaeological
Survey of Canada Paper* No. 73, 1978).
5. See the British Columbia Ministry of Forests Research Branch's map,
Biogeoclimatic Zones of British Columbia 1997 (Victoria, 1997); and The Indian

Affairs Branch of the [Canadian] Department of Indian Affairs and Northern Development's *Linguistic and cultural Affiliations of Canadian Indian Bands* (Ottawa, 1980).

6. Gerald Tande, "Interpreting Fire History in Jasper National Park, Alberta" (pp. 31–34 in Stokes and Dieterich, "Proceedings of the Fire History Workshop . . .," 1980); Stephen Barrett, "Relationship of Indian-caused Fires to the Ecology of Western Montana Forests" (1980a).

7. Barrett and Arno, this volume; Stokes and Dieterich, "Proceedings of the Fire History Workshop . . .,"1980); Henry Wright and Arthur Bailey, *Fire Ecology, United States and Southern Canada* (Toronto, 1982).

8. Harold Lutz, *Aboriginal Man and White Man as Historical Causes of Fires in the Boreal Forest* . . ., Parminter, "A Historical Review of Forest Fire Management in British Columbia"; and Barrett, "Relationship of Indian-caused Fires to the Ecology of Western Montana."

9. Edward House, *A Hunter's Camp-fires* (New York, 1909), cited in Parminter, "A Historical Review . . .," 5.

10. "Reasons" like these are cited or discussed in *The Journal Kept by David Douglas During his Travels in North America 1823–1827* (London, 1914); Stewart, "Burning and Natural Vegetation . . ."; H. Lutz, *Aboriginal Man and White Man as Historical Causes of Fires in the Boreal forest* . . .; Parminter, "A Historical Review . . ."; Barrett, "Relationship of Indian-caused Fires . . ."; Barrett and Arno, this volume; Lewis, "Why Indians Burned . . ."; and Boyd, this volume.

11. Hatter, "Wildlife and People in Interior British Columbia"; Parminter, "A Historical Review . . ."; Cole Harris, "Industry and the Good Life around Idaho Peak" (*Canadian Historical Review* 66(3): 315–43, 1985).

12. George Dawson, "Preliminary Report on the Physical and Geological Features of that Portion of the Rocky Mountains Between latitudes 49 degrees and 51 degrees, 30 minutes" (in *Geological and Natural History Survey of Canada Annual Report*, vol. 1, 1886).

13. See Hatter, "Wildlife and People . . .," on the percentage of burned forests; Harry Whitford and Roland Craig, *Forests of British Columbia* (Ottawa, 1918), 157 on fire prevention policy.

14. Douglas Cole and Bradley Lockner, *The Journals of George M. Dawson, British Columbia, 1875–1878* (Vancouver, 1989). Pp. 48, 130, 199, 203, 206, 214, 229, 247, 262, 320, 327, 329, 346, 350, and 493 cite burnt landscape; pp. 199, 203, and 351–52 note the advantages of burning.

15. The original text in Stl'atl'imx, together with a word-by-word translation, appear in Leo Swoboda's "Lillooet Phonology, Texts and Dictionary" (M.A. thesis, University of British Columbia, 1971), 182–91.

16. For more on Botanie Mountain, see Nancy Turner *et al.,* "Thompson Ethnobotany: Knowledge and Usage of Plants by the Thompson Indians of British Columbia" (*Royal British Columbia Museum Memoir* No. 3, 1990).

17. Turner *et al.,* "Thompson Ethnobotany," 191; see also Boyd (this volume) on burning of hazel bushes.

18. Mary Thomas also noted that morel mushrooms (*Morchella* spp.) flourish after burns too, but said that she did not recall her people eating those in the old days. She learned about their edibility more recently.

19. James Teit, "Traditions of the Thompson River Indians of British Columbia" (*Memoirs of the American Folk-Lore Society* vol. 6, 1898), 72–74.

20. Anonymous, "Colonization of Vancouver Island" (*The Times, London*, May 4, 1849), 18–19. On camas among southeast Vancouver Island Native Peoples, see Nancy Turner and Marcus Bell, "The Ethnobotany of the Coast Salish Indians of Vancouver Island" (*Economic Botany* 25(1): 63–104, 1971); Nancy Turner and Harriet Kuhnlein, "Camas (*Camassia spp.*) and Riceroot (*Fritillaria spp.*): Two Liliaceous 'Root' Foods of the Northwest Coast Indians" (*Ecology of Food and Nutrition* 13(4): 199–219, 1983); and Turner, *Food Plants of Coastal First Peoples* (UBC Press and Royal British Columbia Museum 1995. rev. ed.; orig. 1975).

21. Norton, "The Association Between Anthropogenic Prairies and Important Food Plants . . ."; Floyd Moravets, "Second Growth Douglas Fir Follows Cessation of Indian Fires" (*USDA Forest Service Bulletin* 16(20), 1932).

22. George Vancouver, *A Voyage of Discovery to the Pacific Ocean and Round the World, 1790–5*, vol. 1 (London, 1798), 227–29.

23. Duncan Finlayson, "Fort Victoria Journal" (Hudson's Bay Company Archives ms. B. 226/a/1, Winnipeg). The quotations from James Douglas are from 1) Douglas to John McLoughlin, July 12, 1842 (*The Beaver*, Outfit 273: 4–6, 1943); and 2) Douglas to James Hargrave, February 5, 1843 in George Glazebrook, ed., *The Hargrave Correspondence, 1821–1843* (Toronto, 1938), 420. Both are cited in John Lutz's unpublished "Preparing Eden: Aboriginal Land Use and European Settlement" (paper presented to the 1995 Meeting of the Canadian Historical Association).

24. Wayne Suttles, "The Economic Life of the Coast Salish of Haro and Rosario Straits" (Ph.D. dissertation, University of Washington, 1951a), 59, 60; and "The Early Diffusion of the Potato among the Coast Salish" (*Southwestern Journal of Anthropology* 7(3): 272–88, 1951b), 281. Cole and Lockner, *The Journals of George M. Dawson . . .*, 48, is the source of the Dawson citation.

25. The Tsolum Valley quotation comes from John Hayman, ed., *Robert Brown and the Vancouver Island Exploring Expedition* (Vancouver, 1989), 113. Other evidence for the anthropogenic origin of the Comox prairies is presented in an unpublished term paper by Nick Page, "The Importance of Garry Oak Grasslands as an Example of a Cultural Ecosystem" (Department of Forestry, University of British Columbia, November 1989).

26. W. Colquhon Grant, "Description of Vancouver Island" (*Journal of the Royal Geographic Society* 27: 268–320, 1857), 275.

27. Grant, "Description of Vancouver Island," 275; cited in J. Lutz, "Preparing Eden . . .."

28. Joseph Pemberton, *Facts and Figures Relating to Vancouver Island and British Columbia* (London, 1860), 19; Allan Pritchard, ed., "Letters of a Victorian Naval Officer, 1862–1864" (*BC Studies* 86(1): 32–33, 1990).

29. Franz Boas, "The Religion of the Kwakiutl Indians" (*Columbia University Contributions to Anthropology* 10, 1930), 203. Boas translated the text to English; species not given in original Kwakwala language; only a general term for "fruit" was used.

30. Randy Bouchard, personal communication, January 1991; R. Bouchard and Dorothy Kennedy, *Clayoquot Sound Indian Land Use* (Report prepared for MacMillan Bloedel Limited, Fletcher Challenge Canada, and the British Columbia Ministry of Forests, 1990).

31. Gilbert Sproat, *The Nootka: Scenes and Studies of Savage Life* (Charles Lillard, ed., Victoria, 1987 [orig. 1868]), 17.

32. Ivan Lopatin, "Social Life and Religion of the Indians of Kitimat, British Columbia" (*University of Southern California Social Science Series* 26, 1945), 140.

33. From interviews conducted by David Ellis (personal communications, January 21, 1991 and January 2, 1992).

34. The first two volumes originally were published as *Food Plants of British Columbia Indians; Coastal Peoples* (1975) and *Interior Peoples* (1978). Both were revised and republished in 1995 and 1997 by UBC Press and the Royal British Columbia Museum (Vancouver and Victoria). *Traditional Plant Foods of Canadian Indigenous Peoples* was published by Gordon and Breach Science Publishers, Philadelphia.

35. Hilda Austin [Lytton], personal communication, October 1984; Dorothy Kennedy and Randy Bouchard, "Indian History and Knowledge of the Aspen Grove to Peachland Corridor of the Coquihalla Highway" (Appendix II [pp. 121–35] in *Coquihalla Highway Project, Merritt to Peachland, B.C., Detailed Heritage Resource Inventory and Impact Assessment* (report prepared for the Heritage Conservation Branch, Ministry of Tourism and Design and Survey Branch, Ministry of Transportation and Highways, 1986), 128.

36. E.g., Barrett, "Relationship of Indian-caused Fires . . ."; and Johnson, this volume.

37. Barrett, "Relationship of Indian-caused Fires . . .."

38. Sources include Henry Lewis, "Traditional Indian Uses of Fire in Northern Alberta" (1978) and *A Time for Burning* (1982) on the Slavey; Berrett, "Relationship of Indian-caused Fires . . ." on Salish/Kootenai; Johnson (this volume) on Gitxsan/Wetsuwet'en; and Suttles, "The Economic Life of the Coast Salish of Haro and Rosario Straits" on southern Vancouver Island Salish.

39. Barrett, "Relationship of Indian-caused Fires . . ."; Lewis, "Traditional Uses of Fire in Northern Alberta" and *A Time for Burning*.

40. Eugene Hunn, *Nch'i-Wána, "The Big River": Mid-Columbia Indians and Their Land* (Seattle, 1990), 130.

41. Evelyn Hamilton and H. Kanan Yearley, *Vegetation Development after Clearcutting and Site Preparation in the SBS Zone* (Victoria, 1988).

42. Don Minore, "The Wild Huckleberries of Oregon and Washington—a Dwindling Resource" (*USDA Forest Service Research Paper* No. 143, 1972, 7.

43. See Turner *et al.*, "Thompson Ethnobotany," 127 for the native citations; Minore, "The Wild Huckleberries of Oregon and Washington"; Melissa Connor and Kenneth Cannon, "Forest Fires as a Site Formation Process in the Rocky Mountains of Northwestern Wyoming" (*Archaeology in Montana* 32(2): 1–15, 1991), 5; and plant ecologist Joe Antos (personal communication, 1991), are the authorities on nutrient release and diminished competition after burning.

44. On the revival of traditional plant use, see *People of 'Ksan, Gathering what the Great Nature Provided: Food Traditions of the Gitksan* (Vancouver, 1982); Coqualeetza Education Training Centre, *Upper Sto:lo (Fraser Valley) Plant Gathering* (Sardis, BC, 1981); The People of Port Simpson and School District No. 52 (Prince Rupert), *Port Simpson Foods* (Prince Rupert, 1983); and Marc Matthew, *Foods of the Shuswap People* (Kamloops, 1986). On the nutritional value of traditional foods, see Kuhnlein and Turner, *Traditional Plant Foods of Canadian Indigenous Peoples*.

45. Parminter, "A Historical Review of Forest Fire Management in British Columbia," 3.

46. Connor and Cannon, "Forest Fires as a Site Formation Process," on the detrimental soil effects of intensive burning; Larry Pynn, "Pesticides Hurt Traditional Food, Lillooets Claim" (*The Vancouver Sun*, November 1, 1986, p. A8), and Glenn Bohn, "Haida Elder Tells Board of 2, 4-D Fear" (*The Vancouver Sun*, February 24, 1987, p. B8) on contemporary pesticide problems.

47. Plant ecologist Joe Antos, however, believes that annual burning would reduce or eliminate broom (personal communication, 1991).

48. Suttles, "The Economic Life of the Coast Salish of Haro and Rosario Straits," 59; and Turner *et al.*, "Thompson Ethnobotany," discuss the effects of domestic animals on root grounds in Straits Salish territories and Botanie Valley, respectively. See also White (this volume) and Norton, "The Association between Anthropogenic Prairies and Important Food Plants . . ." on similar effects on Whidbey Island and the western Washington prairies.

49. Jan Timbrook, John Johnson, and David Earle, "Vegetation Burning by the Chumash" (pp. 117–50 in Blackburn and Anderson, *Before the Wilderness* [orig. 1982]).

50. John Walstad, Steven Radosevich, and David Sandberg (eds.), *Natural and Prescribed Fire in Pacific Northwest Forests* (Corvallis, 1990) is a compendium of regional fire ecology research. Clinton Phillips, in "The Relevance of Past Indian Fires to Current Fire Management Programs" (pp. 87–92 in Lotan *et al.*, "Proceedings—Symposium and Workshop on Wilderness Fire"), discuss the differing fire systems of aboriginal and contemporary western peoples; Stephen Arno, in "Ecological Effects and Management Implications of Indian Fires" (pp. 81–87 in Lotan, *ibid.*), notes how fire differentially affects different areas; and Susan Little, in "Conserving Resources and Ameliorating Losses from Prescribed Burning" (pp. 283-96 in Walstad, Radosevich and Sandberg, *Natural and Prescribed Fire in Pacific Northwest Forests*), considers ways to deal with the problems associated with prescribed burning.

Landscape and Environment
Ecological Change in the Intermontane Northwest[1]

William G. Robbins

From time immemorial, humans have been great modifiers of the ecological niches they occupy. That observation also is a proper fit for prehistoric North America, where archaeological evidence shows purposeful human manipulation of the environment to be an incontestable fact. Indeed, the great weight of scientific evidence and hypotheses argue against the notion of the continent as a pristine, Eden-like world where the human imprint was barely perceptible. Scholarly research in the past two decades indicates the existence of sizable prehistoric populations that influenced the extent and composition of forests, established and expanded grassland areas, and altered landscapes through myriad human devices. According to the geographer William Denevan, the important question is "the form and magnitude of environmental modification rather than . . . whether . . . Indians lived in harmony with nature with sustainable systems of resource management."[2]

It also is generally acknowledged that Columbus's voyage in 1492 triggered vast biological and technological changes with worldwide repercussions. In its wake a global network of economic and biological exchanges developed, the "intercontinental energy flows" of which, according to Karl Butzer, favored the emerging centers of the industrial revolution. As the industrializing sector expanded its technological reach, forces were set in motion that introduced immense social and environmental changes. Inexorably, succeeding modes of life—hunting-fishing-gathering, peasant agriculture, and industrial-postindustrial—have increased the extent and scope of human influence in the natural world.[3]

Both natural and cultural processes have been involved in shaping the environments about us. But culture became a factor in environmental change only with the emergence of modern humans during the midpoint of the last glacial period, circa 40,000 years ago, when they were in the process of colonizing most of the earth. For thousands of years, however, population numbers and technological practices limited the human imprint on global modification. With the exception of a possible role in Pleistocene extinctions, human-induced alterations on a broad scale were minor. But with warming conditions and the northward advance of forest ecosystems and plant life during the early Holocene (5,000 to 10,000 years ago), the human imprint on the natural world became much more noticeable. The new climatic conditions expanded the range of ecological niches suitable to human habitation and made it possible for people to manipulate plant and animal species to their advantage. But more than anything else, it was the advent of Neolithic agriculture that accelerated the human role in environmental change in many parts of the world.[4]

Several archaeological finds, including one at Oregon's Fort Rock Cave on the periphery of the Great Basin, indicate that humans first entered the greater Pacific Northwest during the late Pleistocene when glaciers still covered much of the mountainous country of the interior. At that time, some 13,000 years ago, now extinct animals—the giant ground sloth, the giant bison, the camel, and the horse—intermingled with present-day animals—such as antelope, deer, mountain sheep, and a variety of bird life. For reasons that still are the subject of great controversy, several of those late Pleistocene mammals became extinct. Whether the human presence in North America (and in the Pacific Northwest) is responsible for those extinctions remains an open question.[5]

As the great glaciers of the late Pleistocene receded, Lake Missoula periodically burst through its dam of glacial ice and unleashed a series of catastrophic floods through the upper Columbia River drainage. The scouring effects of that huge volume of water created the channeled scablands of eastern Washington, including the famous Grand Coulee. The most recent of those floods probably occurred toward the end of the glacial period. With the recession of the glaciers, conifers such as spruce and fir appeared over broad areas of the interior country, and when the climate began to warm, the conifers receded to higher elevations.[6]

By the sixteenth century, the onset of the modern era, humans had established intensified agricultural ecosystems in many parts of the globe. But economic, environmental, and ecological changes taking place elsewhere were delayed in the Pacific Northwest. Until the very recent past, the region simply was beyond the reach—or at best on the periphery—of the immense, market-induced biological exchanges occurring in the post-Columbian world. Euro-American penetration and conquest on this far edge of North America in fact extends back little more than two centuries. Indeed, what is striking about the region is the very recent and very rapid pace of human-induced environmental disturbance over very extensive areas in a very brief span of time.[7]

For the interior Northwest, the hunting-gathering way of life remained dominant until Europeans began to impose a new set of cultural arrangements on the landscape. The Pacific Northwest was an anomaly in one other respect: Neolithic agricultural practices, as traditionally defined, were absent during the Indian period of domination. Therefore, according to the fisheries and wildlife scientist Dean Shinn, "we are still relatively close to the early history of the region and to the events which caused environmental change there." This historical configuration of events and circumstances provides exceptional opportunities for studying precontact landscapes, for learning about ecological conditions at the onset of large-scale Euro-American migration, and for placing the human-induced environmental changes that have occurred in the industrial age in a broader perspective. In brief, the telescoping of the postcontact history of the region into such a brief span of time makes it possible —through conventional historical records such as journals, diaries, government surveys, and travel accounts— to discern much about ecological conditions at the time of the entry of Euro-Americans. That scholars are increasingly turning to pollen and soil records and traditional archaeological evidence further enriches the potential for building a realistic and viable profile of landscapes and environments.[8]

Once the post-glacial regime established itself, environmental conditions in the intermontane Northwest remained relatively stable for at least 10,000 years—with the exception of the cataclysmic explosion of Mount Mazama (circa 4000 B.C.). For the Plateau culture area of the interior Northwest, the archaeological record permits a consensus of sorts: cultural and social changes were modest until the historical period; subsistence patterns centered on terrestrial and riverine environments. Only the northward spread of Spanish horses in the early eighteenth century, the entry of the market-oriented fur trade in the early nineteenth century, and the introduction of exotic diseases that ravaged indigenous peoples disrupted that stability.[9]

But relative social and cultural stability does not imply the absence of native influence in the natural world. Indeed, extensive archaeological and historical evidence suggests quite the opposite. Native Americans in the Pacific Northwest inhabited a humanized landscape, ecosystems purposefully modified to meet their subsistence needs. Richard White argues that on Whidbey Island in Puget Sound, native people used fire as a tool to enhance the growing of bracken (*Pteridium aquilinum*) and camas (*Camassia quamash*), staple vegetables in their diet. "Rather than being major Indian food sources because they dominated the prairies," he concludes, "camas and bracken more likely dominated the prairies because they were major Indian food sources." There is abundant evidence to indicate equally human-influenced landscapes elsewhere in the region.[10]

Native-modified landscapes extended well beyond the Puget and Willamette lowlands to the eastern slopes of the Cascade Range, where Indians used fire as an effective tool to enhance the production of a variety of foodstuffs, including nutritious herbs and shrubs such as black mountain huckleberry (*Vaccinium membranaceum*) and its near relatives, grouseberry (*V. scoparium*) and blueberry (*V. caespitosum*). Those fire-created niches—both natural and human in origin—also attracted browsing animals such as deer and elk, sources of protein for the Indian diet. Widespread native burning practices, along with lightning-caused fires, created a forest environment of open glades and park-like settings, a descriptive refrain that runs through virtually all of the nineteenth-century travel and survey literature.[11]

The environmental historian Stephen Pyne contends that, except in the extremely arid regions of North America, grassland environments also were shaped by the Indians' calculated and routine use of fire. From the coastal plain of Massachusetts southward to Florida and westward to Texas, from California's Central Valley to Oregon's Willamette Valley, grasslands flourished as a consequence of Indian incendiary activity. Native influences in modifying the grassland environments of the great Columbia plain of eastern Washington and across the high desert country of eastern Oregon also are too obvious to ignore.[12]

Although there is some indication that early Pleistocene hunters in the Northwest used burning thousands of years ago, the practice was widespread by the early historical period; references to fires and burned landscapes appear throughout the early literature of the region. Historical sources do not reveal the ratio of human- to naturally caused fires in the interior Pacific Northwest before large-scale White settlement, but it is obvious that Indian incendiarism was a significant factor in the burning of grassland and forest alike. For desert ecosystems, Lee Eddleman asserts, "Human caused fires were of greater consequence." Other writers agree: fire "was a natural component of the native ecosystem." Early nineteenth-century travel accounts mention fire with such regularity as to create a mental picture of a ravaged, charred, ruined land.[13]

Like much of the early literature of the Pacific Northwest, the journals of Lewis and Clark reveal the complexities of Indian ecology, especially the importance of fire to the horse-mounted hunter-gatherers of the interior country. On their return trip upriver in the spring of 1806, Meriwether Lewis reported that the plains of the Columbia were "covered with a rich virdure of grass and herbs from four to nine inches high" (this would be bunchgrass, *Festuca idahoensis*). As the party drew closer to the Walla Walla River, the journal entries note the absence of firewood, the Indian use of shrubs for fuel, and an abundance of roots for human consumption, and they contain favorable assessments of grass for horses. Writing from some distance up the Walla Walla River, William Clark remarked that a "great portion of these bottoms has been latterly burnt which has entirely distroyed the timbered growth." To attribute all of the early season greenery to Indian burning practices is unreasonable, yet the historical literature shows a fascinating juxtaposition of human incendiary activity in the fall and rich vegetative growth the following year.[14]

It is evident that native people readily fired arid landscapes just as they did the Willamette and Puget lowlands to enhance hunting and the gathering of roots and berries. The Hudson's Bay Company operative Peter Skene Ogden, leading a trapping party through the upper Crooked River and into the Harney Basin in 1826 and 1827, repeatedly declared the country "overrun by fire" and pointed the finger of guilt to what he deemed were native culprits. But Ogden's greatest disappointment about those summer conflagrations centered on the widespread destruction of beaver habitat (and beaver):

> Many small Streams have been discovered in the Mountains and were of long since well supplied with Beaver but unfortunately the natives have destroyed them all and probably by the aid of fire which is certainly a most distructive mode of exterpating them for scarcely ever one escapes particularly when the streams are not wide, and from what I have seen in this my last years travels I will venture to assert without exageration the Natives have distroyed and principally by fire upwards of sixty thousand Beavers and of this number not a Hundred have reached any Establishment but all have been lost.[15]

The explorer-fur trader extraordinaire Ogden saw the regional landscape through a sharply different cultural lens from that of the Paiutes of eastern Oregon. The Indian habit of burning for *Indian purposes*, in his view, was irrational because it led to the destruction of beaver, an animal with a commodity value in distant markets.[16]

John Kirk Townsend, a Philadelphia-based naturalist and traveler on the Oregon Trail, provides one of the most vivid accounts of Indian burning practices in the Columbia River country. When his party camped about 15 miles below the mouth of the Umatilla River on the evening of September 3, 1835, Townsend reported that Indians had "fired the prairie" on the opposite side of the river, thereby brilliantly lighting the night sky:

> Here am I sitting cross-legged on the ground, scribbling by the light of the vast conflagration with as much ease as if I had a ton of oil burning by my side; but my eyes are every moment involuntarily wandering from the paper before me, to contemplate and admire the grandeur of the distant scene. The very heavens themselves appear ignited, and the fragments of ashes and burning grass-blades, ascending and careering about through the glowing firmament, look like brilliant and glorious birds let loose to roam and revel amid this splendid scene.[17]

Standing on a hilltop at the mouth of the Walla Walla River the following spring, the Reverend Samuel Parker described a landscape "covered with the fresh green of spring vegetation." Just a few miles to the north, at the juncture of the Snake River, he remarked again "the fresh verdure, which is springing up, luxuriantly, at this early season." A few years later, looking toward the

Columbia from the western slopes of the Blue Mountains, the United States Army reconnaissance officer John C. Fremont reported that "smoky and unfavorable" weather conditions obstructed "far views with the glass." But before descending to the Walla Walla River, he observed what he deemed to be the salutary aftereffects of burning: "the grass very green and good; the old grass having been burnt off early in the autumn." Both culture and nature were responsible for shaping the ecology of the intermontane region, yet the preponderance of evidence suggests that culture was the major cause of fire.[18]

Although the preceding discussion has focused on the native use of fire in arid landscapes, there is abundant evidence to indicate that culture played an important role in the ecology of the intermontane forests as well. For the greater Blue Mountain area, early travel accounts—many of them Oregon Trail narratives—provide copious testimony to the ecologically intrusive presence of Native Americans throughout the region. The section of the trail from the juncture of the Boise and Snake rivers to the Columbia in particular generated stories of fire and ash. After leaving the Grande Ronde Valley in a northwesterly direction through the Blue Mountains in late August of 1834, John Kirk Townsend remarked about the stately pine trees with an undergrowth of "service bushes and other shrubs." He was offended, however, by the burned grass and trees "blasted by the ravaging fires of the Indians. These fires are yet smouldering, and the smoke from them effectually prevents our viewing the surrounding country."

The ubiquitous and controversial Captain Benjamin Bonneville crisscrossed the Snake River-Blue Mountain country that same year and later made his notes available to Washington Irving, who wrote an account of those travels.

"View on Snake River of Artemesia [sagebrush] Plains." From Osborne Cross, Report of . . . the march of the mounted riflemen, 1849. OrHi # 85436.

According to Irving's version, during the summer months the captain witnessed "the season of setting fires to the prairie"—fire and smoke virtually everywhere. Bonneville's troops subsequently spent two weeks camped in the Grande Ronde Valley because fires in the surrounding hills blocked egress from the area.[19]

Passing through the high country dividing the Powder River and Grande Ronde valleys in August 1835, the missionary Jason Lee described a landscape "covered with a heavy growth of pitch pine [*Pinus ponderosa*], very large, tall, and beautiful." The only distracting feature to the Methodist was the evidence that fire "had recently been making its destructive revages over the whole mountain." After ascending the Blue Mountains and traveling across the summit, Lee reported the party's vision obscured "by smoke, which was [so] dense that we could discern objects only a few yards." Four years later, Thomas Jefferson Farnham followed the west bank of the Snake River and then moved into the hills along a small stream where Indians recently burned had the countryside. The following day he described an atmosphere filled with smoke "as in Indian summer-time in the highlands of New England."[20]

By the time the large emigrant train of 1843 was enroute to the Willamette Valley, newcomers traveling through the interior Northwest were becoming familiar with late summer Indian fires. The trapper James Clyman, who accompanied an 1844 emigrant party to Fort Boise and then pressed on ahead to Oregon, observed "verry Smoky" weather in the Powder River Valley and even worse conditions in the Grande Ronde Valley, where "Indians as is their habit . . . set fire to the grass." Passing northward from the Powder River, Clyman and his group "nearly suffocated with smoke & dust," and upon descending into the Grande Ronde Valley, they witnessed "the whole mountains which surround this vally completely enveloped in fire and Smoke."[21]

There is an ironic twist to much of the scientific and technical literature on the influence of fire in shaping ecosystems in the Pacific Northwest. Virtually all writers recognize that Indians used fire as a tool to fashion grassland and forest environments for a variety of purposes. Despite acknowledging that fact, those same writers discuss "fire and its role in the pristine environment" as if the manipulations of native people were part of nature itself. One authority on fire history, while conceding "significant Indian influence," refers to nineteenth-century forests as "unmanaged" and "natural" environments. In this view, before the advent of modern forest management, Northwest woodlands were not humanized places. As Richard White has observed: "Perhaps the most important decision Europeans made about American nature . . . was that they were not part of it, but Indians were." Moreover, he argues, even when the newcomers encountered human-influenced ecosystems, they "tended to deny that Indians could have created them."[22]

By the early nineteenth century, native people in the interior Northwest had acquired sizable numbers of horses, some tribes—the Yakama, Cayuse, and Nez Perce—possessing especially large herds. Horse populations across western North America originated in the Spanish colonies in what is now New Mexico. When the Pueblo Indians revolted in 1680 and drove the Spanish out of the Rio Grande country, they liberated the Spaniards' horses, and the latter quickly found their way northward. Along the western slope of the Rocky Mountains, the animals were passed from the Utes to the Shoshones on the upper Snake River, to the Flatheads by 1720, and most likely to the Nez Perce and Cayuse in the 1730s.[23]

That the acquisition of horses dramatically increased Indian mobility (and thereby affected Indian economic and social life) is well known; what is more difficult to discern are the extent and magnitude of ecological change that should be attributed to the horse. Some scholars argue that much of the grassland niche in western North America lay vacant and "underutilized" in the wake of the Pleistocene extinctions. The dispersal of horses, according to this view, took place over areas unoccupied by large grazing animals and consequently had little appreciable influence on those settings. Yet the evidence presented here strongly suggests that the introduction of horses, especially as the herds assumed sizable proportions, considerably intensified Indian burning practices. Until the large-scale western emigration of the 1840s, therefore, it seems reasonable to assume that both horses and fire represented an Indian-mediated presence in the landscape.

Early and numerous journal references to the abundance of Indian horses indicate that humans shaped intermontane ecosystems by means other than fire. They had in fact introduced a new species to the region. Struggling through the snow-clad Blue Mountains to the north of the Grande Ronde Valley in the winter of 1911–12, the Astorian Wilson Price Hunt observed on every side of his route "horse-trails used by the Indians." When party members reached the Umatilla River, they visited an Indian camp of thirty-four lodges with an estimated 2,000 horses. The presence of copper kettles and pots about the dwellings and the wearing of bison robes and buckskin leggings indicated extensive travel by horseback and trade with distant peoples. Passing down the arid stretch of the Columbia River between the Umatilla and the Great Falls (Celilo Falls) in September of 1834, John Kirk Townsend reported seeing "large bands of Indian horses . . . beautiful animals . . . almost as wild as deer" and marked with "strange hieroglyphic looking characters" to indicate ownership.[24]

Five years later, Thomas Jefferson Farnham met a Cayuse family in the Blue Mountains returning from a buffalo hunt to the east. The man and woman and their two children had seventeen horses in tow, "splendid animals," Farnham noted, "as large as the best horses of the States, well knit, deep and wide in the shoulders." When he reached the south bank of the Columbia River, he noticed that "groups of Indian horses occasionally appeared." And just prior to the settler movement to the Willamette Valley in the early 1840s, the inveterate preacher-traveler Samuel Parker recorded in his journal that he saw several "bands of Indians' horses" as well as deer and antelope.[25]

When his reconnaissance troop reached the Walla Walla River in October of 1843, John C. Fremont observed "several hundred horses grazing on the hills . . . and as we advanced on the road we met other bands, which the Indians were driving out to pasture also on the hills." A month later, journeying along the eastern slope of the Cascade Mountains, he reported a village of Nez Perce "who appeared to be coming down from the mountains, and had with them fine bands of horses." Major Osborne Cross, on the Umatilla River in September 1849, witnessed everywhere "large droves of horses . . . .stout, well built, and very muscular." And a decade later in the Grande Ronde Valley, George Belshaw observed "quantities of Indians and Poneys" in "this butiful valey."[26]

That Parker and other observers associated horses, deer, and antelope with the natural world points to the pervasive problem of distinguishing between the natural and the unnatural. Horses, of course, were unlike deer and antelope; they were unnatural in the region; they represented Indian cultural adaptations of the relatively recent past; they were large grazing ungulates and unquestionably represented an alien and intrusive element in their adopted environments. Because human agency was responsible for their introduction, the animals should be considered a culturally engendered force shaping the landscape of the Indian Northwest.[27]

After the United States established sovereignty over the country south of the 49th parallel in 1846, the government undertook a series of boundary, military road, and railroad surveys, many of which centered on the Cascade Mountains. Those inquiries provide further evidence of ecosystems heavily influenced by human activity. The reports of the Northwest Boundary Survey Commission offer an excellent description of the transition in forest types on the western and eastern slopes of the Cascades. On the western side, where the human use of fire was less apparent, the timber was dense, "being a heavy growth of pine and fir that in many places stands over a fallen forest not yet decayed." But east of the summit was fire-nurtured ponderosa pine; the commission noted, "the timber becomes more open, and survey operations less difficult."[28]

At the far eastern extreme of Washington Territory, a reconnaissance group under the command of Captain John Mullan examined feasible routes both for military and for railroad passage eastward through the Bitterroot Mountains. In the lower Snake River country, the command frequently traded with local Indian villages for salmon and other supplies and used the numerous

Indian trails to traverse canyons and to gain access to the plateau above. Although the natives lived in permanent villages, the army officials noted that their lodges were covered with buffalo skins and mats, indications of trade and travel east of the mountains. On the slopes above the Palouse River, the Indians harvested service berries (*Amelanchier alnifolia*), wild currants (*Ribes sanguineum*), and gooseberries (*R. divaricatum*) in great abundance; the "luxuriant bunch grass" (*Festuca idahoensis*) that grew everywhere provided excellent feed for the surveyors' horses. Above the scattered groves of trees along the river bottom was "a high, slightly undulating prairie, destitute of timber." Standing atop Steptoe Butte, close to the present border with Idaho, in the summer of 1860, the expedition topographer Theodore Kolecki described the vast area around the mountain as "rolling prairie, very much resembling a stormy sea" with pine timber commencing 4 or 5 miles to the east and stretching to the Bitterroot Mountains.[29]

Lieutenant Henry L. Abbot's survey in the autumn of 1854 of a prospective railroad route from the Sacramento Valley to the Columbia River furnished detailed descriptions of fire-nurtured landscapes, firsthand observations of Indian burning practices, and frequent reference to sizable Indian horse herds. Through the entire route of its travel on the eastern flank of the Cascades from Klamath Lake northward, the Abbot survey found "excellent bunch grass . . . .Whortleberries [the black mountain huckleberry], elder berries [*Sambucus racemosa*] and service berries," species that thrive in the aftermath of fire. A decade later, officials of the Oregon Central Military Wagon Road surveyed a route from Eugene southeast through the Cascade Mountains to

Henry Abbot's narrative credits Indians with excavating water holes and firing the landscape to foster the growth of grass for their horses. (Reports of Explorations . . . for a Railroad . . ., Vol. 6) OrHi # 98638.

the headwaters of the Deschutes River. Although the party struggled through the dense forests on the western slope, once east of the summit the country was flat, the higher elevations "covered with black pine, clover grass in abundance, and great quantities of meadow grounds." The surveyors observed places where the forest had been "killed by fire" and elsewhere found little evidence of undergrowth, either in the "black pine" (lodgepole, *Pinus contorta*) or in the "yellow pine" (*P. ponderosa*) timber to the southeast. On The Dalles-Fort Klamath trail, they saw signs that a large band of horses had camped the previous night, "and from the character of the horse tracks and mockasin tracks accompanying think it is Indians."[30]

The descriptions of landscape in the official reports for the eastern slope of the Washington Cascades read much the same: dense underbrush and trees in the higher elevations, gradually giving way to open spaces and a clean understory in the ponderosa-dominated stands at lower elevations. The botanical section of the 1853–55 railroad surveys through the northern Cascades (which are known as the Stevens report) portrays a forested landscape similar to that located south of the Columbia River. The representation of the ponderosa pine areas is especially striking:

Early ponderosa landscape—not likely pristine. (Reports of Explorations and surveys to Ascertain the Most Practicable and Economical Route for a Railroad from the Mississippi River to the Pacific Ocean, 1853-55, Vol. 12). OrHi # 98640.

There is . . . [so] little underbrush in these forests that a wagon may be drawn through them without difficulty, forming a striking contrast to the dense thickets of the western slopes . . . .The level terraces, covered everywhere with good grass and shaded by fine symmetrical trees of great size, through whose open light foliage the sun's rays penetrate with agreeable mildness, give to these forests the appearance of an immense ornamental park.[31]

But what is most striking about the mid-century railroad survey narratives is their similarity to the later, turn-of-the-century forest reserve reports and the United States Geological Survey (USGS) investigations. Although grazing ungulates—sheep and cattle—had been introduced, and natural and human-caused fired continued to occur, the forested landscape after fifty years of Euro-American habitation looked much the same. In brief, market influences in the forest environment of the interior Northwest still were very limited. On the lower slopes of the central Oregon Cascades, a USGS investigation headed by Harold D. Langille observed forests "of pure growth . . . [which] are generally open, without much litter or undergrowth, and for these reasons are almost immune from fire." In the yellow pine country, the report continued, "the forest floor is often as clean as if it had been cleared, and one may ride or even drive without hindrance. As the hills are approached the brush increases." The investigators estimated that in the "yellow-pine region bordering the timberless area of eastern Oregon," 10% of the timbered area had burned recently and 90% of the forest "at some remote period."[32]

John B. Leiberg's turn-of-the-century survey of the southern Cascades acknowledged both the influence of native burning practices and the effects of fire during the early period of White settlement. The composition of the forest indicated "without any doubt the prevalence of widespread fires throughout this region long before the coming of the white man." But fires during the Indian period of occupancy "were not of such frequent occurrence nor of such magnitude as they have been since the advent of the white man." When settlers learned that burning the forest attracted game, Leiberg surmised, they set the woods on fire. The role of fire in the stands of yellow pine on the eastern slope of the Cascades was clear because of the "noticeable and striking" absence of young growth and underbrush. "The yellow pine," Leiberg concluded, "is by all odds the best fire-resisting tree in the sylva of the North Pacific slope."[33]

Finally, a Division of Forestry inquiry into the influence of sheep grazing in the Cascade Mountains provided yet another turn-of-the-century example of what must be recognized as a humanized landscape. Indian people were "the first manipulators of forest-fires in this region," wrote Frederick V. Coville; in the Willamette Valley they annually burned the savanna grasslands, and in the Cascades, Indian burning practices created what he termed "fire glades."

He thought it an incontestable fact that "at certain seasons it was their custom to set fires in the mountains *intentionally and systematically.*" In traveling the length of the Cascades, Coville concluded that "evidences of fire, recent or remote" had touched every township of forest land. He also reported two relatively new sources of fires—road building and industrial activity, the latter of which had caused a burn of 15,000 to 18,000 acres near the Wood River headwaters in the Fort Klamath region. The conflagration began when a camp of men splitting shakes set several small fires to keep mosquitoes away.[34]

That Wood River fire was only one instance of widespread settler-caused fires during the nineteenth century. Fires "in the early days of settlement," one USGS survey reported, "were more numerous and devastated much larger areas . . . . As time has passed, [however,] the frequency of forest fires in the region has much diminished." With the increasing commodity value of standing timber in the early twentieth century, the effort to curb forest and range fires gained momentum, eventually assuming the form of the prevention crusade symbolized by Smokey the Bear.[35]

With the arrival of ever-increasing numbers of Euro-Americans after 1800, the relative cultural and ecological stability of several millennia in the Pacific

This view of a ponderosa forest shows the open, park-like effect created by periodic burning that so charmed early travelers. (Langille et al., Forest Conditions . . .). OrHi #98635.

Northwest began to erode. Possessing unique social and economic attributes, the newcomers initiated dramatic cultural and biological modifications that continue to the present day. Perhaps the aging former president John Quincy Adams, speaking on the floor of the House of Representatives in favor of settling the Oregon boundary question, expressed that newly emerging set of convictions best: "We claim that country—for what? To make the wilderness blossom as the rose, to establish laws, to increase, multiply, and subdue the earth, which we are commanded to do by the first behest of God Almighty."[36]

The intruders, slowly at first and then gathering momentum, imposed upon the indigenous people and the regional landscape a markedly different cultural vision, one that led to the gradual—sometimes spectacular—modification of ecosystems both east and west of the Cascade Range. In the words of one scientist, the past 150 years have witnessed "an unprecedented acceleration" in the ever-changing ecosystems of the region. And because White settlement was the factor most responsible for precipitating those changes, Richard White asserts, it "destroyed the Indian Northwest."[37]

The worldwide expansion of market capitalism was the great driving force in transforming the human and natural world of the Pacific Northwest. First came the fur men in their quest for beaver pelts, deliberately creating "fur deserts" in one instance to drive competitors away from the region. The fur traders also unknowingly trafficked in other items that brought ecological change, primarily the introduction of exotic plants and human contagions that devastated native populations. To the anthropologist Eugene Hunn, "the history of Indian-white relations in the Columbia Plateau has been first and foremost "a history of the ravages of disease . . . which drastically reduced aboriginal populations." And, he might have added, opened the way for the repeopling of the region.[38]

In both the deliberate and the accidental introduction of exotic plant and animal species, agriculturists were at the forefront of ecological change in North America. Farmers, whether their activities were subsistence or commercial, created artificial, human-imposed ecosystems on the lands they touched. Westering Euro-Americans brought with them cultural practices and familiar plants and animals; the combined effects of that mix began the slow and then accelerated transformation of their newly adopted environments. For the interior Pacific Northwest, where much of that transformation has taken place in this century, the result has been a decisively altered landscape.[39]

In terms of places long occupied by humans, the landscape of the Pacific Northwest is a short-lived enterprise, perhaps 20,000 years old. For a place dominated by Euro-Americans, the time frame narrows to roughly 150 years; for the intermontane Northwest, a century. East of the Cascade Range—as in the more westerly country—complex ecosystems have been modified and simplified drastically as single exotic species replace multiple indigenous species.

By the turn of the century, scientists deplored forest fires, especially those set by sheepmen to extend grazing land. (H. D. Langille et al., *Forest Conditions in the Cascade Range Forest Reserve, Oregon*, 1903). OrHi # 98639.

In the arid country of the Inland Empire, cheatgrass or other annual bromegrass has replaced blue-bunch wheatgrass on land used exclusively for grazing. Elsewhere, on the plateaus and gentle slopes of the Palouse, a monoculture crop—wheat—has replaced everything else. And in the Blue Mountains to the south, logging and suppression of burning have permitted true fir and Douglas-fir to replace some of the great stands of ponderosa pine. With the exception of drought, windstorm, and lightning-caused fires, the spectacular changes in the landscape of the interior Northwest during the past century have been human induced. The striking feature of this story is the abbreviated number of years in which those alterations have taken place, especially the accelerating rate of modification during the past few decades. As public citizens, we all have much to learn about the history of the intricate web of ecological and economic relationships that is part of our daily lives.[40]

Originally published in the *Pacific Northwest Quarterly* 84(4): 140–149 (October 1993)

Notes

1. A longer version of this paper was published as "Eastside forest ecosystem health assessment: An environmental history." Landscape and the intermontane Northwest, vol. 3. (USDA Forest Service General Technical Report PNW-319, 1994).

2. On prehistoric environmental manipulation, see Carl O. Sauer, "Man in the Ecology of Tropical America," *Proceedings of the Ninth Pacific Science Congress,* Vol. 20 (1957), 104–10; William Cronon, *Changes in the Land: Indians, Colonists, and the Ecology of New England* (New York, 1983); and Richard White, *Land Use, Environment, and Social Change: The Shaping of Island County, Washington* (Seattle, 1980). From 1992 (the Columbian sesquicentennial) two geographic overviews are Karl Butzer, "The Americas before and after 1492: An Introduction to Current Geographic Research"; and William Denevan, "The Pristine Myth: The Landscape of the Americas in 1492"; pp. 345-68 and 369-85 in *Annals of the Association of American Geographers,* Vol. 82, no. 3.

3. Butzer, 346; Neil Roberts, *The Holocene: An Environmental History* (New York, 1989), 5. See also Alfred Crosby, *The Columbian Exchange: biological and cultural consequences of 1492.* (Westport, CONN, 1972), and *Ecological Imperialism: the biological expansion of Europe, 900–1900* (Cambridge, 1986).

4. Roberts, 57–113.

5. For a brief account of the Fort Rock and other Northwest archaeological excavations, see Luther S. Cressman, *The Sandal and the Cave: The Indians of Oregon* (1962: rpt. Corvallis, 1981). The greater Pacific Northwest embraces the present states of Washington, Oregon, and Idaho; northern California and Nevada; western Montana; and southern British Columbia. C. Melvin Aikens, *Archaeology of Oregon* (Portland, 1993), 9–10; Roberts, 67; Donald K. Grayson, "Pleistocene Avifaunas and the Overkill Hypothesis," *Science,* Vol. 195, 691–93 (1977); and Paul S. Martin, "The Discovery of America," *Science,* Vol. 179, 969–74 (1973). The Manis mastodon site on the Olympic Peninsula preserves evidence of the contemporaneity of extinct species and early man. See Carl Gustafson, Delbert Gilbow, and Richard Daugherty, "The Manis Mastodon Site: Early Man on the Olympic Peninsula," *Canadian Journal of Archaeology* Vol. 3: 157–64 (1979).

6. Aikens, 41–42; Eugene Hunn, *Nch'i-Wána, "The Big River": Mid-Columbia Indians and Their Land* (Seattle, 1990), 19–21; and John Eliot Allen, *Cataclysms on the Columbia: A layman's guide to the features produced by the catastrophic Bretz floods in the Pacific Northwest* (Portland, 1986).

7. Roberts, 122; Carlos Schwantes argues that "geographical isolation fundamentally shaped the course of Pacific Northwest history." Geography conspired to keep the Northwest "beyond the reach of Europe and the rest of North America" and thereby "contributed to a pronounced time lag in its historical development." See Schwantes, *The Pacific Northwest: An Interpretive History* (Lincoln, NE, 1989), 19.

8. Dean Shinn, "Historical Perspectives on Range Burning in the Inland Pacific Northwest," *Journal of Range Management,* Vol. 33(6): 415-23 (1980), 418, 419 (qtn.). For the absence of Neolithic agriculture in the Pacific Northwest, see Butzer, 348; White, 14–34.

9. Hunn points out that changes in climatic patterns required adjustments in hunting and gathering strategies rather than dramatic economic and social change

(pp. 19, 21). See also Richard White, "The Altered Landscape: Social Change and the Land in the Pacific Northwest," pp. 109-25 in *Regionalism and the Pacific Northwest*, ed. William Robbins, Robert Frank, and Richard Ross (Corvallis, 1983), 110–11; and Hunn, "The Plateau," pp. 9-14 in *The First Oregonians: An Illustrated Collection of Essays on Traditional Lifeways, Federal-Indian Relations, and the State's Native People Today*, ed. Carolyn Buan and Richard Lewis (Portland, 1991), 14.

10. White, *Land Use*, 21 (qtn.), and "The Altered Landscape," 111. For further discussion of Indian fire ecology, see Henry Lewis, "Patterns of Indian Burning in California: Ecology and Ethnohistory," 1973 and 1993 (revised), pp. 55–116 in Thomas Blackburn and Kat Anderson, *Before the Wilderness: Environmental management by native Californians* (Menlo Park, CA: Ballena Press Anthropological Paper no. 40), Robert Boyd, "Strategies of Indian Burning in the Willamette Valley," 1986 and (revised) this volume; and others reprinted in this volume.

11. Hunn, *Nch'i-Wána*, 130–31.

12. Stephen Pyne, *Fire in America: A Cultural History of Wildland and Rural Fire* (Princeton, 1982), 84–85. In Oregon's Willamette Valley, native people used fire in a substantial way to alter the landscape dramatically for their own purposes. See Peter Boag, *Environment and Experience: Settlement Culture in Nineteenth-Century Oregon* (Berkeley, 1992), 12–15.

13. Shinn, 415–17; Lee Eddleman, "Oregon's High Desert—Legacy for Today," 2; and J. Boone Kauffman and D. B. Sapsis, "The Natural Role of Fire in Oregon's High Desert," 15 (2d qtn.), both in *Oregon's High Desert: The Last 100 Years*, Oregon State University, Agricultural Experiment Station, Special Report 841 (Corvallis, 1989).

14. Gary Moulton, ed. *The Journals of the Lewis & Clark Expedition*, vol. 7: March 23–June 9, 1806 (Lincoln, NE, 1991), 131 (lst qtn.), 197 (2d qtn.).

15. Kenneth Davies, ed., *Peter Skene Ogden's Snake Country Journals, 1826–27* (London, 1961), 7 (1st qtn.), 9, 19, 188, and 126–27 (qtn.).

16. Early accounts of the Americas dating from the time of Columbus appraised objects in the physical environment in terms of their value as commodities. See Richard White, "Discovering Nature in North America," *Journal of American History*, Vol. 79(3): 874-91 (1992), 879–80.

17. John Kirk Townsend, *Narrative of a Journey across the Rocky Mountains to the Columbia River . . .* (1839; rpt. Lincoln, 1978), 246.

18. Samuel Parker, *Journal of an Exploring Tour Beyond the Rocky Mountains* (1838; rpt. Minneapolis, 1967), 272 (1st qtn.) and 274 (2d qtn.); Donald Jackson and Mary Lee Spence, eds., *The Expeditions of John Charles Fremont*, Vol. 1 (Urbana, 1970), 550 (1st, 2d qtns.), 551 (3d qtn.); and Eddleman, 2. Except for these early firsthand accounts, there is no body of solid "data" to prove the case one way or the other.

19. Washington Irving, *The Adventures of Captain Bonneville, U.S.A., in the Rocky Mountains and the Far West . . .*, ed. Edgeley Todd (1837; rpt. Norman, OK, 1961), 338–41 (qtn., 338).

20. Lee quoted in Archer Butler Hulbert and Dorothy Printup Hulbert, eds., *The Oregon Crusade: Across Land and Sea to Oregon* (Denver, 1935), 178; and Thomas Farnham, *An 1839 Wagon Train Journal: Travels in the Great Western Prairies, the Anahuac and Rocky Mountains and in the Oregon Territory* (1843; rpt. Monroe, OR, 1977), 73.

21. James Clyman, *Journal of a Mountain Man* (1928; rpt. Missoula, 1984), 120.
22. James Young and B. Abbott Sparks, *Cattle in the Cold Desert* (Logan, UT, 1985), 27 (1st qtn.); James K. Agee, "The Historical Role of Fire in Pacific Northwest Forests," pp. 25-38 in *Natural and Prescribed Fire in Pacific Northwest Forests*, ed. John Walstad, Steven Radosevich, and David Sandberg (Corvallis, 1990), 26 (2d qtns.); and White, "Discovering Nature," 882. One Forest Service employee recalled that in 1909 the Siskiyou forest "was largely as the Indians had left it. It had lots of game in the mountains and fish in the rivers," and it had areas where "practically all the forest had been burned over"; Henry Haefner to Gifford Pinchot, Gifford Pinchot Papers, Series B. Container 986, Manuscript Division, Library of Congress.
23. Francis Haines, "The Northward Spread of Horses among the Plains Indians." *American Anthropologist*, Vol. 40(2-4): 429-37 (1938), 431, 435–36; and Hunn, *Nch'i-Wána*, 22–26.
24. "Wilson Price Hunt's Diary of His Overland Trip Westward to Astoria in 1811–12." pp. 281–328 in *The Discovery of the Oregon Trail: Robert Stuart's Narratives*, ed. Philip Ashton Rollins (New York, 1935), 301 (qtn.), 302; and Townsend, 173. Nearly every Oregon Trail travel account mentions the great number of Indian horses on both sides of the Blue Mountains. Writing from a camp on the Walla Walla River in 1843, James Nesmith mentioned hunting down cattle and horses that strayed during the night, "the Indian horses being so numerous made it difficult for us to find our own"; Nesmith Ankeny, *The West as I Knew It* ([Walla Walla?], 1953), 27.
25. Farnham, 74–75; and Parker, 281.
26. Jackson and Spence, 551 (1st qtn.) and 584 (2d qtn.); Raymond W. Settle, ed., *The March of the Mounted Riflemen . . . as Recorded in the Journals of Major Osborne Cross and George Gibbs and the Official Report of Colonel Loring* (1940; 1989 reprint by The University of Nebraska Press), 229; George Belshaw, *Diary of George Belshaw (Oregon Trail—1853)* (Eugene, 1960), n. pag.
27. Although the literature on Indian horse herds as agents of ecological change is not large, there is a growing body of evidence to suggest that the ecological influence of the rapid spread of horses in western North America was considerable. See Richard White, *The Roots of Dependency: Subsistence, Environment, and Social Change among the Choctaws, Pawnees, and Navajos* (Lincoln, 1983), 100, and 247–48; and Dan Flores, "Bison Ecology and Bison Diplomacy: The Southern Plains from 1800 to 1850," *Journal of American History*, Vol. 78(2): 465-85 (1991), 481.
28. Archibald Campbell to William H. Seward, Secretary of State, Feb. 3, 1869, RG 76, Records Relating to the First Northwest Boundary Survey Commission, 1853–69 , National Archives, T-606, roll 1.
29. John Mullan, *Report on the Construction of a Military Road from Fort Walla-Walla to Fort Benton* (Washington, D.C., 1863), 103 (1st, 2d qtns.), 104 (3d qtn.).
30. *Reports of Explorations and Surveys, to Ascertain the Most Practicable and Economical Route for a Railroad from the Mississippi River to the Pacific Ocean, 1853–55*, 12 vols., 33d Cong., 2d Sess., 1857, SED 78, Vol. 6 (Abbot), p. 75 (Serial 763); and diary of Mrs. Bynon J. Pengra, entries for July 1865, in Stephen Dow Beckham, *The Oregon Central Military Wagon Road: A History and Reconnaissance*, Vol. 1. Heritage Research Associates Report No. 6 (Eugene, 1981), 27 (1st qtn.), 33 (2d qtn.), 28 (3d qtn.).

31. *Reports of Explorations for a Railroad*, Vol. 12, p. 14. The survey through the northern Cascades usually is referred to as the Stevens report because the Washington territorial governor and Indian agent, Isaac Stevens, was in charge.

32. Harold Langille *et al.*, *Forest Conditions in the Cascade Range Forest Reserve, Oregon*, USGS Professional Paper No. 9 (Washington, D.C., 1903), 78 (1st qtns.) and 87 (qtns.).

33. John Leiberg, "Cascade Range and Ashland Forest Reserves and Adjacent Regions," 277 (1st, 2d qtns.), 288 (last qtns.), in USGS annual report, Forestry, 1899, in 56th Cong., 2d Sess., 1900, H.D. 5, Vol. 35, Pt. 5 (Forest Reserves) (Serial 4109). In his study of Indian burning practices in northern Alberta, Henry Lewis found that Native Americans controlled their fires through timing and carefully selecting the places to be burned. See Lewis, "Maskuta: The Ecology of Indian Fires in Northern Alberta," *Western Canadian Journal of Anthropology*, Vol. 7(1): 15-52, (1977).

34. Frederick Coville, *Forest Growth and Sheep Grazing in the Cascade Mountains of Oregon*, USDA Division of Forestry, Bulletin No. 15 (1898), 20 (2d qtn.), 29 (1st, 4th qtns.), 30 (3d qtn., emphasis added), 32, and 33.

35. Leiberg, 277 (qtn.); Eddleman, 2; and Pyne, 161–67.

36. Cf. Hunn, *Nch'i-Wána*, 19; *Congressional Globe*, 29th Cong., 1st Sess., 1846, p. 342.

37. Helmut Buechner, "Some Biotic Changes in the State of Washington, Particularly during the Century 1853–1953," *Research Studies of the State College of Washington*, Vol. 21 (1953), 154; White, "The Altered Landscape," 111.

38. To keep American fur traders away, the Hudson's Bay company officer George Simpson ordered Peter Skene Ogden to create a "fur desert" in the huge drainage of the Snake River; see Schwantes, 60–62. As many as 50,000 native people may have occupied the 260,000 square miles of the Columbia River country. See Hunn, *Nch'i-Wána*, 31–32; for other estimates and Indian population losses, see Robert Boyd, "The Introduction of Infectious Diseases among the Indians of the Pacific Northwest, 1774–1874" (Ph.D. dissertation, University of Washington, 1985), chap. 8.

39. On agriculturists and change, see White, *Land Use*, 35–53.

40. Buechner, 169; and Boyd Wickman, *Forest Health in the Blue Mountains: The Influence of Insects and Disease*, USDA Forest Service, General Technical Report PNW-295 (Portland, 1992), 2. The naturalist Robert Michael Pyle points out that biologists contend that "the rate of species extinction has risen sharply since the introduction of agriculture and industry to the human landscape." See Pyle, "Intimate Relations and the Extinction of Experience," *Left Bank*, No. 2: 61-69 (Summer 1992), 63.

Aboriginal Burning for Vegetation Management in Northwest British Columbia

Leslie Main Johnson[1]

Introduction

Thie Gitxsan and Wet'suwet'en peoples live in the drainage of the Skeena River in Northwest British Columbia. The Gitxsan are a Northwest Coast people who speak a Tsimshian language. The Wet'suwet'en of the Bulkley Valley are Athapaskan speakers who live in close proximity to the Gitxsan and have a long history of interaction and mutual borrowing. Their traditional way of life involved fishing for salmon along the major rivers; hunting and trapping; and gathering of berries, tree cambium, and wild root foods. The Wet'suwet'en village of Hagwilget is 7 km upstream from the Gitxsan village of Gitanmaax. They are culturally similar groups in many ways and occupy a similar environment.

The environment and vegetation of the Gitxsan and Wet'suwet'en territories are transitional between the Northwest Coast and the boreal interior. The landscape is mountainous except where major river valleys occur. It is densely forested with coniferous forests to timberline, except in the valleys around Hazelton, where substantial areas of deciduous and mixed-wood forests occur. The forests are in the interior cedar-hemlock, coastal western hemlock, and mountain hemlock biogeoclimatic zones in the west, and in the sub-boreal spruce and Englemann spruce-subalpine fire biogeoclimatic zones in the east.[2]

The vegetation communities of the Skeena and Bulkley valleys around Hazelton, an ancient center of aboriginal population, show the influence of relatively frequent fires. The vegetation of this area has been designated the "Hazelton variant" (ICHmc3)[3] of the interior-cedar hemlock zone. It is characterized by a high prevalence of seral communities dominated by aspen (*Populus tremuloides* Michx.) and birch (*Betula papyrifera* Marsh.) with scattered conifers, or by pine (*Pinus contorta* Dougl.) stands.[4] The present prevalence of seral vegetation suggests the influence of the aboriginal populations, although certainly settlers, prospectors, and railroad crews contributed as well.[5]

The influence of pre-European burn practices on the local vegetation is corroborated by geologist George Dawson's descriptions of the Skeena in 1879, where he described a distribution of vegetation types quite similar to that found today. At the time of Dawson's visit, significant Euro-Canadian influence on the vegetation probably was confined to the previous two decades.[6] The inference that aboriginal people modified the fire regime of the area also is corroborated by anecdotal accounts of deliberate burning for berry production by Gitxsan and Wet'suwet'en people. Annual spring burning of sites around modern villages continues to the present, largely on reserve land, which, like private land, is not subject to the policies and regulations of the B.C. Forest Service, which suppressed traditional burning practices in the 1930s and 1940s.

The principal berry species managed by burning were black mountain huckleberry (*Vaccinium membranaceum* Dougl.) and lowbush blueberry (*V. caespitosum* Michx.). Soapberries (*Shepherdia canadensis* (L.) Nutt.) also may have been managed by burning in some locations. The other main function of burning was to clear areas around village sites. The clearing of floodplain sites for garden patches by burning is a relatively recent phenomenon.

Methods

To investigate the role of fire in traditional land management, I interviewed fourteen Gitxsan elders and other knowledgeable Gitxsan, and four Wet'suwet'en elders with an interest in traditional practices regarding burning practices. These interviews were conducted in English. Additional information from a fifteenth Gitxsan elder was obtained in 1996. I also monitored and mapped spring burning for the 1991 season in Kitwancool (Gitanyow), Gitwangak, and Gitanmaax (Gitxsan villages); and Hagwilget and Moricetown (Wet'suwet'en villages). I mapped freshly burned areas during weekly visits to the reserves from March 15 through May 7 using large-scale aerial photographs as a base. As background to the ethnographic investigation, I also researched archival sources to define the nature of the regional vegetation and the historical occurrence of fires, and for references to aboriginal burning.

Results

Gitxsan and Wet'suwet'en informants are aware that they formerly used prescribed burning for vegetation management. The most important form of vegetation management by burning was the renewal of berry patches. Berries of many species were the most significant plant foods utilized by the Gitxsan and Wet-suwet-en. In traditional times, the collecting of large stores of berries was a late summer activity that involved the congregation of groups of people at productive berry patches, a sustained harvesting effort, and processing of the berries into large dried berry cakes which were then transported back to village sites for winter provisioning. In the annual round of the Gitxsan and

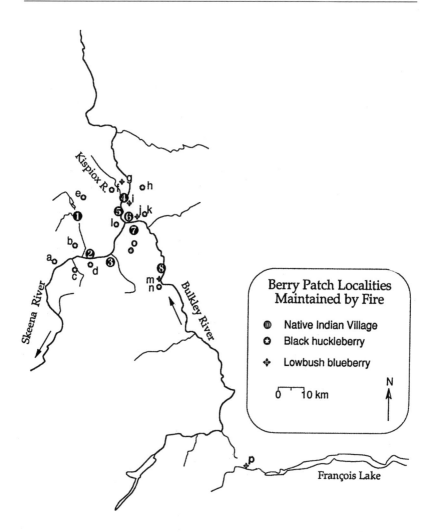

Map 1. *Locations of berry patches identified by consultants as having been managed by
burning. Gitx̲san villages:* (1) *Kitwancool;* (2) *Gitwangak;* (3) *Kitsegukla;* (4)
Kispiox; (5) *Glen Vowell;* (6) *Gitanmaax. Wet'suwet'en villages:* (7) *Hagwilget;* (8)
Moricetown. Berry patches: (a) *Wilson Creek;* (b) *Mountain by Gitwangak;* (c) *Price
Creek;* (d) *Shandilla* (e) *Moonlit Creek;* (f) *Mountain by Kispiox;* (g) *Valley by
Kispiox;* (h) *Cariboo Mountain;* (i) *Flat between Salmon River and Pinenut Creeks;*
(j) *Two Mile;* (k) *Nine Mile Mountain;* (l) *Mountain west of Hazelton;* (m) *Valley by
Moricetown;*(n) *Hills by Trout Creek;* (o) *Nadina Crossing.*

Wet'suwet'en peoples, obtaining enough berries to dry and preserve for the long winters was of paramount importance. Given the low caloric value and small size of individual fresh berries, the location and maintenance of large and productive berry patches with predictable harvests was necessary, so that enough fruit could be collected and processed to be worth the travel time, and the time and effort of picking and drying the fruit.

The principal species used for berry cake production were black huckleberry (supplemented by high-bush blueberry, *Vaccinium ovalifolium* Smith, not preferred because of its lower sugar content), low-bush blueberry, and soapberry. Saskatoons, *Amelanchier alnifolia* Nutt., also were processed for berry cakes.[7] Blueberries and huckleberries also could be preserved for winter in grease. The only species listed above that is not mentioned as being managed by burning is the saskatoon.

Berry patch burning occurred throughout the territories of the Gitxsan and Wet'suwet'en. I have accounts of specific berry patches managed by burning near most of the modern Gitxsan and Wet'suwet'en villages (Map 1, Table 1). In addition, low-elevation areas are reported to have been burned for berries adjacent to Kispiox, Gitanmaax, and Hagwilget, and near Kitsegukla and Moricetown.

Table I. Localities of Known Managed Montane Berry Patches

Designations are English names for the areas; the Gitxsan names for these localities were not collected. The names of informants mentioning each area are given in parentheses.

1. Cariboo Mountain (Sadie Howard)
2. Mtn. by Gitwangak and "Wilson Creek"(several different patches)
3. Mtn. west of Hazelton (Neil Sterritt Jr., Neil Sterritt Sr.)
4. Babine Trail (Nine Mile Mountain) (Percy Sterritt, Alfred Joseph, Elsie Tait)
5. Price Creek (Buddy Williams)
6. Mountain across from Kispiox (Percy Sterritt)
7. Shandilla area (Dora Johnson, Emsley Morgan, Ray Morgan)
8. Ridge up Moonlit Creek east of Kitwancool (Peter Martin)
9. Juniper Creek, Rocher DeBoule "Kslaawt" (Olive Ryan)

Among the Gitxsan and Wet'suwet'en, ownership of resources is primarily through the house group (*Wilp* or *Yikh*), or its matrilineal kinship extension, termed the *wilnat'aahl* in Gitxsan. These corporate institutions own and manage resources such as fishing sites, berry patches, and hunting and trapping territories on behalf of their members. The chief (*Sim'oogit* or *Dineza*) nominally owns and exercises control over the resources. Berry patches were owned and managed under this system, although by common consent the owners of significant berry patches near village sites frequently opened these to all villagers, who later acknowledged the ownership by making small public gifts to the chief of the owning group.[8] Among the duties of the chief was deciding when and where to burn berry patches. Pat Namox (Wet'suwet'en chief Gaslebah) described the duties of a chief:

> When it is the right time he [the chief] burns the berry patches so the berries are fat and plump. If he didn't do that the berry patches would become old and overgrown and there would be berries but they would just be small. But he knows when to burn so that it cleans up just the berry patch and doesn't spread to the trees.

Montane Berry Patches

Black mountain huckleberry does not occur widely in the valley bottoms, and huckleberry patches vary considerably in their productivity. Gitxsan informants refer to traditional berry patches as occurring "half way up the mountain," that is, in the montane and lower subalpine forest zones dominated by conifers (principally western hemlock [*Tsuga heterophylla* (Raf.) Sarg.] and subalpine fir (*Abies lasiocarpa* (Hook.) Nutt.) at about 3,000—4,000 feet in elevation. These berry patches traditionally were burned to maintain or enhance their extent and productivity. Special berry camps adjacent to productive patches were used year after year for harvesting and processing berries.

Traditionally, Gitxsan huckleberry patch burning took place in the early fall. Burning was frequently done by groups of men who were engaged in mountain goat hunting in areas above the berry patches. (Berry harvests were and are conducted by women, while men assisted when not occupied by autumn hunting). In at least some instances, berry patch burning might be done by groups of women. A berry patch adjacent to the village of Kispiox at relatively low elevation is reported to have been burned off by a group of women in the 1920s. Traditionally burning was done by the "father's side" (*wilksi 'wiitxw*) and the service was paid for with a feast (Kathleen Mathews, interview). This is consistent with the ideology of balanced reciprocity between houses that informs most Gitxsan and Wet'suwet'en social relations.[10] In practice, the "father's side" used and had access to the berry resource of the territory it would burn on behalf of spouses and children, and the men likely would be intimately familiar with the territory being managed, although not responsible for managing and regulating the harvest.

Late August and September are mentioned by the Gitxsan as the time when burning was done. At this time, nights are cool and fall frontal storm systems are likely to bring precipitation. Also, in clear weather, night fog or frost usually follow clear, warm weather. Thus the hazard of intense, uncontrolled burning is reduced. Informants agree that in the old days they knew how to burn to avoid extensive wildfire and hot burns. This kind of a burn would severely curtail berry patch production by consumption of the organic surface layer of the soil and the destruction of huckleberry rhizomes. By contrast, a light burn stimulates vigorous sprouting and enhances berry patch production.[11]

Wet'suwet'en informants did not mention fall burning, but apparently did manage black mountain huckleberry patches on the ridges between Trout Creek and Moricetown. The time of year that these patches were burned was not mentioned, but my informant said that those who decided the time for burning could tell when it would rain and would set the fires prior to a rainfall to ensure that they did not spread excessively.

Informants' recollections of burn intervals and the length of time required after a burn for a berry patch to become productive also varied. Some people believe that berry patches were burned every four years to maintain productivity. Others suggest that four years after a burn, the berry patch would be at peak productivity, and that knowledgeable elders (women) would monitor productivity and decide when the next burn was needed. Informants agreed that berry patches now have lost their productivity because of burn suppression by the Forest Service. Olive Ryan said that the berry patch she harvested as a child is all grown over because "The Forestry don't agree with the Native People, you know . . . Big tree now." Both fewer and smaller fruits now are produced in overgrown berry patches.

Huckleberry patches lose their productivity when invaded by taller shrubs and conifers. However, they have extensive rhizome systems and sprout vigorously if the aboveground stems are removed. A surface burn that does not consume the organic soil horizons will stimulate vigorous sprouting of black mountain huckleberry and, within a couple of years, production of large and abundant berries on the new growth.[12]

Low Elevation Berry Patches

The principal berry species was lowbush blueberry. It occurs from valley bottom (ca 450') to timberline (ca 4,500'). This species now is not significantly utilized, perhaps because many formerly productive localities are now private land or farms. It occurs generally on well-drained, droughty, gravelly soils and often is found as an understory in open pine stands. In the vicinity of Hazelton, many areas in the valley bottom formerly were burned for lowbush blueberry production. Most of these areas are either (non-Indian) private land or have undergone forest succession and no longer support a significant lowbush blueberry resource. Anecdotal reports state that formerly the rolling upland between Gitanmaax and Hagwilget looked blue with berries. This area was reported to have been maintained by frequent burning (Alfred Joseph, interview). Today, productive lowbush blueberry localities rarely are encountered.

Lowbush blueberry patches were reported by one elder to have been burned about every four years. Burning for lowbush blueberry may have been done in the spring as well as fall by the Gitxsan. Spring burning is possible for lowland sites; burning in such areas is done soon after the snow melts and before the days lengthen and humidity decreases. Often, more shaded and moister sites still are snow covered, providing effective firebreaks.

Wet'suwet'en elders report spring berry patch burning on the valley flat or lower hills between Hagwilget and Two Mile and adjacent to Moricetown (S. to Evelyn, around Trout Creek). This burning probably was primarily for lowbush blueberry. In addition, hills south of Moricetown may have been burned for black huckleberry. Burning for berries formerly was carried out near Francois Lake also (no specific locality described). No evidence of fall burning by Wet'suwet'en people has yet been obtained.

Soapberry is another low-elevation species that is reported to have been managed by burning. Soapberries are nitrogen-fixing shrubs that typically occur on excessively drained gravelly soils and frequently occur in seral pine stands. Soapberry plants are long lived; however, older stems grow very slowly and fruit sparsely, if at all. Soapberries are highly valued as a feast food; they formed (and still form) an important trade item, as they do not occur on the coast but are utilized in feasts there. Soapberries are relatively laborious to pick; variation in plant productivity therefore is significant. If large volumes of soapberries are desired, a large area of highly productive plants is needed. Both burning and pruning are reported as practices that enhance soapberry productivity by promoting growth of new branches.[13]

Suppression of Berry Patch Burning

Interviews suggest that the last berry patch burns occurred in the early 1930s to early 1940s. Consultants mention that the "forestry" forced the termination of berry patch burning, and that "you would get arrested if you tried to burn a berry patch now." I was told of an instance of a fire crew being mustered to put out a set berry patch fire in 1931 on the mountain just west of Gitwangak. Deliberate suppression of aboriginal burning is documented in the annual Reports of the Prince Rupert Forest District from the 1930s.

> Indian-caused fires have decreased during the past two years. As early as possible in the spring, all Indian settlements were visited and our policy explained in plain words. Notices were written out and posted at Indian trading posts which seemed to get results. Three fires were

started in what we call Siawash [sic] country. Two of these were
extinguished by the Indians before we arrived. The other one was
being fought by Indians and settlers when our patrol arrived on the
scene. . . . It appeared to be of incendiary origin.[14]

An extensive public education and propaganda campaign to reduce forest
fires included indoctrination sessions for Indians on the importance of care
with their camp fires as they returned from the coastal canneries, and special
presentations at pow-wows.[15] Anyone suspected of deliberately setting fires
was subject to criminal prosecution, and several convictions were obtained.
The Forest Service offered rewards for information on incendiary fires to
increase the effectiveness of the law.[16] It also attempted to remove any economic
incentive to start fires by deliberately circulating rumors in Indian communities
that the government lacked money to pay or feed fire-fighting crews, although
the government continued to pay non-Indian fire fighters:

> The Indians are very hard up . . . but our propaganda suggesting that
> no men will be put on fire payrolls appears to have put a stop to the
> usual large number of fires in Siawash country.
>
> The Indians in the back country were told that the Government
> had no money and could not fight fires. Fortunately we had a
> favorable season and were able to stick with this to a large extent.
>
> Recently visible signs of restiveness has been apparent among the
> Red man, presumably due to the gradual infiltration of knowledge that
> the White men are not only paid for fighting fire, but receive their
> board in addition.[17]

Grass and Brush Burning

Burning in the springtime around village sites, on south-facing slopes, and
on floodplain sites to control brush and encourage growth of grass continues
today. I have observed modern spring burning in the Kitwanga River valley
near Kitwancool and adjacent to all of the Gitxsan and Wet'suwet'en villages.
Discussions with informants suggest that this is not a recently introduced
practice, although production of forage for domestic animals and clearing of
floodplain garden sites clearly are associated with post-contact activities.
Informants maintain that they "always" did that. Clearing village sites for
defensive purposes and reducing summer fire hazard may have been pre-contact
reasons for village site burning. It is possible that forage for game species may
have been a motivation as well. Management of rice root (*Fritillaria
camschatcensis* (L.) Ker-Gawl) patches may have been an antecedent of the
modern practice of floodplain garden site burning.[18]

Modern Indian burning is mostly on reserve lands, both because villages
and many garden areas are reserves, and because reserve lands (which are

(Top) Unburned cottonwood floodplain forest at Gitwangak Village, April 16, 1991. (Below) Burned cottonwood floodplain forest across highway from first site, burned April 12, 1991. This area was the location of a smokehouse (now burned down and replaced with a new one) for many years and has undergone repeated burning. Note very sparse cottonwood cover and (burnt) grass understory with very sparse shrubs.

under federal jurisdiction) are not subject to Provincial Forest Service regulation. Many sites around villages are subject to annual burning. Some areas are burned at longer intervals. Decisions as to which areas will be burned and when are largely individual decisions and reflect land ownership of different parcels on reserves. The vegetation burned is either grass or scrub dominated by aspen, hazel (*Corylus cornuta* Marsh.), red osier (*Cornus stolonifera* Michx.), rose (*Rosa acicularis* Lindl.), and willow (*Salix* spp.). Some areas with young lodgepole pine also are burned. The effects of burning are to encourage grass growth, in particular earlier green-up, and to kill or damage above-ground parts of shrub species or young conifers. All the deciduous shrub species resprout after fire and are not eliminated by burning. Succession to forest with a dense shrub understory, however, is retarded by repeated burning.

Floodplain sites in cottonwood (*Populus balsamifera* ssp. *trichocarpa* [Torr. and Gray ex Hook] Brayshaw) forest also may be burned (depending on the location of the house sites, smoke houses, or gardens). The photographs on the facing page show burned and unburned sites in a cottonwood forest. Burning in cottonwood forest thins the canopy by scarring or killing some trees (though mature cottonwoods have thick bark and are fairly fire resistant); eliminates cottonwood reproduction; and suppresses shrub species such as black twinberry (*Lonicera involucrata* (Rich.) Banks), red osier, rose, willow, and hazel.

A relatively recent phenomenon is the clearing of floodplain sites for garden patches by burning. Garden site burning was reported to me by an elder from Kitwancool, and confirms my casual observations of burning in the Kitwanga River valley south of Kitwancool. The practice obviously is a post-contact phenomenon, but may have an antecedent in management of floodplain meadows for rice root bulb production, formerly an important carbohydrate food. Practices that discourage brush and cottonwood invasion would encourage rice root, which occurs today in grassy and herb-dominated openings on the floodplains of the Kitwanga, upper Skeena, and Kispiox rivers. As this plant has not been actively gathered for approximately the past 60 years, it is difficult to gather specific information on harvesting and management practices.

The third type of site burned is steep, south-facing, grassy or brushy slopes. A site adjacent to Gitwangak (Snake Hill; see photograph on page 248), and a site above the Kitwancool garden/floodplain fall into this category, as well as sites in the Bulkely Canyon adjacent to Hagwilget and along Moricetown Canyon.

I observed no differences between Gitxsan and Wet'suwet'en spring burning around village sites, except for the absence of Wet'suwet'en sites in floodplain cottonwood. The lack of Wet'suwet'en cottonwood sites may be due to ecological differences in the village sites, as the two Wet'suwet'en villages are

Snake Hill burn, Gitwangak, March 21, 1991. This south-facing slope is subject to annual spring burning.

located above bedrock canyon fishing sites, which lack extensive floodplain forest. The facing page shows maps of spring burning for Gitwangak and Gitanmaax, Gitxsan villages, and Moricetown, a Wet'suwet'en village, all in the ICHmc3 (Hazelton variant).

The Wet'suwet'en practice spring burning around village sites. There also is evidence of frequent burning of meadows and slopes around other reserves no longer occupied but still utilized for fishing and trapping.

Discussion

Burning by Other Northwest Indian Groups

Nisga'a burning for berry production was reported in the early 1970s, although species managed were not identified. Burning was reported to occur in the spring. The Nisga'a occupy the Nass River drainage to the west of the Gitxsan territories. No information was found on Tsimshian burning. It is likely that the "Canyon Tsimshian" of the Terrace area, whose territories meet the Gitxsan territories between Terrace and Hazelton, once practiced berry patch burning.

The Haisla, despite their wet coastal environment, apparently once burned to enhance berry production. In 1945, the ethnographer of the Haisla wrote, "Berries were especially important, and the Haisla burned areas to encourage their growth." [19] No modern Haisla burning has been observed or reported. The principal berry species used by the Haisla are Alaska blueberry (*Vaccinium alaskaense* Howell), highbush blueberry (*V. ovalifolium* Smith), red huckleberry (*V. parvifolium* Smith), and red elderberry (*Sambucus racemosa* L.). These

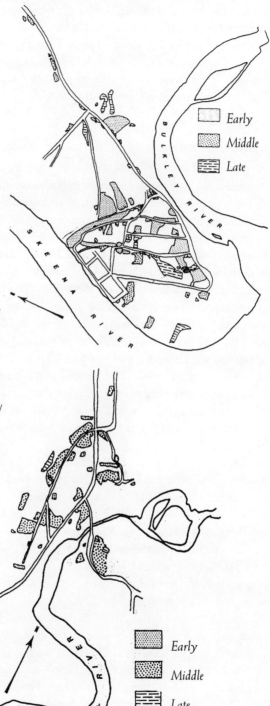

Spring burning 1991, for
Gitanmaax, a Gitx̱san
village (above), and
Moricetown, a Wet'suwet'en
village (below). The sites are
in the ICHmc3 (Hazelton
variant). Early, mid season
and late burned area is
shown. For Gitanmaax,
early = 3/27 and 4/3;
middle = 4/10, and late = 4/
25. For Moricetown, which
is a higher elevation and
slightly later site, early = 4/
3; middle = 4/10 and 4/16;
late = 4/25.

species produce abundantly under partial forest canopies such as those produced by windthrow or avalanche disturbance, and in natural openings bordering wetlands and along streams. They also may respond to fire.

The Dakelhne (Carrier) of British Columbia's central interior practice spring burning of grass and marsh areas at present.[20] Berry patch burning by the Dakelhne has not been reported or observed.

Comparison with Aboriginal Burning Practices in Northwest North America

In other areas, native peoples practiced landscape burning to encourage berry and root crops and seed production. Burning for berry production has been reported for the Nlaka'pamux (Thompson), Stl'atl'imx (Lillooet), Okanagan-Colville, Kootenai, Nuxalk (Bella Coola), Kwakwaka'wakw (Southern Kwakiutl), Nuu-chah-nulth, and Haida. Berry patches were burned by Indians in western Washington. Burning for improvement of berry yield was reported of the Dene-thah (Slavey) Indians of northern Alberta. Burning for production of root crops such as avalanche lily corms (*Erythronium grandiflorum* Pursh.) and camas (*Camassia quamash* (Pursh.) Greene and *C. leichtlinii* (Baker) Wats.) was practiced by the Straits Salish, Stl'atl'imx, and Nlaka'pamux. The Indians of western Washington apparently burned prairies annually to promote root and rhizome production. The Kalapuya Indians of the Willamette Valley burned native grasslands to enhance production of tarweed (*Madia* spp.) seeds, which were collected in quantity for human consumption, and the Wiyot Indians of northern California burned prairies to enhance sunflower seed production.[21]

Certainly the Gitxsan and Wet'suwet'en used fire to manage and enhance production of berry patches. It is not known whether fire was used to enhance root crops. It was possibly a factor in burning valley bottom meadows, the environment where rice root occurs. The other significant root crop, the spiny wood fern (*Dryopteris expansa* [K. B. Presl] Fraser-Jenkins & Jermy), grows best in organic surface horizons and so probably would not be enhanced by burning. Burning around village sites likely would have increased hazelnut production, but no elders have mentioned burning as a factor in hazel abundance or productivity.

Landscape burning was carried out by aboriginal peoples for several reasons other than enhancement of plant food gathering. The Sierra Miwok of California burned areas with California redbud (*Cercis occidentalis* Torr. ex Gray) to produce sprouts suitable for basketry. Deergrass (*Muhlenbergia rigens*) was managed similarly for culm production. The Dene-thah Indians of Alberta burned for a number of reasons, including reduction of fire hazard around living areas, improvement of forage for furbearers and game species, and reduction of brush to promote ease of cross-country travel. The Kalapuya and others used fire as a hunting tool to encircle and drive deer. Various Indian groups of northern California and southern Oregon also are reported to have burned for game management and maintenance of travel corridors. Hazard reduction and enhancement of forage may have been reasons for Gitxsan and Wet'suwet'en burning. Spring burning encourages grass, which was valued in historic times for horse and cattle feed.[22]

Changes in Gitxsan and Wet'suwet'en Use and Collection of Berry Resources

Modern berry collection now focuses on highly productive patches in clearcut areas and on fortuitous natural burns that are accessible by truck. Elders comment that a 1959 burn at "Meziadin" (300 km to the north along Highway 37 from Hazelton) should be reburned. This burn has been invaded heavily by willow 4 to 5 m tall and young pine and spruce, and the highly productive berry area has been reduced significantly in size over the eleven years I have observed it.

The principal species still collected are black mountain huckleberry, highbush blueberry, and soapberry. Lowbush blueberry no longer is an important resource, probably because of changes in both land management and access. Many low-elevation sites have been eliminated by land clearing, gravel pit development, or forest succession. Higher elevation sites are not accessible by logging roads and suppression of burning has allowed forest succession to proceed. Although these changes have occurred, some Gitxsan and Wet'suwet'en families consider the regular burning of brush and grassland, especially berry patches, one of their hereditary, aboriginal rights and, as such, to be part of native land-claims campaigns and negotiations.

Summary and Conclusions

Aboriginal landscape burning was important in northwest British Columbia. It had two main purposes: enhancement of berry patches and reduction of brush around living and gardening areas. Burning was widespread.

Berry patch burning was suppressed by the B.C. Forest Service in the 1930s and early 1940s and has not been practiced since that time. Termination of burning has resulted in forest succession and ecological changes in former berry patches. Land clearing for agriculture and industrial clearcut logging in many lower elevation areas have masked ecological change resulting from diminished fire frequency. Modern Gitxsan and Wet'suwet'en subsistence activities reflect these changes, with lowbush blueberry no longer an important economic species, and black mountain huckleberry collection conditioned by logging disturbance and/or road access. As families are integrated into the market economy of modern Canada, wild berries now play a minor role in annual nutrition, but they retain a high cultural value. They remain required items at many weddings, special family gatherings, and especially at funeral potlatch feasts and totem pole raising feasts.

Originally published in Human Ecology 22(2): 171–188 (1994a)

Acknowledgments

I would like to thank the Gitxsan and Wet'suwet'en people who shared their knowledge about traditional burning practices with me: the late Andy Clifton, Dora Johnson, Alfred Joseph, Sadie Howard, Solomon Marsden, Kathleen Marsden, Peter Martin, the late Art Mathews Sr., Kathleen Mathews, Ray Morgan, the late Emsley Morgan, Roy Morris, Lucy Namox, Pat Namox, Olive Ryan, Neil Sterritt Sr., Neil Sterritt Jr., Percy Sterritt, and the late Buddy Williams. I would like to thank Richard Daly for helpful discussions and Henry T. Lewis for encouragement and support. I also would like to acknowledge Allen Gottesfeld for helpful discussions and support in the field.

Notes

1. Formerly Gottesfeld. University of Alberta, Department of Anthropology, Edmonton, Alberta, Canada T6G 2H4. See also the companion articles by Johnson [Gottesfeld], "Conservation, Territory, and Traditional Beliefs: An Analysis of Gitksan and Wet'suwet'en Subsistence, Northwest British Columbia, Canada" (*Human Ecology* 22(4): 443–65, 1994b), "Wet'suwet'en Ethnobotany: Traditional Plant Uses" (*Journal of Ethnobiology* 14(2): 185–210, 1994c), "The Role of Plant Foods in Traditional Wet'suwet'en Nutrition (*Ecology of Food and Nutrition* 34(2): 149–69, 1995), and (with Sharon Hargus) "Classification and Nomenclature in Wet'suwet'en Ethnobotany: A preliminary examination" (*Journal of Ethnobiology* 18(1), 1999).
2. British Columbia Ministry of Forests and Lands, *Biogeoclimatic and Ecoregion Units of the Prince Rupert Forest Region* (2 maps, 1988).
3. B.C. Ministry of Forests and Lands (*ibid.*).
4. Sybille Haeussler *et al.*, *A Guide to the Interior Cedar-Hemlock Zone, Northwestern Transitional Subzone* (ICHg), *in the Prince Rupert Forest Region, British Columbia* (Victoria, 1985).

5. Lightning-caused ignition is rare in the area, particularly for the valley bottom locations where the "Hazelton variant" is prevalent.

6. George Dawson, *Report on an exploration from Port Simpson on the Pacific coast to Edmonton on the Saskatchewan, embracing a portion of the northern part of British Columbia and the Peace River Country, 1879* (Montreal, 1881).

7. People of 'Ksan, *Gathering What the Great Nature Provided: food traditions of the Gitksan* (Vancouver, 1980).

8. On family ownership, see Richard Daly, *Anthropological opinion on the Nature of the Gitksan and Wet'suwet'en Economy, in Opinion Evidence in Delgamunkw et al. v. the Queen in the Right of the Province of British Columbia and the Attorney-General of Canada* (British Columbia Supreme Court, 0843, Smithers Registry, 1988); the information on public use comes from Richard Daly, personal communication, 1991.

9. Pat Namox, quoted by Antonia Mills in *Eagle Down Is Our Law: Witsuwit'en Law, Feasts, and Land Claims* (Vancouver, 1994), 135–36.

10. R. Daly, personal communication, 1991.

11. Cf. Don Minore, *The Wild Huckleberries of Oregon and Washington—A Dwindling Resource* (USDA Forest Service Research Paper PNW-143, 1972), and *Observations on the Rhizomes and Roots of Vaccinium Membranaceum* (USDA Forest Service Research Note PNW-261, 1975).

12. Minore, 1972 and 1975 *ibid.*

13. Kathleen Marsden, interview notes; Sadie Howard, personal communication.

14. Anonymous, *1932 Annual Report of the Prince Rupert Forest District* (manuscript, Prince Rupert Forest Regional Office Library, Smithers), 3.

15. 1935, 1936, 1940, and 1942 *Annual Reports of the Prince Rupert Forest District.*

16. *Ibid.*, 1933, 1935.

17. *Ibid.*, 1933:3, 1934:4, 1939:4.

18. Euro-Canadian settlers also burned brush and fields (Sheila Ryan, personal communication April 1991; *Annual Reports of the Prince Rupert Forest District*, 1931, 1932). Some non-Indians still burn brush, fields, or roadsides, as well as windrows from modern land clearing.

19. Ivan Lopatin, "Social Life and Religion of the Indians in Kitimat, British Columbia" (*University of Southern California Social Science Series* 26, 1945), 14.

20. Allen Gottesfeld, personal communication, 1992 for Tache/Middle River area and personal observation, 1991, for Stelat'en by Fraser Lake.

21. Sources include Nancy Turner, "Time to Burn" (1991 and this volume, revised); Wayne Suttles, "Variation in Habitat and Culture on the Northwest Coast" (pp. 522–37 in *Proceedings of the 34th International Congress of Americanists,* 1962); Helen H. Norton, "Evidence for bracken fern as a food for aboriginal peoples of western Washington" (*Economic Botany* 33(4): 384–96, 1979a), "The association beween anthropogenic prairies and important food plants in western Washington" (*Northwest Anthropological Research Notes* 13(2): 175–200, 1979b), and Norton *et al.*, "Vegetable food products of the foraging economies of the Pacific Northwest" *(Ecology of Food and Nutrition* 14(3): 219–78, 1984); Henry Lewis, "A Time for Burning" (*Boreal Institute for Northern Studies Occasional Publication* No. 17, 1982); Robert Boyd, "Strategies of Indian Burning in the Willamette Valley" (1986 and this volume, revised); and H. Lewis and Theresa Ferguson, "Yards, corridors and mosaics" (1988 and this volume).

22. Sources include M. Kat Anderson, "California Indian horticulture: Management and use of redbud by the Southern Sierra Miwok" (*Journal of Ethnobiology* 11(1): 145–57, 1991) and "The Ethnobotany of deergrass (*Muhlenbergia rigens*) Poaceae: Its uses and fire management by California Indian Tribes" (*Economic Botany* 50(4): 409–22, 1996); Lewis, "A Time for Burning," and Lewis and Ferguson, "Yards, corridors and mosaics"; and Boyd, "Strategies of Indian Burning in the Willamette Valley."

Burning for a "Fine and Beautiful Open Country"
Native Uses of Fire in Southwestern Oregon

Jeff LaLande and Reg Pullen

In September 1841, while traveling south through the haze-filled Rogue River Valley, members of the United States Exploring Expedition encountered an elderly Indian woman, intently "blowing a brand to set fire to the woods." The small detachment of Navy officers and their associates had struggled during previous days over mountains covered by charred vegetation and through canyons filled with smoke, the result of native-set fires. Expedition artist Titian Ramsay Peale described the woman—who was dressed in a "mantle of antelope or deer skin" and wore a "cup-shaped" basketry cap—as "so busy setting fire to the prairie and mountain ravines that she seemed to disregard us."[1]

The American explorers of 1841 provided the first and almost the only eyewitness written accounts of native use of fire in southwestern Oregon. As Henry Lewis has noted, the area's historic and ethnographic record suffers from a "relative dearth of information . . . .concerning Indian uses of fire" in comparison to the Willamette Valley and especially to northern California. However, the scattered evidence available to us clearly demonstrates the importance of aboriginal fire in southwestern Oregon. Taken together, the few primary historic accounts and the brief mention given by native elders to ethnographers decades later point to the key role of fire in a wide variety of activities. Some of the ethnographic data on fire, gathered early in the twentieth century, never was published and has remained little known; only recently has this information been compiled and presented in an organized fashion.[2]

This paper synthesizes the documentary evidence for the role of fire in the native cultures of southwestern Oregon, focusing on the variety of fire practices in the annual round of subsistence. In addition, it assesses the extent and effect of anthropogenic fire on the area's landscape—fire that, as recalled in the 1930s by Coos Indian Frank Drew, had helped create and maintain a "fine and beautiful open country."[3] The essay concludes by touching briefly on some of the major changes to that landscape that have resulted since the suppression of traditional fire practices.

The Setting

Southwestern Oregon encompasses the drainages of the Umpqua and Rogue rivers, along with those of shorter coastal streams such as the Coos, Coquille, and Chetco. It is a rugged and environmentally distinctive region. Dominated by a jumble of steep mountain ranges (part of the Klamath Mountains geologic province) that are covered by an extensive forest of coniferous trees and evergreen broadleaf shrubs, the area also contains gentler terrain at lower elevations—the Umpqua and Rogue River valleys—that supports open oak woodland and savanna. The most arid portion of the Pacific Northwest west of the Cascade Range crest, geographers and botanists consider the flora of southwestern Oregon (along with adjacent sections of northwestern-most California) to be transitional between the "classic" moist, dense forestlands to the north and the much drier vegetation communities of central California to the south.[4]

Anthropologists long have considered the native groups of southwestern Oregon to have been culturally "transitional" as well, possessing a mix of characteristics that showed influences from more densely populated portions of the Northwest Coast, Plateau, and California culture areas. More recently, however, southwestern Oregon has come to be viewed as a culturally distinctive region. In terms of economic and social organization by the time of Euro-American contact, southwestern Oregon's inhabitants seem to have been most similar to their California neighbors of the Lower Klamath River immediately to the south—the Yurok, Hupa, and Karok.[5]

Native peoples of southwestern Oregon included the Coos and Coquille (or Coquelle) of the area's northern coastal section, as well as the Tututni and Chetco of the southern-most Oregon Coast. Major interior groups included: the Umpqua of the Umpqua Valley; the Applegate (or Dakubetede), Chasta Costa, Galice Creek, and Illinois (or Gusladada) inhabiting the lower Rogue River watershed's Illinois and Applegate valleys and portions of the lower Rogue canyon itself; and the Takelma and Shasta of the main Rogue River Valley (whose territory extended into adjacent drainages to the north and south respectively). (Although inhabiting winter villages on the far side of the Cascade Range, the Klamath visited the upper-most Rogue basin on a regular seasonal basis.) Speaking a wide diversity of languages belonging to three separate linguistic stocks,[6] the various ethnic groups of southwestern Oregon shared many of the same subsistence and social patterns.[7]

In contrast to the Yurok and the other ethnographically well-known northwestern California groups (who remained within their Lower Klamath River homeland after the Euro-American invasion), most of southwestern Oregon's surviving native inhabitants were removed immediately following their defeat in the "Rogue River Indian Wars" of the 1850s. Resettled on distant reservations in the north-central Oregon Coast Range and subjected to the forced assimilation measures of the late nineteenth century, these people suffered a particularly severe break in cultural continuity.[8]

The use of fire, for a variety of purposes, was important to the native people of southwestern Oregon, as it was for hunting/gathering groups living to the north and south of the area. But by the turn of the century, when anthropologists first came to record oral traditions, much information about the uses of fire on that landscape either had been lost, was only dimly remembered, or simply was not sought by the interviewers. Other factors contributed to the relative paucity of knowledge about southwestern Oregon's Indians; among them: the Euro-American historical record for the area began substantially later and was considerably less informative about native cultures than that compiled for the Willamette Valley and other earlier-explored/settled portions of the Pacific Northwest.

Thus, documentary evidence concerning native fire practices in southwestern Oregon is, as Lewis has previously noted, comparatively sparse. To give but one example: although information on use of fire for ritual purposes has been documented in great detail by ethnographic researchers for northwestern California, such religious practices for southwestern Oregon groups can be only indirectly inferred from the historic record, and that from a single, oblique mention in the correspondence of a U.S. Army physician.[9]

The Historic Record: A Hazy View of Native Practices

Although the earliest Euro-American visitors to southwestern Oregon left no direct reference to anthropogenic fire, they did record phenomena that probably resulted from native fire practices. American maritime explorers, cruising along the coast near the present Oregon/California border on August 5, 1788 noted smoke from great fires. Nearly forty years later, Hudson's Bay Company fur trader Peter Skene Ogden was the first to explore the area's interior. Writing in his journal on March 2, 1827, Ogden remarked on the distinct vegetational differences between north-aspect and south-aspect slopes in the Rogue River Valley. Both the smoky coastal skies in 1788 and the open oak woodland of the south-facing hillsides seen along the Rogue in 1827 likely resulted, at least in part, from Indian-set fires.[10]

In June 1828, American trappers led by Jedediah Smith passed northward along the area's rugged coast. Smith's clerk, Harrison Rogers, noted that when the party reached the bank of the Rogue River, Tututni inhabitants on the north side of the river apparently set off a number of fires. Rogers assumed that these were a signal to neighboring groups that strangers were "close at hand."[11]

Despite their first-hand observation of the elderly Indian woman lighting a brush fire near present-day Ashland, Oregon, members of the 1841 U.S. Exploring Expedition obtained little information on the purposes of native fire during their travel through the area. This "sullen and dogged" woman, who carried a "large funnel-shaped" burden basket in addition to the flaming firebrand, remained frustratingly "heedless" of the explorers' inquiries and made no reply. The American explorers did note the Takelmas' use of fire to obtain edible sap from sugar pine (*Pinus lambertiana*) trees; "The Indian manner of gathering . . . large quantities" of the pleasant-tasting substance (described as "much like manna") was "to set fire to the tree['s base] and save the juice as it runs out." But expedition members failed to mention any other subsistence goals of burning. Indeed, anxious about potential hostile encounters with the area's natives, the party's naval officers assumed that most of the fires they encountered in southwestern Oregon had been set simply "to obstruct" the expedition's progress. Whatever the Indians' actual intent may have been in 1841, their fires apparently were numerous, extensive, and difficult to avoid along the Americans' route of travel. On several occasions, the explorers had to skirt flame-filled gullies. Henry Brackenridge, the expedition's botanist, complained that after riding over the still-smoldering forest slopes of one southwestern Oregon mountain crossing the party arrived at camp "as black . . . as so many Negroes from the coast of Africa."[12]

The memoirs of George Riddle, who settled in the Umpqua Valley in the early 1850s, provide some valuable ethnohistoric information; they document that the Cow Creek Indians (a Takelman-speaking group) annually "burned

Indian viewing fire at a distance. "South branch of the Umpqua, September 21st 1841."
From Henry Eld's manuscript Journal of the U.S. Exploring Expedition. Yale Collection
of Western Americana, Beinecke Rare Book and Manuscript Library. Reproduced with
permission.

the grass during the summer." In his single detailed discussion of the purposes of native fire, Riddle told how Cow Creek women ignited entire hillsides of sticky tarweed (*Madia* spp.) in the late summer when its edible seeds had reached maturity. After the quick-moving fire "left the plant standing with the tar burned off," large groups of women then moved through the burn, beating the tarweed stalks over the rim of their burden baskets with wood paddles and thereby gathering copious amounts of seed.[13]

According to Dr. Lorenzo Hubbard, an Army physician during the 1850s, the Tututni ritually burned the hills at the mouth of the Rogue River each spring and fall. This was done, according to Hubbard, "for the purpose, as they say, of inviting the salmon to enter the river"—that is, as a local variant of the "first salmon ceremony" common to most Northwest Coast peoples. A. G. Walling, who mined for gold in southwestern Oregon during the early 1850s, compiled and published the first narrative history of the region. In addition to documenting the Takelmas' use of widespread forest/brushfire as a defensive tactic during the 1853 Indian War, he acknowledged the local "Indian habit of burning over the [ground] surface in order to remove obstructions to their seed and acorn gathering."[14]

"A Southern Oregon Pine Forest": Big Butte Creek watershed, east of Butte Falls, eastern Jackson County, Oregon. Ponderosa pine in the left foreground; sugar pines in the middle-ground; California black oaks on the right. Elderly residents of this relatively gentle portion of the Cascade Range recall that a team-and-wagon formerly could travel easily through the open forest, but that increasing "brush" after 1910–20, coupled with railroad logging, changed the area's appearance dramatically. Rogue River National Forest historic photograph collection, #X-2-43.

By the nineteenth century, with most of the native population long removed from southwestern Oregon, the simple fact that "Indians used to set fire" had become well embedded in the collective memory of Euro-American inhabitants. In 1892, for example, the editor of one local newspaper remarked that "old settlers in Southern Oregon claim that the Indians kept the country looking neater than the whites do" through their frequent burning of the grassy hillsides. Federal forester John Leiberg, surveying the area's timber resources in 1899, noted the evident high frequency of past Indian-set fires in some portions of the forest, but he described them as generally "small and circumscribed" in extent.[15]

Leiberg also remarked with some astonishment on the widespread devastation caused by more recent settler-set fires. Many local settlers had taken up their native predecessors' fire-setting ways. They burned for various reasons—to clear vegetation for mineral prospecting, to facilitate travel through the woods, and to increase browse vegetation for game and rangeland grass for livestock. However, settlers often burned the forest indiscriminately, sometimes causing huge, long-burning conflagrations that filled the main valleys with smoke. The average annual amount of mixed-conifer forestland (as opposed to valley/foothill grassland and oak woodland) in southwestern Oregon burned by Euro-Americans during the late nineteenth and early twentieth centuries probably was far greater than that fired previously by Indians.[16]

After 1910, the U.S.D.A. Forest Service began a concerted campaign to end the fire-setting ways of southwestern Oregon's rural inhabitants. Ironically if not unexpectedly, the agency's attitude toward local "incendiarism" accorded far more respect to the rationale of fire-setting Euro-American ranchers than it did to that of the area's few remaining native inhabitants—whose fires were assumed to result from either stubborn habit or a desire to obtain work on Forest Service fire-fighting crews.[17]

By the early twentieth century, then, the historic record of native-set fire was becoming increasingly sparse and distorted. During this same period, however, the area's ethnographic record began to be compiled, and these personal accounts given by native people further document their uses of fire.

The Ethnographic Record: Burning for Many Purposes

After the turn of the century, various anthropologists[18] interviewed a few elderly individuals who recalled native traditions in southwestern Oregon: Frank Drew (Coos), Frances Johnson (River Takelma), Mollie Orton (Upland Takelma), Sargent Sambo (Shasta), Hoxie Simmons (Applegate/Galice Creek), Coquelle Thompson (Coquille), and others. In aggregate, their recollections provide an informative if incomplete record of the methods and purposes of anthropogenic fire.

Fire was used primarily as part of these hunter/gatherers' annual round, with both short-term and long-term subsistence goals of plant and animal management in mind. However, they also employed fire to meet other needs: as a key component of the native groups' limited horticulture, as well as for communication over long distances.

Fire and Hunting

Groups hunting ungulates, particularly deer (*Odocoileus hemionus*), often employed fire to drive the animals toward desired locations for the kill. In Takelma territory, "[n]ot infrequently mountain forests were set afire" for that purpose. The Shasta set fire to oak woodland hillsides in the early autumn (when the dry leaves provided dependable tinder) in order to encircle herds of deer: "Men went out and set fire in circles . . . [t]he ends of the curved lines . . . did not meet," and in the opening of the U-shaped fire "women stood rattling deer bones," while men concealed themselves in the brush "ready to shoot the deer as they rushed out." The Coquille used fire to drive deer into rope snares: "put [snare] on deer trail—put stick maybe two feet high—deer go—step there—rope goes over neck."[19]

The Applegate Athapascans evidently also used fire during deer hunting. The single available account frames its use in terms of a deer hunter signaling his people to come to the Grayback Mountain vicinity to share the deer he has killed; however, the fire may well have been set primarily for driving the animals. Although residing in winter villages on the east side of the Cascade Range (outside of southwestern Oregon), groups of Klamath Indians regularly crossed the mountains in the late summer to hunt deer. Takelmas of the Rogue River Valley knew that the distant smoke columns rising from the west slope of the Cascades often signaled the presence of Klamath hunters there; the fires apparently were used in driving game.[20]

Fire had longer-term wildlife goals as well, goals that might be years in the future. As has been documented for other groups in the Pacific Northwest and California, Indians of southwestern Oregon employed fire to improve and maintain wildlife habitat. The Tututni periodically burned so as "to produce a better crop of grass to attract wild game."[21] The open, park-like forests that resulted from Indian-set fires were another long-term goal. Coquille men "burned brush out of the hunting places . . . every so often." Coos hunters, who considered such areas "the loveliest of country," set fire "in the mountains to clear away the brush and jungles and so make hunting easier." This created a "fine and beautiful open country . . . where deer [could] be seen at a distance"; the men set these favorite mountain locales afire annually, at the end of the fall hunt.[22]

Fire and Gathering

In an adjacent section of California, the Karoks' frequent use of fire to enhance the growth of edible/useful plants has been described in detail. Among other aims, they set fire to gather tarweed seeds, as well as to manage for huckleberries, hazelnuts, acorns, iris fibers, and beargrass fiber/roots.[23] A few ethnographic accounts demonstrate that southwestern Oregon groups burned with these same goals in mind. The scattered references come from only a few ethnic groups, but such uses of fire almost certainly were widespread throughout the area.

Corroborating Riddle's account for the Cow Creek Indians, Takelma elder Frances Johnson recalled that her people collected the "yellow-flowered tarweed, the stalks of which were first burned . . . to remove the pitchy substance."[24] According to Coquelle Thompson, the Coquille similarly harvested "Indian oats" (a term for tarweed), but with a different sexual division of labor than recorded by Riddle:

> Indian oats used to grow high (sticky grass). They'd . . . just young people (no married people) they take fire. They notice which way wind is blowing at night. 4 or 5 young men go about 100 yards apart—set fire to it—oh, people watch—that stuff burns just like firs. They burn off all those stickers. Then get those black puffed out oats. Gather it with rake into basket with stick . . . Set fire, stalk doesn't burn . . . . Young men carried pitch torches to light it. Lit it after dark—watched it burn—let it stand one day in the sun—didn't usually dance after burning it.[25]
>
> He [C. Thompson] describes wild-oats. It requires 4 or 5 (Indians) to start the fire—they start the fire all around, and this just opened the seeds, did not burn the seeds. The next day about noon they get ready to gather those oats. They had a paddle like a canoe paddle 15" long and they knocked the oats into the basket. The baskets were shallow . . . . About 5 p.m. they quit, pack it home and put the oats on . . . an elkskin blanket.[26]

Coquille men typically burned "Indian oats" and sunflower (*Balsamorhiza* spp., which co-occurred with tarweed) with the same fire, taking care to "not let the fire spread." The Coquille also periodically "burned over berry patches to make good patches," a likely reference to black mountain huckleberry (*Vaccinium membranaceum*).[27]

Hazelnuts (*Corylus cornuta* var. *californica*) were gathered in large quantities by virtually all groups of the area. Tututni headmen had the responsibility for burning hazel patches "[i]n about the middle of the summer . . . [a]ll the hazel nuts fell off and the people went out to pick them up"; the light fires burned off the fuzzy outer coating and roasted the nuts inside the shell. The Coquille burned the hazel patches "every 5 years—in August"; this produced "a big slope of nice hazel nuts." According to Coquelle Thompson, they "had lots of hazel nuts[, e]very year [men] burn it over . . . got baskets and baskets full."[28]

Despite the central importance of acorns in the diet of most groups, southwestern Oregon's ethnographic record (unlike that for northwestern Californian groups such as the Karok, Tolowa, etc.) includes no mention of burning for oak grove management nor other reasons related to acorn gathering. However, the previously described Takelma and Shasta deer-drive fires in oak woodland also would have served the purpose of killing young conifers that otherwise would have grown and eventually overtopped the oak trees.

Although mention of fire for managing beargrass (*Xerophyllum tenax*) is absent from ethnographic accounts, area groups definitely gathered its fibrous leaves for basketry. The Upland Takelma, for instance, regularly utilized a particularly rich patch of beargrass lilies on the west slope of Wagner Butte, near Ashland;[29] as with the Karok, human-set fire almost certainly was a factor in its productivity.

Insects, particularly grasshoppers, were gathered for food by the Takelma and Shasta of the Rogue River Valley. When the grasshopper population was large and concentrated, a grass fire was set that evidently killed massive quantities of the creatures, which were "dried, pounded, and mixed with grass seeds for eating." In the Takelma myth "Coyote in a Hollow Tree," Coyote "discovered a field that had been burnt down." Entering this burned grassy area, he found "numerous grasshoppers . . . lying about"; there Coyote "did nothing but pick them up and eat, eat, eat, eat, eat grasshoppers, everywhere he went about."[30]

Other Uses of Fire

In addition to its use in a variety of subsistence activities, fire had other roles beyond its universal employment for cooking, warmth, and light.

Tobacco (*Nicotiana* spp.), the only plant grown from seed by the Indians of southwestern Oregon and northwestern California, had important social and ritual uses. The Karoks' tobacco horticulture has been thoroughly described by Harrington; they utilized fire to clear a tobacco plot of competing brush and to increase the soil's fertility with the ash from burned pine logs. Applegate Athapascans "burned off the brush and sowed tobacco seeds." Takelma men planted their tobacco "on land from which the brush had been burned away"; Molly Orton told how the Upland Takelma grew tobacco: "ground burned, planted, raked into ashes with bunch of brush."[31]

Regarding ceremonial or ritualistic uses of landscape fire in southwestern Oregon, such as the Tututnis' salmon-invitation fires recorded historically by Hubbard,[32] the ethnographic testimony is silent. Especially considering the well-documented ritual use of fire by neighboring Lower Klamath River peoples such as the Yurok, the lack of ethnographic mention may be due to oversight or accident and not to its actual absence.

Signal fires—to warn of the approach of enemies or other intruders, to proclaim a successful deer hunt—are documented for at least the Takelma and neighboring groups along the middle stretch of the Rogue River and in the adjacent Illinois Valley. Frances Johnson stated that, "[i]f Indians see big fire on that [mountain], the Indians at various villages move—know war is coming."[33] Hoxie Simmons recalled an Applegate hunter who told his relatives: "Whenever you see smoke [on Grayback mountain]come to there. I will have built a fire [there]. You may come for meat for as many [deer or elk] as I have killed."[34]

Some Conclusions about Anthropogenic Fire

In summary, among the Indians of southwestern Oregon, fire played a central role in a variety of subsistence activities.

In both hunting and gathering, fire served as a primary tool that had both immediate returns (e.g., game drives, tarweed harvest) as well as longer-term benefits that might be reaped years in the future (e.g., burning to enhance productivity of a berry field, to prevent the overtopping of an oak grove by conifers, or to create an open hunting area within the brush/tree-choked forest). Some fires doubtless had multiple purposes and varied consequences—driving deer and maintaining the productivity of a favorite plant-gathering locality. Burning also was a key component in growing tobacco. Fire additionally served as a long-distance communication device and as a weapon of war.

Based on the documented setting of brushfires to invite salmon to migrate upriver, additional ritual practices were probable; the incompleteness of the historic/ethnographic record may mask other uses as well.

Although the burning of tobacco plots may have been (as it was in northwestern California) an individual undertaking, most fires typically were group endeavors. And some fires (e.g., the evening blazes that swept across the tarweed fields) possibly had a social component that, similar to other group activities such as game drives, worked to reinforce cooperative and reciprocal ties between families and villages. Perhaps the visual drama of nightfires even involved a shared aesthetic experience among such groups, what one geographer has termed the apparently universal human "sheer love of fires as spectacles."[35]

The record of fire in southwestern Oregon demonstrates that both women and men set fires. Headmen (e.g., the Tututni) traditionally were responsible for some crucial ignitions, such as burning of hazel patches. Thus, skilled leaders knowledgeable about fire likely coordinated the group fire effort. Night burning of grassland (when temperatures were cooler and up-canyon drafts had died down) clearly indicates both a familiarity with fire behavior and a degree of caution. Burning was not indiscriminate, and care apparently was exercised lest "the fire spread."[36] Thus, special measures may have been taken with some fires lest they damage the land's productivity or have other unwanted results. Natives doubtless realized that frequent light burns, selectively set at different times of the year in more diversified environments than now exist, lowered the potential for a high-intensity fire's adverse effects. Frequent low-intensity fire within an area keeps soil nutrients cycling more freely;[37] therefore, long-term observations of site productivity also may have served to encourage anthropogenic fire.

Beyond the topic of anthropogenic fire's objectives in southwestern Oregon is the question of its antiquity and its long-term role in socio-economic organization. Human beings may have brought landscape-scale fire with them to the Americas at the close of the Pleistocene. For example, a sudden, large, and climatically anomalous increase in evidence of fire around 11,000 years ago in the Isthmus of Panama's paleoecological record (i.e., macro/microscopic charcoal fragments, plant phytoliths, fossil pollen) is attributed to ignition of jungle vegetation by the region's first human inhabitants. In southwestern Oregon, fire likewise may have been in the tool-kit of the earliest human arrivals. However, fire may well have increased in importance subsequent to the end of the mid-Holocene "drought" period that lasted from around 8,000 to 4,000 years ago. Archaeologists speculate that this relatively hot, dry climatic episode actually increased the human carrying capacity of southwestern Oregon by encouraging the spread of the valley's drought-tolerant grassland, oak/pine woodland, and pine-dominated transition forest (with their wide variety of edible plants) into higher elevations. This expansion of vegetation communities of central importance to human subsistence would have come at the expense of the much less valuable mixed-conifer forest, which retreated upslope from many mid-elevation areas to moister locales. With the end of the drought period around 4000 B.P., Douglas-fir and white fir forests began to spread back downslope. Human-set fire would have helped to maintain the more fire-resistant oak/pine woodland in the face of encroachment by the returning fir forest.[38]

Focusing on the importance of fire to social organization, archaeologists of Mesolithic Britain recently have proposed a model of its possible ecological and economic consequences: Burning for better and more concentrated areas of game browse increased both the population and locality-specific density of game animals; hence, the predictability of obtaining game from certain areas increased. Growing human dependence on these localized areas of fire-influenced wildlife habitat gradually decreased the mobility and increased the sedentariness and sense of territoriality of various groups. Burns actually may have begun to serve as ethnic territorial markers (i.e., based on sentiments that might be summarized as: "We've burned this place for years; it's ours."). The resultant increased concentration of humans and their dependence on a circumscribed territory marked by past and recent burns may have led to the concept of group land ownership among hunter-gatherers. This model is certainly worth consideration for the complex ethnic territorial situation in southwestern Oregon and elsewhere in the Pacific Northwest.[39]

The geographic extent of anthropogenic fire—"How many acres were burned in an average year or generation?"—is an unanswered (and perhaps unanswerable) question. In the past two decades, we have gone from a near-total blindness to the effects of Indian-set fire to an overdue recognition of its importance. However, it would be wise to admit the ambiguity we face in tracing prehistoric fire origins. Some recent commentators seemingly slight the role of natural fire by implying immense if vague acreages of aboriginal fire in the forests of southwestern Oregon and other coastward portions of the Pacific Northwest.[40]

The tendency (perhaps over-compensating for past foresters' failure to acknowledge the importance of Indian-set fire) to credit most high-frequency/low-intensity prehistoric fire to human ignition and to blame lightning for low-frequency/stand-replacement conflagrations is simplistic and probably incorrect.[41] Writing of California, Lewis concludes that it was "undoubtedly the case that Indians did not set all or even most of [the land] to the torch in any given set of years." Lewis further points out that "[l]arge-scale burning would have reduced the complex of ecotones and consequently the total amount of plant and animal production"; he emphasizes that the "very 'spottiness'" of anthropogenic fire was key to achieving subsistence goals. Moore and Mellars similarly stress that in forested regions, comparatively small-area fires (set for improving browse) better increase the concentration of game, thereby improving the predictability and reliability of the hunt.[41]

More important than the quantity of land burned within a given period was the quality of the burned area—i.e., its productivity and, in the case of game animals, its attractiveness when compared to adjoining areas (which might therefore have called for both restricted size and number of such "hunting grounds" in order to concentrate game animals). Certainly Indian-set fires were a major force in establishing and preserving the vegetational character of lower-elevation savanna, oak woodland, and transition oak/pine forest. However, the higher-elevation berry patches and hunting grounds, although burned regularly, probably accounted for far less acreage. And within the vast mid-elevation, mixed-conifer/mixed-evergreen forest (which accounts for most of southwestern Oregon), the extent of anthropogenic fire likely was far more limited and localized—i.e., confined to creating scattered, small openings. Such openings would have enhanced the growth and productivity of California black oak (*Quercus kelloggii*, a preferred acorn species found at relatively higher-elevation and moister sites than the far more common Oregon white oak [*Q. garryana*] of the main valleys); small openings also provided localized feed for attracting game.[43] Aside from these localities, lightning-caused fire probably deserves more of the credit for the formerly open, park-like stands of most mid-elevation, mixed-conifer forest stands.

The Fire Next Time: Coping with a Changed Landscape

The vegetational landscape of southwestern Oregon has changed dramatically since the nineteenth century. As in many other sections of the Pacific Northwest, twentieth-century fire management policy—with its elimination of traditional anthropogenic fire and suppression of most natural fire—has played a major role in this transformation.

In the main valleys and adjacent foothills, where humans had been the main ignition source for at least 4,000 years, the open landscape brought admiring comment from early settlers. Lindsay Applegate, passing through the area in 1846, likened the Rogue River Valley to "a great meadow, interspersed with groves of oaks which appeared like vast orchards." George Riddle compared the South Umpqua Valley near Cow Creek to "a great wheatfield," remaining green throughout autumn with the new shoots of grass resulting from recent Indian fires. By the mid-twentieth century, many such areas had been invaded by dense thickets of brush and crowded stands of young conifers. The change moved one Klamath man to complain to ethnographer Omer Stewart that "[n]ow I just hear the deer running through the brush at places we used to kill many deer." He pointed out that when the brush "got as thick as it is now, we would burn it off." Modern descendants of southwestern Oregon native groups still recall that burning formerly was a "widespread practice" for a variety of purposes.[44]

continued on page 270

South Fork Canyon of Little Butte Creek, Rogue River National Forest, eastern Jackson County, Oregon. The tall, large-diameter ponderosa pine (approx. 250–300 years old) in the center of the photograph, a remnant of the formerly open pine/oak forest of South Fork Canyon, is crowded by a stand of 40- to 80-year-old Douglas-fir and white fir. (photograph by J. LaLande)

South Fork Canyon of Little Butte Creek. The curving trunk and main branches of the dead California black oak tree testify to the former open quality of this forest. The dense thicket of young Douglas-fir that overtopped the oak in the past ten to twenty years is an artifact of twentieth-century fire suppression. (photograph by J. LaLande)

Vegetational Change in the South Fork Canyon

The South Fork canyon of Little Butte Creek exemplifies the pattern of vegetational change due to twentieth-century fire suppression. Located in the Cascade Range foothills east of the Rogue River Valley, South Fork canyon contains a number of prehistoric archaeological sites along Little Butte Creek, evidence of long-term seasonal hunting and gathering use of the vicinity. At present, the upper portion of the canyon's slopes supports a dense forest dominated by Douglas-fir (*Pseudotsuga menziesii*) and white fir (*Abies concolor*). A hike through almost any of the upper canyon's forested stands reveals a situation common throughout much of southwestern Oregon: The fir stands, by and large, date to between eighty and sixty years of age—i.e., they began growing soon after the era of fire suppression began. And among the thickets of young fir are remnants of the previous transitional-forest community: scattered large-diameter ponderosa pine (*Pinus ponderosa*) and California black oak. This earlier community probably had been maintained by periodic anthropogenic (and natural) fire for centuries.

Ashland Creek watershed, Rogue River National Forest, western Jackson County, Oregon. Recent Forest Service fuelbreak management efforts along Winburn Ridge have resulted in an open, ponderosa pine-dominated forest—recreating the general appearance of the area prior to twentieth-century fire suppression. (photograph by J. LaLande)

Today, many of the South Fork canyon's towering old pines are dying, unable to compete for soil moisture with the thirsty firs crowding below. Most of the massive oaks have been dead for ten or twenty years, overtopped and shaded out by the fast-growing firs. Both ponderosa pine and California black oak are far more fire-tolerant than the comparatively thin-barked young Douglas-fir and white fir, but modern fire suppression in the South Fork canyon changed the equation of survival. A formerly open oak/pine woodland—with an understory rich in edible plants as well as grass and browse for ungulates—has been replaced by a dense, closed-canopy forest of conifers.

***

Nearly fifty years ago, cultural geographer Carl Sauer warned that complete fire protection "accumulates tinder year by year" and that the "longer the accumulation, the greater . . . the fire hazard and the more severe the fire when it results." He then asked "whether well-regulated fires may not have an ecological role beneficent" to modern society "as they did in older days?"[45] Sauer's question finally is being answered affirmatively in southwestern Oregon, as elsewhere. Ecologists, foresters, and fire specialists currently are initiating efforts to recover the "world we have lost" to past fire suppression policies. In the Ashland Creek watershed, for example, the Forest Service now employs selective helicopter logging and periodic burning to help reestablish a more open, pine-dominated (and fire-resistant) forest. Within the recently established Applegate Adaptive Management Area, after years of clearcut and shelterwood harvest with the efficiency-driven goal of even-aged forest management, Forest Service and Bureau of Land Management timber harvest projects now aim to reduce tree density (thinning out the over-stocked stands of young Douglas-fir) and retain species/age diversity, including older pines and oaks.

Along a stretch of the Applegate River, a small portion of National Forest land at Kanaka Gulch has been designated informally as a cultural landscape restoration area. Whereas other "new forestry" endeavors in southwestern Oregon are driven primarily by fire-hazard reduction and other current environmental/economic concerns, a major focus at Kanaka Gulch will be experimental replication of traditional native burning practices, with the ultimate goal of reinvigorating the open oak woodland community and its many culturally important plant species.

The Kanaka Gulch project aims to "achieve the desired condition of cultural landscape restoration"—a landscape "as managed historically by indigenous people"—by reinstating fire as a maintenance tool.[46] It is certain that the elderly woman seen by the U.S. Exploring Expedition with a torch in her hand would have been pleased.

Not previously published

Notes

1. Jessie Poesch (ed.), *Titian Ramsay Peale and his Journals of the Wilkes Expedition* (American Philosophical Society Memoir 52, 1961), 192; Henry Eld, "Journal, Statistics etc. in Oregon and California . . ." (ms., Western Americana Collection, Yale University), entry of September 28, 1841.

2. This essay acknowledges the inspiration and encouragement provided by Henry Lewis's 1990 article, "Reconstructing Patterns of Indian Burning in Southwestern Oregon" (pp. 80–84 in Nan Hannon and Richard Olmo [eds.], *Living with the Land: The Indians of Southwestern Oregon*; Medford: Southern Oregon Historical Society). Lewis found it "eminently reasonable to assume that habitat fires were no less important for the Shasta, Umpqua and other tribes of the . . . southwestern part of the state." He hypothesized that native burning practices in southwestern Oregon (which he describes as a "geographic extension" of the northern Californian environment) "must have been functionally equivalent to those described for . . . the Miwok, Hupa, Tolowa, and Wintun." The historic and ethnographic information presented in this essay support Lewis's hypothesis. Henry Lewis also provided helpful comments on an earlier version of this paper. For a compilation of ethnographic data on southwestern Oregon Indian use of fire, see Reg Pullen, *Overview of the Environment of Native Inhabitants of Southwestern Oregon, Late Prehistoric Era* (Medford, USDI Bureau of Land Management, 1996).

3. In Melville Jacobs, "Coos Ethnological Notes" (Notebook 92, Melville Jacobs Collection, University of Washington Archives, 1932), 66.

4. Thomas Atzet and David Wheeler, *Historical and Ecological Perspectives on Fire Activity in the Klamath Geological Province of the Rogue River and Siskiyou National Forests* (Portland: USDA Forest Service Publication R6-Range-102, 1982).

5. Philip Drucker, "The Tolowa and their Southwest Oregon Kin" (*University of California Publications in American Archaeology and Ethnology* 35(4), 1937).

6. The linguistic stocks included: Hokan (Shasta); Penutian (Takelma, Coos, lower Coquille); and Athapascan (Chetco, Tututni, Galice Creek, Applegate, Chasta Costa, Illinois, upper Umpqua, upper Coquille). See Laurence Thompson and Dale Kinkade, "Languages," pp. 30–51 in Wayne Suttles (ed.), *Northwest Coast*, vol. 7 of the Smithsonian's *Handbook of North American Indians* (Washington, 1990).

7. Recent overviews of southwestern Oregon ethnography include Dennis Gray, "The Takelma and their Athapascan Neighbors: A New Ethnographic Synthesis for the Upper Rogue River Area of Southwestern Oregon" (*University of Oregon Anthropological Paper* No. 37, 1987); Jay Miller and William Seaburg, "Athapascans of Southwestern Oregon," pp. 580–88 in *Northwest Coast*, vol. 7 of the *Handbook of North American Indians*; Jeff LaLande, *The Indians of Southwestern Oregon: An Ethnohistorical Review* (Anthropology Northwest No. 6, Oregon State University, 1991); and Reg Pullen, *Overview of the Environment of Native Inhabitants of Southwestern Oregon*.

8. See Stephen Beckham, *Requiem for a People: the Rogue Indians and the Frontiersmen* (orig. 1971; 1996 reprint by Oregon State University Press); and Early Albert Schwartz, *The Rogue River Indian War and its Aftermath, 1850–1980* (Norman, OK, 1997).

9. See Alfred Kroeber and Edward Gifford, "World Renewal: a Cult System of Native Northwest America" (*University of California Anthropological Records* 13(1),

1949). An 1861 manuscript by Lorenzo Hubbard held by the Bancroft library (quoted below) suggests ritual fire use among lower Rogue Athapascans.

10. See Robert Haswell, in Frederic Howay, *Voyages of the Columbia to the Northwest Coast* . . . (orig. 1941; 1990 reprint by Oregon Historical Society Press, Portland), 30; Jeff LaLande, *First Over the Siskiyous: Peter Skene Ogden's 1826–1827 Journey through the Oregon-California Borderlands* (Portland, 1987).

11. See Harrison Rogers's "Second Journal," pp. 242–75 in Harrison Dale (ed.), *Ashley-Smith explorations and the discovery of a central route to the Pacific, 1822–1829* (Glendale, CA, 1918), 263.

12. *Titian Ramsay Peale and His Journals* . . ., 191–192, 196; Henry Eld, "Journal, Staistics etc . . ."; and Charles Brackenridge, *The Brackenridge Journal for the Oregon Country* (Seattle, 1931), 218–19.

On sugar pine, an even earlier account comes from David Douglas (February 20, 1826; "Sketch of a Journey to the Northwestern Parts of the Continent of North America, During the Years 1824–25–26–27." *Oregon Historical Quarterly* 5: var. pp., 1904, 270–71), and yet another historic description comes from Robert Brown, "On the Vegetable Products, Used by the Northwest American Indians as Food and Medicine, in the Arts, and in Superstitious Rites" (*Transactions of the Edinburgh Botanical Society* 9: 378–96, 1868, 382). All three accounts mention fire as an integral part of the gathering process; Douglas adds that the sap was used "in the same way as sugar is by the civilized nations," and that the seeds were pounded and formed into cakes, "a great delicacy." This singular method of gathering sugar pine apparently didn't survive much beyond the mid-1800s removal of southwestern Oregon Indians to northwest Oregon reservations, where sugar pines are not native; the later anthropological accounts say nothing about it.

13. George Riddle, *Early Days in Oregon: a History of the Riddle Valley* (Riddle, OR, 1920), 37 and 46. Riddle's description of the tarweed harvest is quoted more fully in Boyd (this volume).

14. Hubbard manuscript (1861); A. G. Walling, *History of Southern Oregon* (Portland, 1884), 219 and 334.

15. See Ashland *Tidings,* March 3, 1892; and John Leiberg, *The Cascade Range and Ashland Forest Reserves and Adjacent Regions* (Washington, D.C., 1900).

16. LaLande, *An Environmental History of the Little Applegate River Watershed, Jackson County, Oregon* (Medford, 1995) 35–37.

17. Arthur Ringland, "Report on Fire Protection Problems of the Klamath and Crater National Forests" (Item No. D-9, historical records collection of the Rogue River National Forest, Medford. USDA Forest Service, 1916); Lewis, "Reconstructing Patterns of Indian Burning in Southwestern Oregon," 82–83.

18. Primary among these anthropologists were: Roland Dixon, Cora DuBois, Pliny Goddard, John Peabody Harrington, Catherine Holt, Elizabeth and Melville Jacobs, and Edward Sapir. Both Dixon and Holt focused on the Shasta of the Klamath River canyon in California. However, their main consultant, Sargent Sambo, although he then resided along the Klamath River, had been a member of the Rogue River Valley Shasta band; in many cases, Sambo's information doubtless derives in part from the Shastas of southwestern Oregon.

19. Edward Sapir, "Notes on the Takelma Indians of southwestern Oregon" (*American Anthropologist* 9(2): 251–75, 1907), 260; Roland Dixon, "The Shasta" (*Bulletin of the American Museum of Natural History* 17(5), 1907), 431; Catherine Holt, "Shasta Ethnography" (*University of California Anthropological Records* 3(4),

1946), 310–12; Elizabeth Jacobs, "Upper Coquille Ethnologic Notes" (Jacobs Collection, 1935), notebook 121.

20. Melville Jacobs, "Galice Creek Field Notebooks" (Jacobs Collection, box 104), notebook 126: 97; *The Papers of John Peabody Harrington in the National Anthropological Archives of the Smithsonian Institution* (Kraus International Publications, 1981), microfilm reel 28/frame 430.

21. The Tolowa of the northwestern-most corner of California (whose territory extended a short distance north of the Oregon border) also "burned off the hillsides to improve the hunting grounds"; the "deer frequented such clearings and could be shot most easily." See Drucker, "The Tolowa and Their Southwest Oregon Kin," 232–33. The Chetco people of the extreme southwest corner of Oregon spoke a dialect of Tolowa and were culturally similar to them.

22. Cora DuBois, "Ethnological Document No. 6" [Tututni fieldnotes](Bancroft Library, 1934), Elizabeth Jacobs, "Upper Coquille Ethnologic Notes," notebook 104:100; Melville Jacobs, "Coos Ethnologic Notes" (Jacobs Collection, notebook 92, box 56, 1932), 66.

23. The Karok material is in Sara Schenck and Edward Gifford, "Karok Ethnobotany" (*University of California Anthropological Records* 13(6), 1952), and Gifford, "Karok Field Notes, Part 1" (Ethnological Document No. 174, Bancroft Library, 1939).

24. In Sapir, "Notes on the Takelma Indians . . .," 259.

25. E. Jacobs, "Upper Coquille Ethnologic Notes," notebook 104: 101. Tarweed presently is absent or rare in Coquille territory; it is possible that this account referred to Coquelle Thompson's Upper Umpqua relatives who resided in the interior valleys to the east.

26. Harrington, *Papers,* reel 25/frame 180.

27. Harrington, *Papers,* reel 25/frame 248; E. Jacobs, "Upper Coquille Ethnologic Notes," notebook 104: 110.

The latter is the sole specific ethnographic mention of burning berry fields in southwestern Oregon. This probably reflects the limited topics of the ethnographic interview more than it does the absence of fire for enhancing berry production. For example, although the Klamaths—who annually gathered huckleberries from extensive berry fields in the headwaters of the Rogue River—are known historically to have burned the patches regularly, the most complete ethnography of the Klamath makes no mention of the use of fire for any vegetation or wildlife management purposes. Leiberg, *The Cascade Range and Ashland Forest Reserves . . .,* 331–32; but cf. Leslie Spier, "Klamath Ethnography" (*University of California Publications in American Archaeology and Ethnology* 30, 1930).

28. DuBois [Tututni Fieldnotes]; Harrington *Papers,* reel 26/frame 143; E. Jacobs "Upper Coquille Ethnologic Notes," notebook 104: 101.

29. Harrington, *Papers,* reel 28.

30. Holt, "Shasta Ethnography," 309; see also Sapir, "Notes on the Takelma Indians . . .," 260. Yellowjacket larvae also were collected after the adults had been "smoked out of their holes." "Coyote in a Hollow Tree" appears in Sapir's "Takelma Texts" (*University of Pennsylvania Museum Anthropological Publications* 2(1), 1909), 93 and 95.

31. See Harrington's "Tobacco Among the Karok Indians of California" (*Bureau of American Ethnology Bulletin* No. 94, 1932). The southwestern Oregon sources include Pliny Goddard, "Galice/Applegate Ethnographic Notes" (Jacobs

Collection, Box 104, 1904); Sapir, "Notes on the Takelma Indians . . .," 259; and Anonymous, "Upper Takelma Field Notes from Molly Orton and Elizabeth Harney" (Notebook No. 135, Bancroft Library, n.d.). Again, however, the Tututni were an exception: "Ground not burned over first." (DuBois, [Tututni Field Notes]).

32. Hubbard, 1861 manuscript in Bancroft Library.

33. Harrington, *Papers*, reel 28.

34. M. Jacobs, "Galice Creek Field Notebooks," notebook 126: 97.

35. H. H. Bartlett, "Fire, Primitive Agriculture, and Grazing in the Tropics," pp. 692–720 in William Thomas (ed.), *Man's Role in Changing the Face of the Earth* (Chicago, 1956), 693.

36. Harrington, *Papers,* reel 25/frame 248.

37. T. Atzet, personal communication, 1995.

38. On the Panamanian remains, Dolores Piperno, "The Interpretation of Forest Fires in Paleoecological Records from the Neotropics: Natural or Man-Made?" (paper presented at the 61st Annual Meeting of the Society for American Archaeology, 1996); on the 8000–4000 B.P. drought, C. Melvin Aikens, *Archaeology of Oregon* (USDI Bureau of Land Management, 1993), 226–27; on plant cover dynamics since 4000 B.P. Wallace Woolfenden, "Historical Ecology and the Human Dimension in Ecosystem Management" (typescript, USDA Forest Service, Inyo National Forest, Bishop CA) and LaLande, *An Environmental History of the Little Applegate River Watershed,* 4–5.

39. The Mesolithic Britain hypotheses were presented by Jenny Moore and Paul Mellars in "The Ecological and Economic Consequences of Forest Burning: Some Models for Prehistoric Socio-Economic Change" (Society for American Archaeology, 1996). On prehistoric manipulation of animal populations through fire and its consequences, see also Henry Lewis, "The role of fire in the domestication of plants and animals in Southwest Asia: A hypothesis" (*Man* 7(2): 195–222, 1972).

The Moore-Mellars model also could have some application to the question of native groups' apparent change from originally wide-ranging "foragers" to more sedentary "collectors" later in prehistory. For a detailed discussion of the apparent "forager-to-collector" transformation, see Kathryn Winthrop, "Prehistoric Settlement Patterns in Southwestern Oregon" (Ph.D. dissertation, University of Oregon, 1993).

40. Bob Zybach, "'Voices in the Forest': An Interview with Bob Zybach" (*Evergreen,* March/April 1993: 7–22), and "Forest History and FEMAT Assumptions: A Critical Review of President Clinton's 1994 Northwest Forest Plan" (Corvallis: American Forest and Paper Association and the Northwest Forest Resource Council, 1993); and Doug MacCleery, "Understanding the Role that Humans have Played in Shaping America's Forest and Grassland Landscapes" (*Evergreen*, August 1994: 11–19).

41. Returning to Mesolithic Britain for another analogue, when archaeologists first began to give serious recognition to anthropogenic fire a few decades ago, they produced great, sweeping estimates of the geographic extent of aboriginal incendiarism—acreage figures that have been reduced considerably after years of additional research. Ian Simmons, "Fire and Environment in Later Mesolithic England" (Society for American Archaeology, 1996).

42. Henry Lewis, "Patterns of Indian Burning in California: Ecology and Ethnohistory" (orig. 1973; 1993 revision in Thomas Blackburn and Kat Anderson (eds.), *Before the Wilderness: Environmental Management by Native Californians* (Menlo Park, CA, 55–116); Moore and Mellars, "The Ecological and Economic Consequences of Forest Burning . . .."

43. The practice of concentrating the effects of fire within small, localized areas elsewhere in North America is discussed in Henry Lewis and Theresa Ferguson, "Yards, Corridors, and Mosaics: How to Burn a Boreal Forest" (1988 and this volume).

44. Robert Kentta, [cultural resource specialist, Confederated Tribes of Siletz Indians], personal communication to R. Pullen, 1995. Sue Crispen Shaffer, an elder and tribal leader of the Cow Creek Indians, remembers her Uncle Bob Thomason's practical knowledge of fire:

> When I was a very little girl, I [asked], "When do you do the burning?" His reply was always, "When the time is right." He would sniff the air, also wet his finger and hold it up (although there was no wind that I could perceive), and say, "Not yet" or "It's time." . . . The fires were set annually, but I'm sure on a rotating basis. (Lewis, "Reconstructing Patterns of Indian Burning in Southwestern Oregon," 82–83.)

45. Sauer, "The Agency of Man on Earth," 56.

46. Paul Hosten and Dennis Martinez, "A Preliminary Proposal for Examining the Effects of Fire and Thinning in an Oak Woodland Community at Kanaka Gulch, Applegate Valley, Southwestern Oregon" (report to the Pacific Northwest Research Station, USDA Forest Service, Grants Pass, 1996).

Proto-historical and Historical Spokan Prescribed Burning and Stewardship of Resource Areas

John Alan Ross

Introduction

The relationship between humans and fire is intricate and dramatic, and recently has become a major concern to anthropologists, biologists, foresters, and Indian resource-management personnel.[1] Since Omer Stewart's classic paper of 1956, in which he identified more than 100 Amerind groups that utilized forest and grassland burning, there has been an effort to reexamine existing ethnographies and ethnohistories that make specific reference to Indians who not only recalled such fire-technology, but who practiced burning and were able to provide partial explanations of the effects that prescribed burning had upon the environment and specific plant-animal communities.[2]

Unfortunately, there is a paucity of detailed descriptive data of this trait complex in the ethnographic literature from the Columbia Plateau. Although relatively few early historic references specifically describe prescribed burning,[3] prescribed burning during the late historical period has been studied for some Plateau and neighboring peoples.[4]

For the Spokan (*/spoʔqeʔñi/*)[5] there are some ethnographic data and linguistic classifications on floral/faunal folk taxa[6] that demonstrate that the Spokan understood and practiced the management of indigenous plant-animal associations, and knew how to maintain certain economically significant grassland and forest plant communities by utilizing fire technology. Moreover, it has been documented that the Spokan were cognizant of benefits derived from selective burning.[7] In contrast, most of the area's Euro-American settlers' interpretation and policies suggest that they did not understand the ecological benefits of prescribed burning. By opposing Indian prescribed burning, Euro-Americans created an environmental situation that actually encouraged the heavy accumulation of dead vegetation, windfall, and deadfall; as well as a change in certain species types, seed propagation, and alteration of fire resistance of some plants; increasing diseases caused by bacteria, fungi, parasitic plants, and viruses.

Problems of Gathering and Reconstructing Ethnobiological Taxa

Even though there are Native Americans within the southern Plateau who are conversant in their native language, there are few, if any, who are presently knowledgeable of not only the technology and rituals of controlled burning, but the linguistics unique to these behaviors and strategies. Sadly, many fieldworkers are only too familiar with the response: "Yes, I remember my grandparents talking about how they heard of folks burning certain areas in the spring or early fall, but I can't recall the name used for the people who did the burning." Or, "I saw them burn areas on our way to the mountains when I was young going deer hunting." To use Casson's phrase, "the structure and organization of conceptual categories in folk classification systems" are mostly gone.[8]

Procedures for reconstructing hierarchical nontaxonomic and taxonomic classifications[9] may help retrieve data otherwise not available to the anthropologist. Indigenous taxa may even permit the fieldworker to fill linguistic gaps. Despite the fact that some elders were somewhat familiar with the linguistic nomenclature of plant and animal taxa, the location of pre-reservation resources was often, at best, only general, because of departure from consuming traditional foods and resource-getting patterns. Using even an incomplete taxon as a mnemonic device on occasion permits the ethnographer to assist an elder in recalling forgotten classificatory terms.

It is the purpose of this paper to discuss: 1) why there was either spring or fall burning, or in some instances both; 2) what natural conditions were maintained or purposely altered by this particular biocultural strategy; 3) what major economically significant resource areas amongst the Spokan were affected by prescribed burning; 4) what was the significance of incipient religious specialization and attending rituals of those individuals charged with the responsibility of annual prescribed burning; and 5) why, during the reservation period, did women and berdaches (a man with woman's power to locate productive resource areas) assume the responsibility of maintaining stewardship for nearly all traditions on reservation resource areas.

Strategies and Times of Prescribed Burning

Spokan oral history accounts and early photographic records graphically attest to the fact that there was less accumulated windfall and deadfall on the reservation as late as the 1940s. One may posit that prior to 1913 there were rarely, if any, crown fires, and certainly fewer flying and ground insects, particularly moths and butterflies. It also is obvious that with prescribed burning, tree growth rates, and certain plant successions and locations, have been altered drastically.[10]

The time and location of deliberate burning by the Spokan usually were determined by local soil and moisture conditions, general wind direction, and logistically the location of the resource area during the annual subsistence round. Because of fluctuating variables, the exact time of prescribed burning never was really predictable. Elders had memories of multiple annual burnings of the same resource site, while some areas were not burned for four to five years.[11]

A few elderly Spokan recalled the accounts of their great grandparents (approximately 1830s to 1850s), explaining how most forested areas below 1,000 meters (MSL) were "open," and that prior to reservation confinement, annual prescribed burning served to facilitate ease of travel, communication, and stalking of game.[12] When reflecting upon present forestry practices, now-deceased Spokan-speaking elders lamented to the author about the present condition of many on-reservation forested areas, whereby travel is not only difficult but often dangerous because of the preponderance of windfall, deadfall, and dense understory. In 1972, the author and a ninety-three-year-old Spokan man were laboriously traversing a densely wooded terrace along Chamokane Creek on the Spokane Indian Reservation, looking for a particular plant. The old gentleman stopped, paused in silence, and actually cried as he explained how as a young teenager (circa 1895) he had hunted the terrace and could vividly recall the vegetation as being "open with grasses."

Spokan were aware that in order to maintain open, healthy "park-like" conditions, which were conducive to ungulates, fire-removal of windfall and deadfall and understory fire management was necessary. Elders have frequently stated that a further economic benefit of forest ignition was the reduction of understory vegetation known to effectively compete with grasses that supported ungulates. Prescribed burning was conducted to encourage elk, deer, and even later horse grazing, thereby improving not only game pasturage but visibility when hunting. Spokan were aware that with severe burning, seral shrubs tended to replace conifers and the quantity of forage increased rather dramatically, encouraging utilization by browsing animals. For example, red-stemmed ceanothus (*Ceanothus sanguineus* Pursh.; /k̓ʷlíč̓-t-y/eʔłp/) is the most important browse for deer in some areas, and since this shrub requires the heat of fire to crack its seed and prepare it for germination, burning was essential.[13] Prior to the reservation period, during the fall hunt at higher elevations, fire frequently was used to move game into prearranged areas of predation, and informants cite this as a favored strategy for harvesting mule deer, especially where the region's topography and vegetation were conducive to it. After becoming dependent upon equestrian travel, and until the early 1900s, the Spokan fired the grasses in the area of Cayuse Mountain in early summer to capture wild horses.[14]

Elderly Spokan were adamant in their claims that fire-treated forest areas were more resistant to fires, particularly lightning-induced and, later, crown fires during the early reservation period. Fire management was critical to maintain a healthy state for Douglas-fir (*Pseudotsuga menziesii*—/c̓q/éłp/), lodgepole pine, ponderosa pine, and western white pines (*Pinus monticola* Dougl. ex Lamb.—/cč̓/éy̓łp/), which are subclimax fire types. It was not unusual for Spokan elders to claim that selective burning was performed for the express purpose of maintaining "healthy forest environments" prior to Euro-American settlement.[15]

Stewardship of Specific Resource Areas

Aboriginal stewardship of resource areas was well understood and the indigenous people were fully cognizant of climax vegetations, successions, interdependencies of plant-animal communities, ecotones, and certainly the carrying capacity of a woodland or grassland area.

Trees

Aboriginally, and to the present day, timber and its various byproducts were essential in many ways to Spokan adaptation, particularly the major byproducts such as various species of nuts, mosses, pitch and sap, cambium and barks, stems, branches, and poles.

Ponderosa Pine—A major reason for judicious fire ignition in ponderosa pine (*Pinus ponderosa* Dougl. —/ʔastkʷ/) forests was to prevent any destruction of the lower branches that had been left intact as a means of climbing to storage platform caches to store salmon and other foods.[16] Informants agree ponderosa pine nuts (/ʔ-pilyeʔ/) could be more easily collected after surface burning. Prescribed burning was seen as having no apparent effect upon the nuts of ponderosa, but it benefited the tree itself by controlling the understory. Spokan were aware of how fire in ponderosa stands actually might improve soil permeability by removing accumulated pine needles, which is important because the needles contain poisonous hydrocarbons that makes them detrimental to the growth of young seedlings.[17] In the northern Plateau, seeds (/q̓ʷóxʷ-t/n̓ eʔ/) from the western white pine often were roasted and eaten immediately after burning the understory.

Lodgepole pine—Three major areas on the Spokane Indian Reservation and several off-reservation areas that produced lodgepole pine (*Pinus contorta latifolia*—/kʷkʷlíy̓-t/) were burned annually to reduce the occurrence of an epiphyte known as dwarf mistletoe (*Arceuthobium americanum* Nutt.). Renewed efforts by Spokane tribal foresters to rid regions of this epiphyte involve fire ignition and reflect contemporary policies. The Spokan understood that once this epiphyte colony commences to invade downward, its growth can prevent the desired straight growth and preferred smooth surface of the tree when used for tipi or house construction. Further to the east, lodgepole pine was economically significant as the Flathead traded cleaned, deerhorn-polished lodgepole to western Plains Indians for use as tipi and travois poles.[18]

Willow—Economically, willow (*Salix scouleriana*—/q̓ʷq̓ʷl̓/s/álqʷ/) was an invaluable material, one required for a wide range of purposes (e.g., mats, traps and snares, sweathouse frames, burden baskets, toys and musical instruments, punk wood, and medicine). Willow branches usually were collected by both male and female gatherers in the late spring, a time when it was claimed willow was most pliable, and before the area would be ignited.[19]

Paper Birch and Aspen—It was contended that prescribed burning was done in birch (*Betula papyrifera*—/pcčł-n/álqʷ/) and aspen (*Populus tremuloides*—/m̓lm̓l̓-t/éłp/) groves primarily to reduce the understory, particularly of rose hip bushes (*Rosa* spp.—/xʷxʷy/ép/łp/), which, if not contained, made travel difficult when exploiting the trees for bark or sap.[20]

Lichens—Elderly Spokan women have explained how, when berrying in early autumn at higher elevations, they would gather to collect with their hands and poles any accessible tree lichens (to reduce fire danger as well as for food). Flathead people also gathered lichen as a food, and "to reduce the threat of wildfires which could ignite the lichens and spread into the forest canopy." Lichens (*Alectoria fremontii* Tuck.—/s-q̓ʷl̓ápqn/ and *Alectoria jubata*—/šáw̓-m-qʷn/; commonly known as goat's beard), cooked in an earth oven and processed into long cakes, were an important winter food and the subject of an annual thanksgiving rite among traditional Spokan.[21] In the mid-nineteenth century, roadbuilder John Mullan asked a Coeur d'Alene why he fired a wooded area, and was told that burning destroyed "tree moss" which the deer feed on in winter season, and "By burning the moss the deer are obliged to descend into the valleys for food," thus making them more available for Indian predation.[22]

Root Fields—Informants contended that in the memories of their grandmothers and great grandmothers, the women would burn over camas and other root sites (*Camassia quamash*—/ʔítxʷeʔ/, *Lomatium canbyi*—/č-xíw̓/sšn/, *L. cous*—/s-xʷeʔl/ítxʷeʔ/, *L. farinosum*—/t̓uxʷ/eʔ/) before leaving the harvested fields.

The reasoning for this strategy was clarified through oral history. Women explained how the following year's exploitation of roots would be easier dug if grasses and other organic materials had been burned to create an ash, which they felt "softened," or made more permeable, the sometimes desiccated late summer soils. Further, Spokan were adamant that the traditional root fields would not be encroached upon by competing peripheral grasses and other types of vegetation if they were annually burned.[23]

Large root fields usually were burned by collective effort, whereas smaller fields, particularly medicinal plots or family "owned" root fields, were cared for similarly by a family. It was not unusual for women to return to the same area where they had earlier collected or dug plants and burn over the now-dry plants.[24] Though not delineated here, it must be understood that many other types of root and tuber plants of nutritional, medical, and utilitarian significance benefited from the burning of fields by women after harvest. A major medicinal plant that was protected by ignition was licorice root (*Ligusticum virticillatum*—/ʔey/út/).

Brief mention should be made of balsamroot (*Balsamorhiza sagittata*—/s-múkʷ/eʔ/šn/) and sunflower (*Helianthus annuus* L.—/s-n-čn/čt/qiṅ/), which were the principal plants that provided seeds, tubers, and even stems. Since these plants frequently grew apart and in open areas that made it difficult to ignite the plants effectively with prescribed burning, in the early 1900s people preferred to torch individual plants with kerosene-soaked rags affixed to green wood.[25]

Huckleberry Patches—Recognizing inevitable cultural loss, there still was partial agreement among Spokan elders that early spring burning of vaccinium (*Vaccinium membranaceum* Dougl. ex Torr.— /s-tʼš/łq/éłp/ and *V. caespitosum* —/ssíp-t/) was preferred, since soil moisture normally was higher and heat penetration shallower than in autumn. They also noted that duff at this time invariably has a higher moisture content, and though less combustible, reduced the likelihood of overburning and therefore creating uncontrolled conflagration. Some Spokan elders have stated that the rhizomes were dormant and protected by wet ground, and consequently not harmed by spring burning. However, some elders maintained that late spring snows, or an abnormally high incidence of spring rain, would necessarily postpone any intentional burning until late summer or early fall, which was particularly true with understory or broadcast burning. The berrying patches were not usually burned until later fall when men hunted the berrying areas or traversed the area en route to deer hunting regions.[126]

Huckleberry was one of the few berry crops in which a berdache would locate the site and sometimes direct the women's collective efforts during harvesting. Traditional huckleberry patches were on occasion "owned" by a family, as were the responsibilities of stewardship, though the principles of usufruct applied amongst the Spokan. That is, an extended family was responsible for coordinating with other families or independent groups as to how often and when they would burn an area after harvest. Probably as recently as the 1890s, berdaches were further responsible for coordinating post-harvest burning. Though there was debate amongst informants as to how frequently these areas were ignited, there was consensus that logistics and natural conditions were dominant considerations with frequency of burning. Prescribed burning seldom was pursued annually for berry regions, but usually every fourth or fifth year according to long-term conditions and the presence of other competing flora.[27] Even today, the stewardship of various types of berries is maintained by mechanically or finger pruning the berry plant while harvesting. In remote areas that are considered "family plots," women will severely but carefully prune any dead stock after harvesting the bush.

Tule and Cattail Stands—Though reasons differ slightly for why women would always burn tule (*Scirpus validus* Vahl.—/s-ẏáẏq/) stands after completing their harvest, there is agreement that these particular hydrophytes always grew back taller and straighter than stands not burned. Accumulative experience and knowledge supported the popular notion that ashes improved the plots' fertility because "burnt material was more similar to the earth than unburnt vegetation." Tules, sometimes called the "bamboo of the Plateau," were utilized for bundle boats; house, sleeping, and drying mats; baskets, capes, and hats; storage pit liners; and certain parts as food. Women would travel annually to designated shallow lakes and ponds after a killing frost, frequently assisted by a male berdache.

Villages and Camps; Streams, Springs, and Seeps—A major purpose of Indian ignitions was to rid or reduce a living area of vermin, weeds, and insects, particularly when summer- and autumn-caught dried salmon was returned to permanent riverine villages for winter storage where it attracted yellow jackets and hornets. Most dried salmon was cached on platforms above 10 meters in ponderosa pine trees, beyond most insect flying ranges.[28] Oral accounts explain how habitation sites occasionally were carefully burned over to remove accumulated refuse, or after leaving a temporary ceremonial site. Within a number of Spokan protohistoric, and in some instances probably historical, camp and village sites on the Spokane Indian Reservation adjacent to the Spokane River, there is evidence found with in situ charcoal layers that may have been the result of these occasional ignitions.[29]

Wooded areas and some grasslands near permanent winter riverine villages, and around temporary spring, summer, and certain fall resource sites, were ignited carefully during times of even brief occupancy or utilization. The major concern was to not "overburn" the vegetation immediately bordering streams or contiguous areas with steep gradients because of later accelerated erosion and silt contamination.[30] Water quality was critical if the Spokan were to maintain both an adequate caloric intake from aquatic resources and polyadic trade networks that depended upon salmon. Aboriginally and until dam construction, fish contributed approximately 40 to 50% of total caloric intake in the Spokan diet.[31]

Until the late historical period, the Spokan practiced selective burning near seeps and springs. The burning of surrounding vegetation was so that the water would be "sweeter" and not contaminated by fir or pine needles (/ceme?/), especially western larch needles (*Larix occidentalis*—/caq ls/), which, if concentrated in great quantity in standing water, cause diarrhea. Also, firing surrounding spring or seep vegetation reduced the occurrence of insects.[32]

Deer, Elk, and Antelope—The most important game animals were the mule deer (*Odocoileus hemionus*—/sťúlče?/), whitetail deer (*O. virgianianus*—/č'úlixʷ/), elk (*Cervus canadensis*—/snečtče?/), and antelope (*Antilocapra americana*—/s-ťan/), which provided meat, hide, bone byproducts, antler, and of course marrow, and were hunted collectively most often in the autumn. Three informants have detailed certain strategies employed during deer hunting, stories told by their grandfathers. Methods included the bow and arrow, animal drives, fire surrounds, dead falls, deer jumps, traps and snares, confinement walls, and in winter, running down the deer with a type of bear paw snowshoes.[33]

Fire surrounds probably always involved group hunting. Briefly, in the fall, an individual possessing deer power (/si?ťus/) may dream of a successful hunt and announce his intention to hunting partners who, at dawn, would assist him in strategically placing burnt moccasins and magical bird feathers around the designated area to be fired. The rawhide-secured feathers aided the hunters by pointing to the deer when they attempted to avoid the burnt scent, and further would aid the arrows to their mark. Given topography and vegetation of a southwest facing hill, the fire usually was started at the base after all the hunters, usually thirty to forty men, were encircled in place (/t-cla?qmi/), and when the grass was ignited, orographic winds effectively would push the deer before the fire to a high point where the hunters, waving their arms and shouting, would dispatch the game.[34]

Father Pierre de Smet witnessed neighboring Coeur d'Alene using the fire surround method and driving deer into Lake Coeur d'Alene where the animals were dispatched easily by Indians in highly maneuverable bark canoes.[35] Spokan also may have used this method to drive game into the Spokane River. When rifles were introduced, the surround or circle drive probably declined in popularity to straight drives (/cla?qm/), given the obvious danger the new predation technology presented to participants.

Acquiring Power for Selective Burning

Carefully selected adult males had religious power associated specifically with controlled burning. These individuals ("burners"; /ʔurʼsict/) apparently were afforded complete control over deciding the frequency and strategy of burning economically significant resource areas. "Burners" also were responsible for directing the clearing of trails of unmanageable debris or blow down, and the clearing of important springs and game water seeps within a group's territory. Elders also recalled how their grandfathers would, if necessary, keep game saltlicks open from windblown vegetation.[36] Though women could conduct prescribed burning in certain situations, such as with tule patches and root and berry areas, the author has no knowledge of a Spokan woman ever possessing this unique power.

There were different ways in which a young Spokan man could be designated for training to receive the power (/sumi-xʷ/) for resource stewardship and selective burning. The best memory and reconstruction indicates the person had received recurring dreams of dwelling in the woods with certain animals, or had a close association with an older, consanguineally related male (his sponsor) who already possessed the desired power.[37]

The author worked occasionally for three summers with a Sinkaietk elder, a berdache, who received a special song and sacred paraphernalia from black bear (*Ursus americanus*—/nɫamqeʔ/) that presumably was associated with prescribed burning and with locating huckleberries. Several Entiat and Spokan elders have spoken of certain birds that could assist individuals who were charged with prescribed burning, specifically, the red-headed woodpecker (*Melanerpes erythrocephalus*—/spwalqn/, western meadowlark (*Sturnella neglecta*—/wáwickʷleʔ/), and yellow-shafted flicker (*Colaptes auratu*—/kʷlkʷléceʔ/). One informant thought that anyone knowledgeable of nature would understand why the meadowlark was associated with grassland areas, and the red-headed woodpecker and yellow-shafted flicker were "patron birds" of wooded areas because of their need for standing dead trees for food and nesting. Neither informant was certain as to the exact role of these tutelary birds, only that they could speak to "burners" as well as to other animals to warn them of pending fire.[38]

Reservation Period:
Women Assume the Roles of Stewardship

In 1877, the Northern Pacific Railroad was granted rights through the middle of aboriginal Spokan territory, denying utilization of the lands to the original occupants and forbidding the burning of forest and grasslands for fear of destroying rail-ties and railroad track buildings. Further pressures against prescribed burning began in 1878 when settlers filed homestead claims and bought land once belonging to the Spokan, therefore preventing further Indian use. Spokan oral histories recall that traditional burning first commanded the attention of the area's Euro-Americans when objections were made to Indian incendiarism of traditional root fields and wooded areas near small settler communities and rural areas where cattle and sheep raising was becoming established.[39] By 1900, the U.S. Forest Service had commenced a concerted effort to suppress and control forest fires on federal, and in some instances private, property.

The establishment of the reservation meant the Spokan now were dependent on dwindling fish stock and non-traditional foods acquired through a limited market economy, one based on a monetary system. With more men than women going off the reservation to participate in the market economy, and with women being unable to exploit traditional subsistence activities that were mainly off the reservation, a situation was created in which women had to assume many once-traditional male roles and responsibilities that were essential for fulfilling basic needs. Consequently, women became the major conservators and stewards of those few relatively productive on-reservation resource sites.

In 1914, the first Spokane Indian Reservation manager developed a strict policy that any Spokan who practiced controlled burning would be jailed if apprehended. Even during the 1920s and 1930s, on both the Colville and the Spokane Indian Reservations, the Bureau of Indian Affairs jailed Indian individuals, including several women, who attempted to maintain those few traditional on-reservation berry-picking patches and root fields through prescribed burning. The last time a Spokan woman was arrested was in 1931, by the then-Spokane Indian Tribal Forester who had a vehicle and by chance happened to be in the vicinity of logging roads that facilitated his apprehending the much older woman who was afoot.[40]

Numerous Spokan and Colville women informants have explained that in order to evade apprehension and arrest, they devised simple but effective delayed incendiary devices (/cʔlusnt/) that would ignite many hours after the individual Indian or group had departed from the area. Although these incendiary devices varied according to user, the most common and simple

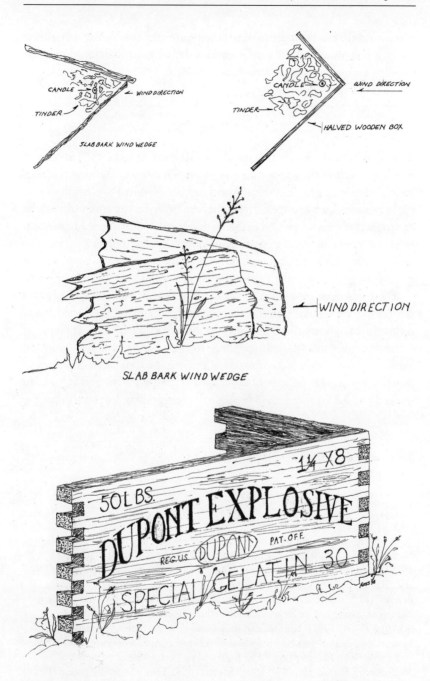

/cʔlusnt/, the "delayed incendiary device" used by Spokan and Colville women to set fires during the early 1900s, when burning in forested areas was prohibited by the government.

was setting a lit candle under an overturned empty fruit or discarded dynamite wooden box, using duff, lichens, shredded dry bark, or abandoned ground-dwelling animal nests as tinder.

Summary

In conclusion, one may say that the aboriginal hunting and gathering Spokan were cognizant of the short- and long-term benefits that burning practices had upon specific ecosystems and associated plant/animal communities that could be modified by culturally induced fire. Prescribed burning reduced the occurrence of crown fires and insect populations, and maintained grassland areas that were conducive to grazing ungulates. Fire ignition was responsible for maintaining rootfields, berrying patches, tule and cattail stands, and of course, many economically significant tree crops and byproducts.

These practices, sometimes under the direction of a few individuals who possessed supernatural power, continued into the historical period when confinement to reservations disrupted the once-traditional annual practice of forest and grassland stewardship. Only recently have several governmental agencies, those concerned with natural resource management, commenced experimenting with policies of controlled burning, practices that were an integral and basic procedure in aboriginal forest/grassland stewardship.

Not previously published

Notes

1. See, for instance, Stephen Arno, "The Historical Role of Fire on the Bitterroot National Forest" (USDA Forest Service Research Paper INT-187, Ogden, UT 1976); Stephen Barrett, "Indians and Fires" (*Western Wildlands* 6(3):17–21, 1980b) and "Relationship of Indian-Caused Fires to the Ecology of Western Montana Forests" (M.S. thesis, University of Montana, 1980a); Barrett and Arno, "Indian Fires as an Ecological Influence in the Northern Rockies" (*Journal of Forestry* 80(10):647–51, 1982); Rexford and Jean Daubenmire, "Forest Vegetation of Eastern Washington and Northern Idaho" (Cooperative Extension Service, WSU, Pullman, 1968); Gordon Day, "The Indian as an Ecological Factor in the Northeastern Forest" (*Ecology* 34(2):329–46, 1953); Omer Stewart, "Forest Fires with a Purpose" (*Southwestern Lore* 20(4):59–64, 1954), "Fire as the First Great Force Employed by Man" (pp. 115–33 in William Thomas (ed.), *Man's Role in Changing the Face of the Earth*, Chicago, 1956), and "Barriers to Understanding the Influence of Use of Fire by Aborigines on Vegetation" (*Proceedings, Tall Timbers Fire Ecology Conference* 2:117–26, 1963); and Harold Weaver, "Reports on Prescribed

Burning on the Colville Indian Reservation, Washington, during 1943 and 1944" (U.S. Dept. of the Interior, 1967).

2. Barrett and Arno "Indian Fires as an Ecological Influence . . ."; George Gruell, "Fire on the Early Landscape: An Annotated Record of Wildland Fires 1776— 1900" (*Northwest Science* 59(2):97–107, 1985); and Douglas Houston, "Wildfires in Northern Yellowstone National Park" (*Ecology* 54(5):1111–17, 1973).

3. See, for example, Hiram Chittenden and Alfred Richandson (eds.), *Life, Letters, and Travels of Father Pierre-Jean deSmet, 1801–1873*, New York, 1969); James C. Cooper, *The Natural History of Washington Territory . . .Being Those Parts of the Final Report on the survey of the Northern Pacific Railroad Route . . .* (New York, 1859); M. J. Elrod, "An Attempt on Mount St. Nicholas" (ms., University of Montana Archives, Missoula, 1906); John Mullan, *Report on the Construction of a Military Road from Fort Benton to Fort Walla Walla*, (36th Cong., 2d Sess., House Ex. Doc. 44, 1861); Warren Ferris, *Life in the Rocky Mountains* (Denver, 1940); and Moulton, Gary (ed.), *Journals of the Lewis & Clark Expedition* (University of Nebraska Press, 1983–).

4. Arno 1976, "The Historical Role of Fire . . ."; Barrett "Relationship of Indian-Caused Fires . . .," "Indians and Fires," and "Indian Fires in the Presettlement Forests of Western Montana" (pp. 35–41 in "Proceedings of the Fire History Workshop, October 20–24, Tucson," USDA Forest Service General Technical Report RM-81, Fort Collins CO, 1978); Daubenmire and Daubenmire, "Forest Vegetation of Eastern Washington . . ."; David French, "Ethnobotany of the Pacific Northwest Indians" (*Economic Botany* 19(4):378–82, 1965); Eugene Hunn and D. French, "Lomatium: A Key Resource for Columbia Plateau Native Subsistence" (*Northwest Science* 55(2):87–94, 1981); Henry Lewis, "Maskuta: The Ecology of Indian Fires in Northern Alberta" (*Western Canadian Journal of Anthropology* 7(1):15–52, 1977) and "Hunter-Gatherers and Problems for Fire History" (pp. 61–62 in USDA Forest Service GTR RM-81, "Proceedings of the Fire History Workshop, 1978"); Stephen Pyne, *Fire in America: A Cultural History of Wildland and Rural Fire* (Princeton, 1982); John A. Ross, "Controlled Burning: Forest management in the aboriginal Columbia Plateau" (paper presented at the 66th Northwest Scientific Association Conference, Corvallis, March 20–24, 1981); Dean Shinn, "Historical Perspectives on Range Burning in the Inland Pacific Northwest" (*Journal of Range Management* 33(6):415–23, 1980); and Howard Weaver, "Slash Disposal on the Colville Indian Reservation" (*Journal of Forestry* 44(2):81–88, 1946), "Effects of Prescribed Burning in Second Growth Ponderosa Pine" (*Journal of Forestry* 55(11)823–826, 1957), and 1967 *ibid.*

5. Including the Lower Spokan /scqesciɬni?/, Middle Spokan /snxʷmene?tey/, and Upper Spokan /sntu?t?lixʷi/: William Elmendorf, "Ethnographic Data from Three Spokan Informants" (unpublished ms. in Elmendorf's possession, 1935–36).

6. E.g., Deane Osterman, "The Ethnoichthyology of the Spokan Indian People" (unpublished M.S. thesis, Eastern Washington University, Cheney, 1995); Ross, "Controlled Burning . . ., " and "An Ethnoarchaeological Survey of the Spokane Indian Reservation" (in possession of the Spokane Indian Tribe, 17 volumes, Wellpinit, 1993a); Ross and Osterman (eds.), "An Ethnographic and Historic Analysis of the Spokan People" (Internal Report to the Spokane Tribe of Indians, 5 volumes, Wellpinit, 1995).

7. John Ross, "Colville and Spokan Field Notes," in the possession of the author (1965–1996); "Controlled Burning . . .," and "Southern Plateau Aboriginal

Utilization and Stewardship of Specific Floral/Faunal Resource Areas" (paper presented at the National Social Science Association Conference, San Antonio, November 10–13, 1993b).

8. Ross, "Colville and Spokan Field Notes"; Ronald Casson, "Cognitive Anthropology" (pp. 61–96 in Philip Bock (ed.), *Handbook of Psychological Anthropology* (Westport, 1994): 69.

9. See B. Stross, "Tzeltal Anatomical Terminology: Semantic Processes," in M. McClaran (ed.), *Mayan Linguistics*, vol. 1, (American Indian Studies Center, UCLA, 1976); cf Brent Berlin, "The Concept of Rank in Ethnobiological Classification: Some Evidence from Aguaruna Folk Botany" (*American Ethnologist* 3(3):381–99, 1976); "Ethnobotanical Classification," (pp. 9–26 in Eleanor Rosch and Barbara Lloyd (eds.), *Cognition and Categorization* (Hillsdale, NJ, 1978); *Ethnobiological Classification: Principles of Categorization of Plants and Animals in Traditional Societies* (Princeton, 1992); B. Berlin, D. E. Breedlove, and P. H. Raven, "General Principles of Classification and Nomenclature in Folk Biology" (*American Anthropologist* 75(1):214–42, 1973), and *Principles of Tzeltal Plant Classification: An Introduction to the Botanical Ethnography of a Mayan-Speaking People of Highland Chiapas* (New York, 1974); Cecil Brown, "Folk Botanical Life-Forms: Their Universality and Growth" (*American Anthropologist* 81(4):791–817, 1979), *Language and Living Things: Uniformities in Folk Classification and Naming* (New Brunswick, NJ, 1984), "The Mode of Subsistence and Folk Biological Taxonomy" (*Current Anthropology* 26(1):43–64, 1985), and "The Growth of Ethnobiological Nomenclature" (*Current Anthropology* 27(1): 1-19, 1986); Eugene Hunn, *Tzeltal Folk Zoology: The Classification of Discontinuities in Nature* (New York, 1977), and "The Utilitarian Factor in Folk Biological Classification" (pp. 117–40 in Janet Dougherty (ed.), *Directions in Cognitive Anthropology* (Urbana, 1985).

10. Frank Grant (ed.), "A Forest and A Tribe in Transition: A History of the Spokane Indian Reservation Forest, 1870—1994" (Missoula: Historical Research Associates, 1994); Ross, "Colville and Spokan Field Notes."

11. Ross, "Field Notes."

12. Ross, "Field Notes."

13. W. R. Moore, "From Fire Control to Fire Management" (*Western Wildlands* 1(3):11–15, 1976).

14. Ross, "Field Notes."

15. Ross, "Field Notes."

16. Ross, "Field Notes."

17. Moore, "From Fire Control to Fire Management."

18. James Samuels, personal communication; John Ross, "Flathead Field Notes," in possession of the author, 1963–64.

19. Ross, "Field Notes."

20. Ross, "Field Notes."

21. Ross, "Field Notes."

22. Ross, "Field Notes"; Barrett, "Relationship of Indian-Caused Fires . . .," 152; Mullan, *Report on the Construction of a Military Road . . .*, 152.

23. Ross, "Field Notes.".

24. Ross, "Controlled Burning . . ."

25. Ross, "Field Notes."

26. Ross, "Field Notes."

27. Ross, "Field Notes."

28. Ross, "Field Notes."
29. Ross, "Field Notes"; "An Ethnoarchaeological Survey of the Spokane Indian Reservation."
30. Ross, "Field Notes."
31. Ross, "Field Notes"; "Southern Plateau Aboriginal Utilization and Stewardship . . ."
32. Ross, "Field Notes."
33. Ross, "Field Notes."
34. Ross, "Field Notes."
35. Chittenden and Richardson, *Life, Letters, and Travels of Father Pierre-Jean de Smet* . . .: 1021–22; see also Nicolas Point in Barrett and Arno, this volume.
36. Ross, "Field Notes."
37. Ross, "Field Notes."
38. Ross, "Field Notes." Similarly, among the Upper Skagit Indians, "One spirit supplied the song to make berries grow, together with the knowledge of how to burn a forest in a carefully controlled way." June Collins, *Valley of the Spirits: The Upper Skagit Indians of Western Washington* (Seattle, 1974), 57.
39. John Fahey, personal communication (1996).
40. Ross, "Field Notes."

Conclusion

Ecological Lessons from Northwest Native Americans

L ike the rest of the Americas, the environment of the Pacific Northwest was not pristine when Europeans first encountered it. It was actively managed and shaped by the hand of its native inhabitants. The primary tool of this indigenous, non-agricultural environmental management was fire. Native Americans used fire purposefully and in patterns that reflected a traditional ecological knowledge that was both broad and deep.

Throughout the pre-White Pacific Northwest, Indian cultures used fire in different yet internally consistent ways. In the "interior valleys province," between the Coast and Cascade ranges, repeated firing maintained open prairie lands where the native peoples' most important wild plant foods grew. In the Columbia Basin, regular firing held back the growth of sagebrush and promoted the growth of bunchgrasses and forbs. Anthropogenic burning kept the understories of the ponderosa pine forests open and extended into higher-elevation, dry eastern forests where fire use was spottier. Along the Cascade crest, Indian-caused fires maintained mountain huckleberry patches, and in the upper Fraser highlands it promoted the growth of important root crops. Along the wet coastline, burning was less common, though locally intense, and mostly associated with the regeneration of various species of wild berries.

Several of the papers in this volume provide glimpses of what once must have been a considerable amount of traditional ecological knowledge underlying regionally patterned uses of fire. Through more than 10,000 years of occupation, Northwest Native Americans learned the intricacies of their local environments and how to use fire to create desired effects. People of Euro-American descent, however, have occupied the lands of the Pacific Northwest for less than 200 years and have been slow to understand the role of fire in Western North American ecosystems. We need to know how our predecessors used fire in the environment so we can best manage those same lands today.[1]

But it must be emphasized that the Indian systems of fire use and the land management systems of the colonizing Whites were fundamentally different. On one level, Indian systems utilized fire primarily to maximize the production of culturally valued species such as camas, huckleberries, and deer. The Euro-American system largely excludes fire and manages instead for valued species such as wheat, timber, and cattle. Although both systems favor particular species, the ecological effects of their practices were different.

We stand to learn at both levels, species and ecological. The most culturally specific and obvious lesson is that, by using Indian practices, we can manage for Indian-favored species, many of which are now in decline. There are several economically useful, underutilized native plants that might be brought back and encouraged through Indian methods. [2] The list is long and includes not only species valued by both Whites and Native Americans, such as the black mountain huckleberry, but also those whose usefulness so far has been overlooked by Whites, such as camas, spring beauty, the lomatiums, white oak acorns, and serviceberry, as well as various basketry materials and medicinal plants. Considering how valuable some of the underutilized species may be, reintroducing Indian methods of land management should be encouraged. Identifying and promoting the use of such plants is one of the major themes in the field of economic botany today. Beyond this practical (and somewhat selfish) reason, we also must recognize that many of these plants were integral parts of the cultural systems of Northwest Native peoples. Their decline has diminished contemporary Indian cultures, and this fact alone constitutes a strong reason to bring them back.

On the other hand, the Native American systems produced environments that were very different from those of the contemporary Northwest. Using fire, Indians set back successional stages among plant communities and produced patchy mosaics across the face of the land. They manipulated the environment without causing drastic changes in species composition. Non-Indian systems, in contrast, are mostly imported and superimposed: plant and animal domesticates evolved in different ecosystems; the land is broken, fertilizer is applied, forests are treated as crops. Thousands of alien species have been introduced to Western American environments, upsetting indigenous ecosystems.

Which system is better, Indian or non-Indian, and what have we to learn? From an anthropological viewpoint, the doctrine of "cultural relativism" tells us that each cultural system, so long as it is internally consistent and promotes the well being of its members, should not be judged—all are equally "good." So whether one digs camas or raises cattle is not the question. What then, becomes the yardstick; what is the ethical measurement? In the case of anthropogenic fire use, it should relate to the health of the environment. We now know that, in Western forests, the incorporation of fire ("natural" or "anthropogenic") has advantages in protection from wildfire and disease outbreaks. Indian systems that judiciously used fire avoided such problems. The elimination of understory buildup that serves as fuel for wildfires, the creation of firebreaks in treeless "yards" and "corridors," and the preventive value of mosaics of different vegetation types and successional stages are all lessons that contemporary forest managers, concerned with destructive, uncontrolled fires, can learn from Native American land management systems.

We can carry this argument a step further. During the past ten years, evolutionary ecologists have reached a consensus on a new measure of ecosystem health—biodiversity. The loss of biodiversity through the global spread of agricultural monocultures and a short list of human-associated plant and animal species, and through deforestation and biological extinctions, is a hallmark of our times. An implicit assumption in many discussions is that foraging peoples did not threaten biodiversity as we do. The judicious use of fire by non-agriculturalists, in fact, may even have promoted ecosystem diversity.

Fire is an important instrument in shaping ecosystems and determining the distribution of species, particularly through the creation of vegetative mosaics and increased heterogeneity.[3]

The papers in this volume demonstrate clearly that Pacific Northwest Indians, using fire, did indeed create environmental mosaics of several different successional stages, each with its own characteristic and varying assemblage of species. Northwest forest ecologist Jerry Franklin believes that "preserving biodiversity in temperate regions requires the maintenance of all successional stages." Each stage, of course, represents a different community of both plants and animals. It stands to reason that land use regimes which maximize the range of successional stages, and hence the different plant and animal communities associated with each, should promote biodiversity.[4] Given the contemporary concern with the threat to old-growth successional communities, Northwesterners have overlooked the fact that early succession communities such as the Indian-managed prairies of the "interior valleys province" have become even more threatened, through agriculture, urbanization, and the invasion of non-native plants. The prairie plant communities described by early explorers are mostly gone; many currently threatened Northwest species inhabited such areas.[5] One of the best ways to encourage such communities may be to reintroduce Indian management methods. In the larger scheme of things, preserving or reestablishing them should promote biodiversity.[6]

Less obvious, but invariably associated with mosaics, are increases in environmental "edges,"—the boundaries of ecological areas—characterized by an overlap, mixing, and diversity of plant and animal species. On the importance of edges, former U.S. Forest Service head Jack Ward Thomas quotes renowned ecologist Aldo Leopold: "game [wildlife] is a phenomenon of edges." In Northwest forests, Thomas argues that besides relatively stable "inherent edges" resulting from topographical features, there are "induced edges" created by environmental disturbances, especially fire. The latter are amenable to human influence. There is potentially great species diversity in forest edge associations when dealing with several possible combinations of a forest edge associations when dealing with several possible combinations of a series of successional stages plus the increased length of border areas that results from increased "patchiness," and jagged, wandering borders. The "yards, corridors, and mosaics" pattern described by Lewis and Ferguson should produce a multiplicity of edges. In this continuum of variations, there is a medium that supports a maximum number of species. Thus, diversity is manipulable, particularly through fire use.[7]

But did foraging peoples really "do it better," or does it just seem that way? The papers in this volume clearly show that they handled their environments differently. But is this different usage really "better," and does it promote more biodiversity? We don't yet know. Ethnobotanist Kat Anderson maintains that among cultures in the

middle part of the cultivation continuum . . . human interaction with nature is most complex and sophisticated . . . [and] there is growing evidence that both biodiversity and the abundance of plants and animals useful to humans commonly reach high levels.[8]

But her colleague Gary Nabhan writes:

It remains unclear whether by favoring certain plants over others, plant diversity increased in particular areas. To my knowledge, no study adequately addresses indigenous peoples' local effects on biological diversity (as opposed to their effects on the abundance of key resources).[9]

In the Northwest, when we look at indigenous versus contemporary methods of land management vis-a-vis biodiversity, the answer *seems* clear: the Indian systems have the edge. But we can't test or quantify this hypothesis, and may never be able to do so given the data left to us today. Measuring relative biodiversity may be a task for those parts of the world such as the Amazon and parts of sub-Saharan Africa where intact foraging systems exist side by side with agricultural systems. In the meantime, in the Pacific Northwest, we must make use of those fragments of information about former and different land management systems that remain available to us: in the historical record and in the memories of our Native American elders. These fragments are what remains of indigenous systems of knowledge that, though different, were extensive and effective. In our search for more and better ways to manage the rich but threatened ecosystems of the Pacific Northwest, it is folly to ignore them.

Notes

1. *Traditional Ecological Knowledge: Wisdom for Sustainable Development*, edited by Nancy Williams and Graham Baines (Canberra, 1988) includes papers by two contributors to this volume, Lewis and Hunn. Nancy Turner also has written on the subject in *The Rainforests of Home: Profile of an North American Bioregion*, edited by Peter Schoonmaker, Bettina von Hagen, and Edward Wolf (Washington, 1997). Eugene Linden's "Lost Tribes, Lost Knowledge" (*Time*, September 23, 1991: 46–55) is a popularized introduction.

Two works that discuss "TEK" among "mid-level" societies like those in this volume are Darrell Posey and William Balee, eds., "Resource Management in Amazonia: Indigenous and Folk Strategies" (*Advances in Economic Botany* vol. 7, 1989) (see especially Posey on Kayapo Indian jungle "resource islands," their composition and maintenance) and Eugene Hunn, *Nch'i Wána, "The Big River": Mid-Columbia Indians and Their Land* (Seattle, 1990), on Sahaptin Indian ethnoecology.

2. Turner, "'A Gift for the Taking': The untapped potential of some food plants of North American native peoples" (*Canadian Journal of Botany* 59(11): 2331–57, 1981).

3. Edward O. Wilson's *Biodiversity* (ed., Washington, D.C., 1988) and *The Diversity of Life* (Cambridge, 1992) are primers on biodiversity. The quotation on fire in ecosystems is from Peter Stahl, "Holocene Biodiversity: An Archaeological Perspective from the Americas" (*Annual Review of Anthropology* 25: 105–26, 1996).

4. Another variable "which heightened biodiversity" in the native forests of California was what ecologist Kat Anderson terms "maximum vertical structural complexity," where, using fire, "forests were manipulated to create areas with a tree, shrub, and herbaceous physiognomy, giving the[m] a layered effect." ("From Tillage to Table: The indigenous cultivation of geophytes for food in California, *Journal of Ethnobiology* 17(2): 149–69, 1997), 163.

5. In the Willamette Valley, it has been estimated that less than 1% of native prairie survives. Endangered, threatened, and proposed for listing endemic prairie species include Bradshaw's lomatium, Nelson's checkermallow, Kincaid's lupine, white-topped aster, Willamette daisy, the pale and peacock larkspurs, and shaggy horkelia. The golden paintbrush is now extinct in Oregon, though it survives in Puget Sound prairies. Several small preserves, from Camassia in West Linn to Fern Ridge reservoir outside Eugene, have been established to maintain native prairie vegetation. Prescribed fire is a management tool in many of them (see John Christy and Edward Alverson, "Saving the Valley's Wet Prairie," *The Nature Conservancy Oregon Chapter Newsletter*, Spring 1994, and *Oregon's Living Landscape: Strategies and opportunities to conserve biodiversity*. Corvallis, 1998, pp. 191–204).

6. Jerry Franklin, "Structural and Functional Diversity in Temperate Forests," pp. 166–75 in Wilson, *Biodiversity*.

7. Jack Ward Thomas, Chris Maser, and Jon Rodiek discuss the edge concept in "Edges—Their Interspersion, Resulting Diversity, and its Measurement," pp. 91–100 in "Proceedings of the Workshop on Nongame Bird Habitat Management in the Coniferous Forests of the Western United States" (*USFS General Technical Report* PNW-64, 1978). For Pacific Northwest forests, forest ecologists David Wallin *et al.* suggest that a management system that replicates pre-contact fire return intervals and fire coverage may be best for "producing conditions suitable for

most, if not all, species . . . present at the time of European settlement." See David Wallin *et al.*, "Comparison of managed and pre-settlement landscape dynamics in forests of the Pacific Northwest, USA" (*Forest Ecology and Management* 85: 291-309, 1996), 292.

8. "Tending the Wilderness" (*Restoration and Management Notes* 14(2): 154-55, 1996), 157. Cultures in the "middle part of the cultivation continuum" would include "complex hunter-gatherers" such as the Indians of the Northwest Coast, and "shifting cultivators" or "horticulturalists" such as the Indians of the North American East Coast and Amazonia.

9. Gary Nabhan, "Cultural Parallax in Viewing North American Habitats," pp. 87–101 in Michael Soule and Gary Lease, eds., *Reinventing Nature?: Responses to Postmodern Deconstruction* (Washington, D.C., 1995) 95–96.

The Contributors

STEPHEN BARRETT is a consulting research forester in Kalispell; STEPHEN ARNO is a research forester at the Intermountain Fire Sciences Laboratory in Missoula. Both have been studying fire ecology in the northern Rockies for more than two decades. Barrett's 1981 master's thesis from the University of Montana, "Relationship of Indian-Caused Fires to the Ecology of Western Montana Forests," provided most of the basic data for this article (originally printed in the *Journal of Forestry* in 1982) as well as 1980's "Indians and Fire" (*Western Wildlands* 6(3): 127–31). See also Barrett's "Fire suppression's effects on forest succession within a central Idaho wilderness (*Western Journal of Applied Forestry* 3(3): 76–80, 1988) and "Comparing the prescribed natural fire program with presettlement fires in the Selway-Bitterroot Wilderness" (by James Brown, Barrett, Arno, and J. Menakis, *International Journal of Wildland Fire* 4(3):157–68, 1994). Stephen Arno's publications include the standard guide *Northwest Trees* (Seattle, 1977); a sampler of works on fire ecology includes "The Historical Role of Fire on the Bitterroot National Forest" (*USFS INT Research Paper* 187, 1979); "Forest Fire History in the Northern Rockies" (*Journal of Forestry* 78(8): 460–65, 1980), "Fire ecology and its management implications in ponderosa pine forests," pp. 133–40 in D. M. Baumgartner and James Lotan, eds., *Ponderosa Pine: The species and its management* (Corvallis, 1988); and in particular, "The Use of Fire in Forest Restoration" (*USFS INT General Technical Report* 341, 1996), a volume resulting from a session at the 1995 Meeting of the Society for Ecological Reconstruction, co-edited with Colin Hardy.

ROBERT BOYD is a consulting anthropologist and ethnohistorian living in Portland. Significant publications include *People of The Dalles: The Indians of Wascopam Mission* (Lincoln NE, 1996) and *The Coming of the Spirit of Pestilence: Introduced diseases and population decline among the Indians of the Northwest Coast, 1774 to 1874* (Seattle, 1999). He also authored the "Demography" chapters in the *Northwest Coast* and *Plateau* volumes of the *Handbook of North American Indians* (Washington, 1990 and 1998).

DAVID FRENCH was professor of anthropology at Reed College in Portland for nearly forty years, and was a noted ethnobotanist, linguist, and expert on the Chinookan and Sahaptin peoples of the Warm Springs Reservation. Prominent among his publications are two papers on Upper Chinookans: "Wasco-Wishram" in Edward Spicer's *Perspectives in American Indian Culture Change* (Chicago, 1961) and "Wasco-Wishram-Cascades" in the *Plateau* volume of the Smithsonian's *Handbook of North American Indians* (with Kathrine French) (Washington, 1998). He also co-authored (with Eugene Hunn and Nancy Turner) the "Ethnobiology" chapter of the *Plateau* volume of the *HNAI*. The present paper was prepared for publication by French's widow, Kathrine, herself a noted ethnographer and expert on the Warm Springs peoples.

EUGENE HUNN is professor of anthropology and American Indian Studies at the University of Washington. Hunn is an ethnographer and cultural ecologist with fieldwork among the Sahaptin peoples of the Columbia River and indigenous peoples of Oaxaca and Chiapas. He also is editor of the *Journal of Ethnobiology*. Relevant publications include *Resource Managers: North American and Australian hunter-gatherers* (co-edited with Nancy Williams, Boulder, 1982) and *Nch'i-Wána, the "Big River": Mid-Columbia Indians and their Land* (Seattle, 1990). With David French, he co-authored the "Western Columbia River Sahaptins" chapter in the *Plateau* volume of the *Handbook of North American Indians* (Washington, 1998). A summary of Hunn's continuing work with Sahaptin ethnogeography is "Columbia Plateau Indian Place Names: what do they teach us?" (*Journal of Linguistic Anthropology* 6(1): 3–26, 1996).

LESLIE MAIN JOHNSON is a Grant-Notley Post-doctoral Fellow in the Department of Anthropology at the University of Alberta. Her Ph.D. dissertation (1997) is "Health, Wholeness, and the Land: Gitxsan Traditional Plant Use and Healing." Several years of ethnobotanical and ethnoecological fieldwork among the Gitxsan and Wet'suwet'en peoples has resulted in a series of journal articles: in addition to the above, which first appeared in *Human Ecology* in 1994, they include "Conservation, Territory and Traditional Beliefs: an analysis of Gitksan and Wet'suwet'en subsistence, Northwest British Columbia, Canada" (*Human Ecology* 22(4): 443–65, 1994b); "Wet'suwet'en Ethnobotany: Traditional Plant Uses" (*Journal of Ethnobiology* 14(2): 185–210, 1994c); "The Role of Plant Foods in Traditional Wet'suwet'en Nutrition" (*Ecology of Food and Nutrition* 34(2): 149–69, 1995); and (with Sharon Hargus) "Classification and Nomenclature in Wet'suwet'en Ethnobotany: a preliminary examination" (*Journal of Ethnobiology* 18(1), 1999.

JEFF LALANDE is a historian/archaeologist with the U.S. Forest Service, Medford; REG PULLEN is a consulting anthropologist in Bandon. The interests of these two researchers converged in the early 1990s on the topic of Indian fire use: LaLande's *An Environmental History of the Little Applegate River Watershed* (USFS Medford, 1995) documented local Indian fire use and change in plant cover with fire suppression; and Pullen's *Overview of the environment of Native Inhabitants of southwestern Oregon, late prehistoric era* (BLM Medford, 1996), thoroughly surveyed the historic and ethnographic literature on Indian land use in the region. See also LaLande's *First Over the Siskiyous: Peter Skene Ogden's 1826–1827 Journey through the Oregon-California borderlands* (Portland, 1987) and *The Indians of Southwestern Oregon: An ethnohistorical review* (Corvallis, 1991); and Pullen's "The Identification of Early Prehistoric Settlement Patterns along the Coast of Southwest Oregon" (M.A. thesis, anthropology, Oregon State University, 1982).

ESTELLA LEOPOLD is professor (Department of Botany and Quaternary Research Center) at the University of Washington and one of the region's foremost palynologists. A selection of her important papers includes "Development and

Affinities of Tertiary Floras in the Rocky Mountains" (with Harry McGintie), pp. 147–200 in Alan Graham, ed., *Floristics and Paleofloristics of Asia and Eastern North America* (New York, 1972); "Comparative age of grassland and steppe east and west of the northern Rocky Mountains (with M. F. Denton, *Annals of the Missouri Botanical Garden* 74: 841–67, 1987); "Late Cenozoic Palynology," pp. 377–438 in Robert Tschudy and Richard Scott, eds., *Aspects of Palynology* (New York, 1969); and "Late Cenozoic Patterns of Plant Extinction," pp. 203–46 in Paul Martin and Herbert Wright, eds., *Pleistocene Extinctions: The search for a cause* (New Haven, 1967).

HENRY LEWIS is emeritus professor of anthropology at the University of Alberta, and is the most prolific and influential researcher on fire use among foraging peoples. His seminal 1973 paper, "Patterns of Indian Burning in California," reawakened the anthropological community to the cultural and ecological importance of non-agricultural fire and was the inspiration for several of the papers in this volume. A second cross-cultural study by Lewis, "Fire Technology and Resource Management in Aboriginal North America and Australia" (Hunn and Williams 1982), which examines how the seasonality and frequency of indigenous burning varies in the different environments of northern Alberta, California and Oregon, and Australia, might be read profitably in tandem with this volume's "Yards, Corridors, and Mosaics." Other important and relevant papers are listed in the introduction (fn. 36). THERESA FERGUSON, a student of Lewis, received her M.A. from the University of Alberta in 1979. Her thesis was entitled "Productivity and Predictability of Resource Yield: Aboriginal Controlled Burning in the Boreal Forest." She is a sessional instructor in anthropology at the University of Alberta.

HELEN H. NORTON is a practicing anthropologist in Anacortes, WA. Her Ph.D. dissertation was "Women and Resources on the Northwest Coast: Documentation from the 18th and early 19th centuries" (University of Washington, 1985). Her most important work on anthropogenic fire was "The Association between Anthropogenic Prairies and Important food Plants in Western Washington" (*Northwest Anthropological Research Notes* 13(2): 175–200, 1979. Other relevant articles include "Evidence for Bracken Fern as a food for aboriginal peoples of western Washington" (*Economic Botany* 33(4): 384–96, 1979) and "Vegetable food products of the foraging economies of the Pacific Northwest" (with Eugene Hunn, Charlene Martinsen, and Patrick Keely, *Ecology of Food and Nutrition* 14(3): 219–28, 1984).

WILLIAM ROBBINS is professor of history and associate dean of the College of Arts and Sciences at Oregon State University. The present contribution, which appeared in the *Pacific Northwest Quarterly* in 1993, is a slightly revised version of the first twelve pages of "Landscape and the Intermontane Northwest: An Environmental History," by Robbins and Donald Wolf, a report prepared for the U.S. Forest Service (*PNW-GTR*-319, 1994). The second half of this report deals with more recent developments: population growth and railroads, mining and livestock, and the development of the timber industry. Other significant publications by Robbins include his environmental history of Oregon: *Landscapes of Promise: The Oregon story, 1800–1940* (Seattle, 1997), *Colony and Empire: The capitalist transformation of the American West* (Lawrence KN, 1994), and *American Forestry: A history of national, state, and private cooperation* (Lincoln NE, 1985).

JOHN ROSS is professor and curator of the museum of anthropology at Eastern Washington University in Cheney. He has worked with the Spokan and Colville peoples for several decades and written several reports for their internal use. He is author of the Spokane chapter in the *Plateau* volume of the Smithsonian's *Handbook of North American Indians* (Washington, 1998).

NANCY TURNER, professor of environmental studies at the University of Victoria, is an internationally recognized ethnobotanist and prolific author of several important studies on economically important plants of British Columbia First Nations. Her two standard works on the ethnobotany of B.C.'s coastal and interior peoples, originally published in 1975 and 1978, recently have been revised and reprinted as *Food Plants of Coastal First Peoples* and *Food Plants of Interior First Peoples* (Royal British Columbia Museum, Victoria, and UBC Press, Vancouver, 1995 and 1997). Turner has written more specialized ethnobotanies (singly authored and in collaboration) on Vancouver Island Salish, Kwak'waka'wakw (southern Kwakiutl), Nuxalk (Bella Coola), Okanagan-Colville, Hesquiat, Nitinaht, Nlaka'pamux (Thompson), and Stl'atl'imx (Lillooet), as well as important species soapberry, springbank clover and Pacific silverweed, camas and riceroot, cottonwood mushroom, cow parsnip, wood ferns, and the various "famine foods" of the Native Northwest. Important integrative studies include *Plants in British Columbia Indian Technology* (Victoria, 1979); "A Gift for the Taking: the untapped potential of some food plants of North American native peoples" (*Canadian Journal of Botany* 59(11): 2331–57, 1981); and *Traditional Plant Foods of Canadian Indigenous Peoples: Nutrition, botany, and use* (with Harriet Kuhnlein, Philadelphia, 1991). She is co-editor (with Douglas Deur) of the forthcoming *"Keeping it Living": Traditional plant tending and cultivation on the Northwest Coast.*

RICHARD WHITE is professor of history at Stanford University. He is one of the founding cadre of practitioners of the "new" history of the American West, and in the vanguard of environmental historians. Among his several books, *The Roots of Dependency: Subsistence, environment, and social change among the Choctaws, Pawnees, and Navajos* (Nebraska, 1983) discusses fire use by Indians in the Southeast and Great Plains, and *"It's Your Misfortune and None of My Own": A new history of the American West* (Oklahoma, 1993) places Indian fire and environmental management in its proper context in the flow of Western American history.

Index